The Rise of the Russian

Studying the interplay between ideology and politics in Russian governance, from the former USSR to contemporary Russia, this book examines why, despite the prohibition of state ideology in the 1993 Russian Constitution, Russian hawks endured beyond the 1991 regime change and have risen to political prominence as the chief ideologues of Russia's confrontation against the West. Departing from realist and constructivist explanations of foreign policy focused on Vladimir Putin, Juliette Faure highlights the influence of elite groups with diverse strategic cultures and reveals how, even under authoritarian rule, a competitive space exists where rival elites contest their visions of national interests. Demonstrating the regime's strategic use of ideological ambiguity to maintain policy flexibility, Faure offers a fresh lens on the domestic factors that have played into the Russian regime's decision to wage war against Ukraine and their implications for international security, regional stability, and the global balance of power.

JULIETTE FAURE is a National Fund for Scientific Research (FNRS) postdoctoral researcher at the Université Libre de Bruxelles and earned a PhD in political science from Sciences Po in 2022. She received the Michael Freeden Prize for best article published in the *Journal of Political Ideologies* and is coeditor of the *Routledge Handbook of Ideology Analysis* (2025).

The Rise of the Russian Hawks

Ideology and Politics from the Late Soviet Union to Putin's Russia

JULIETTE FAURE
National Fund for Scientific Research (FNRS) – Université Libre de Bruxelles

CAMBRIDGE
UNIVERSITY PRESS

CAMBRIDGE
UNIVERSITY PRESS

Shaftesbury Road, Cambridge CB2 8EA, United Kingdom

One Liberty Plaza, 20th Floor, New York, NY 10006, USA

477 Williamstown Road, Port Melbourne, VIC 3207, Australia

314–321, 3rd Floor, Plot 3, Splendor Forum, Jasola District Centre,
New Delhi – 110025, India

103 Penang Road, #05–06/07, Visioncrest Commercial, Singapore 238467

Cambridge University Press is part of Cambridge University Press & Assessment,
a department of the University of Cambridge.

We share the University's mission to contribute to society through the pursuit of
education, learning and research at the highest international levels of excellence.

www.cambridge.org
Information on this title: www.cambridge.org/9781009542685

DOI: 10.1017/9781009542661

When citing this work, please include a reference to the
DOI 10.1017/9781009542661

First published 2025

A catalogue record for this publication is available from the British Library

A Cataloging-in-Publication data record for this book is available from the Library of Congress

ISBN 978-1-009-54268-5 Hardback
ISBN 978-1-009-54264-7 Paperback

Contents

Acknowledgments

I would first like to express my deepest gratitude to my PhD supervisors, Kathy Rousselet and Philippe Portier, for their constant support and invaluable guidance throughout my research journey.

I am very appreciative of Sciences Po and the Center for International Studies (CERI) research center, where I originally conceived this research, for their financial support and for providing me with an inspiring work environment. My special thanks go to the Sciences Po library staff, in particular Isabelle Blanchemaison-Karanov, for their kindness and permanent readiness to help. I also benefited from research grants from the Centre d'études franco-russe and the University Consortium that allowed me to conduct fieldwork in Russia.

I thank Andrei Melville for having welcomed me as a visiting student at the Higher School of Economics in Moscow during one semester and for having taken the time to discuss my work. I am also deeply grateful to the Davis Center for Russian and Eurasian Studies at Harvard University, and especially to Alexandra Vacroux, for accepting me as a visiting fellow. Access to Harvard Library's resources has tremendously facilitated my work on Soviet archives.

My research benefited immensely from fieldwork I conducted in Russia on several occasions. I thank all the interviewees who took the time to meet me and share with me information and personal memories. My life in Moscow would not have been as fascinating without the warmth, generosity, and intellectual fervor of my Russian friends Eva, Denis, Vadim, Sergei, Anna, Nikita, Dmitrii, Aleksei, and Tatiana. It is still a shock to realize how the world we lived in, where war was a distant past, has been tragically crushed by the brutal application of the ideology studied in this book.

Over the years of this research, I also had the chance to meet scholars who have provided important comments on my work and have encouraged me to present and publish it. I would like to express my deep appreciation to Timur Atnashev, Thierry Balzacq, Mark Bassin, Valentin Behr, Anemona Constantin, Alicja Curanović,

Dmitrii Dorogov, Marc Elie, Clémentine Fauconnier, Gilles Favarel-Garrigues, Michael Freeden, Paul Forman, Isabelle Gouarné, Alex Graef, Samuel Greene, Michael Hagemeister, Mathieu Hauchecorne, Mathew Humphrey, Marlène Laruelle, Françoise Lesourd, Alexander Lutsenko, Marius Ostrowski, Benoît Pelopidas, Richard Sakwa, Olivier Schmitt, Yulia Sineokaya, Pierre-Louis Six, Kristina Stoeckl, Mikhail Suslov, Apolline Taillandier, and Paul Zawadzki.

I thank the *Revue française de science politique* for granting me permission to include portions of my article in this manuscript, specifically in Chapters 3 to 7.[1] Likewise, I extend my gratitude to Taylor & Francis Ltd for granting permission to reprint parts of my article published in the *Journal of Political Ideologies*, specifically in Chapters 2 through 4.[2]

The path toward the writing of this book has been enlightened by the company of friends and peers, with whom I have shared the joys and laments of academic life, in particular Anna Gromada, Benjamin Tainturier, Édouard Girard, Sergei Fediunin, Denis Lisin, Morvan Lallouet, Maxime Audinet, Jusmeet Singh, Rodolphe Droalin, and Thomas Blonski.

A special thank-you to David Laycock, Francis Godard, and Guillaume Sauvé for their invaluable feedback on my manuscript and for the inspiring mentorship they have provided throughout my academic journey.

I extend my gratitude to my editors at Cambridge University Press, John Haslam and Carrie Parkinson, for their trust and guidance in helping me publish my first book. I am also thankful to the two anonymous reviewers for their thoughtful engagement with my manuscript and for their constructive comments.

Thank you to my friends, to my parents, to Philippe Buhannic, to all my large and wonderful family, and to Maxime for their love and support, which gave me the joy of writing and achieving this work.

Finally, I thank my grandmother, Anne-Marie Dousset, for having been a model intellectual, combining philosophical sensitivity, humor, and wonder in the face of the world. This book is dedicated to her.

1 Juliette Faure, "La carrière des faucons russes. Sociohistoire de l'ascension d'un réseau d'idées politico-intellectuel en contexte autoritaire (1991–2022)," *Revue française de science politique* 73, no. 6 (2024): 883–901, https://shs.cairn.info/revue-francaise-de-science-politique-2023-6-page-883?lang=fr.

2 Juliette Faure, "A Russian Version of Reactionary Modernism: Aleksandr Prokhanov's 'spiritualization of technology'," *Journal of Political Ideologies* 26, no 3 (2021): 356–379, www.tandfonline.com/doi/full/10.1080/13569317.2021.1885591?scroll=top&needAccess=true.

Transliteration

The book uses the transcription system Passport 2013 ICAO to transliterate Russian, except for surnames conventionally transcribed otherwise (e.g., Boris Yeltsin, Konstantin Tsiolkovsky).

The table below shows the romanization of Russian letters that do not have equivalents in the Latin alphabet:

Russian alphabet	Transliteration
ё	e
ж	zh
й	i
с	s
х	kh
ц	ts
ч	ch
ш	sh
щ	shch
ъ	ie
ы	y
ь	-
э	e
ю	iu
я	ia

1 *Introduction*

September 6, 2019. Moscow International Book Fair, Center for the Exhibition of Achievements of National Economy (Vystavka dostizhenii narodnogo khoziaistva, VDNKh), Moscow. Aleksandr Prokhanov, eighty-one years old, sits at the center of the stage, his face inexpressive, behind the table where his latest book, *The Fifth Stalin*, is displayed. Above the stage, a massive screen projects a loop of illustrations from the book: a series of black-and-white drawings that blend religious medieval iconography with Soviet aesthetics. They portray Joseph Stalin in various situations: alongside Orthodox saints; as a schoolteacher facing Vladimir Putin and Dmitrii Medvedev, who sit in the front row sheepishly copying the lesson's title marked on the blackboard in capital letters: "MOBILIZATION"; or on a large nuclear warhead with the inscription "ZA STALINA" ("FOR STALIN").

The book's editor, Sergei Dmitriev, director of the publishing house Veche, takes the floor. As he explains, the book commemorates the upcoming 140th anniversary of Stalin's birth. It is a collection of articles by Prokhanov and illustrations by Gennadii Zhivotov, originally published in the newspaper *Zavtra*, fervently glorifying Stalin.

In the conference room, about twenty "Night Wolves," members of Russia's largest motorcycle club, are seated in three rows. They are easily recognizable: shaved heads, biker vests adorned with various pins, and the club's symbol – a wolf's head roaring in a lunar white circle with its mane twirling in orange and red flames – on their backs. Besides them, the audience includes several men with long beards, dressed in black, mimicking the style of the Eurasian philosopher Aleksandr Dugin, and a few other smart men in suits. These are probably the "technocrats from the defense industry" that a journalist identified among the conference's participants, in a report later published by *Zavtra*.[1]

[1] Vladimir Vinnikov, "'Russkii reaktor' na VDNKh," *Zavtra*, September 12, 2019, https://zavtra.ru/blogs/pyatij_stalin_gryadyot. Unless otherwise mentioned, all translations from Russian or French are mine.

"This book is not a commemoration," remarks Prokhanov, "it is a premonition. Premonition of a new appearance of Stalin. Stalin is coming!"

He further elaborates on the book's title. In Russian history, as he explains, four empires have arisen: Kievan Rus, Muscovite Russia, the Romanov empire, and the Soviet Union. Each of them, Prokhanov claims, gave birth to a Stalinian leader: Prince Vladimir, Ivan the Terrible, Peter the Great, and Joseph Stalin.

"But the Stalinist empire," he continues, "of which I consider myself a son, was destroyed in 1991 … And now again, in some miraculous way, a new Russian state has started to emerge from this 'black hole.' I call it the fifth Russian empire."

On the stage, the roundtable speakers also include a prominent figure from the younger generation of communist politicians, Iurii Afonin (1977–), deputy chairman of the Communist Party of the Russian Federation and a member of the State Duma. Next to him sits Aleksandr Zaldostanov, the leader of the Night Wolves, known as The Surgeon, who is personally acquainted with Putin. Decked out in the same gear as his gang, he, however, is the only one to sport long, curly hair, held in place by a tight black cap. During his speech, he explains that, at Prokhanov's request, he has passed a letter to Putin asking for the restoration of the name Stalingrad to the city of Volgograd. He smiles and adds: "In front of me, Putin read Prokhanov's letter to the end and said: 'Someday this will happen.'"

This event, which I attended during my fourth field research visit to Russia, illustrates several defining attributes of the Russian hawks: They seek to reconfigure the relationship between Orthodox conservatism and Soviet military-technological might, they span various social sectors and generations, and their ideas circulate from ideologues to policy circles through a network of actors made up of disparate members of the intellectual and political elite.

1.1 Who Are the Russian Hawks?

"Hawk" is originally a Cold War expression used in the American context to refer to those who support a well-financed, aggressive military. By contrast with doves' emphasis on cooperation to avoid war, hawks maintain a competitive understanding of international politics.

They argue for constant military buildup to establish a posture of superior strength and to deter the opponent.[2] As providers of justification for the use of force to defend national security interests over the adversary's, hawks are known as the war machine's chief ideologues.

In the post-Soviet context, the term has occasionally been used to describe Stalinist ideologues advocating for the restoration of a Russian empire,[3] as well as members of the "party of war" within the political and military elite who promoted the use of military force against Chechen secessionists in 1994.[4] I also use this term to designate the group of ideologues examined in this book, including Prokhanov and others, who from the beginning of their careers in the Soviet Union have portrayed the military as the natural carrier of their ideas. At the core of their ideology is a reflection on the modernization processes of the Soviet Union and subsequently Russia. In stark contrast to Western modernization theories, which began to spread during Nikita Khrushchev's Thaw and assumed that technoscientific modernization would eventually lead to the Soviet state's liberalization and convergence with the West, they were committed to preserving the uniqueness of the Soviet path. Throughout the period studied, from the Soviet Union to contemporary Russia, these hawks have been adamant about the "wartime" context faced by their country in its confrontation with the West and have focused on reinvigorating a state ideology to mobilize the nation. To them, the military is the quintessential venue for realizing their conception of the Russian national idea, defined in radical opposition to the West and understood as a blend of technological power and religious conservatism in service of a strong and imperial state. Further, "hawks" alludes to the symbol of the Russian tsarist empire, the double-headed eagle, which these ideologues have revitalized in the post-Soviet context as

2 Graham T. Allison, Albert Carnesale, and Joseph S. Nye, "Hawks, Doves and Owls: A New Perspective on Avoiding Nuclear War," *International Affairs* 61, no. 4 (1985): 581–89; Bruce Russett, "Doves, Hawks, and U.S. Public Opinion," *Political Science Quarterly* 105, no. 4 (1990): 515–38.

3 Vitalii I. Goldanskii, "Russia's 'Red-Brown' Hawks," *Bulletin of the Atomic Scientists* 5 (1993): 24–27.

4 John B. Dunlop, *The Moscow Bombings of September 1999: Examinations of Russian Terrorist Attacks at the Onset of Vladimir Putin's Rule* (Stuttgart: ibidem-Verlag, 2014), 14.

they have aimed to merge historical narratives and imperial legacies to forge a renewed "fifth empire."[5]

The Russian hawks' advocacy of a mix of technological modernization, religious conservatism, and state patriotism form an ideological language, which I have termed "modernist conservatism." Instead of classic Russian conservatism, modernist conservatism resembles the type of political ideology that Jeffrey Herf identifies in the context of Weimar Germany as "reactionary modernism."[6] As Herf explains, the theorists of the German Conservative Revolution, such as Oswald Spengler, Ernst Jünger, and Carl Schmitt, framed an illiberal and nationalist ideology of modernity by embracing technological progress while rejecting Enlightenment's liberal and secular conception of reason.

Modernist conservatism is still the ideological flagship of the Izborskii Klub, the hawks' central and largest think tank in today's Russia. Created in 2012, the club comprises intellectual, economic, political, religious, and military elites advocating the restoration of Russia's imperial great-power status, drawing on both religious conservatism and techno-military might. While the hawks were marginal in the 1990s, the regime has increasingly relied on their ideas to justify the authoritarian consolidation of strong state power, to enforce a social discipline based on traditional values, and to pursue an imperialist foreign policy, which culminated in the annexation of Crimea in 2014 and the 2022 invasion of Ukraine. Since the start of the war, the Izborskii Klub has been actively engaged in propaganda work stressing the "military-technological," "spiritual," and "ideological" dimensions of what they picture as a "battle of civilizations" between Russia and the West.[7]

This book represents an attempt to understand why, despite the prohibition of state ideology in the Russian Constitution of 1993, Russian hawks have endured across the 1991 regime change and have risen to political prominence as the chief ideologues of Russia's confrontation against the West. The ascent of hawks from the fringes to the center of Russian political discourse underscores broader shifts in societal attitudes and governmental strategies. By tracing the trajectory of these

[5] See, for instance, the cover page of issue 1 of the Izborskii Klub's journal, published in 2024.
[6] Jeffrey Herf, *Reactionary Modernism: Technology, Culture, and Politics in Weimar and the Third Reich* (Cambridge: Cambridge University Press, 2003).
[7] "Vremia Dugina. Otkliki Chlenov Izborskogo Kluba," Izborskii Klub website, September 2, 2022, https://izborsk-club.ru/23275.

ideologues and examining the mechanisms through which their ideas were translated into state policies, this study aims to elucidate the continuity and evolution of the interplay between ideology and politics in Russian governance from the end of the USSR to contemporary times. In doing so, it provides insights into the ideological underpinnings of Russia's foreign posture and its implications for international security, regional stability, and the global balance of power.

1.2 Sources

While studies on contemporary Russian conservatism have usually revolved around institutions such as the Communist Party of the Russian Federation and the Russian Orthodox Church, the concept of the Russian hawks highlights the role of intellectuals in shaping and spreading beliefs through various intellectual, cultural, and political vehicles. I distinguish between two generations of Russian hawks: The first generation began their activities as public intellectuals in the late Soviet Union, around the 1970s, while the second entered the public scene in the late 1990s. Moreover, although the literature on conservative intellectuals has often spotlighted the Eurasianist philosopher Aleksandr Dugin, I place particular emphasis on Aleksandr Prokhanov (1938–), who has held a leading position among the first generation of Russian hawks as the founder of their main media mouthpieces.[8] By contrast with Dugin, whose popularity and visibility in Russia are limited to intellectual circles, Prokhanov is an author of literature well known to the general public.[9] Besides him, I also pay particular

[8] For studies focused on Dugin, see, for instance, Jacob Kipp, "Aleksandr Dugin and the Ideology of National Revival: Geopolitics, Eurasianism and the Conservative Revolution," *European Security* 11, no. 3 (2002): 91–125; Marlène Laruelle, "A Textbook Case of Doctrinal Entrepreneurship: Aleksandr Dugin," in *Russian Nationalism* (London; New York: Routledge, Taylor & Francis Group, 2019), 95–133; Anton Shekhovtsov and Andreas Umland, "Is Aleksandr Dugin a Traditionalist? 'Neo-Eurasianism' and Perennial Philosophy," *The Russian Review* 68, no. 4 (2009): 662–78; Dmitry Shlapentokh, "Alexander Dugin's Views of Russian History: Collapse and Revival," *Journal of Contemporary Central and Eastern Europe* 25, no. 3 (2017): 331–43.

[9] For this reason, Prokhanov has been studied in greater detail by scholars in literature rather than in political science. Edmund Griffiths's recently published book is a remarkable exception. See Edmund Griffiths, *Aleksandr Prokhanov and Post-Soviet Esotericism* (Stuttgart: ibidem Verlag, 2023).

attention to one of the leading members of the younger generation of Russian hawks, Vitalii Averianov, who is the chief conceptualizer of the concept of "dynamic conservatism," blending technological modernity and religious conservatism. Averianov is also one of the founders of the first conservative think tank in contemporary Russia, the "Institute of Dynamic Conservatism."

Following the social history of ideas approach, I use a mixed method of inquiry that combines discourse analysis with empirically grounded research on idea producers. For the Soviet period, my archival sources comprise the newspapers that were used by the Russian hawks as forums for sociopolitical debates, such as *Literaturnaia gazeta*, *Nash sovremennik*, and *Literaturnaia Rossiia*. For the years 1991–99, my sources include the newspapers founded by Prokhanov, *Den* (1990–93) and *Zavtra* (1993–), which served as the rallying points for modernist conservatives. For the period 2000–20, I also review the online archives of the internet media platforms used by the younger generation of Russian hawks, such as the web newspaper *Russkii zhurnal*, and their personal blogs on the social networking service Livejournal (Zhivoi Zhurnal). From 2009 onward, I use the online archives of the institutions created by Russian hawks, first the Institute of Dynamic Conservatism (Institut dinamicheskogo konservatizma, IDK) (2009–12) and then the Izborskii Klub (2012–), which have recorded their publications and transcripts of roundtables on their websites.[10] I have also reviewed the archives of the Izborskii Klub's monthly journal, *Izborskii Klub: Russkie strategii.*[11]

In addition to ideational content, the archives of the IDK's and the Izborskii Klub's websites record in detail the routine activities of the institutions and their members over the period 2009–20.[12] These data include the list of roundtables and conferences that the organizations have hosted, the list of participants that have attended them and the list of meetings held by the leaders of the organizations with political, economic, or religious actors. Reviewing these archives, therefore, provides important information on the audience and socialization of Russian hawks. In particular, these data enable me to track the

10 See http://dynacon.ru and https://izborsk-club.ru.

11 The archives can be accessed here: https://izborsk-club.ru/magazine#2013.

12 See the section "Materials of the IDK Website (2009–2012)" ("Materialy saita IDK (2009–2012)"): www.dynacon.ru/arh_idk/ and the section "Chronology of the Club's Events" ("Khronologiia meropriiatii kluba") in each issue of the Izborskii Klub's journals.

IDK's and Izborskii Klub's connections with policy circles through the analysis of their mentions of interaction and cooperation with policymakers or political institutions.

Moreover, by contrast with most studies on Russian conservatism, the interpretation developed in this book benefits from the rich and original materials retrieved during interviews and ethnographic observations, which I gathered during several fieldwork visits in Russia from 2017 to 2019. These materials are especially valuable today as access to the Russian field has been challenged since 2020 owing to Covid-19 travel restrictions and the start of the war.

There were many challenges involved in my fieldwork. The first difficulty was to get in touch with a social group far away from my personal environment in the sensitive political context of hostility and mistrust that prevailed between Russia and the West following Russia's annexation of Crimea in 2014. Another difficulty related to the conditions brought about by my immersion in an antipathic cultural milieu as an isolated stranger. As scholars have highlighted, exposure to "extreme" or "repugnant" cultural milieus challenges ethnographic methodological processes, which rely on a certain openness and interpersonal empathy to allow access to the respondents and the smooth running of the interviews.[13] In this respect, I concur with other French female researchers on Russian right-wing political and ideological milieus who have noted that the status of foreigner, "exotic" to the cultural milieu covered by the research, helps to neutralize personal reactions and establish a more professional ethnographic posture.[14]

In total, I conducted thirty-two semistructured oral interviews in the Russian language. The first category of interviewers was composed of members of the two generations of Russian hawks, including Izborskii

13 Susan Harding, "Representing Fundamentalism: The Problem of the Repugnant Cultural Other," *Social Research* 58, no. 2 (1991): 373–93; Magali Boumaza, "L'expérience d'une jeune chercheuse en 'milieu extrême': Une enquête au Front National," *Regards sociologiques* 22 (2001): 105–21; Véra Nikolski, "La valeur heuristique de l'empathie dans l'étude des engagements 'répugnants,'" *Genèses* 84, no. 3 (2011): 113–26; Clémentine Fauconnier, "Enquêter sur le parti Russie Unie : De la défiance politique à l'illégitimité scientifique? L'apport critique de l'étude des objets antipathiques," *Terrains/Théories* 10 (2019).

14 Nikolski, "La valeur heuristique," 20; Fauconnier, "Enquêter sur le parti Russie unie," 7.

Klub members and "Young Conservatives."[15] Some of the key questions I asked related to the context that led them to start authoring public speech, the reason behind turning points in their intellectual trajectory, the individuals whom they related to as *edinomyshlenniki* (like-minded persons) at specific points in their life, the rival groups that they targeted in their publications, the incentives that led them to coalesce with other ideologues, their routine practices as part of a group of ideologues, and so on. A second category of interviews was aimed at gaining insight into the perception of the hawks by other members of Russia's contemporary intellectual and political elites.[16]

The fieldwork also included ethnographic observations such as attending events organized by the Izborskii Klub as a group or separately by its members. My goal here was to identify the type of audience that Russian hawks attracted in the public space and to get insight into the more affective, emotional dimension of their identity as a group.

1.3 A Social History of the Russian Hawks' Ideas

Whereas studies on contemporary Russian conservatism focus exclusively on the post-Soviet context,[17] I look at Russian modernist

15 The list of these interviewees is available in Annex 1, but the material quoted from interviews is anonymized.

16 See Annex 1. Some of them are anonymized. They are identified by a letter (e.g., "A.", "B.") and by their professional occupation.

17 Marlène Laruelle, ed., *Le rouge et le noir: Extrême droite et nationalisme en Russie* (Paris: CNRS Éditions, 2007); Marlène Laruelle, *Russian Eurasianism: An Ideology of Empire* (Washington, DC: Woodrow Wilson Center Press, 2008); Marlène Laruelle, *In the Name of the Nation: Nationalism and Politics in Contemporary Russia* (New York: Palgrave Macmillan, 2009); Marlène Laruelle, *Russian Nationalism: Imaginaries, Doctrines, and Political Battlefields* (London: Routledge, 2019); Thomas Parland, *The Extreme Nationalist Threat in Russia: The Growing Influence of Western Rightist Ideas* (London: Routledge Curzon, 2004); Véra Nikolski, *National-bolchevisme et néo-eurasisme dans la Russie contemporaine: La carrière militante d'une idéologie* (Paris: Mare & Martin, 2013). Andrei P. Tsygankov, *The Strong State in Russia: Development and Crisis* (Oxford: Oxford University Press, 2014); Pål Kolstø and Helge Blakkisrud, eds., *The New Russian Nationalism: Imperialism, Ethnicity and Authoritarianism 2000–15* (Edinburgh: Edinburgh University Press, 2016); Katharina Bluhm and Mihai Varga, eds., *New Conservatives in Russia and East Central Europe* (Abingdon: Routledge, 2019); Mikhail Suslov and Dmitry Uzlaner, eds., *Contemporary Russian Conservatism: Problems, Paradoxes, and Perspectives* (Boston: Brill, 2020).

conservatism as an ideological product that was formed over a period encompassing the late Soviet Union to contemporary Russia. In this respect, my research builds a bridge between the historiography of the late Soviet period and the literature on post-Soviet Russia.[18] Moreover, contrary to classic intellectual histories of Russian conservatism,[19] I draw on recent attempts to develop a method for the study of political ideas by combining a contextualist interpretation of discourses with an analysis of the social conditions of their production and circulation.

In the early 2000s, the American sociologists Charles Camic and Neil Gross defined this approach as the "new sociology of ideas."[20] Likewise, in France, a group of scholars has recently laid down the key principles for a new "social history of political ideas."[21] The social history of ideas builds on the historiographical movement formed by the Cambridge School in the 1970s. Representatives of this school have argued that ideas are not purely abstract constructions; rather, they "intervene" in specific historical contexts.[22] Quentin Skinner has particularly emphasized that understanding the meaning of ideas involves the identification of their argumentative context. The study of ideas, he argues, should reveal the "broader networks of beliefs"

[18] Walter Laqueur, *Black Hundred: The Rise of the Extreme Right in Russia* (New York: HarperCollins, 1993); John B. Dunlop, *The Rise of Russia and the Fall of the Soviet Empire* (Princeton: Princeton University Press, 1993); James P. Scanlan, ed., *Russian Thought after Communism: The Recovery of a Philosophical Heritage* (Armonk, NY: M. E. Sharpe, 1994); Yitzhak M. Brudny, *Reinventing Russia: Russian Nationalism and the Soviet State, 1953–1991* (Cambridge, MA: Harvard University Press, 1998); Nikolai Mitrokhin, *Russkaia Partiia: Dvizhenie russkikh natsionalistov v SSSR 1953–1985 gody* (Moscow: Novoe literaturnoe obozrenie, 2003).

[19] Richard Pipes, *Russian Conservatism and Its Critics: A Study in Political Culture* (New Haven: Yale University Press, 2005); Paul Robinson, *Russian Conservatism* (Ithaca, NY: Northern Illinois University Press, 2019); Glenn Diesen, *Russian Conservatism: Managing Change under Permanent Revolution* (Lanham, MD: Rowman & Littlefield, 2021).

[20] Charles Camic and Neil Gross, "The New Sociology of Ideas," in *The Blackwell Companion to Sociology*, ed. Judith R. Blau (Oxford: Blackwell Publishing, 2001), 236–49.

[21] Arnault Skornicki and Jérôme Tournadre, *La nouvelle histoire des idées politiques* (Paris: La Découverte, 2015); Chloé Gaboriaux and Arnault Skornicki, eds., *Vers une histoire sociale des idées politiques* (Villeneuve-d'Ascq, France: Presses universitaires du Septentrion, 2017).

[22] Quentin Skinner, "Interpretation and the Understanding of Speech Acts," in *Visions of Politics: Volume 1; Regarding Method* (Cambridge: Cambridge University Press, 2002), 116.

and "intellectual frameworks" that form the discursive environment in which ideas occur.[23]

A key aspect of this method is to understand what authors were "doing in writing" by retrieving the intention and performative meaning of their discourse. This approach led me to look at the Soviet genesis of the ideas upheld by contemporary Russian hawks, whose lives and professional careers spread over the 1991 change in regime. Their ideology is based on a thread of ideas that has not been systematically theorized through a core set of works but is rather spread across a series of documents including newspaper articles, political manifestos, blog articles, doctrines, and essays. Most of these sources belong to the specifically Russian discursive genre of *publicistika*, which roughly translates as sociopolitical journalism. A central part of the analysis of these texts, therefore, includes the reconstitution of the broader discursive context composed by the articles and authors to which they referred and reacted.

Unlike the Cambridge School's essentially semantic definition of discursive contexts, however, I follow up on the sociological turn in the study of ideas that has also brought to the fore the social processes that shape the production and circulation of ideas. Based on the concept of field developed by Pierre Bourdieu, this sociology of ideas locates discourses within a social space of idea production, structured by specific rules and by the power relations between the groups that compete with each other for the distribution of the field's capital.[24] As Camic and Gross put it, idea producers are engaged in "historically specific struggles with one another" to establish their "legitimacy and respectability."[25]

In this respect, by contrast with studies based on a fixed definition of Russian conservatism as a stream of ideas maintained unchanged throughout history, I focus on the specific trend of Russian modernist conservatism as the doctrinal language of a group whose theoretical definition and relation toward other groups are evolving and contested.

23 Quentin Skinner, "Introduction: Seeing Things Their Way," in *Visions of Politics: Volume 1; Regarding Method* (Cambridge: Cambridge University Press, 2002), 4–5.
24 Pierre Bourdieu, "Champ intellectuel et projet créateur," *Les temps modernes* 246 (1966): 865–906; Pierre Bourdieu, "Le fonctionnement du champ intellectuel," *Regards Sociologiques* 17/18 (1999): 5–27.
25 Camic and Gross, "New Sociology of Ideas," 248.

First, Russian modernist conservatism operates in the intellectual field of idea production in confrontation with other groups carrying rival worldviews, such as antimodern conservatism or liberalism. In this regard, in addition to the analysis of their concepts and ideas, I identify the evolving position of the hawks within the intellectual field, which I determine from attributes such as their generation, education, professional trajectory, institutional memberships, and places of publication. Second, as an action-oriented program aimed at becoming a state ideology, Russian modernist conservatism plays in the political space of competition for influence over policy choices, in interaction with other concurrent groups.

1.4 Modernist Conservatism: An Illiberal Ideology of Modernity Formed across the 1991 Regime Change

Instead of the standard historiographical distinction between the Soviet and post-Soviet periods, I highlight the need to comprehend Russian modernist conservatism as addressing an argumentative context spanning from the 1960s until today. As I argue, this timeline corresponds to the unfolding of a convergence horizon between Russia and the West, against which Russian modernist conservatism reacted by designing an alternative to Russia's engagement on a shared path with Western modernity.

Early sociological theories of modernity, as found in the work of Max Weber, Emile Durkheim, and Karl Marx, defined modernity as a historically and geographically situated phenomenon that arose in Western Europe in the eighteenth century. As Shmuel Eisenstadt has highlighted, these "original" theories characterized modernity as having two major dimensions.[26] The structural, or organizational, dimension refers to changes such as urbanization, industrialization, spread of education and literacy, demographic revolution, increased scale of communication, development of science and technology, and the differentiation of the social structure into distinct sectors of activity. The institutional dimension refers to the development of a new political community, the nation-state, of new capitalist political

[26] S. N. Eisenstadt, "Multiple Modernities in an Age of Globalization," *Canadian Journal of Sociology/Cahiers Canadiens de sociologie* 24, no. 2 (1999): 284.

economies, and of a new cultural program based on secularization, rationalization, and individualization.

In the 1950s and 1960s, Western modernization theorists such as Talcott Parsons, Daniel Bell, and Alex Inkeles singled out the structural aspects of the Soviet system to argue that it shared certain features with modern industrial societies.[27] They emphasized tendencies such as the growth of scientific knowledge and technical expertise associated with claims to intellectual autonomy, the professionalization of the Soviet economy, and the role of the occupational structure, social class, and upward mobility as central factors in Soviet life. Moreover, on their visits to Moscow in the 1960s, Robert Merton, Parsons, and George Fischer acknowledged the emergence of a new Soviet sociology, whose empirical turn and efforts to import structural functionalism departed from orthodox Marxist–Leninist ideological frameworks. As Parsons put it, the growing autonomy of Soviet sociology and economic rationality was evidence of the "secularization" of Soviet social sciences and its separation from ideology.[28] In contrast to the view of the Soviet Union as a totalitarian exceptionalism, American sociologists contended that the requirements of economic and industrial growth would lead to the "end of ideology" and the eventual convergence of the Soviet system with the institutional aspects of Western societies.[29]

Similar reflections were developed inside the Soviet bloc. An intense dialogue took place across the Iron Curtain between postwar Western and Soviet social sciences on the issue of modernization.[30] Scholars have increasingly used the label "late socialism" to refer to the period that followed Nikita Khrushchev's de-Stalinization speech at the Twentieth Congress of the Communist Party in 1956.[31] The liberalizing effects of

[27] David C. Engerman, *Know Your Enemy: The Rise and Fall of America's Soviet Experts* (Cary, NC: Oxford University Press, 2009), 180–205.

[28] Engerman, *Know Your Enemy*, 197.

[29] Daniel Bell, "The 'End of Ideology' in the USSR?" in *Marxist Ideology in the Contemporary World: Its Appeals and Paradoxes*, ed. Milorad Drachkovich (Stanford: F. A. Praeger Pall Mall Press, 1966).

[30] Isabelle Gouarné and Olessia Kirtchik, "La 'modernité' des sciences sociales soviétiques," *Revue d'histoire des sciences humaines* 40 (2022): 5.

[31] See "Chapter 1: Late Socialism; An Eternal State," in *Everything Was Forever, until It Was No More: The Last Soviet Generation, ed.* Alexei Yurchak (Princeton: Princeton University Press, 2005), 1–35; Neringa Klumbyte and Gulnaz Sharafutdinova, "Introduction: What Was Late

this speech brought considerable changes from the early Soviet period and led to growing correspondences between Soviet society and some of the sociocultural features of Western modernity such as intellectual liberalization and pluralization, the professionalization of the social sciences, and the individualization of lifestyles.

First, Khrushchev's Thaw was accompanied by the liberalization and pluralization of Soviet intellectual life. Phenomena such as the loosening of party control over scientific production and the mass circulation of "thick journals" (*tolstye zhurnaly*), used as forums for sociopolitical arguments, fostered the opening up of posttotalitarian enclaves of public debate.[32] Soviet intellectuals gained steady, although controlled, access to non-Marxist intellectual references, such as Western authors and the prerevolutionary Russian philosophical heritage.[33] The discovery of these alternative sources inspired the emergence of the dissident movement of defenders of rights (*pravozashchitniki* or *zakonniki*) as well as various types of "other-thinking" (*inakomyslie*) that revisited the Marxist–Leninist creed. While they still abided by Marxism–Leninism as the official reference, these nonconformist worldviews sought to combine it with other forms of thought.[34]

Relatedly, the de-Stalinization program enhanced another sociocultural feature associated with modernity, that is, the professionalization of scientific discourse. Remarkable progress was made to separate

Socialism?" in *Soviet Society in the Era of Late Socialism, 1964–1985*, ed. Neringa Klumbyte and Gulnaz Sharafutdinova (Blue Ridge Summit, PA: Lexington Books, 2012), 6–18.

32 Paul R. Josephson, "Soviet Scientists and the State: Politics, Ideology, and Fundamental Research from Stalin to Gorbachev," *Social Research* 59, no. 3 (1992): 590; Yitzhak M. Brudny, *Reinventing Russia: Russian Nationalism and the Soviet State, 1953–1991*, Russian Research Center Studies 91 (Cambridge, MA: Harvard University Press, 1998), 31.

33 Vladislav Zubok, *Zhivago's Children: The Last Russian Intelligentsia* (Cambridge, MA: Belknap Press of Harvard University Press, 2009), 135; Brudny, *Reinventing Russia.*

34 Janina Markiewicz-Lagneau, "La fin de l'intelligentsia? Formation et transformation de l'intelligentsia soviétique," *Revue d'études comparatives Est-Ouest* 7, no. 4 (1976): 7–71. See also Mikhail Epstein's two volumes on Marxist revisionism and non-Marxist thought in the late Soviet period: Mikhail Epstein, *The Phoenix of Philosophy: Russian Thought of the Late Soviet Period (1953–1991)* (New York: Bloomsbury Academic, 2019); Mikhail Epstein, *Ideas against Ideocracy: Non-Marxist Thought of the Late Soviet Period (1953–1991)* (New York: Bloomsbury Academic, 2022).

scientific expertise from ideological and political considerations.[35] Moreover, the authorities' new perception of social sciences as a resource for policymaking increasingly challenged the grip of ideology over political decisions.[36]

Finally, modernity in its sociocultural aspects also reached Soviet society more broadly through the progressive individualization and Westernization of lifestyles and behaviors. Scholars have emphasized the impact of major programs such as Khrushchev's new housing policy – which involved mass individual housing construction – and the development of an automobile industry on the spread of individualistic values such as consumerism, personal well-being, and worker welfare.[37] In addition, Khrushchev's doctrine of "peaceful coexistence" with the West resulted in the transition of Soviet society to controlled interaction with Western values in various sectors and social milieus. Western modern art and culture, for instance, were on display in Moscow during the Picasso exhibition in 1956 and the American jazz music concerts held at the 1957 World Youth Festival.[38]

The development of these aspects of modernity in the late Soviet Union, however, was an ambivalent process that brought contradictions to the Marxist–Leninist foundations of the Soviet political system. The Soviet authorities' commitment to reform was characterized by a nonlinear chronology, partial consistency, and limited

35 Olessia Kirtchik and Mariana Heredia, "Social and Behavioral Sciences under Dictatorship," in *International Encyclopedia of the Social & Behavioral Sciences (Second Edition)*, ed. James D. Wright (Oxford: Elsevier, 2015), 141; Martine Mespoulet, "La 'renaissance' de la sociologie en URSS (1958–1972): Une voie étroite entre matérialisme historique et 'recherches sociologiques concrètes,'" *Revue d'histoire des sciences humaines* 16, no. 1 (2007): 57–86.

36 Kirtchik and Heredia, "Social and Behavioral Sciences under Dictatorship," 142.

37 Christine Varga-Harris, "Forging Citizenship on the Home Front: Reviving the Socialist Contract and Constructing Soviet Identity during the Thaw," in *The Dilemmas of De-Stalinization: Negotiating Cultural and Social Change in the Khrushchev Era*, ed. Polly Jones (London: Routledge, 2006), 101–16; Susan E. Reid, "Khrushchev Modern," *Cahiers du monde russe* 47, no. 1–2 (2006): 227–68; Nordica Nettleton, "Driving towards Communist Consumerism," *Cahiers du monde russe* 47, no. 1–2 (2006): 131–51.

38 Eleonory Gilburd, "Picasso in Thaw Culture," *Cahiers du monde russe* 47, no. 1–2 (2006); Pia Koivunen, "The 1957 Moscow Youth Festival: Propagating a New, Peaceful Image of the Soviet Union," in *Soviet State and Society under Nikita Khrushchev*, ed. Melanie Ilic and Jeremy Smith (London: Routledge, 2009), 46–65.

application to certain sectors.[39] Polly Jones particularly highlights the authorities' paradoxical, concurrent promotion of a new Soviet individual (*lichnost*) and their fear of "disengagement from collective pursuits."[40] Similar dilemmas attended the modernization of the social sciences, which stood on a narrow path between the liberalization of knowledge production and the repressive political control over its conformity with Marxist–Leninist dogmas.[41]

In contrast to the view of the Soviet system as a rigid and monolithic bloc, therefore, the late Soviet period was marked by conflicting dynamics: the dispersion of values shared with Western liberal modernity and the preservation of idiosyncratic features of the Soviet authoritarian order.[42] The dual nature of Soviet modernity reached a climax in the Brezhnev era. Indeed, while Leonid Brezhnev's coming to power in 1964 has commonly been associated with an authoritarian crackdown and stagnation, research has shown that the maturing of Soviet modernity in these three aspects – intellectual autonomy, scientific professionalization, and individualization – continued under Brezhnev's regime, along with repressive policies of state control and censorship seeking to maintain the status quo.[43]

This paradoxical situation led some Soviet intellectuals to call for ideological reform. Toward the end of the 1960s, the Czech philosopher Radovan Richta and his fellow social scientists from the Prague Academy of Sciences reassessed some of the key epistemological principles of Marxism–Leninism to adjust them to the postindustrial development of Soviet society. They advocated reform of the state ideology

39 Polly Jones, "Introduction: The Dilemmas of De-Stalinization," in *The Dilemmas of De-Stalinization: Negotiating Cultural and Social Change in the Khrushchev Era* (London: Routledge, 2006), 12.

40 Jones, "Introduction: The Dilemmas of De-Stalinization," 9. See also Oleg Kharkhordin, "The Individual in Mature Soviet Society," in *The Collective and the Individual in Russia* (Berkeley: University of California Press, 1999), 329–54.

41 Mespoulet, "La 'renaissance' de la sociologie en URSS (1958–1972);" Gouarné and Kirtchik, "La 'modernité' des sciences sociales soviétiques."

42 For an instance of the view of the Soviet system as a monolithic ideocracy, see Graeme Gill, *Symbolism and Regime Change in Russia* (Cambridge: Cambridge University Press, 2013), 3.

43 Edwin Bacon and Mark Sandle, eds., *Brezhnev Reconsidered* (Houndmills: Palgrave Macmillan, 2002); Dina Fainberg and Artemy Kalinovsky, eds., *Reconsidering Stagnation in the Brezhnev Era: Ideology and Exchange* (Lanham, MD: Lexington Books, 2016).

to account for the changed conditions of the Soviet socioeconomic order, where the new role of the scientific intelligentsia as the key growth factor seriously challenged the Marxist class structure based on proletarian forces.[44] In particular, instead of the Marxist causal-material linear philosophy of history, they admitted a "potentially open-ended horizon of change."[45] As Jenny Andersson has noted, the discourse of the Richta group bore a certain similarity to Daniel Bell's writings on the postindustrial convergence of societies, which cited Richta extensively.[46]

These calls for ideological reforms, which resulted in the Prague Spring of 1968, were eventually crushed by the regime. However, debate over the definition and directions of Soviet modernization continued throughout the 1970s in a discursive space formed in between dissident thought and official state ideology, where Soviet intellectual elites could contribute nonconformist thinking to public sociopolitical debates while remaining established thinkers in the existing system.[47] Under these conditions, the conception of Soviet modernity as engaged on a developmental path shared with the West and leading to the two systems' ultimate convergence remained influential among reformist intellectual and political elites.[48]

It was precisely to react against this view that other Soviet intellectuals coined an alternative vision of modernity. By contrast with the convergence approach, which linked the technological modernization

[44] The volume edited by Radovan Richta, *Civilization at the Crossroads: Social and Human Implications of the Scientific and Technological Revolution*, was published in Czech in 1966, in French in 1967, and in English in 1969. See Jenny Andersson, "Bridging the Iron Curtain: Futurology as Dissidence and Control," in *The Future of the World: Futurology, Futurists, and the Struggle for the Post-Cold War Imagination* (Oxford: Oxford University Press, 2018), 123.

[45] Andersson, "Bridging the Iron Curtain," 128–29.

[46] Andersson, "Bridging the Iron Curtain," 134–35.

[47] Mark Sandle, "A Triumph of Ideological Hairdressing? Intellectual Life in the Brezhnev Era Reconsidered," in Bacon and Sandle, *Brezhnev Reconsidered*, 144; Yurchak, *Everything Was Forever, until It Was No More*, 25.

[48] Eglė Rindzevičiūtė, *The Power of Systems: How Policy Sciences Opened Up the Cold War World* (Ithaca, NY: Cornell University Press, 2016); Sergei I. Zhuk, "'Academic Détente': IREX Files, Academic Reports, and 'American' Adventures of Soviet Americanists during the Brezhnev Era," *Cahiers du monde russe* 54, no. 1–2 (2013): 297–328; Sari Autio-Sarasmo, "Stagnation or Not? The Brezhnev Leadership and East–West Interaction," in Fainberg and Kalinovsky, *Reconsidering Stagnation in the Brezhnev Era*, 87–104.

of the Soviet state with its ultimate liberalization and was used by reformist Soviet elites to justify dialogue, peaceful coexistence, and cooperation with the West, they aimed to maintain the Soviet Union in confrontation with the West. They sought to "reenchant" Soviet modernity with non-Marxist conservative and nationalistic ideological sources preserving the specificity of Russia's path. In doing, they connected elements of paradigms formerly held as incompatible, including Soviet technoscientific modernity, religious Russophile conservatism, and Stalinian state patriotism. The construction of this distinctive configuration of concepts was the birth act of Russian modernist conservatism as an ideological language.[49]

Outside the Soviet and Russian cultural areas, similar types of ideological languages also emerged around the same period to frame an alternative to Western modernity. In China and Turkey, for instance, political leaders and intellectuals have coined a comparable model of strong state power resting on a blend of traditional conservative and spiritual values with economic and technological developmental goals.

Post-Mao Chinese society, indeed, also faced a new phase of modernity following rural decollectivization and the development of a freer labor market in the late 1970s.[50] In the 1980s, Chinese society experimented with what Anne-Marie Brady calls an "age of enlightenment," marked by intense intellectual polarization over the "westernization" of the Chinese path.[51] The Chinese Communist Party (CCP) sought to "Sinicize Marxism" by combining Confucianism and communism in its efforts to design an alternative to the American doctrine of "peaceful evolution," according to which exposure to Western ideas and lifestyles would lead communist systems to merge with the dominant Western model of modernity.[52] Moreover, as Lawrence Sullivan argues, following the crackdown of the proreform faction in the CCP in 1989, Chinese leaders further embraced a conservative ideology

[49] My identification of Russian modernist conservatism as a new form of ideology is based on Michael Freeden's definition, according to which ideologies are forms of political thinking built around "distinctive configurations of concepts." Michael Freeden, *Ideologies and Political Theory: A Conceptual Approach* (Oxford: Clarendon Press, 2008), 4.

[50] Anne-Marie Brady, *Marketing Dictatorship: Propaganda and Thought Work in Contemporary China* (Lanham, MD: Rowman & Littlefield, 2009), 66.

[51] Brady, *Marketing Dictatorship*, 60.

[52] Anne-Marie Brady, ed., *China's Thought Management*, Routledge Studies on China in Transition 40 (Abingdon: Routledge, 2012), 58–70.

similar to "reactionary modernism," combining an illiberal political model with modern technology.[53]

In Turkey, a comparable ideological hybrid, the "Turkish–Islamic Synthesis," was formed in the 1970s by a right-wing intellectual society, the "Intellectuals' Hearth," to address the intellectual and social developments of modernity. The synthesis was meant as a counterreaction to the radical left-wing protest movements that had occurred in France in 1968 and were paralleled in Turkey.[54] It sought to overcome divides between secular nationalism and Islamism to unify the diverse right-wing forces against communism and the Westernization assumed by Kemalism. Since the military coup of September 1980, Zeynep Bursa-Millet shows, this eclectic synthesis has been used as the official ideology of the state and has inspired a series of education and economic reforms.[55]

Conservative reconsiderations of modernity also arose in Western contexts in the 1970s, following the postwar acceleration of individualization, technological progress, and globalization. Western societies' experience of growing sociocultural polarization, economic crises, and ecological risks triggered value uncertainty over some of the founding ideals of modernity such as the nation-state, rational progress, and growth. Sociologists have identified this period as a second phase of modernity, or late modernity, where modernity starts to question its own premises.[56] In the words of Ulrich Beck, Anthony Giddens, and Scott Lash, "late modernity" is characterized by its "self-reflexivity," that is, its capacity to "take itself as object of reflection."[57] This

[53] Lawrence R. Sullivan, "Reactionary Modernism in China: Cultural Conservatism and Technical Economism in Communist Ideology and Policy Since June 1989," in *The Aftermath of the 1989 Tiananmen Crisis for Mainland China*, ed. Bih-jaw Lin (Routledge, 1993), 15–38.

[54] Zeynep Bursa-Millet, "Le foyer des intellectuels: Sociohistoire d'un club d'influence de droite dans la Turquie du XXe siècle" (PhD diss., Paris, Ecole des Hautes Études en Sciences Sociales, 2020), 19.

[55] Bursa-Millet, "Le foyer des intellectuels," 18.

[56] Ulrich Beck, Anthony Giddens and Scott Lash, *Reflexive Modernization: Politics, Tradition and Aesthetics in the Modern Social Order* (Stanford, CA: Stanford University Press, 1994); Zygmunt Bauman, *Liquid Modernity* (Cambridge: Polity Press, 2000).

[57] Scott Lash, "Reflexivity and Its Doubles: Structures, Aesthetics, Community," in Beck, Giddens and Lash, *Reflexive Modernization*, 112; Ulrich Beck, Wolfgang Bonss and Christoph Lau, "The Theory of Reflexive Modernization: Problematic, Hypotheses and Research Programme," *Theory, Culture & Society* 20, no. 2 (2003): 6.

problematization of modernity has fed the resurgence of new conservative movements, such as the German Deutsche Volksunion, founded in 1971, the French Front National, founded in 1972, and the American "Moral Majority," created in 1979. These radical right movements were not characterized by a rejection of modernity in its entirety but rather selectively opposed the sociocultural changes brought about by the second phase of modernity.[58] An important body of literature has covered the rising popularity of these antiliberal or illiberal political movements in Europe and the United States over the past fifty years.[59]

The study of Russian modernist conservatism, therefore, opens ways to cross-cultural comparisons of illiberal ideologies of modernity that seek to frame an alternative path to postindustrial modernity emancipated from the sociocultural dimensions of the Western liberal model. In this respect, this ideology falls within the framework of "multiple modernities" developed by Eisenstadt to account for the multiplication, from around the 1960s, of understandings of modernity that have challenged the formerly homogenic vision of modernity as a Western-centered concept.[60] Eisenstadt identifies "communist Soviet" and "fascist/national-socialist" systems as the "first distinct, ideological, 'alternative' modernities."[61] Johann Arnason further theorizes the Soviet project as a "practical alternative to the existing Western version of modernity" that sought to "improve on shared ideas of modernity," such as a growth-oriented economy, modern state-building and scientific progress, albeit through its own distinctive patterns.[62] Proponents of the multiple modernities framework, however, argue that Soviet modernity eventually failed as an alternative to Western modernity. Arnason states that Soviet modernity turned into a "defunct model," a "distinctive but ultimately self-destructive version of modernity, rather

[58] Michael Minkenberg, "The Renewal of the Radical Right: Between Modernity and Anti-modernity," *Government and Opposition* 35, no. 2 (April 2000): 177.

[59] For a selection of the most recent publications, see Theda Skocpol, *The Tea Party and the Remaking of Republican Conservatism* (New York: Oxford University Press, 2016); Roger Eatwell and Matthew Goodwin, *National Populism: The Revolt against Liberal Democracy* (London: Pelican, 2018); Pippa Norris and Ronald Inglehart, *Cultural Backlash: Trump, Brexit, and Authoritarian Populism* (New York: Cambridge University Press, 2019).

[60] S. N. Eisenstadt, "Multiple Modernities," *Daedalus* 129, no. 1 (2000): 24.

[61] Eisenstadt, "Multiple Modernities," 11.

[62] Johann P. Arnason, "Communism and Modernity," *Daedalus* 129, no. 1 (2000): 70–71.

than a sustained deviation from the modernizing mainstream."[63] Likewise, Michael David-Fox writes that Soviet communism was "a failed modernity" in that it was "not able to resolve its deepest problems and perpetuate itself during its seven-decade life cycle, and it ultimately vanished as an alternative."[64]

In contrast with this historiography of Soviet modernity, which reads it backward from 1991 as a failed and self-destructive project, I analyze the phenomenon of Russian modernist conservatism as an ideological attempt to frame an alternative to Western modernity, whose mix of elements of Soviet modernity with conservative ideological resources remained active and influential as a political language across the change in regime. Russian modernist conservatism's recombination of Soviet technological modernity with traditional conservative values was maintained and consolidated after the collapse of the Soviet Union. This book suggests a method of inquiry into the production and circulation of modernist conservatism, which could be used beyond the Russian case study to reflect on other contexts where alternative conservative ideologies of modernity have risen to contest liberal standards.

1.5 From Ideological Fringes to Policy Prominence: Tracking the Career of an Idea Network in an Authoritarian Context

Russian modernist conservatism has grown in response to a growingly pressing political and geopolitical issue faced by the Soviet and then Russian regime – the horizon of convergence through postindustrial modernization – with the aim of becoming a state ideology that must guide the leaders' choices. The relation of Russian hawks to the state, therefore, has not merely been discursive; it has also been socially worked up by actions through which they have sought to play a part in setting policy agendas, inserting norms and concepts in official discourse, and legitimizing political decisions.

63 Arnason, "Communism and Modernity," 61; See also Richard Sakwa, "Modernisation, Neo-modernisation, and Comparative Democratisation in Russia," *East European Politics* 28, no. 1 (2012): 49.

64 Michael David-Fox, *Crossing Borders: Modernity, Ideology, and Culture in Russia and the Soviet Union* (Pittsburgh, PA: University of Pittsburgh Press, 2015), 9.

Despite the centralized and patrimonial character of the regime that has unfolded in post-Soviet Russia, scholars have emphasized the persistence of a moderately pluralist, policy-consequential competition between elite groups. They have described Russia as a "network state" to highlight the reliance of the regime on various informal elite networks whose interaction contributes to the country's governance by organizing the distribution of resources through a system of coercion and reward.[65] These models of Russia as a network state, however, exclude intellectuals from any role by focusing exclusively on the political and economic pursuits of elite groups such as oligarchs, party bosses, and government officials. Furthermore, Henry Hale's influential study on post-Soviet patronal politics posits elite networks as displacing ideology, by drawing individuals away from collectivities bound by abstract principles and into collectivities based on personalized exchange of material gains.[66] Instead, my analysis of the formation of the Russian hawks puts forward the concept of "idea network" to highlight that ideology is a key dimension, alongside material factors, that determines the construction of elite networks.

In this attempt, I follow in the footsteps of authors who have restored the significance of ideology as a form of symbolic language constitutive of social life. This approach seeks to reach a balance between idealism, which views ideas as pure value commitment to norms, and structuralism, which understands ideas as instruments concealing material interests. By contrast, authors such as Karl Mannheim have defined ideology as a collective practice that is dependent on group existence and is rooted in action. As Mannheim explains, ideology is a collection of shared meanings and evaluative interpretations that contains a "crystallization of the experiences of a certain group" and defines membership in this group.[67] More recently, Michael Freeden has linked the study of ideological recombination with the processes of

[65] Vadim Kononenko and Arkadii Moshes, *Russia as a Network State: What Works in Russia When State Institutions Do Not?* (New York: Palgrave Macmillan, 2011); Alena V. Ledeneva, *Can Russia Modernise?: Sistema, Power Networks and Informal Governance* (Cambridge: Cambridge University Press, 2013); Henry E. Hale, *Patronal Politics: Eurasian Regime Dynamics in Comparative Perspective*, Problems of International Politics (Cambridge: Cambridge University Press, 2014).

[66] Hale, *Patronal Politics*, 9–10.

[67] Karl Mannheim, *Ideology and Utopia: An Introduction to the Sociology of Knowledge* (Mansfield Center, CT: Martino Publishing, 2015), 19.

mutation of groups from which ideologies emerge.[68] This perspective stresses the relational aspect of ideology as a variety of group language that has a meaning in relation to the ideology of other groups.

Likewise, I understand modernist conservatism as the collective language that has provided symbolic representation to the Russian hawks by organizing their common reaction to late modern developments. Starting in the late Soviet Union, modernist conservatism provided a rallying "magnet" sealing a common group identity for various intellectual and political elites opposing convergence with the West.[69] The unity of the coalition was formed as much on a set of common reactions and experiences as on a common pledge to gain hegemony over other elite groups. Despite the eclecticism of this coalition, the consolidation of modernist conservatism as their common language performatively forged their sense of group belonging and carried it through the collapse of the Soviet Union. Not only did Russian hawks sustain and expand as a social group across two generations in post-Soviet Russia but they also managed to reach new constituencies among intellectual, political, and cultural elite groups.

Ideology, therefore, plays a structuring role in the Russian political system, since it defines and substantiates the identity and contours of elite groups whose interaction, administered under the authoritarian control of the executive power, shapes the power system organizing the distribution of resources.[70]

This approach addresses an important debate in political science regarding how to assess the influence of ideas over policy decisions. In the Russian case, some scholars assume that the regime's policy decisions are rooted in ideological considerations. They use discourse analyses to demonstrate the political leaders' progressive endorsement of an increasingly assertive conservative state ideology.[71] Others, by

[68] Michael Freeden, "Confronting the Chimera of a 'Post-Ideological' Age," *Critical Review of International Social and Political Philosophy* 8, no. 2 (June 2005): 257.

[69] On ideas as "magnets," see Daniel Béland and Robert Henry Cox, "Ideas as Coalition Magnets: Coalition Building, Policy Entrepreneurs, and Power Relations," *Journal of European Public Policy* 23, no. 3 (2016): 428–45.

[70] I thank Aleksandr Lutsenko for helping me formulate this argument.

[71] See, for instance, Aleksei Chadaev, *Putin. Ego ideologiia* (Moscow: Evropa, 2006) and Maria Engström, "Contemporary Russian Messianism and New Russian Foreign Policy," *Contemporary Security Policy* 35, no. 3 (2014): 356–79.

contrast, expose the regime's lack of genuine adhesion to ideological values and principles. They have pointed to the Kremlin's mere instrumental and cynical use of ideology as a cover, hiding pragmatic goals such as legitimizing a ruling circle holding onto power and attracting international support for Russia among conservative political audiences.[72]

Instead, I demonstrate that the rise of the Russian hawks' ideas to policy prominence was the result of the reconfiguration of the Soviet and then Russian elite networks, which ensued from conflicts and negotiations taking place over the past sixty years across intellectual and political milieus. I therefore depart from strictly realist approaches that only consider material interests and capabilities as explanatory variables affecting policy decisions. Further, I also highlight what culturalist approaches may not be so good at seeing – the interactional and competitive process through which idea producers seek policy influence.

Contrary to the view that pits the Soviet state ideology against the post-Soviet ideological vacuum,[73] I show that, starting from the mid-1990s, the Russian regime has resumed Soviet practices of state sponsorship of ideology production. However, unlike in Soviet times, the post-Soviet regime does not rely on an institutionalized ideological apparatus but rather on transactional relations with idea networks across intellectual and political elites.

By focusing on the public career of the Russian hawks, I highlight the sociohistorical processes through which they have evolved from the fringes to an hegemonic position able to contribute to the

72 See, for instance, Marlène Laruelle, 'Conservatism as the Kremlin's New Toolkit: An Ideology at the Lowest Cost,' *Russian Analytical Digest* 138 (2013): 2–4; Anton Shekhovtsov, *Russia and the Western Far Right: Tango Noir* (London: Routledge, 2017) and Mark Galeotti, *We Need to Talk about Putin: Why the West Gets Him Wrong, and How to Get Him Right* (London: Ebury Publishing, 2019).

73 For works carrying on this view, see Artemy Magun, *Negative Revolution: Modern Political Subject and Its Fate after the Cold War* (New York: Bloomsbury Academic, 2013); Serguei Oushakine, "In the State of Post-Soviet Aphasia: Symbolic Development in Contemporary Russia," *Europe-Asia Studies* 52, no. 6 (2000): 1003; Stephen Hanson, *Post-Imperial Democracies: Ideology and Party Formation in Third Republic France, Weimar Germany, and Post-Soviet Russia* (New York: Cambridge University Press, 2010); Graeme Gill, *Symbolism and Regime Change in Russia* (Cambridge: Cambridge University Press, 2013), 11, 212.

justification of major policy choices in contemporary Russia.[74] Their rise resulted from the strategy of cultural influence that they deployed to gain recognition and legitimacy in the public space by investing a set of relational, discursive, and institutional resources. On the other hand, their ascension was fostered by their top-down cooptation by decision-makers seeking legitimizing and mobilizing resources for the regime's distinction from Western liberalism. Analysis of their public career shows that they have been increasingly able, starting from the 2000s, to compete against more liberal groups for access to state-sponsored resources such as media visibility, honorific status recognition and financial support. The creation of the Izborskii Klub in 2012 provided official institutional shape to the Russian hawks as an idea network across various elite groups. The regime, however, has remained committed to the maintenance of a competitive environment for ideology production, where the Izborskii Klub has coexisted with liberal-inclined elite networks.

Beyond the Russian context, this research contributes a study of the transformation of the use of ideology in contemporary authoritarian regimes. As authors have highlighted in the Chinese and Iranian contexts, I show that, instead of fixing a single state ideology, authoritarian leaders maintain ideological polarization within elite groups and selectively coopt them to ensure a degree of policy flexibility and sustain themselves in changing strategic environments.[75]

1.6 Structure of the Book

Chapter 2 demonstrates that Russian hawks first theorized modernist conservatism in the late Soviet Union as an attempt to confront the convergence horizon predicted by Western liberal modernization

[74] Although I use a relational approach to analyze the evolution of the position of the Russian hawks relative to that of other groups, my focus on the particularities of the hawks' career limits the scope of my research to one ideological group in a broader environment of ideology production. A more comprehensive understanding of that environment would require similar in-depth investigations into the socio-intellectual career of the Russian hawks' alternatives.

[75] See, for instance, Wendy Ramadan-Alban and Thierry Balzacq, "Pivotal Powers: Iran," in *Comparative Grand Strategy: A Framework and Cases*, ed. Thierry Balzacq, Peter Dombrowski, and Simon Reich (Oxford: Oxford University Press, 2019) and Zhu Xufeng, "The Influence of Think Tanks in the Chinese Policy Process: Different Ways and Mechanisms," *Asian Survey* 49, no. 2 (2009): 333–57.

theories. They aimed to reenchant Soviet modernity through the decontestation of the relationship between technological modernity and spirituality. As they view it, this new ideological language should serve to reinvigorate the Soviet state ideology and maintain it as an alternative to the Western model of modernity. The chapter shows that, in contrast to the description of the Soviet state ideology as a rigid monolith, modernist conservatism's ideas were selectively dispersed in official sites of ideology production such as the Komsomol.

Chapter 3 argues that, starting from 1985, the Russian hawks consolidated as an idea network built around their common opposition to *perestroika*. Modernist conservatism served as the ideological magnet of this eclectic group aggregating national-conservative intellectuals with pro–status quo members of the Soviet political and military establishment. The newspapers *Den* (1990–93) and *Zavtra* (1993–) became the intellectual and social fabrics of the group's identity and cohesion, which were maintained across the 1991 regime change. The chapter demonstrates that some of the hawks' ideas spread in the ruling elites' discourse as early as in the mid-1990s to legitimate the authoritarian nature of the turn to a superpresidential system and to foster the construction of post-Soviet state patriotism.

Chapter 4 shows how the Russian hawks' ideas moved from the fringes to the center of the public scene in the early 2000s. It investigates the 2001–2002 controversy that surrounded the publication of a novel written by one of the most radical conservative ideologues, Aleksandr Prokhanov. It demonstrates that the controversy reconfigured the formerly consensual distinction between legitimate and transgressive public discourse. It explains that the intellectual legitimation of Prokhanov thrived on Russia's political and intellectual elites' backlash against the legacy of the 1990s and the standards of Western liberalism. The controversy eventually contributed to normalizing modernist conservatism, which gained a new audience among the younger generation of intellectuals.

Chapter 5 demonstrates that in the years 2000–2005 a new generation of Russian hawks born around the 1970s, the "Young Conservatives," acquired a reputation as professional media intellectuals and developed a new type of collective ideological entrepreneurship. They naturalized modernist conservatism's eclectic blend of concepts into a full-fledged ideology, "dynamic conservatism." Moreover, they established themselves as a legitimate stratum of Russia's intellectual elites contributing public policy recommendations.

Chapter 6 shows that Russian hawks entered the regime's market for ideology in the years 2005–12. Transactional relations were established between modernist conservatives and the ruling party, whereby the former's ideological discourse was sponsored as a strategic resource for the regime's legitimation against oppositional forces and for its distinction against the Western model of liberal democracy. In 2012, the creation of the Izborskii Klub provided institutional form to this interelite network aimed at gaining policy influence over more liberal-inclined elite networks.

Chapter 7 finds that, from 2012 to 2022, the Izborskii Klub evolved from a state-sponsored think tank, whose ideas were used as legitimizing sources for the regime's policy decisions, to a private lobby group competing for hegemony over the definition of Russia's grand strategy. The alternative state promotion and demotion of the club demonstrates the executive power's limited and contextual endorsement of ideological narratives and its principled commitment to maintaining a certain degree of pluralism and policy flexibility through the attribution of shifting power weights to different elite blocs.

Chapter 8 discusses how the Russian regime's invasion of Ukraine in February 2022 concretely enacted Russian hawks' conception of Russia as an imperial great power that should rely on its technological and military might to assert its civilizational distinction from the West. This chapter argues that the Russian regime has restored elements reminiscent of the Soviet-style "vertical," facilitating the propagation of norms and principles through a bureaucratic chain of command. However, the regime has not completely reconstructed a cohesive institutionalized state apparatus. Its doctrinal framework remains adaptable. In addition to official state-led initiatives, the regime continues to oversee ideology formation through interactions and transactions with a variety of nonstate ideological entrepreneurs. This involvement of diverse actors across state and nonstate realms fostered maintains a certain degree of polarization within policy circles. Moreover, the hawks' production of narratives justifying Russia's imperialism and war violence has encountered resistance from recent intellectual emigrants who have established organizations in exile dedicated to fostering critical thinking and dissent within intellectual circles.

In conclusion, Chapter 9 highlights that the book has shown that the Russian regime, from the mid-1990s onward, has revived Soviet practices of sponsorship of ideology production. Instead of the Soviet institutionalization of an ideological apparatus, however, the current regime has outsourced it to clubs and think tanks outside the administration or party institutions. This challenges the common narrative that identifies a distinct conservative turning point in the Russian regime from 2012 onward. Instead, the book argues that this shift should be viewed within a broader and more gradual evolution of the relationship between decision-makers and "ideas networks." The second implication is that regime support for ideology production aimed not at consolidating a unique state ideology but at cultivating and authoritatively controlling a certain degree of ideological pluralism. While an ideological core consolidated over the years in official discourse around key concepts such as strong state power and the multipolarity of the world order, additional ideological content remained fluid. This practice of "managed ideological pluralism" through the promotion or demotion of different idea networks maintained a range of lines and narratives available to justify various policy courses.

2 *Reenchanting Soviet Modernity (1960–1985)*

The spiritualization, deification, or, more simply, humanization of technology, is the ethical mission of contemporary art.

Aleksandr Prokhanov, "Ne oshibitsia v diagnoze," 1980

Following the Second World War, a new phase of scientific and technological modernity unfolded with the rise of nuclear, space, and cybernetics technologies. The technoscientific revolution and the rise of postindustrialism, led by scientific elites, challenged the key foundations of the Soviet socioeconomic order. The Soviet economy had previously relied on the working classes at the center of the mechanization of industry and agriculture, yet scientific and technocratic elites had gradually become the main drivers of economic growth. Starting from the 1960s, the prediction, by Western modernization theories, that technological development would lead the Soviet society to eventually converge with the Western model of political and economic institutions became a major concern for Soviet intellectuals.

This chapter studies the period between Nikita Khrushchev's Thaw and Mikhail Gorbachev's coming to power in 1985. The liberalization policies led by Khrushchev provided more freedom for intellectuals to argue about the consequences of the technological modernization of the Soviet society by voicing nonconformist, even critical, views. The pluralization of ideological languages and their contestation of Marxism–Leninism as an established dogma proliferated in the intellectual space of "other-thinking" (*inakomyslie*) that grew in between dissent and conformism.[1] On the one hand, liberal-inclined intellectuals advocated

[1] For instances of "other-thinking" in this period, see Vladislav Zubok, *Zhivago's Children: The Last Russian Intelligentsia* (Cambridge, MA: Belknap Press of Harvard University Press, 2009), 39; Mark Sandle, "A Triumph of Ideological Hairdressing? Intellectual Life in the Brezhnev Era Reconsidered," in *Brezhnev Reconsidered*, ed. Edwin Bacon and Mark Sandle (London: Palgrave

the diffusion of democratic values associated with science, such as transparency and freedom of expression, to sociopolitical domains. On the other hand, nationalist and conservative voices rose to denounce the impact of technological progress on the destruction of Russia's traditional cultural, moral, and religious values. Throughout the 1960s and 1970s, various intellectuals framed a third path that I term "modernist conservatism" because it reconfigured the ideological affinities between technological modernity, spirituality, and Soviet state patriotism.

Modernist conservatism reacted to the convergence horizon by seeking to reenchant the state Marxist–Leninist ideology through its spiritualization, in order to maintain a specifically Soviet path to modernity. In contrast to the liberal secular conception of technology, modernist conservatives framed an alternative path to modernity by blending technoscientific progress with the promotion of the country's distinct cultural and religious identity. In doing so, they embraced a spiritual approach to technological progress that had been developed by thinkers between the end of the nineteenth century and the beginning of the twentieth, whose ideas spread in the 1970s under the label "Russian cosmism." Although they relied on non-Marxist intellectual sources such as Orthodox spirituality and Russian cosmism, modernist conservatives aimed to use them to fix and legitimize the Soviet alternative to Western modernity. This critical, yet loyal, reinterpretation of the state ideology was characteristic of late Soviet intellectuals' attempt to seek a "conciliation path" between Marxism and other philosophical currents.[2]

This chapter focuses on three major theorizers of modernist conservatism: Vasilii Zakharchenko (1915–99), Aleksandr Prokhanov (1938–), and Valerii Skurlatov (1938–).[3] Through their dual

Macmillan UK, 2002), pp. 1–21; Alexei Yurchak, *Everything Was Forever, until It Was No More: The Last Soviet Generation* (Princeton, NJ: Princeton University Press, 2005); Benjamin Nathans, "The Dictatorship of Reason: Aleksandr Vol'Pin and the Idea of Rights under 'Developed Socialism,'" *Slavic Review* 66, no. 4 (2007): 630–63; Mikhail Epstein, *Ideas against Ideocracy: Non-Marxist Thought of the Late Soviet Period (1953–1991)* (New York: Bloomsbury Academic, 2022).

2 Sociologist Janina Markiewicz-Lagneau has coined the expression "integrated nonconformism" to define this attitude. See Janina Markiewicz-Lagneau, "La fin de l'intelligentsia? Formation et transformation de l'intelligentsia soviétique," *Revue d'études comparatives Est-Ouest* 7, no. 4 (1976): 65.

3 I have conducted interviews in Russian with Aleksandr Prokhanov (2019, in Moscow, semistructured oral interview) and Valerii Skurlatov (2021, written interview over emails due to Covid-related travel restrictions).

membership in intellectual and political milieus, they were able to spread modernist conservatism from informal study groups to public sites of idea production such as newspapers and state organizations like the Komsomol, the youth division of the Communist Party, thereby feeding the political system with alternative sources of ideological underpinning. Eventually, the new hybrid ideology they framed, blending technological modernity with spirituality, found resonance in official state ideological work to the extent that it put forward the Soviet Union's distinct identity in opposition to the West.

2.1 The "Convergence Horizon": A Major Concern for Soviet Elites

2.1.1 A Growing Intellectual and Political Debate about Technological Modernity

By the mid-1960s the social impact of the scientific and technological revolution had become a major concern for the Soviet elite. Debates over the consequences of the new stage of modernity were permitted by Khrushchev's relaxation of censorship. Indeed, with the partial release of the state's control and greater informal access to non-Marxist thinking, intellectuals were able to detach themselves from the collective official metanarrative. Khrushchev's Thaw therefore empowered intellectuals with greater freedom to contribute to sociopolitical debates with nonconformist, even critical, thinking.[4] The newly founded, mass-circulation journals, distributed in hundreds of thousands of copies, became major forums where intellectuals were able to confront each other's views.[5] In 1966, Radovan Richta (1924–83), a philosopher at the Academy of Sciences of

[4] Carole Sigman, for instance, mentions the formation of places of liberal "heterodox thought" in the 1960s, which later served as the founding bases for the creation of informal political clubs during perestroika. Carole Sigman, *Clubs politiques et perestroïka en Russie: Subversion sans dissidence* (Paris: Karthala, 2009), 56.

[5] Yitzhak Brudny uses the expression "politics by culture" to describe the practice whereby Soviet intellectuals would use seemingly nonpolitical venues such as literary journals to hold sociopolitical debates. Yitzhak M. Brudny, *Reinventing Russia: Russian Nationalism and the Soviet State, 1953–1991* (Cambridge, MA: Harvard University Press, 1998), 13.

Czechoslovakia, published a series of articles on the consequences of the scientific and technological revolution for the Soviet social order. He edited a volume entitled *Civilization at the Crossroads: Social and Human Implications of the Scientific and Technological Revolution* to highlight the changes in the class structure of Soviet society as "knowledge classes" progressively replaced the "working class" as the main productive forces:

> Science is emerging as the leading variable in the national economy and the vital dimension in the growth of civilization. There are signs of a new ("post-industrial") type of growth with a new dynamic stemming from continuing structural changes in the productive forces, with the amount of means of production and humanpower becoming less important than their changing quality and degree of utilization.[6]

The task of addressing the social changes prompted by the scientific and technological revolution was a central motive behind the reform communism agenda requested by the leaders of the Prague Spring in 1968.[7]

Brezhnev's repression of the Prague Spring was followed by censorship measures directed at social studies, which had argued for ideological reforms as a consequence of the scientific and technological revolution.[8] As Marxist–Leninist ideology was increasingly losing its mobilization power and grasp on social reality, the Brezhnev regime advocated the achievement of technical goals such as the scientific management of society, bureaucratic efficiency, and economic rationalization.[9] However, debate over the definition and directions of Soviet modernization continued throughout the 1970s in a discursive space formed in between dissident thought and official state ideology, where Soviet intellectual elites could contribute nonconformist

6 Cited in Daniel Bell, *Coming of Post-Industrial Society* (New York: Basic Books, 1973), 113.

7 Vitezslav Sommer, "'Are We Still Behaving as Revolutionaries?': Radovan Richta, Theory of Revolution and Dilemmas of Reform Communism in Czechoslovakia," *Studies in East European Thought* 69 (2017): 93–110.

8 The only permitted analyses of these changes were provided by the newly created sociological department of the Academy of Sciences, the Institute of Concrete Social Research, founded in 1968.

9 Egle Rindzevičiūtė, "The Future as an Intellectual Technology in the Soviet Union: From Centralised Planning to Reflexive Management," *Cahiers du monde russe* 56, no. 1 (March 2015): 117.

thinking while remaining established thinkers in the existing system.[10] The contestation over Marxist–Leninism's inability to address the changed conditions of Soviet modernity resulted in the proliferation of new ideological languages.

On the one hand, the conception of Soviet modernity as engaged on a developmental path shared with the West and leading to the two systems' ultimate convergence remained influential among liberal-inclined elites. In particular, famous scientists such as the physicists Andrei Sakharov (1921–89) and Andrei Tverdokhlebov (1940–2011) and the biologist Zhores Medvedev (1925–2018) promoted a liberal and democratic understanding of science as a universal rational method requiring greater transparency and individual freedoms. They were among the leaders of the dissident movement that advocated democratic reforms and human rights.[11] In literature, a liberal trend represented by Iurii Trifonov (1925–81) and Anatolii Rybakov (1911–98) was concerned with urban social issues and the critique of Stalin's legacy.

On the other hand, conservative voices, inspired by the rediscovery of the prerevolutionary religious and Slavophile philosophy, voiced concerns over the moral and cultural decline provoked by technological modernity. The literary journal *Nash sovremennik* became the mouthpiece of this conservative attitude, which was notably advocated by the "village writers."[12] This literary movement put forward an idealized vision of prerevolutionary Russia and promoted traditions, religious values, moral codes, and ancient peasant virtues.[13] In their view, scientific and technological progress had led to the destruction of nature, the westernization of the country, the passing of traditions,

[10] See Sandle, "Triumph of Ideological Hairdressing?" 144 and Yurchak, *Everything Was Forever*, 25.

[11] See for instance Andrei Sakharov's article on progress, pacific coexistence and intellectual freedom: Andrei Sakharov, "Rasmyshleniia o progresse, mirnom sosushchestvovanii i intellektualnoi svobode," published in *Samizdat* in 1968. On the local liberal subculture developed in scientific cities, see Paul R. Josephson, *New Atlantis Revisited: Akademgorodok, the Siberian City of Science* (Princeton, NJ: Princeton University Press, 1997), xv.

[12] Famous village prose writers included Fedor Abramov (1920–83), Viktor Astafev (1924–2001), Valentin Rasputin (1937–2015), and Vladimir Soloukhin (1924–97).

[13] For a detailed study of the village prose movement, see Kathleen F. Parthé, *Russian Village Prose: The Radiant Past* (Princeton, NJ: Princeton University Press, 1992).

and a deepening moral crisis. Yitzhak Brudny has shown that, despite the heightened censorship, village prose writers were granted "unprecedented freedom"[14] to discuss their ideas in leading journals.[15] By the 1970s, the village prose had turned into a predominantly nationalist movement with anti-Western and anti-Semitic overtones. They voiced their concerns on issues such as the use of chemical fertilizers, the pollution of Lake Baikal by industrial factories, and the state's project of diverting Siberian rivers.[16] Valentin Rasputin's novel *Farewell to Matyora* (1976), which told the story of the flooding of a village and its Orthodox church as a result of the construction of a hydroelectric power plant, is one of the most prominent examples of the ecological consciousness of conservative village writers.

In contrast to both technocritical conservatism and liberal progressivism, an alternative spiritual conception of science, compatible with the preservation of a specifically national modernization model, progressively formed around the rehabilitation of the reputation and works of cosmist scientists and philosophers.

2.1.2 Russian Cosmism: A New Philosophical Hybrid of Science and Religion

In the 1960s and 1970s, a group of scholars started promoting the work of authors from the end of the nineteenth century and the beginning of the twentieth, such as the philosopher Nikolai Fedorov (1829–1903) and the scientists Konstantin Tsiolkovskii (1857–1935), and Vladimir Vernadskii (1863–1945). In contrast to both secular positivism and religious traditionalism, Fedorov's model of "active Christianity" claimed that modern science could contribute to the achievement of Christian eschatology.[17] His main work, *The Philosophy of the Common Cause*,

[14] The state promotion of village prose varied in intensity under the Brezhnev regime. It was mainly motivated by the fact that, in contrast to the liberal trend of literature, village prose was not considered a threat to the authoritarian nature of the regime and that it put forward anti-Western views. See Brudny, *Reinventing Russia*, 16, 57.

[15] For instance, in 1969, the journal *Voprosy literatury* held a debate over the political legacy of nineteenth-century nationalist and Slavophile thought. See Brudny, *Reinventing Russia*, 86.

[16] Brudny, *Reinventing Russia*, 137–38.

[17] As put by the sociologist Boris Knorre, Fedorov's religious philosophy is a case of "Orthodox modernism." Boris Knorre, "Fedorovskoe religiozno-filosofskoe dvizhenie kak primer religioznogo modernizma," *Russian Review* 10 (2006).

which was published posthumously in 1906–13, advocated the use of scientific and technological progress to direct the evolution of the universe toward the spiritualization of the world and the achievement of universal salvation. In his view, technological progress would usher in a new age where humanity was able to regulate the cosmos and realize the promises of the Bible, including transforming human nature toward its deification, reaching immortality and resurrecting the dead. Following him, Vernadskii, the founder of modern geochemistry, and Tsiolkovskii, a pioneer of astronautic theory, also developed a spiritualist understanding of the end goal of science.[18]

The cosmist roots of the Soviet enthusiasm for science and technology were purged in the early 1930s as a result of the rise of the totalitarian application of the party's Marxist–Leninist ideology to all spheres of cultural and intellectual production. However, Khrushchev's Thaw led to the rediscovery and timid circulation of some of Fedorov's ideas. In the 1960s, Olga Setnitskaia, the daughter of one of Fedorov's leading disciples, Nikolai Setnitskii (1888–1937), introduced the work of Fedorov to philosophers and scientists such as the biologist and president of the Belarusian Academy of Sciences, Vasilii Kuprevich, and the futurologist Igor Zabelin.[19] During this period, Kuprevich and other authors periodically published articles covering issues such as life extension, resuscitation, immortality, and cryonics in the newspapers *Nauka i zhizn* (*Science and Life*), *Komsomolskaia pravda*, *Moskovskii komsomolets*, and *Literaturnaia gazeta*.[20] In 1965, the publishing house Progress edited a translation of Pierre Teilhard de Chardin's philosophical and theological essay *The Human Phenomenon*, in which he developed the concept of "noosphere," coauthored with Vernadskii, according to which human intelligence would become the driver and the organizing principle of the next geological phase after the biosphere. In addition, in 1966, the first annual readings in memory of Tsiolkovskii were held in his hometown, Kaluga. These readings were subsequently held

[18] Michael Hagemeister, "The Conquest of Space and the Bliss of Atoms: Konstantin Tsiolkovskii," in *Cosmic Enthusiasm: The Cultural Impact of Soviet Space Exploration since the 1950s*, ed. Eva Maurer et al. (New York: Palgrave Macmillan, 2011), pp. 27–41.

[19] Anastasiia Gacheva, *Russkii kosmizm v ideiakh i litsakh* (Moscow: Akademicheskii Proekt, 2019), 413–14.

[20] See Gacheva, *Russkii kosmizm*, 413–14.

every year and served as a platform for the circulation and discussion of nonconformist cosmist thinkers.[21]

The first definition of the label "Russian cosmism" in a print publication appeared in 1970, in the fifth volume of the *Philosophical Encyclopedia*. According to Hagemeister, this volume of the *Philosophical Encyclopedia* was "known among experts to be particularly liberal and free of ideological condemnations."[22] In an article devoted to Vernadskii, the philosopher Renata Galtseva stated that the core of his common lineage and collectivity as part of "Russian cosmism" laid in a set of "natural-philosophical ideas" that considered "the human and the Universe as a single self-regulated system (homeostatis)" and that advocated the use of human intelligence to seek the "transformation of the cosmos."[23] In 1972, during an annual conference devoted to Tsiolkovskii, the historian of religious philosophy Nikolai Gavriushin also contributed a definition of Russian cosmism as a "worldview characterized by a brightly pronounced anti-geocentric orientation and a belief in the unlimited creative capacity of human beings."[24]

Throughout the 1970s, Russian cosmism was studied by a group of scholars who went on to turn the theoretical label into an active, although informal, intellectual movement. This community comprised a wide range of intellectuals such as philosophers Boris Slavin (1941–) and Iurii Linnik (1944–2018), the engineer Oleg Avdykovich (1925–89), the linguist Marika Melkumian (dates unknown), art critic Valerii Baidin (1948–), the theologian Valentin Nikitin (1947–2017), and the psychiatrist Lazar Sukharebskii (1899–1986). The leading organizer of this community, the philologist and specialist in Russian philosophical history Svetlana Semenova (1941–2014), fixed the core concept of Russian cosmism around the idea of "active evolution."[25]

21 Hagemeister, "Le 'cosmisme russe,' 'philosophie de l'avenir?'" *Slavica Occitania* 46 (December 2018): 61.
22 Private communication.
23 Galtseva's original definition in Russian is cited in Michael Hagemeister, "Le 'cosmisme russe,'" 58. Translation from Russian is mine.
24 Nikolai Gavriushin, "Iz istorii russkogo kosmizma," *Trudy V i VI chtenii, posviashchennykh razrabotke nauchnogo naslediia i razvitiiu tvorchestva K. E. Tsiolkovskogo* (1972): 104.
25 For more biographical information on Svetlana Semenova, see Anya Bernstein, *The Future of Immortality: Remaking Life and Death in Contemporary Russia*, Princeton Studies in Culture and Technology (Princeton, NJ: Princeton University Press, 2019), 117.

As she explains, the concept is based on the idea that humanity is destined to orient the development of the universe according to its divinely predetermined path toward the spiritualization of the human and the world.[26]

The name "Russian cosmism" did not correspond to a structured theoretical school of thought but rather retrospectively brought together an eclectic set of thinkers under a single label. For this reason, Michael Hagemeister regards Russian cosmism as a typical case of an "invented tradition" devoid of heuristic value.[27] However, Russian cosmism should instead be considered as a meaning-making symbolic construction, the meaning of which primarily addressed the debates stemming from the context of late Soviet society. The spiritual vision of scientific progress promoted by Russian cosmism provided an alternative to the growing opposition between technological modernity and the revival of Russian prerevolutionary conservative philosophy. Moreover, the making of Russian cosmism as a philosophy of history, which reads the evolution of humanity in light of an eschatological teleology, aimed to provide an alternative to the exhaustion of materialistic Soviet modernity under Brezhnev's regime. As noticed by one of the scholars involved in the theorization of Russian cosmism, the choice of the terms "Russian cosmism," instead of "Soviet cosmism" or simply "cosmism," aimed to reaffirm the "Russian philosophical consciousness," which had been absent since 1917.[28] They further claimed that the intellectual interest in Fedorov at that time was part of a search for "an alternative to the old Soviet ideology, including a moral alternative."[29] Moreover, the Russian cosmists' interest in heterodox, esoteric discourse on science and spirituality matched what Mikhail Epstein identifies as the "religious renaissance" of the 1970s. As he puts it, a "phenomenon of post-atheist religiosity" took place in the "'mundane' spiritual life and in contemporary thought," rather

[26] See the introduction in Svetlana Semenova and Anastasiia Gacheva (eds.), *Russkii kosmizm: Antologiia filosofskoi mysli* (Moscow: Pedagogika Press, 1993). For a more detailed presentation of Semenova's and other Soviet thinkers' interpretation of Russian cosmism, see Epstein, *Ideas against Ideocracy*, 135–50.

[27] Michael Hagemeister, "The Hybrid Ideology: Historian Michael Hagemeister Traces the Trajectory of Russian Cosmism," interview by Andrey Shental, INRUSSIA, http://inrussia.com/the-hybrid-ideology.

[28] Author interview, Zoom, 2020. [29] Author interview.

than in churches and in traditional religious doctrines.[30] This new, "minimal religion" emphasized the believer's direct relationship with God, "here and now." Appeals to "spirituality" (*dukhovnost*) never ceased during the Soviet period, despite the regime promoting a secularized meaning of the word, mainly relying on humanistic values.[31] The concept of spirituality regained its religious content in the nonconformist discourses of the 1970s, which were phrased in opposition to institutionalized religions, in "reaction to atheism" and at times in "opposition to the Soviet regime."[32] Indeed, Semenova's story of her personal encounter with Fedorov's thought demonstrates the spiritual dimension of her "conversion" to the Russian cosmist system of thought. In an interview given in 2004 to *Literaturnaia gazeta*, she described her first reading of Fedorov's *Philosophy of the Common Cause* as an event that "radically changed her life" and "pierced" her "as a revelation of the evolutionary vanguard of the Earth and of the entire human race":

> Fedorov's teachings appeared to me clear and harmonious, like a beautiful Temple, visibly bearing the wealth of its metaphysical, ethical-aesthetic, practical message to the sons and daughters of men.[33]

Like other mystical and theosophical movements gaining in popularity at that time throughout the Eastern bloc, Russian cosmism's esotericism, parascience, and spiritual eschatology were characteristic of a desecularization of modernity. In this regard, while Russian cosmism embraced a diverse set of authors and ideas, it also provided a meaning-making symbolic paradigm embedded in the context of its emergence in and answer to Soviet modernity. Beyond the strictly Soviet context, Russian cosmism was also illustrative of a broader evolution of secularized societies in the early 1970s, which witnessed both upsurges of traditional religions and a rise of "new religious movements" outside

30 Mikhail Epstein, "Minimal Religion (1982)," in *Russian Postmodernism: New Perspectives on Post-Soviet Culture*, ed. Mikhail Epstein, Alexander Genis and Slobodanka Vladiv-Glover (New York: Berghahn Books, 2016), pp. 282–83.

31 Kathy Rousselet, "'Dukhovnost' in Russia's Politics," *Religion, State and Society* 48, no. 1 (2020): 41–42.

32 Rousselet, "'Dukhovnost' in Russia's Politics," 43.

33 Svetlana Semenova, "Filosofstvovat—znachit uchitsia ne umirat," interview by Aleksandr Iakovkev, *Literaturnaia gazeta* 10, no. 5870 (March 19, 2002).

church institutions.[34] The development of Russian cosmism as an intellectual movement in the 1970s thus undermines claims of Soviet culture's exceptionalism and instead highlights its contribution to a global intellectual history of modernity.

2.2 A New Conservative Ideology Based on the "Spiritualization of Technology"

2.2.1 Three Founding Conceptualizers of Modernist Conservatism

The absence of an open public sphere to discuss the definition and use of Russian cosmism allowed for varied amateur understandings of this label. In these circumstances, several intellectuals, including Vasilii Zakharchenko (1915–99), Aleksandr Prokhanov (1938–), and Valerii Skurlatov (1938–), played a key role in influencing its interpretation and circulation among intellectual and political milieus. In the context of the late Soviet society's debate over technological modernity, they drew on Russian cosmism as a theoretical foundation for producing a newfound compatibility between national-conservatism and Soviet technocratism. Against Western modernization theories advocating a universal model of liberal secular modernity, they drew on Russian cosmism's syncretic vision of science and spirituality to argue that technological progress can marry Russian traditional religious values and serve the development of an authoritarian state. In doing so, they formed a new type of nonconformist thinking, modernist conservatism.

Analysis of the biographical trajectories of these three intellectuals highlights some of the key factors that led them to embrace heterodox, theoretically eclectic worldviews. Despite their initial scientific background, they all subsequently changed their career paths toward social sciences and the humanities. Moreover, they benefited from the progressive individualization of life choices to connect to informal intellectual circles and to enjoy greater leeway in the management of

[34] For an exploration of the upsurges of traditional religions in various cultural contexts, see Peter L. Berger (ed.), *The Desecularization of the World: Resurgent Religion and World Politics* (Washington, DC: Ethics and Public Policy Center W. B. Eerdmans, 1999).

their professional itinerary and belief systems.[35] Finally, their membership in both nonconformist milieus and the establishment cultivated their dual commitment to unorthodox worldviews and loyalist state patriotism.

2.2.1.1 Vasilii Zakharchenko

Zakharchenko graduated from the Moscow Power Engineering Institute in 1937 and from the Maxim Gorky Literature Institute in 1941.[36] As a member of what Brudny terms the "purge generation," born between approximately 1910 and 1919, Zakharchenko mainly accessed the ideas of Russian cosmists through literature and science fiction.[37] In 1949, he became the editor-in-chief of the journal *Tekhnika i molodezhi*, a mass audience popular science magazine with a circulation of about 1.5 million copies. In this position, Zakharchenko proved to be what historian Lewis Siegelbaum terms a "cosmic enthusiast *par excellence*."[38] Under his leadership, the magazine became a central forum for discussions about science fiction and fantasy. Topics covered by the journal included technical business analyses and scientific expertise by academics as well as articles devoted to contact with aliens, telepathy, telekinesis, human paranormal abilities, and weapons of the future. The journal also published science fiction writers such as Ivan Efremov, who built on Fedorov's ideas in his novel *Andromeda Nebula* (1957).[39]

In addition to his prominent position on the cultural scene as the editor-in-chief of *Tekhnika i molodezhi*, Zakharchenko was also able to convey his cosmic enthusiasm to the highest ranks of the

35 See Oleg Kharkhordin, "The Individual in Mature Soviet Society," in *The Collective and the Individual in Russia* (Berkeley, Los Angeles, London: University of California Press, 1999), pp. 329–54.

36 "Zakharchenko Vasilii Dmitrievich—Bolchaia entsiklopediia russkogo naroda," Institut Russkoi Tsivilizatsii, https://web.archive.org/web/20120417200250/http://www.rusinst.ru/articletext.asp?rzd=1&id=5816&abc=1.

37 Brudny, *Reinventing Russia*, 36.

38 Lewis H. Siegelbaum, "Sputnik Goes to Brussels: The Exhibition of a Soviet Technological Wonder," in *Soviet Space Culture: Cosmic Enthusiasm in Socialist Societies*, ed. Eva Maurer et al. (New York: Palgrave Macmillan, 2011), p. 175.

39 Matthias Schwartz, "A Dream Come True: Close Encounters with Outer Space in Soviet Popular Scientific Journals of the 1950s and 1960s," in *Soviet Space Culture: Cosmic Enthusiasm in Socialist Societies*, ed. Eva Maurer et al. (New York: Palgrave Macmillan, 2011), p. 242.

bureaucratic state hierarchy. In 1957, he held an influential role as one of the thirty members of the consultative council for the organization of the Soviet pavilion displayed at the Brussels World Fair in 1958. As reported by Siegelbaum, Zakharchenko's proposals had the most "far-reaching consequences" by pushing for the adoption of replicas of the satellite *Sputnik* as the major masterpieces of the pavilion.[40] Zakharchenko was also well positioned in influential national-conservative organizations at the crossroads of intellectual and political networks. In 1965, Zakharchenko played an important role as one of the initiators of the All-Russian Society for the Protection of Historical and Cultural Monuments (Vserossiiskoe obshchestvo okhrany pamiatnikov istorii i kultury, VOOPIK), where he headed the section dedicated to monuments related to technology.[41] VOOPIK had been created under the supervision of the Council of Ministers of the Russian Soviet Republic and with the active support of the Komsomol.[42] The organization became one of the leading advocates of national-conservative issues.[43] Zakharchenko was also a key member of the "Russian Party," which gathered intellectuals and members of the political establishment around nationalist ideas.[44]

2.2.1.2 Valerii Skurlatov

Skurlatov graduated from the Physics Department of the Moscow State University in 1961. His intellectual socialization into heterodox thinking primarily took place in academic institutions. From 1962 to 1965, he was a graduate student at the Institute of Philosophy of the Academy of Sciences,[45] which is where he first became acquainted with one of his mentors, the philosopher Evald Ilienkov. Ilienkov had authored an essay entitled *The Cosmology of Spirit*, which develops the idea of a human-led cosmic eschatology. Skurlatov also claimed that he was able to access the original edition of Fedorov's

40 Siegelbaum, "Sputnik Goes to Brussels," 176.

41 "Zakharchenko Vasilii Dmitrievich." In the 1970s, VOOPIK grew into a mass organization, with seven million members in 1972.

42 Nikolai Mitrokhin, *Russkaia Partiia: Dvizhenie russkikh natsionalistov v SSSR 1953–1985 gody* (Moscow: Novoe literaturnoe obozrenie, 2003).

43 Brudny, *Reinventing Russia*, 70.

44 Mitrokhin, *Russkaia Partiia*, 8.

45 He later received a PhD from the Institute for African Studies of the Academy of Sciences in 1971. V. A. Nikerov, *Kto est kto: Russkoe izdanie; Biograzicheskii innovatsionnii spravoshnik* (Moscow: Astreia, 2009).

essay *The Philosophy of the Common Cause* in the library of the institute.[46] Skurlatov's social circle at the time included other young researchers studying Russian cosmist thinkers such as his close friend Igor Kolchenko, who defended his PhD in the history of sciences on "Konstantin Tsiolkovskii as a Thinker" in 1968.[47]

Similar to Zakharchenko, Skurlatov developed a dual membership of intellectual and political milieus in the 1960s. In parallel to his studies at the Institute of Philosophy, Skurlatov and his friends Iurii Lunkov and Igor Kolchenko organized the "Young Marxist University" under the aegis of the Komsomol. From 1963 to 1965, the Young Marxist University held seminars and conferences in the Moscow State University and in the House of Unions for young graduates from higher educational institutions. Some of the participants in the university's program, such as Sergei Khoruzhii (1941–2020) and Georgii Gachev (1929–2008), the husband of Svetlana Semenova, subsequently became well-known intellectual figures.[48] Despite its "Marxist" etiquette, the university was a place where nonconformist ideas, such as Russian cosmism, were dissimulated through rhetorical strategies that allowed them to circulate. As Skurlatov explained, the "Marxist" label served as a cover for what were in fact intellectual discussions of heterodox philosophers:

> We pragmatically called our rally the Young Marxist University (YMU) in order to have scope for action in a communist country. The magic word "Marxism" then opened the hearts of almost all intellectuals and public figures in the world. But I was fond of the ideas of Friedrich Nietzsche, while Igor Kolchenko professed Orthodoxy and the ideas of Russian cosmism.[49]

Although the original work of the Russian cosmists had not yet been published at that time, the Young Marxist University's curriculum in

46 Valerii Skurlatov, "Pravaia Vera i odin iz ee provozvestnikov Nikolai Fedorovich Fedorov (1829–1903)," Livejournal, October 9, 2019, https://surlatov.livejournal.com/5683435.html.

47 Valerii Skurlatov, "Vspominaia Igoria Kolchenko," Livejournal, May 29, 2012, https://skurlatov.livejournal.com/1509991.html.

48 Valerii Skurlatov, "Interviu so mnoi o filosofii," Livejournal, May 18, 2011, https://skurlatov.livejournal.com/1229402.html.

49 Valerii Skurlatov, "Universitet Molodogo Marksista: Ego kratkaia istoriia i programma," Livejournal, April 30, 2010, https://skurlatov.livejournal.com/899852.html.

1965 did include the study of Teilhard de Chardin, the French priest and paleontologist who was close to Vernadskii's ideas and whose magnum opus, *The Phenomenon of Man*, had just been translated into Russian.[50]

Skurlatov also used his position as the leading organizer of a youth institution to spread some of his cosmist ideas within the ranks of the Komsomol's hierarchy. In 1965, he circulated a programmatic text entitled "A Code of Morals" among Komsomol executives. According to Skurlatov, the "Code of Morals" aimed to "give a new impetus to the Komsomol ideology" and was written upon the instructions of his "friend and patron Vasilii Trushin, who [later] became the last Minister of Internal Affairs in the USSR."[51] As Skurlatov acknowledged, the "Code of Morals" was directed against the destalinization of the country started by Khrushchev in 1956, which he associated with the "collapse of the spiritual foundation of the Russian person" and its exposure to the "temptation of consumerism."[52] The text advocated a militarist, xenophobic, and sexist ethics, recommending corporal punishment to educate young people and the sterilization of Russian women who had had sexual intercourse with foreigners.[53] It also contained Fedorovian themes such the promotion of a "cult of ancestors," a "cult of immortality," and "the transformation of mankind."[54]

The "Code of Morals" provoked a scandal that resulted in Skurlatov's exclusion from the Communist Party and his expulsion from the Institute of Philosophy. However, this did not prevent him from pursuing a successful career in prestigious academic institutions in the 1970s and 1980s, which suggested that he continued to enjoy some support from the political authorities.[55] Indeed, in addi-

50 The brochure of the university's program was reproduced by Skurlatov at https://skurlatov.livejournal.com/899852.html.

51 Valerii Skurlatov, "Politik ne dolzhen dumat o dengakh i smerti," interview by Aleksei Alikin, Russkaia Planeta, March 13, 2014, https://rusplt.ru/policy/interview-Skurlatov-8611.html.

52 Valerii Skurlatov, "Perechityvaia 'Ustav Nrava,'" Livejournal, November 4, 2006, https://skurlatov.livejournal.com/148680.html.

53 Walter Laqueur, *Black Hundred: The Rise of the Extreme Right in Russia* (New York: Harper Collins, 1993), 114.

54 The text is reproduced on Skurlatov's blog. See Skurlatov, "Perechityvaia 'Ustav Nrava.'"

55 He held several positions in academia as a researcher at the All-Russian Institute for Scientific and Technical Information (1965–68), assistant director of the Institute for African Studies of the Academy of Sciences (1971–73),

tion to his established academic position, Skurlatov was reportedly a KGB informer, implying he had a close connection to the Soviet state apparatus.[56] He also continued to publish articles advocating ultranationalist and cosmist ideas. Zakharchenko's journal, *Tekhnika i molodezhi*, where Skurlatov served as scientific editor in 1968–71, became one of his main publishing platforms. He authored articles on Russians' Aryan origins, as well as science fiction novels inspired by "Russian pagan pre-history."[57] Skurlatov was also one of the permanent authors of the science fiction almanacs *Tainy vekov* and *Dorogami tysiacheletii*, edited by the publishing house of the Komsomol, Molodaia Gvardiia.

2.2.1.3 Aleksandr Prokhanov

Unlike Zakharchenko and Skurlatov, Prokhanov's intellectual formation mainly took place outside academic institutions. First and foremost, Prokhanov's worldview was shaped by his family origins. Although he described his family as atheistic, Prokhanov was inspired by the religiosity of his ancestors, who belonged to evangelical groups that had split away from the Russian Orthodox Church. Prokhanov particularly related to his great uncle, Ivan Prokhanov (1869–1935), who founded the All-Russian Union of Evangelical Christians in 1908 and attempted to construct a socialist Christian city, "Evangelsk," in the 1920s.[58]

Prokhanov was introduced to an eclectic set of philosophies and social theories as he interacted with various intellectual circles.

as head of the Department of Philosophy and Methodology of History at the Institute of Scientific Information on Social Sciences of the Academy of Sciences (1973–78), as associate professor of the Department of Philosophy at the Peoples' Friendship University (1981–87) and finally, as the head of the Department of Developing Countries and member of the Academic Council of the Diplomatic Academy of the Ministry of Foreign Affairs (1978–83). Nikerov, *Kto est kto*.

[56] John Dunlop noted that, in 1990, "former KGB major-general Oleg Kalugin ... identified Skurlatov as having in the past served as a KGB informer." See John B. Dunlop, *The Rise of Russia and the Fall of the Soviet Empire* (Princeton, NJ: Princeton University Press, 1993), 110.

[57] See Viktor Chnirelman, *Russkoe rodnoverie: Neoiazychestvo i natsionalizm v sovremennoi Rossii* (Moscow: BBI, 2012), 115.

[58] Prokhanov acknowledged his great uncle as one of his mentors during an interview with Lev Danilkin. See Lev Danilkin, *Chelovek s iaitsom, zhizn i mnenie Aleksandra Prokhanova* (Moscow: Ad Marginem, 2007), 20.

During the second half of the 1950s, while studying at the Moscow Aviation Institute, he became a habitué of literary "Bohemian" salons, where, as he reported, "erotica and decadence united with mystical Orthodoxy."[59] Prokhanov also mentioned meeting with "followers of Fedorov" (*fedorovtsy*) and being influenced by the *Philosophy of the Common Task* early on.[60] In addition, Prokhanov's worldview was strongly shaped by his stay in the city of Pskov, located near the Estonian border. Here, he became involved with a team of architects dedicated to restoring medieval churches destroyed in the Second World War. This experience sparked Prokhanov's interest in Russia's historical and religious heritage predating the revolution. Moreover, he became acquainted with a local subculture that had emerged in Pskov, centered on a nonconformist community of poets, writers, philosophers, and historians. In 1962, Prokhanov abandoned his career as an engineer and settled in the city of Istra, an hour and a half from Moscow, where he worked for three years as a forester.[61] He recalled these years as a transformative period of acquaintance with rural folklore that helped him acquire his "vocabulary" as a writer.[62] It was also where Prokhanov met another of his life mentors, Lev Lebedev (1935–98), who was working as a historian in the local museum of the New Jerusalem Monastery. While Khrushchev's antireligious campaign was at its peak, Lebedev introduced Prokhanov to Orthodoxy. Lebedev later became a priest and baptized Prokhanov in 1974.[63]

Other figures played a key role in the formation of Prokhanov's nonconformist worldview in the 1960s. First, Prokhanov was a regular visitor to the "Iuzhinskii Circle," a private, informal venue held in Moscow at the house of the writer and philosopher Iurii Mamleev (1931–2015). The circle was attended by a company of "esotericists" and "mystics" who discussed Gnosticism, magic, and metaphysics. Their readings included the traditionalist philosophers René Guénon and Julius Evola, as well as Oriental religious texts such as

59 Quoted in Danilkin, *Chelovek s iaitsom*, 67–70.
60 Aleksandr Prokhanov, "Khozhdenie v ogon," *Zavtra*, December 10, 2011, http://zavtra.ru/blogs/hozhdenie-v-ogon.
61 Prokhanov, "Khozhdenie v ogon."
62 Quoted in Danilkin, *Chelovek s iaitsom*, 153.
63 Danilkin, *Chelovek s iaitsom*, 140.

the Mahabharata.[64] Prokhanov recounted their meetings as radically subversive and iconoclastic:

> [We] conjured, mocked, recited poems, drank vodka, defamed the authorities, broke the taboo not only of Soviet ethics and Soviet ideology, but also of everything that had been sealed over thousands of centuries of culture.[65]

Prokhanov's mentors at that time also included Konstantin Pchelnikov (1924–2001), an avant-garde constructivist architect who had fallen out of favor under Khrushchev. Through Pchelnikov, Prokhanov reconnected with early Soviet technocratism that held technology as the "highest form of culture" and as a "panacea for social and economic problems."[66] As Prokhanov acknowledged, Pchelnikov transmitted to him his futurist and holistic conception of technology, which he regarded as an all-pervading and expanding power turning the world into a "technosphere."[67] Echoing Vernadskii's theory of the "noosphere," Pchelnikov's technosphere conceives of technology as an autonomous force emancipated from human agency and able to direct the universe's evolution.

In addition to his socialization into these informal subcultures, Prokhanov entered the intellectual establishment in 1968, when he became a correspondent for *Literaturnaia gazeta*, one of the most prominent Soviet newspapers. In 1969, he was sent to the Damanskii Island to report on the military conflict at the border with China. He referred to this experience as a decisive turning point in his life, after which he became a staunch promoter of the Soviet state and the Soviet army.[68] Subsequently, Prokhanov regularly reported on security and defense issues and celebrated the expansion of Soviet military and technological power. His status as a war reporter led him to establish connections with the military establishment and to undertake regular field

64 On the Iuzhinskii Circle, see Marlene Laruelle, "The Iuzhinskii Circle: Far-Right Metaphysics in the Soviet Underground and Its Legacy Today," *Russian Review* 74 (2015): 563–80.

65 See Prokhanov's tribute to Mamleev following his death in 2015: Aleksandr Prokhanov, "Umer glavnii 'metafizicheskii realist,'" *Izborskii klub* (blog), October 28, 2015, https://izborsk-club.ru/7534.

66 Paul R. Josephson, "Rockets, Reactors and Soviet Culture," in *Science and the Soviet Social Order*, ed. Loren Graham (Cambridge, MA: Harvard University Press, 1990), p. 164.

67 Danilkin, *Chelovek s iaitsom*, 258.

68 Prokhanov, "Khozhdenie v ogon."

trips to strategic sites of the Soviet military-technological complex. In his report on the mines of Donbass, for instance, Prokhanov concluded that "new technology ... ennobles [humankind]."[69] In another article, entitled "Air Villages," he wrote a laudatory description of the impact of aviation on the development of life in remote rural areas.[70] He also developed an enthusiastic narrative of the transformative effect of the army and its new technologies on life in villages.[71]

On top of his work as a journalist, Prokhanov also made his way in the literary field as a writer throughout the 1970s. His first novel, *Idu v put moi* (*I Am Going My Way*), published in 1971, illustrates Prokhanov's association with various intellectual and military circles, which led him to develop an original literary style. The novel, indeed, was prefaced by the liberal Iurii Trifonov, but was akin to village prose, as it portrayed a romantic vision of the folklore and life in the countryside.

Prokhanov's career as a writer and journalist for one of the most prominent newspapers of the intelligentsia offered him a publishing platform with a massive audience. In this capacity, he became the most vocal and accomplished theorizer of modernist conservatism.

2.2.2 Aleksandr Prokhanov's Theorization of Modernist Conservatism

Throughout the 1970s, Prokhanov expressed an increasing dissatisfaction with the domination of a backward-looking, antimodern worldview among conservatives. While he was influenced by the conservative and prerevolutionary legacy disclosed by the village prose movement, he did not express the feelings of pain and deprivation that were typical of this "emotional community."[72] Rather, his enthu-

69 Aleksandr Prokhanov, "Muchketovskii rudnik: Spustia polveka," *Literaturnaia gazeta* 45 (November 5, 1969): 10.

70 Aleksandr Prokhanov, "Vozduchnye proselki," *Literaturnaia gazeta* 32 (August 6, 1969): 12.

71 Aleksandr Prokhanov, "Polk prikhodit v gorodok," *Literaturnaia gazeta* 8 (February 18, 1970): 11.

72 On the cementing role of the "emotional vocabulary" of pain and loss in the cohesion of the national-conservative community in the late Soviet Union, see Anna Razuvalova, "The Plot Device of Conspiracy in Nikolay Burlyaev's Film Lermontov and A Director's Diary: On the 'Ethnography of the Emotions' of the National-Conservative Community," *Forum for Anthropology and Culture* 12 (2016): 161–85.

siasm for new technologies and industrial aesthetics and his faith in historical progress and the Soviet future excluded him from village prose circles that saw him as a technocrat. Prokhanov's divergence from village prose writers was also generational. As Brudny explains, village prose writers were the first intellectual elite from the "purge and wartime generation" (born between 1920 and 1925), who mainly came from rural backgrounds.[73] They reacted strongly against Khrushchev's cult of science and antireligious campaign. In contrast, Prokhanov was one of the youngest representatives of the "postwar generation," which Brudny situates as those born between 1926 and 1938.[74] In addition, Prokhanov was born into an urban intelligentsia family. Finally, Prokhanov's divergence from the village prose movement stemmed from his marginal position as a young new entrant in the literary scene. While rural writers were firmly established as a dominant school, benefiting from a mass audience and state promotion, Prokhanov sought to gain recognition by establishing himself as the founder of an innovative avant-garde.[75]

Prokhanov's originality as an author can be seen in the way he combined journalistic methods with a lyrical and poetic writing style. Prokhanov used materials gathered during field trips such as official documents, tape recordings, and interviews to provide technical descriptions of facts and social reality. But he combined this social and technical realism with a romantic organicist view of the world and the frequent use of poetic metaphors.[76] In that sense, Prokhanov's practices as a journalist matched the principles of the "new journalism" or "narrative nonfiction" also emerging in the West at the time. In contrast to standard journalistic methods, "new journalism" was

[73] Brudny, *Reinventing Russia*, 34, 42, 46.

[74] Brudny, *Reinventing Russia*, 34. An outstanding outlier in this generational classification is Valentin Rasputin (1937–2015), who became one of the most renowned conservative village prose writers, although he belonged to the postwar generation.

[75] The print runs of books by village prose writers illustrate their mass popularity: In the years 1971–82, Viktor Astafev sold 13,737,840 books, Iurii Bondarev sold 6,627,780 books, and Valentin Rasputin sold 3,478,600 books. The major literary journals used by village prose writers were also issued in massive numbers – *Nash sovremennik* (336,000), *Molodaia gvardiia* (870,000), *Moskva* (500,000) (monthly circulation, 1982); see Brudny, *Reinventing Russia*, 105–7.

[76] See, for instance, his article on the construction of Tobolsk's petrochemical plant: Prokhanov, "Posredi Sibiri," *Literaturnaia gazeta* 22 (April 13, 1977): 10.

about using narrative, aesthetic, and literary devices to report on the social reality.[77] In 1974, Prokhanov's methods stirred a debate with the literary critic Vladimir Gusev. Against Prokhanov's promotion of the fundamental role of "facts" and "documents" for artistic practices, Gusev argued that "art [had] a more responsible task than just finding a document."[78]

At the end of the 1970s, when he had become a well-known writer and journalist, Prokhanov provoked a major controversy in the literary scene as he theorized his worldviews in a mass-audience debate about nature and technology. Against the conservatives' moral and ecological critique of technological modernity, Prokhanov articulated a modernist conservatism based on the "spiritualization of technology" advocated by Russian cosmists.

In 1978, *Literaturnaia gazeta* held a roundtable of writers to discuss their views on the issue of "modern ecology," the status of nature, and the definition of a "reasonable attitude toward nature."[79] In opposition to other participants,[80] Prokhanov stepped into the debate as a "technocrat," which he defined as a "person who, in the conflict between nature and technology, often takes the side of the latter."[81] Other writers instead advocated a classic conservationist approach to nature, emphasizing the need for authors to acquire a "deep awareness in the field of ecology," to "inspire respect for nature," and to view the "attitude of human to human" and the "attitude of human to nature" as one single "moral code."[82] Prokhanov denounced this attitude toward nature as an "arrière-garde" reaction. In contrast to classic conservatism, he advocated an organicist conception of the Earth system, wherein humankind, nature, and technology were interrelated components of a single whole:

77 The principles of the "new journalism" were spelled out by Tom Wolfe in essays published in 1973. See Tom Wolfe and E. W. Johnson, *The New Journalism*, 1st ed. (New York: Harper & Row, 1973).

78 Aleksandr Prokhanov and Vladimir Gusev, "Iz reki po imeni—'Fakt,'" 2 (January 9, 1974): 5.

79 Andrei Bitov et al., "Kruglii stol—I khram, i masterskaia!" *Literaturnaia gazeta* 14 (April 5, 1978): 4–5.

80 Andrei Bitov, Oleg Volkov, Iurii Dmitriev, Petr Dudochkin, Leonid Korobkov, and Vladimir Chivilikhin.

81 Bitov et al., "Kruglii stol—I khram, i masterskaia!"

82 These arguments were phrased respectively by Vladimir Chivilikhin (1928–84), Iurii Dmitriev (1926–89), and Petr Dudochkin (1915–?).

Earth is a kind of global organism, which includes components of nature, human spiritual and psychological structure, and technology. The task of humanity is to ensure the smooth functioning of this complex "machine." If one of the components fails, disaster will ensue.[83]

In this view, the conceptual and philosophical distinction between nature and technique, the innate and the fabricated, is dissolved into a broader organicism, which includes technology as part of life processes:

Technology, just like nature, must also be loved and protected. It is also complex and contradictory. It is also a part of our life.[84]

Prokhanov's position was criticized by the other participants. Vladimir Chivilikhin, one of the leading Russophile nationalist writers, for instance, stated that the "introduction of technology on an equal footing with nature and the spiritual and cultural life of the human" was a "meaningless, unnecessary and unrealistic task."[85]

In 1979, Prokhanov went on to publish an article entitled "Metaphor of Modernity" in *Literaturnaia gazeta* that fully theorized his modernist conservative worldview. He explicitly framed his article in opposition to the domination of *passéism* among conservative village prose writers.[86] The disclaimer of liability added by the journal's editors to what they described as a "polemical piece" that would "cause disagreement and well-grounded objections" is an indication of the daring character of this manifesto, which was oriented against what was then the best-established and most popular literary movement.[87]

Prokhanov's article began by highlighting the important role played by village prose writers, calling them "excellent masters" for their success at "maintaining tradition." However, he called into question the village prose's inability to account for the scientific and technical transformations taking place in Soviet society. In his view, by sticking to the "snobbery" of a literary tradition set on fixing the "sick, grieving soul" of a passing rural world, the "elite village

83 Bitov et al., "Kruglii stol—I khram, i masterskaia!"
84 Bitov et al., "Kruglii stol—I khram, i masterskaia!"
85 Bitov et al., "Kruglii stol—I khram, i masterskaia!"
86 Aleksandr Prokhanov, "Metafora sovremennosti": 4.
87 This disclaimer of liability, which concludes with the words "Let the truth be born in a dispute, in a lively, interested exchange of opinions!" also testified to the journal's commitment to fostering a pluralist public debate. Prokhanov, "Metafora sovremennosti."

prose" failed to sustain the task of culture, which was to embrace and conquer modernity with an artistic language. He called on writers to abandon their "comfort" and explore contemporary society. Prokhanov enthusiastically praised modernity in its entirety, including in its most controversial and damaging aspects, such as the "peasant-technocrat" living in "modern technicized villages," "the new army," the "new Moscow," the "'tasteless' high-rise buildings," and the "atomic submarines." He claimed that it was necessary to drop the "antithesis between the 'machine' and 'spirit'" in order to reconcile traditional values with a technologically advanced society. According to him, writers needed to develop a "new vocabulary" in order to artistically craft a "metaphor of modernity" that would qualify neither as romantic nostalgia nor technical realism but rather as a search for a poetic, symbolic, and imaginative description of modernity. In support of his ideas, Prokhanov referred to the cosmist thinkers Fedorov and Vernadskii:

> The spirit breathes where it wants! People always knew about that. Those who painfully experienced the cultural divide of Russia, who looked for ways to unify the extremes, to spiritualize and not to reject the machine, knew this. Fedorov knew this, when he tried to build a huge spiritual teaching based on science and space technology. Vernadskii knew this, when he connected humanity, cosmos and technology under the crystal dome of the noosphere.[88]

While Fedorovian, spiritualist, and organicist visions of technological modernity had inspired early Soviet science fiction, they were rare among writers in the Brezhnev era, especially in village prose circles.[89] In Brudny's view, Prokhanov's article "constituted the greatest challenge that village prose nationalism faced during the Brezhnev era."[90]

A year-long controversy ensued, during which writers and literary critics reacted to Prokhanov's position in the journals *Literaturnaia*

88 Prokhanov, "Metafora sovremennosti."

89 Katerina Clark noted a few exceptions, such as Chinghiz Aitmatov's *The Day Longer than an Age Doth Last* (1980), which sought to reach a "fine line between traditionalist ethos and technological amelioration." She also found Fedorovian themes of immortality and "occult and folk remedies" in Anatolii Kim's *Gurin's Utopia* (1979). Katerina Clark, "The Changing Image of Science and Technology in Soviet Literature," in *Science and the Soviet Social Order* (Cambridge, MA: Harvard University Press, 1990).

90 Brudny, *Reinventing Russia*, 157.

gazeta and *Literaturnaia ucheba*.[91] A majority of authors strongly opposed Prokhanov's arguments. In substance, most critics sought to discredit Prokhanov as a "technocrat"[92] and disagreed with him by stressing the primacy of moral and cultural values over technology. In his answer to critics, Prokhanov built on the concept of technosphere developed by his friend and architect Pchelnikov to further claim that reality was destined to be dominated by an "all-pervading 'total' technology."[93] In Prokhanov's view, however, the point was to strike a balance between human agency and technological power by seeking the "spiritualization [*odukhotvorenie*], deification [*obozhestvlenie*] or, more simply, the humanization [*ochelovechenie*] of technology."[94]

Prokhanov's ideas were not rejected unanimously. Among his critics, Vladimir Gusev also acknowledged Prokhanov as a "bright and talented person."[95] A few authors also concurred with Prokhanov's critique of village prose as a gloomy and outdated literary trend.[96]

While the village prose was at its peak of popularity, this major literary and intellectual controversy indicated an ongoing change in the value hierarchies and attitudes toward technological modernity in conservative intellectual milieus. Moreover, the year-long discussion about Prokhanov's ideas held in mass-audience literary journals increased his visibility and caused him to rise him from an outlier

91 Around fifteen articles were published in *Literaturnaia gazeta* in 1979–80 in reaction to Prokhanov's piece.
92 Vladimir Gusev, "Zemlia i nebo," *Literaturnaia gazeta* 38 (September 19, 1979): 4.
93 Aleksandr Prokhanov, "Ne oshibitsia v diagnoze," *Literaturnaia ucheba* 3 (1980).
94 Prokhanov, "Ne oshibitsia v diagnoze." In contrast to both the "noosphere" and the "technosphere," a leading figure of Russian liberal nationalism, the literary scholar Dmitrii Likhachev, coined the concept of "homosphere" to designate a sphere of activity based on human creative spirituality that regulates humans' interaction with each other, with nature, and with the universe. Dmitrii Likhachev, "Gomosfera—termin nashikh dnei," *Ogonek* 36 (1984): 17–19.
95 Gusev, "Zemlia i nebo."
96 See Viktor Kovalenko, "Etot strogii sudiia—vremia," *Literaturnaia gazeta* 46 (October 3, 1979): 4; Albert Ustinov, "Kto 'pervii paren na derevne?'" *Literaturnaia gazeta* (October 19, 1979): 4; Anatolii Pogribnii, "Gde iskat orientiry?" *Literaturnaia gazeta* 48 (November 28, 1979): 6; Adyl Iakubov, "V ozhidanii analiticheskogo romana," *Literaturnaia gazeta* 43 (October 24, 1979): 4; Vladimir Bondarenko, "V novuiu derevniu—na Telege?" *Literaturnaia gazeta* 49 (December 5, 1979): 4.

to an opinion-maker among conservative intellectuals. According to Brudny, this debate turned out to be the "stepping stone in his meteoric rise to a position as one of the most prominent figures in the Russian nationalist movement in the 1980s."[97] In the years that followed, Prokhanov became well known for his romantic, spiritual apologia for the Soviet military-industrial complex, thereby establishing modernist conservatism as a new variant of nonconformist loyalism.

2.3 Modernist Conservatism's Controlled Dispersion inside the Soviet State Ideology

2.3.1 Modernist Conservatism as Ideological Underpinning of the Soviet System

Similar to other forms of nonconformism practiced by late Soviet intellectuals, the unconventional character of modernist conservatism was not framed as a rupture with the Soviet system. Rather, Prokhanov aimed to use spiritual and conservative values as alternative ideological underpinning of the Soviet political system. Indeed, in the context of Brezhnev's stagnation and lack of vision for the Soviet future, his references to cosmist authors such as Fedorov and Vernadskii was intended to fix what he perceived as a decrepit state ideology.

Prokhanov applied his advocacy for the "spiritualization of technology" to the entire military-industrial complex in a series of articles devoted to the Soviet defense industry.[98] His description of a nuclear rocket in his article on the "nuclear shield" is a case in point:

> The rocket is a part of nature and cosmos, an expression of ancient human aspirations, from the caves of rock paintings, through delusion, darkness and great sacrifices. It contains the soul of infantrymen, who fell in battles, and of the unborn future generations.[99]

Although nonconformist, his ideas provided intellectual repertoires to support and justify the state's defense and security policies.

[97] Brudny, *Reinventing Russia*, 155.

[98] Aleksandr Prokhanov, "Iadernii shchit," *Literaturnaia gazeta* 46 (November 17, 1982): 10; Aleksandr Prokhanov, "Krasnye zvezdy nad okeanom," *Literaturnaia gazeta* 29 (July 21, 1982): 10; Aleksandr Prokhanov, "Poliarnii kupol," *Literaturnaia gazeta* 36 (September 7, 1983): 12; Aleksandr Prokhanov, "Eskadra," *Literaturnaia gazeta* 38 (September 19, 1984): 11.

[99] Prokhanov, "Iadernii shchit."

In particular, Prokhanov's discourse contributed to the justification of the arms race and military-technological investments at a time when the social benefits of both the nuclear and the space programs were increasingly being questioned inside the country.[100] Prokhanov also played a key role as the champion of the Soviet state during the Afghan war. In 1980–81, he published a series of articles reporting from Afghanistan in which he actively contradicted the critical narratives of the Western media by propagating an idealized vision of the Soviet military invasion, praising the Soviet army as the protector of the local population.[101] As a journalist for *Literaturnaia gazeta*, Prokhanov lent legitimacy to the official narrative of the war by retranscribing the thoughts of the political officers within the pages of one of the most reputable intellectual platforms:

> The political instructor of one of the formations, Viktor Alekseevich Lavrischev, told me—Our soldiers came to Afghanistan in peace, with goodness. When we entered the country, residents greeted us with fruit and flat cakes. I remember one old man crouched down to the tank and kissed the dusty armor. We do not distance ourselves from the local population, we meet with them, we show films about the Soviet Union, about Lenin, about the revolution. Our army does not interfere in the internal processes taking place in Afghanistan.[102]

In return for his contribution to state propaganda, Prokhanov was a journalist officially acclaimed by the authorities. In 1980, he was awarded the prize of the Union of Journalists for his reporting on the

[100] See Prokhanov, "Iadernii shchit." As put by Paul Josephson, "public criticism of the Soviet nuclear power programmes predates Chernobyl by some 8 years." See Paul R. Josephson, "Rockets, Reactors and Soviet Culture," 190

[101] Aleksandr Prokhanov, "Pobedy trudnii put," *Literaturnaia gazeta* 52 (December 24, 1980): 14; Aleksandr Prokhanov, "Soldaty revoliutsii," *Literaturnaia gazeta* 16 (April 16, 1980): 14; Aleksandr Prokhanov, "Chto tvoriat bandity," *Literaturnaia gazeta* 9 (February 27, 1980): 9; Aleksandr Prokhanov, "Vremia pakhoty i seba," *Literaturnaia gazeta* 12 (March 19, 1980): 9; Aleksandr Prokhanov, "Edinye v revoliutsii," *Literaturnaia gazeta* 19 (May 7, 1980): 14; Aleksandr Prokhanov, "Vybor—revoliutsiia," *Literaturnaia gazeta* 33 (June 18, 1980): 14; Aleksandr Prokhanov, "Za plugom," *Literaturnaia gazeta* 7 (February 11, 1981): 15; Aleksandr Prokhanov, "Plemena i puli," *Literaturnaia gazeta* 5 (January 28,1981): 14; Aleksandr Prokhanov, "Vstrechi na Maivande," *Literaturnaia gazeta* 17 (April 12, 1981): 7; Aleksandr Prokhanov, "Razgromlena banda," *Literaturnaia gazeta* 2 (January 7, 1981): 14.

[102] Prokhanov, "Vremia pakhoty i seba."

Afghan war. Prokhanov subsequently covered many other war fronts as a journalist until the mid-1980s.[103]

However, despite his allegiance to the regime, Prokhanov's nonconformist spiritual fervor was inconsistent with the official ideological canons displayed in Soviet realism. In addition, he reportedly refused to become a member of the Communist Party, instead claiming for himself the status of an artist "outside the system."[104] Prokhanov's self-representation as an artist is reflected in his writing style, which sought to estheticize technology by attributing emotional and spiritual qualities to it. In that sense, Prokhanov sought to convey his visions through a unique language based on aesthetics and imagination rather than rational arguments. His description of a nuclear rocket launch provides a good illustration of his singular, flowery, mystical, and metaphorical writing style applied to military technologies:

> Slowly, in white hot vapors, a huge granite-sharpened tusk moves out, like the Aleksandr Column,[105] but instead of an angel, it has a pointed white-mercury head. It squeezes out on a roaring flame, turning the air into crackling scrolls, blowing out giant daggers of fire, speeding up, interrupting a chandelier dazzling in the sky, instantly decreasing, curling up into a disappearing torch. [The rocket] passed through the clouds, illuminating them with a crimson glow, burning a small hole. The wound of the clouds has disappeared. Membranes hurt. It flies somewhere, dropping the steps, sending an electronic plume of information to the ground. At the place of take-off, there is a charred steel womb with scraps of molten metal, which has emitted both an earthly and a heavenly body.[106]

103 The other war fronts included Angola, Namibia, Cambodia, Mozambique, and Nicaragua. See Aleksandr Prokhanov, "Angola—novyi Vetnam?" *Literaturnaia gazeta* 33 (September 16, 1981): 9; Aleksandr Prokhanov, "Eshche odna neobiavlennaia," *Literaturnaia gazeta* 23 (June 3, 1981): 14; Aleksandr Prokhanov, "Namibiia, ty budech svobodnoi!" *Literaturnaia gazeta* 26 (June 24, 1981): 15; Aleksandr Prokhanov, "Sokhi i puli," *Literaturnaia gazeta* 30 (June 28, 1982): 14; Aleksandr Prokhanov, "Vstaiushchaia iz Prakha," *Literaturnaia gazeta* 23 (June 9, 1982): 14; Aleksandr Prokhanov, "Pust rasisty ne smykaiut nochami glaz," *Literaturnaia gazeta* 15 (April 14, 1982): 14; Aleksandr Prokhanov, "Vystoiat!" *Literaturnaia gazeta* 50 (December 15, 1982): 14.

104 Aleksandr Prokhanov, interview by Vladimir Pozner, Efir 1, 2010, www.1tv.ru/shows/pozner/vypuski/gost-aleksandr-prohanov-pozner-vypusk-ot-18-05-2010?start=0.

105 The Aleksandr Column is a monument that was raised for Emperor Aleksandr I in the Palace Square of Saint Petersburg.

106 Prokhanov, "Iadernii shchit."

Prokhanov's discourse, therefore, thrived on the late Soviet intellectual practice of nonconformist loyalism to establish modernist conservatism as an alternative ideological underpinning of the Soviet system.

2.3.2 *Russian Cosmism's Local Hybridization with the State Ideology*

Instead of descriptions of the Brezhnev regime's ideological stagnation,[107] Mikhail Epstein has highlighted that it was in fact paired with the semantic expansion of the state ideology. As he put it, Marxist Soviet ideology as a system "constantly changed and expanded its set of ideas" in order to retain the then-flourishing alternative philosophical systems and maintain its power.[108] As Yitzhak Brudny has also shown, the Soviet ideological system established interactions with intellectual producers of alternative ideological resources. In particular, the Brezhnev regime implemented a set of inclusionary politics toward nationalist and conservative intellectuals.[109]

Partisans of Russian cosmism also benefited from the state's overture to alternative ideological resources. In the words of one of the active members of Semenova's study group on Russian cosmism, party leaders at that time were "looking for an alternative to the communist ideology" and considered "the topic of cosmism" a "fashionable alternative" and a likely "tactical, popular doctrine."[110] Another eyewitness of this period and scholar of cosmism, Nikolai Gavriushin, also testified to the interest in cosmist ideas coming from high-ranking officials in the party's propaganda department.[111] Indeed, while the Marxist–Leninist dogmas had been increasingly challenged by the socioeconomic developments brought by scientific advances, Russian cosmism arguably provided the political authorities with a useful vision of technological development that was compatible with

[107] See Nikolai Mitrokhin, *Russkaia Partiia*, 547; Stephen Hanson, *Post-Imperial Democracies: Ideology and Party Formation in Third Republic France, Weimar Germany, and Post-Soviet Russia* (Cambridge: Cambridge University Press, 2010), 187.

[108] See Mikhail Epstein, "Relativistic Patterns in Totalitarian Thinking: The Linguistic Games of Soviet Ideology," in *After the Future*, 155–61.

[109] Brudny, *Reinventing Russia.* [110] Author interview, Zoom, 2020.

[111] Nikolai Gavriushin, "A byl li 'Russkii Kosmizm'?" *Voprosy istorii estestvoznaniia i techniki* 3 (n.d.): 1993.

the preservation of the specificity of the Soviet path. As Hagemeister says, the proponents of Russian cosmism emphasized the "specifically national character of this worldview" and considered that the concept of organic development of human and the universe was "rooted in the uniquely Russian archetype of 'all-unity' (*vseedinstvo*)."[112] In contrast to the Western convergence thesis, therefore, Russian cosmism offered a culture-specific view of the Soviet path to technological modernization. In addition, given the exhaustion of the regime's vision of a socialist future, Russian cosmism revived early Soviet utopian constructivism and provided a new philosophical basis for belief in progress.

The opening of the state ideological system to some of the cosmists' ideas was visible in the evolution of activities organized by scholars of Russian cosmism. By the end of the 1970s, these scholars were able to shift from informal, private meetings to public settings.[113] The Komsomol was at the forefront of some of the official state initiatives to normalize cosmist ideas in the public sphere. In 1978, the Komsomol's publishing house, Molodaia Gvardiia, provided a space in their building to hold the art exhibition "Time. Space. Human," displaying the work of the cosmist art group "Amaravella." Despite this implicit support, party ideologues still maintained formal control over the production of discourse. To comply with official standards, the heterodox, nonconformist aspects of Russian cosmism were articulated within the constraints of publicly authorized discourse. These rhetorical strategies of production of forbidden content under the guise of apparent conformity were commonplace in intellectual circles of the late Soviet system. As Alexei Yurchak has shown, intellectuals used the appearance of a ritualized theoretical discourse in seeming conformity with the established dogma to convey ideas that challenged dominant ways of thinking.[114]

In an interview, a scholar of cosmism, who played a key role in organizing the exhibition, recalled seeking approval from officials of the Komsomol's Central Committee.[115] Their negotiations with authorities is a case in point. When questioned by KGB officials about

112 Michael Hagemeister, "Russian Cosmism in the 1920s and Today," in *The Occult in Russian and Soviet Culture*, ed. Bernice G. Rosenthal (Ithaca, NY: Cornell University Press, 1997), p. 186.
113 Gacheva, *Russkii kosmizm v ideiakh i litsakh*, 414–15.
114 Yurchak, *Everything Was Forever*, 286. 115 Author interview, Zoom, 2020.

the "mystical" themes depicted in the artworks, they contextualized their significance within the broader context of the scientific competition between the Soviet Union and the United States:

> I was constantly asked provocative questions about mysticism. I said, you know, this is not mysticism, this is fantasy. We know nothing about infinity, space and the universe. This is an attempt to grasp and visualize what is impossible to convey in words. I constantly emphasized the difference between verbal and visual. At that time, the cosmos was a prestigious topic due to the competition between Gagarin's flight and the American Apollo Lunar missions ... I said that this exhibition represented an artistic advantage for the Soviet Union over America.[116]

The official status granted to the exhibition by the Central Committee of the Komsomol allowed it to travel across the country and become a national cultural event.

Molodaia Gvardiia also granted permission for the first official publication of original works by Fedorov, issuing in 1979 an anthology of Russian social utopia with short, ideologically selected extracts of Fedorov's work.[117] In the period that followed, publications on cosmism adhered to what the historian of Russian philosophy James Scanlan describes as the "common paradigm" of the Russian philosophical renaissance in the Soviet Union.[118] Thus, while individuals were increasingly able to publish works on cosmism, they put forward its least controversial aspects. In 1977, Semenova's first article on Fedorov, published in the journal *Prometei*, focused on biographical information about the philosopher and its relation to twentieth-century literature.[119] In later publications, she looked at the influence of Fedorov's ideas on famous Soviet writers such as Maksim Gorkii and Andrei Platonov. From 1979 to 1985, Semenova also delivered a number of public lectures on Fedorov and Russian cosmism in public research institutes, houses of culture, museums, and libraries.[120] According to a participant's account, these lectures typically drew

116 Author interview. 117 Hagemeister, "Le 'cosmisme russe,'" 59.

118 James P. Scanlan, ed., *Russian Thought after Communism: The Recovery of a Philosophical Heritage* (Armonk, NY: M. E. Sharpe, 1994), 26.

119 Semenova and Gacheva, *Russkii kosmizm*, 416.

120 For instance, such events occurred at the House of Scientists in Moscow, at the Institute for the Design of Metallurgical Plants, and at the House of Scientific and Technical Propaganda. Gacheva, *Russkii kosmizm v ideiakh i litsakh*, 417–19.

between 100 and 300 participants, mostly young people and members of the Muscovite intelligentsia.[121] As they further observed, Semenova used rhetorical strategies in her public speech to avoid censorship constraints. While her lecture notes were designed to adhere to the lines allowed by the authorities, she used the questions and answers session to develop the themes she was really interested in.[122] In a later interview, Semenova recounted the end of the 1970s as a period of expansion for Russian cosmism and a surge of interest in Fedorov's ideas, perceived as an "exciting spiritual alternative to official ideology":

> It became possible to publish a whole set of articles both in the Muscovite press and in provincial journals, where the eye of editing and censorship was not so vigilant. Every year, "Federovian" evenings were held in front of different audiences, where discourses impossible to print were heard and a unique atmosphere of intense spirituality was created.[123]

Zakharchenko and Skurlatov also relied on their memberships of different intellectual and political networks to act as intermediaries and organizers of venues for the public dissemination of Russian cosmism. VOOPIK and the Russian Party partly supported the activities of Semenova's study group on Russian cosmism.[124] In 1982, VOOPIK provided institutional cover for the organization of an evening in memory of Fedorov at the Institute of Organic and Nonorganic Chemistry.[125] Two central members of the Russian Party, Vadim Kozhinov and Piotr Palievskii, were also pressing for the publication of Fedorov's writings. As reported by Semenova, Fedorov served as the spearhead of a more general campaign to "break through the officially permissible revolutionary democratic canon of Russian philosophy."[126]

The circulation of Russian cosmist ideas, from informal intellectual circles to public sites of ideological production, mirrored the evolution of Soviet state ideology from a rigid metanarrative to an adaptive system seeking to expand by integrating diverse meanings. However, this evolution was not a linear process and was attended by dilemmas

[121] Author interview, Zoom, 2020. [122] Author interview.
[123] Semenova, "Filosofstvovat—znachit uchitsia ne umirat."
[124] Hagemeister, "Le 'cosmisme russe,'" 61.
[125] Valerii Baidin, *Nepodvizhnoe stranstvie, povest-vospominanie* (Moscow: Vikmo-M, 2018), 284.
[126] Semenova, "Filosofstvovat—znachit uchitsia ne umirat."

and setbacks. In 1982, the publication of Fedorov's work by the Institute of Philosophy of the Academy of Sciences provoked a major scandal.[127] In the foreword to the book, Semenova provided an uncensored introduction to Fedorov's thought, including the ideas of active evolution, noosphere and cosmic thought. In the aftermath of the publication, a series of articles denounced the volume as "ideological sabotage" and Fedorov's philosophy as a "mystical," "prophetic" heresy.[128] These vocal reactions resulted in the book being banned from distribution and led to the imposition of sanctions against its editors. The fallout from the publication of Fedorov's volume underscored the continued contentious character of cosmist ideas, which only received sporadic support in local public sites and within limited circles of the political and intellectual establishment.

2.4 Conclusion

This chapter has shown how advocates of late Soviet modernist conservatism built new conceptual affinities between conservatism and technological modernity, leading to the apologia for technology from a romantic, organic, and spiritual perspective. They blended their interest in the revival of conservative and nationalist cultural repertoires with enthusiasm for Soviet scientific and technological achievements. This new ideological rearrangement sought to reenchant Soviet modernity in reaction to Marxism–Leninism's growing inability to reflect the socioeconomic changes brought by technological modernity and in opposition to the convergence horizon predicted by Western modernization theories. The chapter has also demonstrated that the eclectic character of Soviet conservative modernism originated from the specific conditions of an authoritatively controlled public sphere, where informal access to nonconformist thinking led to amateur patchworks of ideas. Faced with the constraints of public discourse in an authoritarian context, modernist conservatism was formed within the limits of integrated nonconformism, defined by its

[127] Nikolai Fedorov, *Sochineniia*, ed. Arsenii Gulyga, introduction by S. G. Semenova (Moscow: Mysl, 1982).

[128] See Hagemeister, "Le 'cosmisme russe,'" 60; Gacheva, *Russkii kosmizm v ideiakh i litsakh*, 418; Semenova, "Filosofstvovat—znachit uchitsia ne umirat."

loyalty to the political authorities and its symbolic heterodoxy relative to state ideology.

Moreover, this chapter has examined how the circulation of modernist conservatism contributed to intellectual change in the Soviet authoritarian context. A major controversy triggered by modernist conservative ideas propelled a new polarization in conservative intellectuals' attitudes toward technological modernity. The chapter has also found that modernist conservatism's ideas were dispersed in social venues – exhibitions, conferences, publications – at the crossroads of political and intellectual milieus. These relations between intellectuals and the political establishment have reconfigured some of the publicly admitted values and meanings displayed in official sites of ideology production. In contrast to the perception of Soviet state ideology as a rigid Soviet Marxism, therefore, the chapter has shown that some of the strategic discourse used to justify the Soviet defense industry and its military competition with the United States included nonconformist, prerevolutionary spiritual and cultural values.

The next chapter looks at how the theorizers of modernist conservatism invested new lines of action as the Soviet system transitioned toward a competitive political environment in the aftermath of *perestroika*. It shows how modernist conservatism was used as an ideological arrangement for the conservation of a group's identity, aggregating national-conservative intellectuals and the conservative forces of the Soviet establishment against the growing hegemony of liberal reformists.

3 *The Emergence of the Russian Hawks as an Idea Network (1985–1999)*

We have the following task: to connect what seems to be incompatible.

Aleksandr Prokhanov,
"Ia ne khotel govorit o Gorbacheve," 1994

Chapter 2 has shown how the social and historical processes affecting late Soviet society prompted new debates over the relationship between classic conservatism and technological modernity. Following the launch of Mikhail Gorbachev's program of liberalizing reforms in 1985, the democratization of the public sphere, stirred by the freedom of the press and the first free elections, polarized debates between advocates and opponents of reforms. Under these circumstances, national-conservative intellectuals merged forces with the pro–status quo members of the political and military establishment against the growing hegemony of liberal reformists. Despite its sociological and ideological eclecticism, the unity of this coalition was cemented from 1987 to 1993 by its experience of political struggle against the liberals, promoting the evolution of their country toward a shared path with Western modernity based on values such as democracy, human rights, and a market economy. These anti-liberal forces formed the basis of the Russian hawks as an idea network aggregating Soviet technocratism with classic conservatism. Nodal individuals and social forums, such as Aleksandr Prokhanov and his newspapers, *Den* and *Zavtra*, organized the common materials of this network – its collective actions, emotions, and ideas – into a full-fledged ideological culture, modernist conservatism.

While traveling between the frontiers of Soviet and post-Soviet society, modernist conservatism consolidated itself by serving as the symbolic rallying structure that provided representation to this eclectic elite network. Russian modernist conservatism, therefore, was not devised as an abstract theoretical system but acquired consistency as a stylized discourse that accompanied the processes of mutation of a group and performatively forged that group's shared protest into a collective identity. In this respect, Russian modernist conservatism belongs to the type of ideas that Daniel Béland and Robert Henry have defined as "coalition magnet," for they appeal to a diversity of constituencies and facilitate the construction of a political coalition.[1]

This chapter's findings challenge some of the central assumptions in political science accounts of ideological production in the post-Soviet period. One commonplace claim, among Russian and Western analysts alike, holds that Russian society transitioned from an ideocratic regime, based on an all-encompassing and consistent state doctrine, to a post-Soviet ideological vacuum, marked by a general rejection of ideology and the proliferation of inconsistent, vague political identities.[2] In contrast to this narrative, the chapter shows the permeability of scattered elements of Soviet ideology across the institutional collapse of the Soviet Union and their reconfiguration in post-Soviet discourse. The fuzziness of post-Soviet modernist conservatism cannot be treated as a symptom of the ideological nullity allegedly resulting from the dissolution of Soviet ideology.[3] The chapter instead highlights the operational character of modernist conservatism as an ideological arrangement that successfully carried the continuity of an elite network despite the institutional collapse of the Soviet Union. Moreover, the strategy of cultural mobilization that the Russian hawks deployed over the course of the 1990s to challenge the media dominance of liberals contributed to their growing recognition in the

[1] Daniel Béland and Robert Henry Cox, "Ideas as Coalition Magnets: Coalition Building, Policy Entrepreneurs, and Power Relations," *Journal of European Public Policy* 23, no. 3 (2016): 429.

[2] For works carrying on this view, see Artemy Magun, *Negative Revolution: Modern Political Subject and Its Fate after the Cold War* (New York: Bloomsbury Academic, 2013); Serguei Oushakine, "In the State of Post-Soviet Aphasia: Symbolic Development in Contemporary Russia," *Europe-Asia Studies* 52, no. 6 (2000): 1003; Stephen Hanson, *Post-Imperial Democracies: Ideology and Party Formation in Third Republic France, Weimar Germany, and Post-Soviet Russia* (New York: Cambridge University Press, 2010); Graeme Gill, *Symbolism and Regime Change in Russia* (Cambridge: Cambridge University Press, 2013).

[3] In this regard, I follow on Michael Freeden's argument against the "chimera of a 'post-ideological' age." As he contends, the internal malleability of contemporary ideologies "must not be confused with the fragility of ideology in general." See Michael Freeden, "Confronting the Chimera of a 'Post-Ideological' Age," *Critical Review of International Social and Political Philosophy* 8, no. 2 (2005): 259.

public sphere. The political career of their ideas, from extremist political opposition to dispersion in the regime's official state patriotism, disclosed their capacity to contribute to the ideological underpinning of the post-Soviet political system and to a sense of belonging that extended beyond the limits of the group.

3.1 An Idea Network Formed across Intellectual and Political Elites (1985–1993)

3.1.1 The Electoral Marriage of Russophile Nationalism with Soviet Patriotism (1985–1991)

The Russian hawks' network of antiliberal forces was formed in the context of the cultural and political struggle between elite groups brought about by *perestroika*. The early period of *perestroika*, from around the spring of 1985 to the fall of 1986, was widely acclaimed by national-conservative and liberal intellectuals alike as necessary to address what they perceived as the decay of the Soviet economy and society.[4] Yitzhak Brudny has shown that, during this period, Russian national-conservatives, inclined toward the prerevolutionary monarchy, the Russian Orthodox Church, and ethnic Russian national interests, were the most influential group among the Russian intelligentsia.[5] In an effort to gain their support in favor of his reform agenda, Gorbachev sought to address some of their main concerns, such as the fight against alcoholism and the abandonment of the Siberian rivers' diversion project.[6] Conversely, the national-conservatives supported some of the liberalizing reforms such as those allowing the freer circulation of literature and philosophical works. However, they shared the concerns of the partisans of the established order over the Westernization of Soviet society and its effect on the disintegration of traditional moral values.[7]

[4] The historical delimitation of this first phase of *perestroika* was suggested by the historian Geoffrey Hosking. See Geoffrey A. Hosking, *The Awakening of the Soviet Union* (London: Mandarin, 1991), 139–41.

[5] Yitzhak M. Brudny, *Reinventing Russia: Russian Nationalism and the Soviet State, 1953–1991* (Cambridge, MA: Harvard University Press, 1998), 193.

[6] See John B. Dunlop, *The Rise of Russia and the Fall of the Soviet Empire* (Princeton, NJ: Princeton University Press, 1993), 13.

[7] Brudny, *Reinventing Russia*, 200.

By the second half of 1986, the new phase of reforms, which was based on the slogan *glasnost* ("openness"), met with considerable opposition in the national-conservative ranks and caused major divisions among the intellectual elite. Indeed, *glasnost* was paired with the regime's shift of cooptation toward the liberal reformist intelligentsia, which was focused on fighting the Stalinist legacy and promoting economic reforms.[8] Meanwhile, the progressive discursive and institutional waning of the Communist monopoly led to the emergence of new coalitions across social groups, blurring the barriers between intellectual circles and official party members.[9] Over the course of 1987, national-conservatives progressively coalesced with pro–status quo members of the political and military establishment as part of their common opposition to liberal cultural and economic policies.

The growing struggle between promoters and adversaries of *perestroika* took place within the Central Committee of the Communist Party, where Aleksandr Iakovlev, the advocate of radical reform and long-time adversary of Russian nationalism, had gained influence over Egor Ligachev, the "patron" of the national-conservatives.[10] The political polarization of the Kremlin's hierarchy was also reflected in the competition for influence and control over media and cultural institutions. Starting from 1987, the Writers' Union of the Russian Soviet Federative Socialist Republic (RSFSR) served as the institutional base for the growing outcry of national-conservatives and members of the Soviet establishment against the hegemony of liberal reformists.[11] At the tribune of the Writers' Union, leading nationalist figures such as Iurii Bondarev and Sergei Mikhalkov recommended the fusion of these two social segments into a single antiliberal opposition

8 On the implementation, starting from the end of 1986, of Gorbachev's "New Thinking," see Robert English, *Russia and the Idea of the West: Gorbachev, Intellectuals, and the End of the Cold War* (Columbia University Press, 2000) and Archie Brown, *Seven Years That Changed the World: Perestroika in Perspective* (Oxford New York: Oxford University Press, 2007).

9 On how informal liberal clubs were formed across intellectual and political circles, see Carole Sigman, *Clubs politiques et perestroïka en Russie: Subversion sans dissidence*, Recherches Internationales (Paris: Karthala, 2009).

10 Dunlop, *Rise of Russia and the Fall of the Soviet Empire*, 124.

11 The nationalist organization Pamiat, which was created in 1980, also became a central platform organizing a "national-patriotic front." By contrast with modernist conservatives, however, Pamiat was dominated by traditionalist and monarchist conservatives. See Walter Laqueur, *Black Hundred: The Rise of the Extreme Right in Russia* (New York: HarperCollins, 1993), 204.

against Gorbachev. This alliance merged contradictory ideas, such as the national-conservatives' nostalgia for prerevolutionary Russian Orthodox monarchy and its rejection as reactionary by radical communists and neo-Stalinists.[12] However, their mutual situational opposition against the liberals rearranged the value hierarchies guiding their worldviews and gained primacy over their past disagreements. In a series of conferences held at the RSFSR and the All-Union Writers' Unions in 1987, Prokhanov, Mikhalkov, and Bondarev emphasized the main causes that had brought their coalition together. These included concerns over the growing Westernization of Soviet society and the propagation of mass culture, the association of market reforms and capitalism with criminality and theft, the need to protect the integrity of the Soviet state and its status as a military superpower, the promotion of national and spiritual values, ethnic Russian solidarity, and rabid anti-Semitism.[13]

The polarization of the Soviet intelligentsia was prominently depicted by Prokhanov in his article "Kultura khram, a ne strelbishche," published in *Literaturnaia Rossiia* in 1988, in which he argued that the unity of Soviet culture and ideology had been dissolved into "two fragments." On the one hand, he described national-conservatives as "guardians" (*okhraniteli*) who were concerned with the conservation of the prerevolutionary traditions and "eternal constants of culture." Prokhanov blamed them for their backward-looking attitude and their opposition to technological progress. On the other hand, Prokhanov condemned the left-wing "Western-oriented liberals" as enemies of their own people for seeking to "transplant the organs" of another culture and society onto Russia.[14] Prokhanov's portrait of the two poles of society provoked one of the most significant backlashes against *perestroika*. Indeed, the article inspired Nina Andreeva's famous open

[12] Dunlop, *Rise of Russia and the Fall of the Soviet Empire*, 129.

[13] Scholarship on late Soviet and post-Soviet conservatism has highlighted the significant role of anti-Semitism as a unifying factor within the antiliberal opposition. See Dunlop, *Rise of Russia and the Fall of the Soviet Empire*; Brudny, *Reinventing Russia*; Laqueur, *Black Hundred*; Wayne Allensworth, *The Russian Question: Nationalism, Modernization, and Post-Communist Russia* (Lanham, MD: Rowman & Littlefield, 1998); Thomas Parland, *The Extreme Nationalist Threat in Russia: The Growing Influence of Western Rightist Ideas* (London: Routledge Curzon, 2004).

[14] Aleksandr Prokhanov, "Kultura khram, a ne strelbishche," *Literaturnaia Rossiia*, January 22, 1988.

letter, "I Cannot Forsake My Principles," published on March 13, 1988, in *Sovetskaia Rossiia*.[15] As Guillaume Sauvé has explained, this letter reacted to the increased circulation of the values advocated by the liberal intelligentsia, such as universalism, democracy, and market mechanisms, into Gorbachev's discourse and the media.[16] In contrast, Andreeva, a chemistry professor from Leningrad, sought to legitimize the Soviet social order and the Soviet history, including Stalin's legacy, against the liberals' critical revisions, "falsifications," and demands for "repentance." Explicitly quoting Prokhanov, the article includes a lengthy discussion of the division of society between "left-liberals" and conservative "guardians," accusing both of being adversaries of "socialist values." Instead, Andreeva asserts a rigorous Marxist–Leninist position, according to which the "socialist construction" of the country should be determined by "the leading role of the party" and the "working class."[17] The article's subsequent publication in a range of other outlets, and hence its resonance throughout Soviet society, was facilitated by Ligachev, the patron of the conservatives within the Politburo.[18] For a short time, the wide publication of Andreeva's piece was interpreted as a victory for Ligachev within the party and an official change of course.[19] However, Gorbachev was able to command a firm counterreaction, prompting a two-day Politburo reunion to obtain the members' condemnation of the letter and reaffirmation of their support for reforms. This indirect confrontation within the party

[15] *Sovetskaia Rossiia* was the official paper of the RSFSR government. On the filiation between Andreeva's letter and Prokhanov's article, see Timur Atnashev, "Perekliuchaia Rezhimy Publichnosti: Kak Nina Andreeva Sodeistvovala Prevrashcheniiu Glasnosti v Svobodu Slova," *Novoe literaturnoe obozrenie* 151 (2018): 462.

[16] Guillaume Sauvé, *Subir la victoire : Essor et chute de l'intelligentsia libérale en Russie, 1987–1993* (Paris: Éditions EHESS, 2019), 91. The English translation of the book is scheduled for release by Cornell University Press in 2025 under the title *Suffering Victory: Soviet Liberals and the Failure of Democracy in Russia, 1987–1993*.

[17] Nina Andreeva, "Ne mogu postupatsa printsipami," *Sovetskaia Rossiia*, March 13, 1988.

[18] Dunlop, *Rise of Russia and the Fall of the Soviet Empire*, 127.

[19] According to historians Dusko Doder and Louise Branson, this episode constituted the "gravest challenge to Gorbachev's leadership." Dusko Doder and Louise Branson, *Gorbachev: Heretic in the Kremlin* (New York: Viking, 1990), 304. The journalist David Remnick, who wrote a long report on this affair, called it a "silent coup." David Remnick, "The Counterrevolutionary," *New York Review of Books*, March 25, 1993.

through public controversies shows how the divisions of the intelligentsia cut across political struggles for domination over the party line. Subsequently, the polarization across both political and intellectual institutions intensified. The journals *Molodaia gvardiia* and *Nash sovremennik* firmed up the unity of their editorial lines as the leading tribunes for the antiliberal intelligentsia, in direct confrontation with the liberal outlets *Ogonek* and *Moskovskii novosti*.[20]

Despite the conservative opposition, the Nineteenth Party Conference, held in June–July 1988, launched a third phase of democratizing reforms, which established a parliament elected by secret competitive ballots, the Congress of People's Deputies of the Soviet Union. While antiliberal forces progressively lost ground in the Kremlin's hierarchy – Ligachev was demoted from second-ranking Politburo member in the fall of 1988[21] – the political liberalization launched by Gorbachev moved their power struggle into the realm of competitive electoral campaigns.

The regime's approval of political pluralism and competition was a turning point in the organization of the antiliberal coalition. As put by Brudny, conservative intellectuals had primarily practiced "politics by culture" by using literary and cultural platforms to contribute to sociopolitical debates.[22] In contrast to their liberal counterparts, who had started to form ad hoc prodemocracy clubs and had been involved in the organization of meetings and demonstrations since 1986, conservative intellectuals lacked operational support for the circulation of their ideas among a popular audience. In the run-up to the first free elections of the Congress of People's Deputies of the USSR in 1989, they had to adjust their organizational strategy to undertake what John Dunlop has termed a "move to the people," which would test the adhesion of the electorate to their program.[23] The series of organizations created ahead of the elections institutionally enacted the alliance of conservative intellectuals with the pro–status quo forces of the Soviet establishment. Despite the ideological bones of contention between them, their alignment on an "empire-saving" strategy meant they had to rearrange their set of values by

[20] Brudny mentions the publication by *Nash sovremennik* of an interview with *Molodaia gvardiia*'s editor-in-chief, Anatolii Ivanov, in May 1988, as a symbolic act of this solidarity. Brudny, *Reinventing Russia*, 208.

[21] Brudny, *Reinventing Russia*, 211. [22] Brudny, *Reinventing Russia*, 13.

[23] Dunlop, *Rise of Russia and the Fall of the Soviet Empire*, 130.

establishing the preservation of the state as their main priority.[24] The results of the 1989 elections to the USSR Congress of People's Deputies reflected the strong political polarization of Soviet society. While Communist Party members kept a large majority of seats, central figures from both the liberal and the national-conservative intelligentsia were also elected.[25]

In the aftermath of these elections, the alliance of anti-*perestroika* forces further consolidated around the defense of ethnic Russian interests. In particular, the coalition reacted against the emergence of ethnonationalist popular fronts in the Caucasus, Moldavia, and the Baltics, which rejected russification policies and asked for greater independence. As a counterreaction, they put forward an agenda focused on ethnic Russian sentiments, the discrimination suffered by the RSFSR compared to other Soviet republics, and the demographic decline of ethnic Russians.[26] In this context, former divisions between various trends of conservatism, such as between Prokhanov's modernist conservatism and the village writers' critique of modernity, dissolved. The "Letter of the Russian Writers," published in 1990 in *Literaturnaia Rossiia* and *Moskovskii literator*, is evidence of their realignment along a Russian nationalist agenda, with anti-Semitic accusations against the prevailing "Russophobia" and "idealization of Zionist ideology" in the mass media.[27]

In the run-up to the March 1990 elections of the RSFSR Congress of People's Deputies, the anti-*perestroika* coalition was institutionally established for the first time with the creation of the United Council of Russia. This coalition included both national-conservative associations and the Moscow and Leningrad United Workers' Front, which had just been created by anti-Gorbachev factions within the Communist Party.[28] The coalition campaigned for the elections under the name of the Bloc of Social-Patriotic Movements of Russia. However, they were severely defeated by the democratic coalition

[24] Dunlop, *Rise of Russia and the Fall of the Soviet Empire*, 143.

[25] For an overview of the elected liberal deputies, see Sauvé, *Subir la victoire*, 124. On the elected figures among national-conservatives, see Brudny, *Reinventing Russia*, 227–28.

[26] Brudny, *Reinventing Russia*, 220–21.

[27] Norman N. Shneidman, *Russian Literature, 1988–1994: The End of an Era* (Toronto: University of Toronto Press, 2016), 8.

[28] Brudny, *Reinventing Russia*, 236–37.

DemRossia. Only sixteen of the sixty-one candidates put forward by the Patriotic Bloc secured enough votes to compete in the second round of the elections, and none of the remaining candidates was elected on the second ballot.[29]

The electoral and media campaign of the anti-*perestroika* coalition, therefore, failed to achieve its goals. From 1987 to 1991, the domination of the liberal intelligentsia in the media and in political institutions remained unchallenged. In the aftermath of their electoral defeat in 1990, one of the main leaders of the coalition, Iurii Bondarenko, argued to end the association of national-conservatives with the antireformist establishment, identifying this as the cause of the unpopularity of their ideas. However, his voice was a minority within the movement, with most members instead choosing to strengthen the alliance.[30]

Following the revocation of the one-party system in February 1990, the antiliberal coalition settled in a new partisan organization: the Communist Party of the RSFSR (CP RSFSR). Headed by Ivan Polozkov, the CP RSFSR aimed to provide an alternative to the CPSU, which was dominated by reformists.[31] The CP RSFSR further entrenched the partnership between national-conservative intellectuals and the antireform Soviet political establishment. Gennadii Ziuganov, who was the deputy head of the ideological department of the CPSU, was elected secretary for ideology of the CP RSFSR. Under his leadership, prominent nationalist figures became actively involved in the ideological construction of the party. They used the label "national-patriots" to identify themselves in opposition to the liberals.[32] In addition to Ziuganov, the theater director Sergei Kurginian was one of the major ideological sources of inspiration for the leader of the CP RSFSR,

29 In contrast, DemRossia won 148 seats and the Communist Party won 920 seats.

30 Brudny, *Reinventing Russia*, 247.

31 New conservative political coalitions also formed in the Soviet and Russian Congresses, which had become the centers of political activity. At the union level, Colonel Viktor Alksnis founded the Soiuz parliamentary faction in early 1990 to advocate for the preservation of the unity of the Soviet Union. By December 1990, the faction had 561 adherents in the USSR Congress out of a total of 2,250 deputies. Soiuz cooperated closely with the Russian parliamentary faction Rossiia, led by Sergei Baburin. Dunlop, *Rise of Russia and the Fall of the Soviet Empire*, 149–50.

32 In February 1991, Ziuganov founded the Council of National-Patriotic Movements of Russia.

Polozkov.[33] Similar to Ziuganov, Kurginian advocated a synthesis of nationalism and communism, and of conservatism and modernization. He put together his ideas in the manifesto *Postperestroika*, published in the fall of 1990. The document pitted Russia's imperial and collectivist civilizational values against the individualistic West and recommended an authoritarian postindustrial technological breakthrough directed by a religious, cosmist philosophy of history.[34] Likewise, Prokhanov acquired a central role as conceptualizer of the national-patriots' ideological identity. As Timur Atnashev has highlighted, Prokhanov was one of the first intellectuals to use the word "conservative" to designate the association of Russophile nationalism with Soviet patriotism.[35] Prokhanov promoted the army as the basis for a state ideology combining "technology, rationalism, [and] organization" with conservative "social ideals" of "patriotism," "national integrity" and "the traditional Russian idea of self-sacrifice and the creation of a Great Power."[36] Moreover, Prokhanov's promotion of binding ideals such as "Russian statehood" (*russkaia gosudarstvennost*) and the "Russian idea" (*russkaia ideia*) drew on an eclectic set of religious and spiritual references, including Russian Orthodoxy, Russian pantheism, and Russian cosmism.[37]

The RSFSR presidential elections held in June 1991, however, were a sweeping victory for Yeltsin, who won 58.6 percent of the vote, while the platform of the CP RSFSR was clearly rejected.[38] Following their failure to achieve electoral results, the unity of the group was maintained until 1993 by their common experience of protest and agitational politics against the collapse of the Soviet Union and, following this, Boris Yeltsin's government of post-Soviet Russia.

33 Since the end of the 1980s, Kurginian had promoted himself as an ideological counselor, recommending party reforms and scenarios for the country's future that were discussed by the Communist Party organizations.

34 Sergei Kurginian, ed., *Postperestroika: Kontseptualnaia model razvitiia nashego obshchestva, politicheskikh partii i obshchestvennykh organizatsii* (Moscow: Politizdat, 1990).

35 Timur Atnashev, "Utopicheskii konservatizm v epokhu pozdnei perestroiki: Otpuskaia vozhzhi istorii," *Sotsiologiia Vlasti* 29, no. 2 (2017): 36.

36 See Jeff Gleisner, "Keeping the West at Bay: A Conversation with Alexander Prokhanov," *Detente* 9–10 (December 1987).

37 Aleksandr Prokhanov, "Zametki konservatora: II: Ruskii faktor," *Nash sovremennik* 5 (1990): 89.

38 The CP RSFSR's candidate, Nikolai Ryzhkov, finished second, with only 17.2 percent of the vote. Brudny, *Reinventing Russia*, 257.

3.1.2 A "National-Patriotic" Opposition Bound by Political Protest (1991–1993)

After their ultimate electoral defeat, the national-patriots entered a period of political protest. They turned to direct and illegal political action. On July 23, 1991, a group of eleven signatories issued a public call, "A Word to the People" ("Slovo k narodu"), which provided the ideological justification for the organization of the August coup against Gorbachev. The text painted a catastrophic picture of the "disintegration" of the state and economy, called for the unification of all social groups to "save the state," and announced the organization of a movement to take power.[39] The list of signatories spanned the entire range of the antiliberal coalition, including members of the armed forces, the CP RSFSR's leadership, and conservative writers. It also included two leading organizers of the coup: Vasilii Starodubtsev, chairman of the USSR Union of Peasants, and Aleksandr Tiziakov, president of the Association of USSR State Industries.[40] The putsch was an attempt to prevent Gorbachev's signature of a new union treaty and to replace his government with a "State Committee for the State of Emergency." It was quickly defeated by the resistance led by Yeltsin.[41]

After the fall of the Soviet Union in December 1991, the antiliberal opposition coalesced against Yeltsin, the president of Russia. Their cohesion as a group built on a mix of common emotions, ideas, and actions – their resentment at the collapse of the Soviet Union, their rejection of the post-Soviet elites, and their organization of mass demonstrations against the regime. They established a common platform, the "National Salvation Front," and used mobilization resources – direct political action and collective statements – to articulate their claims in the public sphere. During the entire month of June 1992, for instance, the opposition organized pickets in front of Ostankino, Moscow's radio and television tower, to protest their exclusion from public programs.[42] The opposition also organized anti-Yeltsin ral-

[39] Alexander Prokhanov, "Slovo k narodu," *Sovetskaia Rossiia*, July 23, 1991, http://zavtra.ru/cgi/veil/data/denlit/050/12.html.

[40] Other signatories were General Varennikov; General Boris Gromov, first deputy chairman of the USSR Ministry of Internal Affairs; Gennadii Ziuganov; Iurii Blokhin, the leader of Soiuz; and the leading conservative intellectuals Iurii Bondarev, Eduard Volodin, and Valentin Rasputin.

[41] For a detailed analysis of the coup, see the chapter "Anatomy of a Failed Coup" in Dunlop, *Rise of Russia and the Fall of the Soviet Empire*, 186–255.

[42] See *Den*'s coverage of the event in *Den* 54 (1992): 1.

lies and processions during national holidays, which were severely repressed by the police.[43] The Defender of the Fatherland Day, on February 23, became a major symbolic mobilization anniversary.

The experience of protests and sanctions provided the foundations on which the national-patriots based their post-Soviet collective identity. Their first public statement, entitled "Statement by the 'Left' and 'Right' Opposition," was written in reaction to the repression of the February 23, 1992, protests. This text and other public statements framed a traumatic narrative of the fall of the Soviet Union and a catastrophic portrait of post-Soviet Russia as subjected to "unprecedented destruction and desecration."[44] In a move characteristic of what sociologist Howard Becker has designated as "moral crusaders" engaged in a "holy war," they denounced existing rules as illegitimate and presented themselves as the protectors of the country's sacred values.[45] While they faced prosecution for their actions, they returned these charges against the regime and presented their agitational activities as rightful and legitimate.[46]

From 1991 to 1993, therefore, the national-patriots acquired a stock of common memories, emotions, and interpretations of key events that sealed their sense of group belonging. During this period, Prokhanov's newspaper *Den* was the media mouthpiece of the opposition and played an instrumental role in shaping the consistency of its political culture.

3.2 The Newspaper *Den* as the Fabric of the Coalition's Ideological Magnet

3.2.1 Den *as a Rallying Social Forum for the Antiliberal Coalition*

Building on the recognition he had gained among national-conservative intellectuals, and his well-established connections with the Soviet

[43] Violent confrontations with the police took place on May 1 and on Victory Day, May 8, 1993. See *Den* 98 and 99.

[44] "Zaiavlenie 'levoi' i 'pravoi' oppozitsii," *Den*, February 1992; "Zaiavlenie obedinennoi oppozitsii," *Den*, August 1992; "Obrashchenie k grazhdanam Rossii orgkomiteta Fronta Natsionalnogo Spaseniia," *Den*, October 1992.

[45] Howard Becker, *Outsiders: Studies in the Sociology of Deviance* (New York: Free Press, 1991), 147–48.

[46] "Zaiavlenie obedinennoi oppozitsii."

political and military apparatus, Prokhanov became one of the major ideological architects of the *anti-perestroika* forces. He founded his own newspaper, *Den*, to provide a media platform in which the diverse beliefs of the group could rally together under the same flag. As with the emergence of opposition parties, the newspaper's foundation was allowed by the liberalization enacted in 1990. The "Law on the Press and Other Means of Mass Information" ended official censorship and ensured the freedom of press. *Den* was designated by the conservative board of the USSR Writers' Union as its new official organ. Its publication was sponsored by conservative members of the army, and its office was located in a military building.[47] Starting from 1992, it received financial support from entrepreneurs and directors of industries.[48]

With "the newspaper of the spiritual opposition" as the title on its front page, *Den* endorsed a Gramscian understanding of political struggle according to which ideas can use extraparliamentary, cultural means to compete for hegemony. It therefore perpetuated the "politics by culture" strategy of Soviet intellectuals at a time when interest in intellectual politics was increasingly being replaced by a focus on electoral politics, as demonstrated by the sharp decline in the circulation of thick journals.[49] However, with a circulation of around 150,000 issues over the period of its operation, from 1991 to 1993, *Den* compared favorably with some of the major liberal and conservative publishing outlets.[50]

Den aimed to gather varied antiliberal authors, cutting across a wide ideological spectrum and diverse professional backgrounds. *Den*'s contributors included monarchist Orthodox Slavophiles like Vladimir Osipov (1938–2020); Father Dmitrii Dudko and Metropolitan Ioann; national-communists like Ziuganov and Kurginian; national-conservatives like Valentin Rasputin, Vladimir Soloukhin, and Vadim Kozhinov; Islamic traditionalists like Geidar Dzhemal and Samil Sultanov; Eurasianists like Aleksandr Dugin and Lev Gumilev; neo-Nazi ultranationalists like Aleksandr Barkashov; constructivist

47 Shneidman, *Russian Literature, 1988–1994*, 25; Laqueur, *Black Hundred*, 139.

48 Aleksandr Prokhanov, "S novym godom, liudi russkie!" *Den*, December 1992.

49 Brudny, *Reinventing Russia*, 252.

50 From 1991 to 1993, *Nash sovremennik*'s circulation declined from 280,000 to 60,000 issues, and *Literaturnaia gazeta*'s circulation dropped from 1,500,000 to 210,000 issues.

technocrats like Konstantin Pchelnikov; and former Soviet dissidents disillusioned with liberalism like Aleksandr Zinovev and Eduard Limonov. One group of authors belonged to the "Sixtiers" generation, that is, those born between 1925 and 1945 who had first engaged in the cultural field and publication activities in journals in the 1960s, in the aftermath of Khrushchev's Thaw.[51] This group is represented by the founding fathers of national-conservative journals such as Vladimir Osipov, the founder of the Soviet *samizdat* Orthodox journal *Veche* in 1971; Father Dmitrii Dudko (1922–2004), who was a regular author for *Veche*; and Valentin Rasputin (1937–2015), Vladimir Soloukhin (1924–97), and Vadim Kozhinov (1930–2001), who were members of the editorial board of *Nash sovremennik*. Others, such as Eduard Limonov and Aleksandr Zinovev, who had been dissidents or exiled in the West, were new entrants to the field of ideological essay-writing in the early 1990s. In addition, some authors already had an established reputation, such as the well-known village prose writer Valentin Rasputin and the exiled writer Eduard Limonov, whose works had been translated in France and the United States. On the other hand, names such as Aleksandr Dugin, Geidar Dzhemal, and Shamil Sultanov were largely unknown to the public at that time. *Den*'s contributors also came from diverse professional backgrounds, including military commanders, clerics, scientists and scholars, politicians, and businessmen.

This diversity of sociological backgrounds testifies to the eclecticism of the antiliberal coalition. It also attests to Prokhanov's ability to act as a network entrepreneur, tapping into his involvement in multiple milieus in order to connect them together. This network in turn expanded through the network of its members and, beyond the Soviet environment, was able to reach out and engage with foreign political leaders such as Jean-Marie Le Pen, the founder of the French extreme-right political party Front National,[52] and intellectuals such as the French Alain de Benoist and the Belgian Robert Steuckers, theorizers of the European "New Right."[53]

[51] V. M. Zubok, *Zhivago's Children: The Last Russian Intelligentsia* (Cambridge, MA: Belknap Press of Harvard University Press, 2009).
[52] See Le Pen's interview with Dugin in *Den* 29 (1991).
[53] "'Predal Rossiiu—Predal Evraziiu!,' Kruglyi stol, Aleksandr Dugin, Alain de Benoist, Robert Stoikers, Aleksandr Prokhanov, Eduard Volodin, Gennadii Ziuganov," *Den* 50 (1992): 3.

Den directly contributed to the cohesion of the national-patriots across the 1991 regime change by offering a headquarters for their socialization and an editorial space where their ideas were brought together. The newspaper regularly held roundtables, where major authors and leaders of the opposition consolidated their identity as a group by engaging in joint discussions on their collective identity.[54] In June 1992, for instance, a roundtable entitled "We Are Ready for Power" brought together all the leaders of the opposition (Sergei Baburin, Gennadii Ziuganov, Albert Makashov, Nikolai Pavlov, Aleksandr Sterligov, Ilia Konstantinov). These venues offered a concrete setting for the socialization of the group's members and helped foster affective relationships between the group's members. The newspaper also served as a means of recruiting followers and young adherents to the group's identity.[55]

3.2.2 Den *as the Ideological Fabric of the Hawks' Common Group Style*

In the first official issue of the paper, published in January 1991, Prokhanov's editorial introduced *Den* as the center of the alternative to the "collapse of the liberal utopia." In contrast to civil war, economic criminality, and political dictatorship, which he associated with liberal policies, Prokhanov called on all forces of society to unite as a "new collective entity," a "single creative whole."[56] To that end, the editorial line of the newspaper embraced a traditionalist worldview pleading for a fundamental normative unity and permanence of values across varied ideological paradigms:

> *Den* will enable the difficult, lengthy reconciliation of artists. "Left" and "right," "liberal" and "conservative"—all this means something in the parliaments, but not in the libraries, in the praying homes, in the families, where most people serve the eternal trinity—truth, good and beauty.[57]

[54] "Vpered, k konservatizmu! Kruglyi stol glavnykh redaktorov patrioticheskikh izdanii," *Den* 15 (1991); "'Predal Rossiiu—Predal Evraziiu!'"; "'My gotovy k vlasty,' kruglyi stol lidery oppozitsii: Sergei Baburin, Gennadii Ziuganov, Albert Makashov, Nikolai Pavlov, Aleksandr Sterligov, Ilia Konstantinov," *Zavtra* 54 (1992): 1–2.

[55] "'Novy Pravye?' Za kruglym stolom redaktsii gazety 'Den'—Molodye pisateli," *Den* 10 (1991): 5.

[56] Aleksandr Prokhanov, "Krakh liberalnoi utopii," *Den*, January 1991.

[57] Aleksandr Prokhanov, "Skovz sumerki," *Den*, Probnyi nomer (November 1990): 1.

Den strengthened the hawks' unity by discursively feeding a defining divide between them ("like-minded people," *edinomyshlenniki*) and "the others." This confrontation created a sense of group belonging by pitting the group's common opposition against, and alienation from, the rest of society. While *Den*'s authors railed against their exclusion from the public sphere, they were still arguably directly engaged in the construction of the political order. Indeed, *Den*'s language helped shape and solidify the content of the ideological labels structuring the post-Soviet political cleavages between two groups in society, described as the "conservatives," "traditionalists," and "patriots" on the one hand, and the "democrats," "liberals," and "traitors" on the other.[58] Through their application of these labels to specific groups and individuals, *Den*'s authors stabilized and substantiated these identities. In addition, they expanded the relevance and significance of these existential divisions between groups – "one of us"/"not one of us" (*nashi/nenashi*) – to any field of activity, such as art and literature, thereby expanding the frontiers of the political struggle.[59]

The competition between *Den*'s ideas and those promoted by liberal groups was manifested in concrete institutions. In the media, *Den* pitted itself as the main adversary of *Literaturnaia gazeta* by publishing articles that had been rejected by the latter's editorial board.[60] *Den*'s most virulent attacks against the media, however, were directed against the state television and radio broadcasting companies. Prokhanov took particular issue with the state media's description of the national-patriots as "fascists." In reaction, he turned the accusations against the media by depicting the opposition as a heroic and victimized group engaged in a struggle against a demonized liberal rival:

> Close-up genitals, pederasty poetry, the cult of Satan, everything that is ugly, shameful, corrupting, cultivating a low instinct, lust, interest in perversion in a person—this is the whole program on television, persistently destroying national ethics, chastity and the search for knowledge and faith. The result of this telepedagogy is child prostitution, an overflow of drug addiction, cult of violence, complete neglect of the beauty, kindness and light preached by Russian culture, Russian theater, and Russian music.[61]

[58] Prokhanov, "Krakh liberalnoi utopii."
[59] Aleksandr Dugin, "Erotizm i imperiia," *Den* 21 (1991): 16.
[60] See *Den* 2 (1991), where Svetlana Selivanova, a former member of the editorial board of *Literaturanaia gazeta*, explains her decision to resign.
[61] Aleksandr Prokhanov, "22 iiunia, rovno v 4 chasa," *Den*, June 1993.

Den used similar tactics to delegitimize the political elite. The paper coined the nickname "Bloody Boris" for Yeltsin in reaction to the repression of the mass protests organized in February 1992 and May 1993.[62] In the run-up to the elections in 1993, *Den* also formulated a series of slogans against Yeltsin such as "Yeltsin is the destruction of the USSR," "Yeltsin is the occupation of Russia," "Yeltsin is a criminal society," and "Yeltsin is the collapse of culture."[63] In contrast, *Den*'s op-eds eulogized the opposition and narrated their actions as part of a heroic epic: "The Democrats in the prefectures and city halls mess around, steal, and get drunk. We, statesmen, will return the state to the people."[64] And: "We were driven by fear for a dying state, pain for a ruined people, love for the only and beloved Russia, religious and unshakable faith in her future light."[65] *Den*, therefore, established the unity of the opposition via a "self-justifying rationale" for the group, turning its protest into a form of principled, righteous behavior.[66] Under the heading "Prokhanov against Yeltsin," the newspaper reported extensively on the government's attempt to sanction and close it down, and on its success at avoiding the enforcement of rules.[67]

Den also supplied important identity markers for the hawks by establishing their past actions and experiences as points of reference defining the history of the movement and binding its participants together: "February 23, 1993, will go down in the history of the Russian resistance, in the history of the restoration of the great state."[68]

In the end, *Den* organized the common materials of the group – its shared experiences and its differences from other groups – into a full-fledged ideological culture. *Den*'s symbolic identity – provided

62 See the frontpage headlines of *Den* 98 (1993). 63 See *Den* 94 (1993): 2.
64 Aleksandr Prokhanov, "A ty gotov postoiat za Rossiiu?" *Den*, October 1992.
65 Prokhanov, "S Novym Godom, liudi russkie!"
66 On the self-justifying rationale used by deviant groups, see Becker, *Outsiders*, 38–39.
67 In August 1993, *Den* was eventually put on trial by the Ministry of Press and Information for the publication of materials inciting sedition, such as articles calling for the introduction of a state of emergency or encouraging a rebellion by ethnic Russians in the Baltics. The newspaper held a series of protest actions such as picketing in front of the ministry, and the accusations were ultimately withdrawn. See Aleksandr Prokhanov, "'Zavtra'—Rubezh soprotivleniia," *Zavtra*, September 1994.
68 Aleksandr Prokhanov, "Trista tysiach krasno-korichnevykh," *Den*, February 1993.

by its name, its founding manifesto, its slogan, its specific language, the recurring theoretical references, and the categories used to pit the newspaper's identity against others – helped substantiate the coalition's boundaries and form its common interpretations, attitudes, and reactions to events.

Den aimed to order the hawks' diverse worldviews into a unique perspective built around a single concern: "how to preserve Russia and preserve the state."[69] Prokhanov championed this attempt to assemble the opposition into a unique ideological framework, which he termed "the ideology of resistance," the "ideology of national salvation," or "the ideology of reconciliation." He thereby aimed to subsume internal contradictions within the coalition under broader rallying categories, such as the "patriots" (*patrioty*) and the "partisans of the state" (*gosudarstvenniki*). *Den* became the platform where this synthesis of eclecticism took concrete shape. The newspaper combined elements of classic Orthodox Slavophile conservatism, neo-Soviet industrialism, and post-Soviet counterculture by including special features targeting the respective audience of these ideas, such as "Symbol of Faith," "Technocrats," and "Rock and the Russian Resistance." *Den*, therefore, served as a rallying platform for both the social and ideological construction of the hawks' collective identity.

3.3 The Russian Hawks between Opposition and Competition with Yeltsin's New Course (1993–1999)

3.3.1 October 1993: The Collapse of the Bipolarization between the Antiliberal Forces and the Regime

Over the year 1993, the defining lines of Russian politics shifted as a rapprochement took place between Yeltsin's deceived allies in power and the antiliberal extraparliamentary coalition. The former, whom John Dunlop has termed "democratic statists," had been key supporters of Yeltsin during his presidential campaign and the failed August coup in 1991.[70] They included Aleksandr Rutskoi, Russia's vice-president, and Ruslan Khasbulatov, the chair of the Supreme Soviet. They grew

69 Aleksandr Prokhanov, "'Den'—100! Slovo glavnogo redaktora," *Den*, May 1993.

70 Dunlop, *Rise of Russia and the Fall of the Soviet Empire*, 184–85.

increasingly critical of Yeltsin after the signing of the Belovezh Accords in December 1991 that dissolved the Soviet Union. They opposed the creation of the Commonwealth of Independent States, which they perceived as diminishing the status of Russia as a great power. In addition, they strongly rejected Prime Minister Egor Gaidar's shock therapy program of accelerated liberalization reforms.[71] Throughout 1993, they increasingly clashed with Yeltsin over his proposed constitution, which granted more powers to the president, and eventually rallied the voice of the antiliberal opposition.[72] The institutional stand-off between the legislature and the executive reached a peak on September 21, when Yeltsin unconstitutionally declared the dissolution of the Supreme Soviet and the Congress of People's Deputies and announced that a constitutional referendum would subsequently take place. In reaction, the parliament impeached Yeltsin and proclaimed Rutskoi as acting president. Mass protests, headed by hawkish opposition movements such as the National Salvation Front, took to the streets in support of the parliament. On October 4, after ten days of violent street fighting, the army, acting on Yeltsin's orders, shelled the barricades organized around the parliament building and arrested the opposition leaders.[73] In the aftermath, Yeltsin issued a series of decrees banning the main opposition organizations and newspapers, including *Den*. Russia's new constitution, which enacted a superpresidential regime, was subsequently adopted by referendum in December 1993.[74]

The events of October 1993 blurred the past bipolar opposition between the antiliberal forces and Yeltsin's regime. Yeltsin's unconstitutional revocation of the legislature's powers and his authoritarian use of armed force to defeat the opposition challenged

[71] See Celestine Bohlen, "Yeltsin Deputy Calls Reforms 'Economic Genocide,'" *New York Times*, February 9, 1992.

[72] In May 1993, numerous members of parliament joined the anti-Yeltsin demonstrations. In September, *Den* published an interview with Khasbulatov by Prokhanov. See *Den* 115 (1993): 1, 2.

[73] The toll of the 1993 October crisis was around 150 dead and 400 wounded. This was the deadliest street fighting event in Russian history since the Russian Revolution. Myriam Désert, "Russia, October 1993: Twenty Years Later, Evaluating the Crisis," *TEPSIS Papers* (2014): 2.

[74] On the deleterious effects of superpresidentialism on Russia's democratic development, see M. Steven Fish, "The Institutional Problem; Superpresidentialism," in *Democracy Derailed in Russia: The Failure of Open Politics* (Cambridge: Cambridge University Press, 2005).

the liberal democratic ideals claimed by his coalition, "Democratic Russia."[75] Conversely, the alignment of the legislative institutions with the extraparliamentary protests consolidated the opposition's self-justifying rationale. In an article on the October barricades, Prokhanov embraced a legalist form of language, highlighting the righteousness of the opposition:

> I cannot call for retaliatory violence, I cannot call the people to arms. Our weapon is law, political will, fearlessness. The deputies behaved courageously, they could not be intimidated, they could not be bribed.[76]

This picture was further established by Prokhanov's op-ed in the first issue of his new newspaper *Zavtra*, *Den*'s successor: "We start our work under the conditions of dictatorship ... These two cultures, ours and theirs [*nasha i ikh*] must not interact with each other."[77]

This narrative was seconded by Rutskoi and Khasbulatov, who joined the national-patriotic opposition against Yeltsin. In an interview with Prokhanov, Rutskoi enhanced his critique of Yeltsin's regime as unlawful and "fascist":

> We acted strictly within the framework of the law. We were the legislature and, criticizing the other side for violating constitutional legality, we ourselves had to act strictly within its framework ... To surround parliament with barbed wire, throw armed men from head to foot against parliamentarians and their defenders, shoot women and children—only a fascist regime could do that.[78]

October 1993, therefore, provided a key symbolic date rallying the anti-Yeltsin forces and providing them with added legitimacy. On the other hand, this date was the last moment of collective effervescence of the opposition. The armed repression of street protests marked the failure of the opposition's strategy of direct action against the regime and pointed to its organizational weakness.[79] In addition, October

[75] Sauvé, *Subir la victoire*, 221.
[76] Aleksandr Prokhanov, "Snachala—Ipatevskii Dom, a potom—Vsiu Rossiiu ...," *Zavtra* 1 (October 1993).
[77] Aleksandr Prokhanov, "Slovo redaktora," *Zavtra* 1 (1993).
[78] Aleksandr Prokhanov and Ruslan Khasbulatov, "Rabota—Dlia Rossii," *Zavtra*, May 1994.
[79] Leading figures of the opposition blamed their failure on their lack of organizational autonomy. See Aleksandr Prokhanov and Ilia Konstantinov, "Oktiabr byl moim glavnym postupkom," *Zavtra*, September 1994.

1993 provoked divisions between partisans of greater antisystem radicalism and advocates of electoral politics. On the one hand, party leaders such as Ziuganov, the leader of the Communist Party, Viktor Anpilov, the leader of the Labor Party, and Sergei Baburin, the leader of the "Russian unity" bloc in the Supreme Soviet, chose to focus on electoral politics. They expressed lassitude for street protests and their physical repression. As put by Anpilov: "We are not political masochists. We do not want the authorities to persecute us all the time."[80] On the other hand, grassroots militant organizations became more radicalized by positioning themselves as an extraparliamentary antisystem opposition. Aleksandr Barkashov's neo-Nazi and paramilitary movement, Russian National Unity, was one of the key leaders of this trend calling for social protest.[81] Similarly, Dugin and Limonov transitioned to a more revolutionary approach to opposition. They cooperated in the creation of the National-Bolshevik Party in 1994 to elaborate an alternative youth counterculture that celebrated the use of violence against the political order.[82]

In addition, Yeltsin's authoritarian crackdown on the opposition was paradoxically paired with a reversal of his attitude to some of their key ideas. The dispersion of these ideas within official public discourse caused a new challenge to the opposition, by opening a field of competition for the appropriation of "patriotic" ideas.

3.3.2 Yeltsin's New Courting Policy toward Patriotic Ideas

The year 1993 marked a conservative turn in Yeltsin's rule. First, the military resolution of the October conflict was paired with the army's increased influence over domestic politics. On November 2, the president's Security Council adopted Russia's first military doctrine, which stated that the armed forces can be involved in the management of armed violence and protection of strategic facilities on

80 Viktor Anpilov and Aleksandr Prokhanov, "Ne pokorimsia!" *Zavtra*, April 1994.

81 Sven Gunnar Simonsen, "Aleksandr Barkashov and Russian National Unity: Blackshirt Friends of the Nation," *Nationalities Papers* 24, no. 4 (1996): 625–39.

82 See Chapter 6 in Véra Nikolski, *National-bolchevisme et néo-eurasisme dans la Russie contemporaine: La carrière militante d'une idéologie* (Paris: Mare & Martin, 2013).

Russian territory.[83] As spelled out by Lieutenant-General Goncharov during an interview with Prokhanov, this military doctrine reestablished the army as a "legal means of political struggle" and inaugurated an important shift away from the slogan "keep the army out of politics," which had prevailed since the 1991 August coup.[84]

The increased prestige and role granted to the army addressed some of the hawks' key requests. Prokhanov's enthusiastic perception of this evolution is representative. He acknowledged that the military doctrine "carried elements of our state ideology"[85] and argued that the ideology and political values of the "patriots" had begun "to enter the ruling consciousness."[86] Moreover, the post–October 1993 environment led to a dispersion of antiliberal ideas in the public sphere and in official speech. The first evidence of this came in December 1993, with the results of the legislative elections signaling a major backlash against pro-Yeltsin liberal forces and bringing nationalist and patriotic programs to the fore. Vladimir Zhirinovskii's rightist LDPR came in first place, with 22.9 percent of the vote, while Ziuganov's CPRF won 12.40 percent of the vote. Gaidar's electoral bloc, "Voice of Russia," which included the Democratic Russia coalition, only received 15.5 percent of the vote. These results testified to the popular rejection of the "shock therapy" program and the rise of nationalist sentiments in Russian society.

The electoral success of conservative programs resulted in a significant modification of Yeltsin's agenda in favor of patriotic ideas. This new course was signified by the economic program announced by Prime Minister Viktor Chernomyrdin in January, which implemented more protectionist and social measures involving increased budgetary spending. This policy move resulted in the resignation of First Deputy Prime Minister Gaidar and Minister of Finance Boris Fedorov, the main architects of the "shock therapy." Subsequently, Fedorov founded his own political party, "Forward, Russia!" which opened the way for a liberal opposition to Yeltsin. Yeltsin's new centrism,

83 See "The Basic Provisions of the Military Doctrine of the Russian Federation," https://fas.org/nuke/guide/russia/doctrine/russia-mil-doc.html.

84 Aleksandr Prokhanov, "Armiia i narod: Posle krovi ('Krgulyi stol' s Generalami Rossisskoi Armii)," *Zavtra*, November 1993.

85 Nikolai Ryzhkov and Aleksandr Prokhanov, "Ia ne khotel govorit o Gorbacheve," *Zavtra*, February 1994.

86 Prokhanov, "Armiia i narod."

therefore, was paired with the evolution of the political spectrum from bipolarization to pluralization.

Yeltsin's change of course included a shift in his approach toward the national-patriotic opposition, from confrontation to engagement. He initiated outreach efforts by granting amnesty to the instigators of the August 1991 coup and the October 1993 crisis.[87] In April, Yeltsin's proposed "Agreement on Civic Accord" sought to end "civil confrontation" and establish a truce among political parties.[88] This initiative marked a new dividing line among opposition parties, between those who signed the agreement, such as Zhirinovskii's LDPR, and those who refused to take part in what they perceived as cooperation with the regime, such as Ziuganov's Communist Party.[89] Like Ziuganov, Prokhanov firmly rejected Yeltsin's outreach to the patriotic opposition's ideas, denouncing this evolution as a cynical and populist move:

> Yesterday's ruthless destroyers of Russia are literally turning into "strong" statesmen and "tough" patriots before our very eyes. Recent supporters of the "wild market" now openly dissociate themselves from it, ranting about the importance of "pragmatic" government regulation. Let's be frank: despite the complete inability to bring the country out of the crisis, they still have a chance to fool the people once again, relying on the powerful support of the ruling regime, the mafia and the media that serve them.[90]

These new diverging attitudes toward the regime particularly crystallized during the Chechen war, which was launched by Yeltsin in December 1994 against the secessionist government of Dzhokhar Dudaiev. To a first group, comprising Zhirinovskii, Limonov, and Barkashov, the defense of Russian ethnic interests against the separatist Chechen community and support for the actions of the Russian armed forces trumped their opposition to Yeltsin's regime. On the other hand, Prokhanov's newspaper, which had advocated multiethnic state patriotism and Russian cooperation with the Muslim world, condemned the interethnic divisions fostered by the war.[91] Both

[87] Thomas Parland, *The Extreme Nationalist Threat in Russia*, 57.
[88] "Dogovor ob obshchestvennom soglasii," *Kommersant* 78 (April 29, 1994).
[89] Parland, *Extreme Nationalist Threat in Russia*, 57.
[90] Aleksandr Rutskoi and Aleksandr Prokhanov, "Razgovor s otkrytym zabrolom," *Zavtra*, September 1994.
[91] See *Den* 20 (1992), section "Slav-Islamic Academy," and the article by Ayatollah Khomeini in *Den* 12 (1992).

Ziuganov and Prokhanov denounced the regime's instrumental use of war as a strategy to foster support for Yeltsin and as a distortion of true Russian patriotism. Early in January 1995, *Zavtra* ran with the headline "The Enemy of the Russian Army Is Not the Chechen, But the 'Democrat.'"[92] The major rift within the ranks of the opposition over the issue of cooperation with the regime was vocally displayed in *Zavtra*, where long-time allies and pillars of the anti-Yeltsin coalition expressed their conflicting views on the Chechen campaign.[93]

In addition, Yeltsin's politics of national reconciliation led him to court some of the key themes of the patriotic opposition. The organization of the fiftieth anniversary of the victory in the Second World War, in 1995, was directed toward this purpose. During the ceremony, a statue of Marshal Georgii Zhukov, a prominent war hero acclaimed by both communists and Orthodox conservatives, was erected outside the Historical Museum in Moscow.[94] Other key measures glorified the role of the army and the church, such as the construction of a war memorial park and an Orthodox church, "Saint George the Victorious," on Poklonnaia Hill, a few miles from the center of Moscow.[95] On the date of the anniversary, Poklonnaia Hill hosted the first military parade of the post-Soviet period. Another symbolic policy aimed at national reconciliation was the creation of the security services, the "FSB," in 1995, the official emblem of which combined the tsarist double-headed eagle and the Soviet secret police's shield and sword.[96] As Prokhanov put it, the hawks viewed this change in Yeltsin's style as an appropriation of their ideas:

> We see an amazing transformation of one Yeltsin into another, at least in words. The vocabulary, the thoughts with which he filled his speech, have been previously common in the publications of our newspapers. This is partly our ideas, our ideals, tendencies, for which we were whipped with scourges, were surrounded by OMON [a special police unit].[97]

92 See *Zavtra* 58 (1995).

93 See *Zavtra* 60 (1995); "Chechenskii raskol, kruglii stol," *Zavtra* 64 (February 1995): 3.

94 Wendy Slater, "Russia's Imagined History: Visions of the Soviet Past and the New 'Russian Idea,'" *Journal of Communist Studies and Transition Politics* 14, no. 4 (1998): 82.

95 Parland, *The Extreme Nationalist Threat in Russia*, 59.

96 Julie Fedor, *Russia and the Cult of State Security: The Chekist Tradition, from Lenin to Putin* (London: Routledge, 2013), 122.

97 Aleksandr Prokhanov and Vladimir Isakov, "Byt russkim—Eto dar," *Zavtra*, March 1994.

The competition between anti-Yeltsin hawkish discourse and the regime's version of state patriotism intensified during the elections in 1995 and 1996. In the run-up to the legislative elections in 1995, Prime Minister Chernomyrdin founded a pro-Yeltsin political party, Our Home – Russia, with the financial support of large corporations and oligarchs. The party put forward a liberal-conservative, centrist program, which advocated neoliberal economic policies while also appealing to the protection of Russia's cultural traditions.[98] However, the results of the election enforced the anti-Yeltsin conservative opposition's meteoric rise in popular support: Ziuganov's CPRF came first, with 22.3 percent of the vote, and Zhirinovskii's LDPR came second, with 11.18 percent of the vote, leaving Chernomyrdin's party to finish third, with 10.13 percent of the vote. During the following presidential elections in 1996, Yeltsin beat Ziuganov by a wafer-thin margin in the first round, with the two receiving 35.8 and 32.5 percent of the vote, respectively. While Yeltsin won the second round, he would nevertheless be faced with a CPRF parliamentary majority until 1999. Throughout this period, a new *modus vivendi* settled between the government and the opposition. On the one hand, in parallel to liberal economic policies, Yeltsin pursued his outreach to some of the key themes of the national-patriotic opposition. In 1996, his decision to establish a commission to define a post-Soviet "Russian idea" was one of his most visible efforts to do so. His call to "think about what national ideal, what national ideology is the most important for Russia" grappled with one of the long-term concerns of the national-patriots.[99] This proposition was paired with further efforts to celebrate Russia's past and traditions and rally Russia's conflicting identities. In 1997, during his radio-broadcast speech celebrating the eightieth anniversary of the creation of the state security organs, Yeltsin enacted a paradigmatic change in the official attitude toward the Soviet past.[100] In a parallel move, in 1998, Yeltsin paid tribute to Russia's prerevolutionary past during the burial ceremony of the tsar's family, which was organized by First Deputy Prime Minister Boris Nemtsov under the supervision of the Orthodox national-conservative intellectual Viktor Aksiuchits.[101] On the other

[98] Aleksei Gariavin et al., *Istoriia Gosudarstvennogo Upravleniia* (Moscow: Direkt-Media, 2018), 340.

[99] Kathleen E. Smith, *Mythmaking in the New Russia: Politics and Memory in the Yeltsin Era* (Ithaca, NY: Cornell University Press, 2002), 158.

[100] Fedor, *Russia and the Cult of State Security*, 126.

[101] Smith, *Mythmaking in the New Russia*, 167.

hand, after 1996, part of the patriotic opposition also engaged in a more pragmatic form of cooperation with the regime. Zhirinovskii was reported to be willing to offer his support to the regime in exchange for bribes and other financial inducements. His party ceased to be regarded as an opposition party by other liberal and conservative opposition parties.[102] Ziuganov's Communist Party relied on its comfortable integration in the power structures – through its parliamentary majority and leadership (CPRF members Gennadii Seleznev and Egor Stroev were respectively chair of the Duma and speaker of the Council of the Federation) – to lobby and enter into negotiations with the regime.[103] The power position of Ziuganov's party also benefited the normalization of former opposition outsiders, such as Aleksandr Dugin, who set aside the National-Bolshevik Party's revolutionary strategy to become adviser for geopolitical issues to Duma Speaker Seleznev.[104]

Zavtra's editorial line, however, remained fiercely critical of Yeltsin's regime. In Prokhanov's view, cooperation with the authorities neutralized the mobilization potential of the patriotic ideas and surrendered it to the benefit of the regime.[105] Instead, *Zavtra* sought to conquer cultural hegemony in the public sphere through demonization of the ruling elites and promotion of the national-patriotic opposition as the carrier group of the Russian population's traumas and grievances.[106]

3.3.3 The Russian Hawks' Mobilization Strategy to Gain Cultural Hegemony

Prokhanov launched the newspaper *Zavtra* in 1993 with the slogan "The newspaper of the Russian state," illustrating its dismissal of the

102 Zhirinovskii clearly manifested his alignment with the government in April 1999, when his party refused to participate in the impeachment vote against Yeltsin. See Parland, *Extreme Nationalist Threat in Russia*, 158.

103 Parland, *Extreme Nationalist Threat in Russia*, 83.

104 Parland, *Extreme Nationalist Threat in Russia*, 83. In 1997, Prokhanov wrote: "Now it seems that Ziuganov is cramped in a coat of 'compromise' style." Aleksandr Prokhanov, "Ne verte koldunam Svanidze i Kiselidze!" *Zavtra*, April 1997.

105 Aleksandr Prokhanov and Gennadii Ziuganov, "Odna oppozitsiia—Dva vzgliada," *Zavtra* 6 (1998).

106 The concept of "carrier group" is borrowed from Max Weber's sociology of religion and reused in Jeffrey Alexander's cultural sociology in Jeffrey C. Alexander, *The Meanings of Social Life: A Cultural Sociology* (Oxford: Oxford University Press, 2003), 93–94.

incumbent regime and its claim to represent the "real" essence of the Russian state in a separate space. Prokhanov built on his personal access to the different opposition groups to sustain a space in which they could be brought together despite their divergences:

> Our newspaper *Den* ... has always set itself the goal of accumulating forces and uniting ... And now we still have the following task: to connect what seems to be incompatible.[107]

The newspaper's columns gave representation to the different attitudes of the opposition. The section "The Third Rome or the Republic of Rus" ("Tretii Rim ili Respublika Rus"), for instance, published articles on the Russian idea ranging from ethnic nationalist programs to Eurasian imperialism.[108] Moreover, *Zavtra* supported both the parliamentary and the extraparliamentary opposition. During the legislative elections in December 1993, *Zavtra* campaigned for the different national-patriotic opposition parties. Despite the competition between Rutskoi's, Ziuganov's, and Baburin's electoral blocs, *Zavtra* gathered them together as members of the same group with the headline: "Ours Are in the Duma!"[109] In parallel, *Zavtra* also showed support for the revolutionary opposition with the publication of the "Declaration of the Revolutionary Opposition" by Barkashov, Dugin, Limonov, Letov, and others in June 1994.

Zavtra's eclecticism provoked disagreements within the opposition and, as the director of the newspaper, Prokhanov played a key role in advocating a conciliatory pragmatism. In early 1993, for instance, Kurginian split with *Zavtra* over his rejection of the newspaper's support for the occult and neo-Nazi ideas propagated by Dugin. Against Kurginian's principled position, Prokhanov exposed the newspaper's commitment to an overarching philosophy of "victory," which prioritized the unity of the opposition over its consistency.[110] On the other hand, Prokhanov also addressed critiques against Ziuganov's moderation by defending Ziuganov's ability to

[107] Ryzhkov and Prokhanov, "Ia ne khotel govorit o Gorbacheve."

[108] Aleksandr Prokhanov, "Tretii Rim ili Respublika Rus: Priglashenie k diskussii," *Zavtra*, June 1995.

[109] See *Zavtra* 4 (1993). See also, ahead of the legislative elections in 1995: "'V Dumu!': Zhirinovskii, Ziuganov, Rutskoi, Skokov," *Zavtra* 93 (1995).

[110] Sergei Kurginian, "Esli khotim zhit," *Zavtra* 81 (1993); Aleksandr Prokhanov, "Esli khotim pobedit," *Zavtra* 81 (1993).

structure the Communist Party and provide an organizational basis for the opposition.[111]

In answer to the divisions of the opposition and its competition with official state patriotism, *Zavtra*'s editorial line sought to maintain sources of group membership for the various antiliberal forces.[112] In 1994–95, Prokhanov held a series of interviews with the various leaders of the opposition, during which they reflected on the opposition's definition and their relationship with political power. The interviews highlighted several elements maintaining the opposition's common ground: a shared stock of memories and emotions, a quasi-religious understanding of their unity and destiny, and a conspiratorial view of politics uniting them against outside enemies.

First, the respondents expressed a common nostalgia for their experience of protests during the years 1991–93. They highlighted the formative role of these years and their continued influence as the founding myth of their movement. They referred to the specific dates on which mass demonstrations were held, such as February 23 or May 1, as shared memories and key identity markers.[113] Prokhanov also sought to translate their common exposure to repression and physical injury into attributes of group belonging. He pitted opposition figures as martyrs and sacrificial figures who had been "beaten," "captured and tortured in prison."[114] He consequently highlighted *Zavtra*'s status as a victim of repression and leading organizer of the resistance.[115] Prokhanov stressed the essential role of the group's "suffering" as the common bond of the opposition, reflecting the entire society's suffering:

> The idea of unity is not a dream. This is the tendency of the society itself. There is one and only one face: the face of a person who is suffering for its nation, the face of a Russian, robbed, destroyed, and socially suffering.[116]

[111] Aleksandr Prokhanov, "Ziuganov," *Zavtra*, September 1995.

[112] Besides *Zavtra*, other organizations were created to maintain the unity of the antiliberal forces, such as the Congress of Russian Communities, led by Dmitrii Rogozin and Aleksandr Lebed, which aimed at forming electoral blocs for legislative elections.

[113] See, for instance, Stanislas Terekhov and Aleksandr Prokhanov, "Ostaius russkim ofitserom," *Zavtra*, July 1994.

[114] See, for instance, Prokhanov's portrait of Anpilov in Anpilov and Prokhanov, "Ne pokorimsia!"

[115] On *Zavtra*'s leading role as a resistance fighter and victim of repression, see Prokhanov, "'Zavtra'—Rubezh soprotivleniia."

[116] Prokhanov and Konstantinov, "Oktiabr byl moim glavnym postupkom."

Prokhanov's highlighting of the hawks' shared stock of experiences and common emotions, therefore, was instrumental in continuing to hold the community together.

Moreover, the series of interviews also shows that the respondents shared a dual adherence to spiritual values and to the goal of shaping Russia's path as a modernized, alternative great power to the Western model of development. Rutskoi, the leader of the "social-patriotic" movement Derzhava (Power), stated his commitment to the "revival of Russia as a great power within the borders of the USSR," which, in his view, required the restoration "of our primordially Orthodox way of life ... based on morality and spirituality."[117] Likewise, Baburin, the leader of the nationalist Russian All People's Union, promoted "patriotic traditionalism" as his party program, which centered on "the idea of the Russian path" and held Orthodoxy as "the mystical philosophy from which, in essence, Russia flowed."[118] Similar views were also advocated by Zhirinovskii, who called for the revival of the "remnant of the Russian Empire and the communist USSR – a powerful military industry, a powerful army, the heroic spirit of the Russian people" and the preservation of the "spiritual world of the Orthodox Slavs" in opposition to the "disintegrated" West.[119] Oleg Shenin, the chairman of the Council of the Union of Communist Parties, argued for the creation of a "Russian alternative to 'sustainable development'" based on a "post-industrial breakthrough" and "new cardinal strategic ideas of a technocultural nature," further calling for the rediscovery of "Russian cosmism and its connection with communist ideology."[120] The appeal to a religious, eschatological vision of history provided a narrative to maintain the opposition's unity despite its historic experience of disintegration and defeat. As Barkashov argued:

> The events that are taking place in our country are certainly of a metaphysical nature. It is almost pointless to try to measure up to them, to evaluate from the point of view of political benefits.[121]

117 Rutskoi and Prokhanov, "Razgovor s otkrytym zabrolom."
118 Sergei Baburin and Aleksandr Prokhanov, "Volia, Pobeda," *Zavtra*, July 1995.
119 Vladimir Zhirinovskii and Aleksandr Prokhanov, "Ia vvedu v Kreml," *Zavtra*, February 1994.
120 Oleg Shenin and Aleksandr Prokhanov, "Zovu prodolzhat borbu," *Zavtra*, June 1995.
121 Aleksandr Barkashov and Aleksandr Prokhanov, "Slava Rossii!" *Zavtra*, March 1994.

Prokhanov also put forward the "metaphysical meaning" of October 1993, interpreting the opposition's political failure as part of a broader divine plan:

Not being a theologian and not having a prophetic gift, I nevertheless keenly felt the metaphysical meaning of what happened in the fall of 1993, when it was not just the political system that broke, not just a period of history, but the invisible axis around which revolved the universe. All the events of those days—deaths, exploits, conflagrations—seemed to me like a mystery in which Russian life went its Way of the Cross.[122]

Zavtra strengthened its links with Orthodox clerics, such as the monarchist Metropolitan Ioann (Snychev) of Saint Petersburg and Ladoga, who served as authoritative support of this religious interpretation of the opposition's mission. During an interview with Metropolitan Ioann, Prokhanov clearly spelled out his understanding of an Orthodox "providential" philosophy of history providing a positive meaning to negative events:

I was directly involved with this, my friends suffered. My heart initially felt trouble, tragedy. And in the first days after the fire, the tank shooting, the burial of victims, I felt horror, human horror. And then this horror was replaced by sadness, apathy, despondency ... But as time passed ... despondency began to give way to a strange sensation of light. There was a hope that these victims, these deaths were not just a bloody absurdity. This has a providential, Russian Orthodox meaning.

The martyrs, who spoke out for the faith, some for the Fatherland, some for the people, did not die in vain. Their death expiates the abomination around us, filth, disgusting, theft, decay. The October events became a luminous explosion.[123]

In his response, Metropolitan Ioann backed these views and promoted an interpretation of October 1993 as part of a cathartic and eschatological Orthodox meaning of Russian history:

The doctrine of the Orthodox Church says that any moral improvement is possible only through sorrow ... All Russian history is catastrophic. Cataclysm upon cataclysm, disaster upon disaster. The Russian people, carrying through the centuries the Orthodox idea of embodying the truths of

122 Aleksandr Prokhanov, "Mistika vosstaniia," *Zavtra*, September 1996.
123 Metropolitan Ioann and Aleksandr Prokhanov, "Rossiia: Podnozhie prestola gospodnia," *Zavtra*, March 1994.

faith, ideals of righteousness and mercy into the surrounding life, endlessly "wade" through the circumstances that hinder it in this.[124]

Finally, *Zavtra*'s production of group belonging relied on conspirationist narratives pitting the unity of national-patriots against the supposed assaults of domestic and foreign enemies. *Zavtra* developed an extremely fierce and aggressive form of rhetoric against Yeltsin's regime. Yeltsin's economic policies were regularly compared to "genocide."[125] In 1995, one of *Zavtra*'s headlines was titled "Yeltsin Killed 2,200,000 Russians."[126] By contrast, the patriotic opposition was depicted as the righteous protector of "Russian civilization," engaged in resistance against the ruling elites, described as "murderers," "butchers," "perjurers," "molesters," "perverts," and so on.[127] Prokhanov's rhetoric also included personal shaming and degradation of the main figures of the ruling elites. In one article, he described Prime Minister Chernomyrdin as:

> a Soviet tycoon, covered with the even fat of success, with a well-fed uterine laugh, fearful and merciless, loyal and secretly vain. When he speaks, it seems that two frogs are fighting to the death in his mouth, and in his head the two hemispheres are trying to swap places.[128]

Elsewhere, Prokhanov further substantiated the image of Yeltsin as the personal enemy of the Russian people, responsible for all their suffering:

> [Yeltsin] dismembered the Great Soviet Union, sent 30 million Russians into scattering, deprived Russia of half of its space with oil fields, uranium and gold mines. ... He skillfully and deftly created hell for the people, starved them to death, poisoned them with diseases, strangled them with poverty, eyes and ears with multi-colored putty made by NTV.[129]

124 Ioann and Prokhanov, "Rossiia."
125 Aleksandr Prokhanov and Valentin Chikin, "Ot patrioticheskogo informbiuro," *Zavtra* 4 (1997); Mikhail Karaulnik, "Eltsinizm: Eto genotsid," *Zavtra* 20 (1997).
126 *Zavtra* 35, no. 91 (1995).
127 Aleksandr Prokhanov, "My—Iz russkoi tsivilizatsii," *Zavtra*, August 1996, and Aleksandr Prokhanov, "Zagnannykh prezidentov pristrelivaiut, ne pravda li?" *Zavtra*, October 1996.
128 Aleksandr Prokhanov, "Chernobyl na Ukraine: Chernomydrin v Rossii," *Zavtra*, August 1998.
129 Aleksandr Prokhanov, "Kostikov obratil Eltsina v katolichestvo," *Zavtra*, July 1997.

Finally, Prokhanov targeted the country's national state corporation for having "ruined" the Soviet Union and "devoured the untold richness of the Motherland."[130]

Zavtra's delegitimization and demonization of the ruling elites helped feed popular stereotypes about post-Soviet politics, such as the corruption and criminalization of politics, the theft of the country's resources by mighty oligarchs, the influence of tycoons on the regime, and the manipulation of the people's opinions by media corporations. Prokhanov's prophesying tone evoking the country's catastrophic state and his literary use of burlesque metaphors to ridicule the authorities played an important role in estheticizing these ideas. As Anna Razuvalova explains, Prokhanov's language is an example of the creation of a "master narrative of social suffering."[131] It aimed to fix the traumatic character of post-Soviet Russia's political life and frame *Zavtra* as the medium of the representation of society's mass emotions and collective grievances.

Conspiracy theories also became privileged linguistic devices among *Zavtra* authors to feed their opposition between "us" and "them," the "Russian people" and the "regime." Dugin played a central role in coining a "science of conspiracies" (*konspirologiia*).[132] Likewise, as Edmund Griffiths has highlighted, the inner logic driving Prokhanov's discourse in the 1990s was that of esotericism, assuming the existence of "an inner truth, known only to a few and radically separate from the outward sense presented to the masses."[133] In particular, Prokhanov has actively propagated the theory of the "organizational weapon," according to which the collapse of the Soviet Union was orchestrated from the outside, by a "system of economic, ideological, psychological and perhaps even parapsychological sources of influence."[134]

130 Prokhanov, "Chernobyl na Ukraine, Chernomydrin v Rossii."
131 Anna Razuvalova, "Conspiracy Theory and Neoconservative PR Strategies in the 2000–2010s: The Case of Aleksandr Prokhanov," in *"Truth" and Fiction. Conspiracy Theories in Eastern European Culture and Literature*, ed. Peter Deutschmann, Jens Herlth, and Alois Woldan (Stuttgart: ibidem Verlag, 2020), 147.
132 See Aleksandr Dugin, *Konspirologiia: Nauka o zagovorakh, tainykh obshchestvakh i okkultnoi voine* (Moscow: Arktogea, 1993).
133 Edmund Griffiths, *Aleksandr Prokhanov and Post-Soviet Esotericism* (Stuttgart: ibidem Verlag, 2023), 86.
134 Leonid Shebarshin and Aleksandr Prokhanov, "Shef razvedki v gostiakh u 'Dnia,'" *Zavtra*, August 1991.

His contempt for the post-Soviet political order as a treacherous usurpation of power was supported by blunt anti-Semitism:

> The reality in which today's Russian life is taking place is a genocide carried out by the World Bank, the International Monetary Fund, a group of Moscow bankers, the World Jewish Congress, Chubais, Nemtsov, Prime Minister Chernomyrdin and the apocalyptic Yeltsin, which knocks out the Russian people in the interests of the "golden billion" whole.[135]

Moreover, as Razuvalova points out, Prokhanov's conspiracy theories carried a "set of authoritarian ideas" that undermined "the rational legal sources of political power" in favor of the defense of "the sacred and mysterious nature of power."[136] Indeed, Prokhanov portrayed the role of the patriotic opposition as engaged in a sacred, God-commanded mission to reestablish the organic, eternal and authentic Russian identity:

> We are the ones who survived the slaughter. Who, in August 1991 and in October 1993, brought out of the pogroms and fire the shrines and tablets containing the sacred texts, the genetic codes, the scientific and religious formulas of Russian civilization. Our mission is to find each other, come together, put together these split tables, glue the torn and burnt scrolls and again reveal the general formula according to which on this part of the earth, through all shocks and invasions, all satanic intrigues, Divine providence is carried out.[137]

At the end of the 1990s, *Zavtra*'s uncompromising discourse against the regime attracted a new audience outside the conservative opposition's ranks. The 1998 government's default, the devaluation of the ruble, and the ensuing financial crisis led to the resignation of Prime Minister Sergei Kirienko and bolstered the Russian people's opposition to capitalist economic reforms.[138] Subsequently, in 1999, anti-Western attitudes became predominant in Russian public opinion in reaction to NATO's extension to Hungary, Poland, and the Czech Republic and to NATO's military operations against Serbia without

135 Aleksandr Prokhanov, "Russkoe soprotivlenie: Proroki i lidery," *Zavtra*, March 1998.
136 Razuvalova, "Conspiracy Theory and Neoconservative PR Strategies in the 2000–2010s," 161.
137 Prokhanov, "My—Iz russkoi tsivilizatsii."
138 Parland, *Extreme Nationalist Threat in Russia*, 156.

a United Nations mandate.[139] *Zavtra* reported extensively on the conflict in Yugoslavia and fed virulent anti-American sentiments.[140] Criticism of the West also grew significantly in important liberal media outlets such as *Izvestiia* and *Segodnia*.[141] In this context, the national-patriots met with opposing segments of opinion around the same protest actions and position. This is well illustrated by *Zavtra*'s reporting on the anti-NATO demonstrations held in 1999:

> The NATO bombings rallied in anti-American protest not only ordinary people, but also musicians who were previously on opposite sides of the barricades. All of them in one way or another oppose US aggression, and this cannot but rejoice.[142]

3.4 Conclusion

This chapter has demonstrated that the Russian hawks' network was formed in the late Soviet Union by aggregating national-conservative intellectuals and antireformist members of the Soviet military and political establishment opposing *perestroika*. The network was not elaborated as a completely consistent ideological coalition but rather was shaped by the shared experiences, representations, language, and emotions built through the group's common political struggle against liberals. Conversely, the fabric of the group's sociability and ideological cohesion – coordinated by Prokhanov's newspapers *Den* and *Zavtra* – became a performative source of group identity.

This chapter has also shown that Yeltsin's authoritarian crackdown on the October 1993 protests marked a turning point after which the regime used some of the hawks' defining ideas – such as the preservation of Russia's cultural and traditional values, the search

[139] As reported by the sociologist Denis Volkov, "The U.S. first took its place at the number one spot on Russians' list of countries that 'pose a risk to Russia's security': 23% held this opinion in 1998, and 35% in 1999. 75% of Russians agreed with the statement that 'the U.S. is taking advantage of Russia's troubles to turn it into a second-class country,' and 60% were confident that the U.S. wanted Russia to break into several parts." See Denis Volkov, "The Evolution of Anti-Americanism in Russia," Carnegie Moscow Center, https://carnegie.ru/commentary/60457.

[140] See, for instance, Aleksandr Prokhanov, "Eltsin, Zachem Razbombil Belgrad?" *Zavtra*, March 1999.

[141] Parland, *Extreme Nationalist Threat in Russia*, 163.

[142] *Zavtra* 15 (1999).

for a post-Soviet national idea – as ideological underpinning of the construction of official state patriotism. Moreover, by the end of the 1990s, the evolution of the Russian public opinion toward anti-Western and antiliberal views demonstrated the hawks' success at framing their discourse as a carrier narrative of the society's grievances and demands. In 2001–2002, the controversy that followed the success and literary award won by Prokhanov's satirical novel about post-Soviet politics, *Mister Hexogen*, further disclosed the growing appeal of Prokhanov's language beyond the opposition ranks, to elitist and popular audiences alike.

4 *From Fringe to Mainstream*
The Mister Hexogen *Controversy (2001–2002)*

In the late 1980s – early 1990s ... happiness was understood in such a way that we would merge in ecstasy with Europe, with the European mentality in its various manifestations ... It turned out that it was not for sale. Trying to make a Russian version of Derrida, a Russian version of Deleuze, or a Russian version of Putnam is not a good strategy ... Apparently, what is productive is what is called self-reliance. Searching for some "mental" basis in one's own national culture. Why are we interesting? Because we are different, we have our own way of intellectual and cultural evolution. And not because we can assimilate this or that European intellectual tradition and then retell it.

At one time, everyone was very much excited by the West. And this excitement turned into subsequent monstrous disappointment.

Aleksandr Ivanov, "'Kultura Dvizhetsia Vzryvami'," 2002

As explained in Chapter 3, after the collapse of the Soviet Union, Aleksandr Prokhanov acquired leadership and charismatic authority among oppositional antiliberal milieus. His audience, however, was limited to the readership of his newspaper *Zavtra*, which was widely perceived as a marginal, extremist outlet. In October 2001, Prokhanov started issuing a literary novel, *Mister Hexogen*, as a special supplement to his newspaper. The novel portrayed a bitter, cynical, and violent vision of post-Soviet politics. Under barely disguised fictional characters, it recounted the September 1999 apartment bombings[1] as a conspiracy orchestrated by Boris Yeltsin's entourage to legitimate the Second Chechen War (August 1999–April 2000) and propel Vladimir

[1] In September 1999, a series of explosions hit apartment buildings across Russia, which were attributed to rebel Chechen groups. For an in-depth analysis of these events, see John B. Dunlop, *The Moscow Bombings of September 1999: Examinations of Russian Terrorist Attacks at the Onset of Vladimir Putin's Rule* (Stuttgart: ibidem-Verlag, 2014).

Putin to power. Throughout the novel, the main protagonist, ex-KGB officer Viktor Beloseltsev, who is remobilized to carry on this special operation, recovers from the depression and loss of purpose he experienced after the Soviet collapse as he returns to a life devoted to a collective and utopian mission. The novel uses certain stylistic characteristics of Russian postmodernism, such as irony and conspiracy narratives, to blur the barriers between reality and fantasy, while also featuring Prokhanov's ultraconservative ideological views.[2] With clear anti-Semitic and xenophobic themes, the novel paints an apologetic vision of the Stalinist state based on the omnipotence of the security services, the sacrifice of the people, and the technological modernization of the country. Furthermore, it marries this neo-Soviet political aesthetics with Orthodox beliefs and a cosmist, esoteric understanding of history.[3]

In March 2002, a few months after Prokhanov's novel was serialized in newspaper format, the publishing house Ad Marginem released it as a book. Widely regarded as an intellectual and progressive institution, Ad Marginem had built its reputation throughout the 1990s as the publisher of the first Russian-language editions of works by Michel Foucault and Gilles Deleuze and of the postmodern conceptualist Russian writer Vladimir Sorokin.[4] The publication of Prokhanov's novel by a prestigious intellectual institution came as a major surprise in the literary field. Prokhanov had been dismissed from the realm of legitimate literature during the 1990s, yet Ad Marginem's editors promoted a new reading of his work, arguing that his mix of "hyper-Soviet" and "futuristic" themes should be considered part of a literary "new wave."[5] Shortly after its publication, in May 2002,

[2] For a detailed examination of Russian postmodernism, see Mikhail Epstein, "The Origins and Meaning of Russian Postmodernism," in *After the Future: The Paradoxes of Postmodernism and Contemporary Russian Culture*, Critical Perspectives on Modern Culture (Amherst: University of Massachusetts Press, 1995), 188–212.

[3] For a more complete literary analysis of *Mister Hexogen*, see Keith Livers, "The Tower or the Labyrinth: Conspiracy, Occult, and Empire-Nostalgia in the Work of Viktor Pelevin and Aleksandr Prokhanov," *Russian Review* 69, no. 3 (2010): 477–503.

[4] See the presentation of the history of the publishing house in the "About Us" section of its website: "O nas," https://admarginem.ru/o-nas.

[5] Aleksandr Ivanov and Mikhail Kotomin, "'Kultura Dvizhetsia Vzryvami'. Beseda s Glavnoi 'Ad Marginem' Aleksandrom Ivanovym i Vedushchim Redaktorom Izdatelstva Mikhailom Kotominym," *Zavtra*, May 2002, https://web.archive.org/web/20060507143406/http://geksogen.ru/r61.html.

Prokhanov's novel was awarded the National Bestseller Prize. Over the year, the book was released in two editions, with a total distribution of 110,000 copies. The book's success and publicity triggered a controversy among literary critics, political scholars, and journalists. Because of the dual nature of the book – as both a political pamphlet and a literary novel – this controversy extended beyond purely literary issues to also include concerns about the morality of publishing such views.

While the Russian cultural scene of the 1990s clearly pitted "liberal-democrats" against "national-patriots," during the *Mister Hexogen* controversy part of the former liberal establishment sided with Prokhanov's challenge to the standards and norms of post-Soviet society. The controversy, therefore, broke the formerly prevailing consensus that viewed Prokhanov as an extremist outsider and resulted in his intellectual legitimization in the public sphere. Some of the key components of Prokhanov's hawkish ideology – such as critique of the Western model of modernity, rehabilitation of Russia as the heir of the Soviet Union's great power status, and the promotion of Russia's primordial national cultural values and militarist moral codes – gained a new audience, especially among the younger generation of intellectuals born in the 1970s.

This chapter demonstrates that Prokhanov's ascension in the early 2000s reflected changes in the value system ruling legitimate discourse in the Russian public sphere, as part of the intellectual and political elites started rejecting Western liberalism and the legacy of the 1990s to promote a Russia-specific national popular culture. In this respect, Prokhanov's move from the fringes to the center stage of the public sphere is a marker of the Russian development of the cultural backlash against globalization that also manifested in other Western and non-Western contexts.[6]

The chapter is based on a review of over a hundred press articles devoted to Prokhanov's novel and published during the period from November 2001 until June 2002. These articles were authored by literary specialists (critics, scholars) as well as journalists. They appeared

[6] Stanley Hoffman, for instance, identified the September 11 terrorist attacks as the "beginning of a new era," in reaction to the 1990s decade marked by the progress of economic, cultural, and political globalization. Stanley Hoffmann, "Clash of Globalizations," *Foreign Affairs* 81, no. 4 (2002): 104–15.

in most major Russian media outlets, either online or in print.[7] They are listed and accessible on the website devoted to Prokhanov's novel, "geksogen.ru."[8]

4.1 *Mister Hexogen*: A Catalyst in the New Culture War against the 1990s

4.1.1 A State-Sponsored Political Backlash against the Legacy of the 1990s

By the end of the 1990s, Russia's experience of economic crisis and of a brutal devaluation of the ruble, NATO's extension to Hungary, Poland, and the Czech Republic, and NATO's military intervention during the Kosovo crisis without a mandate from the United Nations had stirred up anticapitalist and anti-Western sentiments in the Russian elites and population. Kevin Livers, for instance, has stressed that the financial crisis of 1988 resulted in the Russian elite's "extraordinary pessimism" and "disillusionment about the possibilities of democratic reforms."[9] As also reported by figures from the polling and research institute the Levada Center, in 1999, 75 percent of Russians agreed with the statement that "the U.S. is taking advantage of Russia's troubles to turn it into a second-class country," and 60 percent were confident that "the U.S. wanted Russia to break into several parts."[10] In addition, as emphasized by Thomas Parland, the unanimous support of the Duma for the military operation against Chechnya launched by then-Prime Minister Putin in September 1999 fostered "an atmosphere of patriotic ecstasy."[11]

In this context, the campaign for the presidential elections held in March 2000 resulted in what Sergei Prozorov has described as the dispersion of conservatism as an "hegemonic discourse" in Russian

[7] Such as *Izvestiia*, *Nezavisimaia gazeta*, *Russkhii zhurnal*, *Kommersant*, *Ezhenedelnyi zhurnal*, *Knizhnoe obozrenie*, *Komsomolskaia pravda*, and *Vremia MN*.

[8] The reviews are listed on the webpage "Retsenzii," geksogen.ru, https://web.archive.org/web/20060507143508/http:/geksogen.ru/recen_1.html.

[9] Livers, "Tower or the Labyrinth," 481.

[10] See Denis Volkov, "The Evolution of Anti-Americanism in Russia," Carnegie Moscow Center, https://carnegie.ru/commentary/60457.

[11] Thomas Parland, *The Extreme Nationalist Threat in Russia: The Growing Influence of Western Rightist Ideas* (London: Routledge Curzon, 2004), 156.

politics.[12] The evolution of the political parties' programs toward conservative values even reached the liberal end of the political spectrum. As an example of this evolution, Prozorov refers to the programmatic shift of the liberal party Union of Right Forces, which was set in motion by Sergei Ulyukaev's article "The Right Turn," published in 1999.[13] Likewise, a conservative turn was enforced by Putin's platform, which the political scientist Leonid Poliakov defined as a "liberal–conservative" synthesis.[14] Indeed, Putin's program, laid down in the article "Russia at the Turn of the Millennium" published in December 1999, married a liberal socioeconomic agenda with a conservative definition of the "Russian idea" as characterized by "primordial, traditional Russian values" such as "patriotism," "great power status" (*derzhavnost*), "statehood" (*gosudarstvennichestvo*) and social solidarity.[15]

Although Putin was positioned as the direct heir to the Yeltsin regime, his first mandate as president in 2000–2004 selectively departed from Yeltsin's legacy.[16] As Richard Sakwa has pointed out, Putin built his presidency on the idea that in the 1990s the Russian state lost its capacity to manage affairs, leading to economic decline and the rise of powerful special interests threatening governance.[17]

12 Sergei Prozorov, "Russian Conservatism in the Putin Presidency: The Dispersion of a Hegemonic Discourse," *Journal of Political Ideologies* 10, no. 2 (2005): 121–43.

13 Prozorov, "Russian Conservatism in the Putin Presidency," 125.

14 See Leonid Poliakov, "Liberalnyi Konservator," *Nezavisimaia Gazeta*, February 2, 2000, www.ng.ru/ideas/2000-02-02/8_conserve.html. As explained by Philipp Boobbyer, early twentieth-century Russian thinkers Petr Struve (1870–1944) and Semen Frank (1877–1950) already identified themselves with the etiquette "liberal-conservative," as they sought to combine strong state power with the development of a strong civil society, private property, and the rule of law. See Philip Boobbyer, "Russian Liberal Conservatism," in *Russian Nationalism, Past and Present*, ed. Geoffrey Hosking and Robert Service (Basingstoke: Macmillan Press, 1998), 36–37. The etiquette was first used in post-Soviet politics in the early 1990s and associated with figures such as Boris Nemtsov. See Katharina Bluhm, "Modernization, Geopolitics and the New Russian Conservatives," *Arbeitspapiere Des Osteuropa-Instituts (Abteilung Soziologie), Freie Universität Berlin* 1 (2016): 7.

15 Vladimir Putin, "Rossiia na rubezhe tysiacheletii," *Nezavisimaia gazeta*, December 30, 1999, www.ng.ru/politics/1999-12-30/4_millenium.html.

16 On Putin's leadership as a mix of continuity and remedial politics toward Yeltsin's legacy, see Richard Sakwa, "Putin's Leadership: Character and Consequences," *Europe-Asia Studies* 60, no. 6 (2008): 881.

17 Sakwa, *Putin Redux: Power and Contradiction in Contemporary Russia* (Abingdon: Routledge, 2014), 1.

In Sakwa's words, Putin regarded the 1990s as a "Time of Troubles" that needed to be "overcome."[18] Instead of the polarization between the "liberals" and the "national-conservatives" that had defined Russian politics in the 1990s, Putin sought to build a new ideological hegemony around what Prozorov has qualified as "a nodal point of conservatism."[19] The 2000 Law on State Symbols, which established the tricolor republican flag while also restoring the imperial two-headed eagle as the state emblem and the Soviet anthem with new lyrics, illustrated this attempt at building a political consensus beyond former divides. Putin's new style was hailed by the leaders of the national-patriotic opposition as an opening to some of their key ideas. Prokhanov, for instance, acclaimed Putin's rule as an attempt to build a "new imperial centralism."[20]

Harley Balzer has put forward the concept of "managed pluralism" to qualify Putin's regime's balance between authoritarian and liberal principles, which Balzer interprets as an endeavor to limit "the diverse cultural influences accompanying globalization while still reaping economic benefits from the international economy."[21] As Balzer shows, Putin introduced constraints and norms in various policy sectors – religion, the media, the party system, labor unions, business associations, civil society, and federal relations – to strengthen the centralized executive authority and limit dissent. In particular, Putin took concreate measures to limit the power of oligarchs associated with Yeltsin's entourage by nationalizing some of their major economic assets. In 2000, Vladimir Gusinskii, a media tycoon, was arrested, and his TV channel, NTV, was acquired by the public holding Gazprom Media. Putin's election was also shortly followed by the emigration of Boris Berezovskii, an oligarch close to Yeltsin, and the acquisition by the state of his TV Channel One.[22]

18 Sakwa, *Putin Redux*, 1.

19 Prozorov, "Russian Conservatism in the Putin Presidency," 121.

20 Aleksandr Prokhanov, "Rossiia—Imperiia sveta," *Zavtra*, June 11, 2001, http://zavtra.ru/blogs/2001-06-1211.

21 Harley Balzer, "Managed Pluralism: Vladimir Putin's Emerging Regime," *Post-Soviet Affairs* 19, no. 3 (2003): 191.

22 As put by Sakwa, Putin's campaign against the oligarchs was selective. It was primarily targeted at those who criticized him or threatened his power by their control of the media. Richard Sakwa, *Putin: Russia's Choice* (London; New York: Routledge, 2004), 100.

Putin's patrimonial type of governance aimed at countering any opposition to the regime and destabilization of the state.[23] As Sakwa has described, from the very beginning Putin's statecraft relied on a "vertical," dirigiste and paternalistic form of tutelary control over the party system, the legislative and judicial bodies, the business community and the civil society.[24] The regime's top-down organization of a "cooperative relationship between the state and society" was supported by the administration's attempt to create and coopt social movements in line with a range of symbolic values such as respect for Russia's history, state patriotism, and self-assertion abroad.[25]

This new, all-encompassing managerial role claimed by the state also applied to cultural life and, more specifically, to literature. Moral and political values have progressively interfered in the appraisal of literary works, leading to repressive censorship measures and collective actions against works dubbed "dangerous" owing to their immoral content.[26] This shifting environment for arts and literature was signaled by several prosecutions of publishers and writers in the years 2001–2002. In 2001, the Russian Ministry of Press threatened two publishers (Ad Marginem and Kolonna Publications) with the revocation of their license because of their publication of the writers Baian Shirianov and Ilia Masodov, whose works allegedly contained "murders, mockery of corpses and obscene scenes."[27] In addition, throughout 2002, the new youth movement "Walking Together" (Idushchie vmeste), funded by the presidential administration, launched a moral crusade against the major representatives of post-Soviet postmodernism such as Vladimir Sorokin, Viktor Pelevin, and Viktor Erofeev.[28]

[23] As an illustration of Putin's patrimonial politics, Sakwa mentions the development of the presidential party, United Russia, as subordinate to the regime and deprived of any political autonomy. Sakwa, *Putin Redux*, 19.

[24] See Sakwa, *Putin Redux*, 30–32. [25] Sakwa, *Putin Redux*, 31, 47.

[26] Fedor Yermolov, "Free Speech and the Attack on Vladimir Sorokin," Ofitsialnyi sait Vladimira Sorokina, August 13, 2002, https://srkn.ru/criticism/yermolov.shtml.

[27] Denis Kurenov, "Szhech, utopit i zapretit: Kto i pochemu zhaluetsia na khudozhestvennuiu literaturu v Rossii XXI veka?" yuga.ru, October 16, 2016, www.yuga.ru/articles/culture/7577.html.

[28] On the identification of these authors as representatives of Russian postmodernism, see Epstein, "The Origins and Meaning of Russian Postmodernism" and Mark Lipovetskii, *Paralogii: Transformatsii (post) modernistkogo diskursa v russkoi kulture 1920–2000-kh godov* (Moscow: Novoe literaturnoe obozrenie, 2008).

The movement particularly targeted Sorokin and denounced what it perceived as immorality and pornography in his novel *Blue Salo*, which Ad Marginem had published in 1999. The group staged public rallies during which participants mimicked Inquisition scenes – tearing copies of *Blue Salo* and offering in exchange books by Boris Vasiliev, a writer of war prose, recounting his experience of the Second World War.[29] A member of the Walking Together movement even took the case to court, charging Sorokin with violation of Article 242 of the Criminal Code for disseminating pornography.[30]

The publication of Prokhanov's *Mister Hexogen*, therefore, occurred in a context where literature had increasingly become used by ruling elites for the promotion of specific moral values. The state-led cultural backlash against the West and against the legacy of the 1990s provided a favorable environment for the circulation of the hawks' discourse. An early signal of this evolution was the possibility given to Aleksandr Dugin in 2000 to regularly contribute to an official governmental website, strana.ru.[31] Likewise, while Prokhanov was largely considered an outsider in post-Soviet literature, the pejorative stereotypes about post-Soviet democracy depicted in his work gained increased popularity. Some of the literary critics endorsing Prokhanov emphasized what they viewed as a refreshing alternative to the rest of post-Soviet literature, which they deemed to be "dull" and "faded."[32] In contrast, they valued the provocative, extremist, and violent rejection of the 1990s offered by Prokhanov, enthusiastically praising its "massively violent energy," "madness," and "mixture of horror and delight."[33]

Conversely, Prokhanov's detractors underlined what they perceived as an artificially inflated popularity of his work and suggested that his novel was used as an instrument of political calculations. The

[29] Yermolov, "Free Speech and the Attack on Vladimir Sorokin."
[30] The charges were eventually dismissed by the court. Accusations against Baian Chirianov's book *Pilotazh* were also taken to the court. See Yermolov, "Free Speech and the Attack on Vladimir Sorokin."
[31] Marlène Laruelle, "Alexandre Dugin : Esquisse d'un eurasisme d'extrême-droite en Russie post-soviétique," *Revue d'études comparatives Est-Ouest* 32, no. 3 (2001): 92.
[32] Liza Novikova, "Knigi za nedeliu," *Kommersant*, April 10, 2002, https://web.archive.org/web/20050216130611/http://geksogen.ru/r26.html.
[33] This verbatim about Prokhanov's novel was listed by Sergei Chuprinin. See Sergei Chuprinin, "Posle draki. Urok prikladnoi konspirologii," *Znamia*, no. 10 (2002), https://magazines.gorky.media/znamia/2002/10/posle-draki.html.

success of *Mister Hexogen* was one of the cases where concerns were raised over the influence of the state's tutelary role in the literary field. Moreover, it was one of the first instances where the concept of "political technologies" was applied to the post-Soviet literary scene. This expression had appeared in the mid-1990s to designate the communication and electoral strategies developed by consultants to ensure the election of certain politicians and to counter any opposition. During a roundtable held at the Institute of Philosophy of the Russian Academy of Sciences in reaction to the publication of *Mister Hexogen*, the scholar Mikhail Ryklin argued that Prokhanov offered "a great advantage for political strategists who are interested in introducing certain stereotypes [about the 1990s]."[34] Another researcher from the institute, Sergei Zemlianoi, viewed Prokhanov's success as the result of the application of the Doctrine of Information Security, which was adopted by the regime in 2002.[35] Moreover, the philosopher and art critic Igor Chubarov added that "the publication of this novel should be considered primarily and even solely as an event in the field of PR [public relations] technologies of the current Russian government."[36] He further described Prokhanov as a representative of a "pseudo-opposition," providing the regime with a way to "distract society from struggle."[37]

The controversy triggered by *Mister Hexogen*, therefore, revealed growing concerns over the use of literature as a battlefield for the promotion of moral and political values. Alongside a state-led rejection of 1990s culture, Ad Marginem's decision to publish Prokhanov also reflected a profound disillusionment with the Western values they had previously embraced, marking a significant U-turn in their editorial stance.

[34] "K publikatsii knigi 'Gospodin Geksogen' A. Prokhanova v izdatelstve Ad Marginem. Obsuzhdenie v sektore 'analticheskoi antropologii' IF RAN," Anthropology.rinet.ru, June 13, 2002, https://web.archive.org/web/20080407224154/http:/anthropology.rinet.ru/drupal/node.php?id=56.

[35] The Doctrine of Information Security is a "synthesis of official positions on the objectives, tasks, principles, and principal measures for ensuring the information security of the Russian Federation." See Douglas Carman, "Translation and Analysis of the Doctrine of Information Security of the Russian Federation: Mass Media and the Politics of Identity," *Washington International Law Journal* 11, no. 2 (2002): 347.

[36] "K publikatsii knigi 'Gospodin Geksogen' A. Prokhanova v Izdatelstve Ad Marginem. Obsuzhdenie v sektore 'analticheskoi antropologii' IF RAN."

[37] "K publikatsii knigi 'Gospodin Geksogen' A. Prokhanova v izdatelstve Ad Marginem. Obsuzhdenie v sektore 'analticheskoi antropologii' IF RAN."

4.1.2 *The Revision of Liberal Intellectuals' Identity through Rejection of Western Values*

Ad Marginem was created as an independent publishing house in 1993 by Aleksandr Ivanov (1956–), a PhD in philosophy, who had previous professional editing experience as the director of the series "Philosophy on the Edge" in the state publishing house Kultura in the early 1990s. Ad Marginem's foundational works specialized in philosophy and included the first Russian editions of twentieth-century Western philosophers such as Martin Heidegger, Michel Foucault, Gilles Deleuze, Walter Benjamin and Roland Barthes.[38] At the end of the 1990s, Ad Marginem enlarged its repertoire to literary works, with Russian postmodern writers such as Vladimir Sorokin and the translation of Western writers such as the Swiss Christian Kracht, the Italian Aldo Nove, and the French-American Jonathan Littell. In contrast to this selection of well-established, internationally acclaimed writers, the publishers' decision to issue Prokhanov's novel in 2002 clearly marked an important turning point in their editorial policy. Ivanov and the editor-in-chief Mikhail Kotomin explained the drivers of this change during two interviews conducted in 2002: one with the liberal critic Nikolai Aleksandrov and the other with *Zavtra* journalist Aleksei Smirnov. Beside affirming their choice with claims that Prokhanov's prose is of a "very high quality" and that *Mister Hexogen* is a "huge plot novel,"[39] Ivanov and Kotomin stressed that they had aimed for a commercial and intellectual reorientation of their publishing strategy.

First, working with Prokhanov was part of their effort to publish more domestic writers to attract new, larger readerships. Ad Marginem sought to compensate for the lack of market demand for books in the "humanities" (*gumanitarnaia mysl*)[40] and to gain access to markets

[38] "O nas."

[39] Ivanov and Kotomin, "'Kultura Dvizhetsia Vzryvami'. Beseda s Glavnoi 'Ad Marginem' Aleksandrom Ivanovym i Vedushchim Redaktorom Izdatelstva Mikhailom Kotominym."

[40] Ivanov, "Prokhanov kak pevets ruinirovannoi sovetskoi imperii."
The roundtable held at the Institute of Philosophy in June 2002 also pondered the reasons related to market strategies, which explained the publication of Prokhanov's prose by an "intellectual publisher." Referring to his experience as the member of the editorial board of the philosophical journal *Logos*, Igor Chubarov mentioned the general contraction of available financial resources for intellectual publications: "We must recall the history of the 1990s. The fact is that the maximum number of buyers of philosophical literature

overseas. As an editor of translated works, Ivanov contended, he used to attend the Frankfurt Book Fair, the world's largest book trade fair, mostly "to buy the rights to publications, to find out what was new," without an opportunity to sell original works. However, publishing domestic literature allowed him to change his market position and offer his own selection to Frankfurt.[41] In 2003, the year after the publication of *Mister Hexogen*, Prokhanov was indeed introduced at the Frankfurt Book Fair by Boris Groys, a well-known German art critic and philosopher.[42] The success of Prokhanov's marketization to foreign audiences, however, was limited, as his novel was only translated into Polish and Chinese.

Moreover, Ad Marginem's decision to specifically publish Prokhanov aimed to foster an intellectual rebranding of the publishing house from its Western-oriented liberal leftist identity to a Russia-specific form of left-wing populism. Indeed, Ivanov claimed that the publication of Prokhanov's novel was a political statement in itself, consistent with his self-conception as "a left-wing publisher."[43] More precisely, publishing Prokhanov corresponded to Ivanov's changing definition of "left-wing" values, which, in the early 2000s, entailed the rejection of his former enthusiasm for Western culture and, instead, the promotion of Russian national culture. This reaction, as mentioned earlier, was typical of the general cultural backlash against liberalism and the West that occurred among the Russian elite at that time.[44] As Ivanov recounted, in the late 1980s and early 1990s he was one

in the country is about one thousand or two thousand people ... In these conditions, there is no way to survive. What choice is there? This is an endless search for sponsors, which is what we do at Logos. The publishing house 'Ad Marginem' existed as long as large grants were given." See "K publikatsii knigi 'Gospodin Geksogen' A. Prokhanova v izdatelstve Ad Marginem. Obsuzhdenie v sektore 'analticheskoi antropologii' IF RAN."

41 Ivanov, "Prokhanov kak pevets ruinirovannoi sovetskoi imperii."

42 Ilia Kukulin, "Reaktsiia dissotsiatsii: Legitimatsia ultrapravogo diskursa v sovremennoi rossiiskoi literature," in *Russkii natsionalizm: Sotsialnyi i kulturnyi kontekst*, ed. Marlène Laruelle (Moscow: Novoe literaturnoe obozrenie, 2008), 257–338.

43 Ivanov and Kotomin, "'Kultura Dvizhetsia Vzryvami'. Beseda s Glavnoi 'Ad Marginem' Aleksandrom Ivanovym i Vedushchim Redaktorom Izdatelstva Mikhailom Kotominym."

44 On the increasingly negative image of liberalism in public discourse in the 2000s, see Olga Malinova, "Encounters with Liberalism in Post-Soviet Russia," in *In Search of European Liberalisms: Concepts, Languages, Ideologies*, ed. Michael Freeden (New York: Berghahn Books, 2019), 292–94.

of the leading promoters of what he termed the "European mentality." He described the initial mission of Ad Marginem as "an attempt to install a European left tradition" and referred to this period as a "wonderful, romantic time," driven by the desire to "merge in ecstasy with Europe." However, alluding to the commercial decline in the sales of philosophy and social science books in the 1990s, he concluded: "It turned out that [the European mentality] was not for sale" and publishing "the Russian version of Derrida, Deleuze and Putnam was not a very good strategy as a whole."[45] Along with economic concerns, Ivanov also based the company's strategic reorientation on a moral critique of the liberal values of the 1990s. As he put it, "at one time, everyone was very much excited by the West. And this excitement grew into a subsequent monstrous disappointment." Ivanov held capitalism and consumerism as responsible for a "decline in interest for Russia." He further associated the "need to play by Western standards" with Russia's loss of self-identity and reflection "on the concept of dignity."[46] By contrast, Ivanov viewed Prokhanov's virulent critique of the 1990s as an answer to the "very serious crisis on-going within the liberal ideology" and its "ideological deficit." He argued:

> The actual effect of the exploding bomb from *Hexogen* is due to the fact that the novel fell into the very core of the social, cultural, economic, ideological problems that Russia faced at the beginning of this millennium ... It seems to me that Prokhanov's novel is about this. *Mister Hexogen*, as a true worldview novel, is powerful in that it raises a central question: what happened to us in the nineties?[47]

In place of Western values, Ivanov sought to promote Russia's "self-reliance" and specific "path of intellectual and cultural development."[48] Thus, while he had started as a left-wing intellectual well-read in

45 Ivanov and Kotomin, "'Kultura Dvizhetsia Vzryvami'. Beseda s Glavnoi 'Ad Marginem' Aleksandrom Ivanovym i Vedushchim Redaktorom Izdatelstva Mikhailom Kotominym."

46 Ivanov and Kotomin, "'Kultura Dvizhetsia Vzryvami'. Beseda s Glavnoi 'Ad Marginem' Aleksandrom Ivanovym i Vedushchim Redaktorom Izdatelstva Mikhailom Kotominym."

47 Aleksandr Ivanov, "Vopros kak otvet," *Zavtra* 476 (December 30, 2002), https://web.archive.org/web/20080831151656/http:/www.zavtra.ru/cgi/veil/data/zavtra/03/476/62.html.

48 Ivanov and Kotomin, "Kultura dvizhetsia vzryvami." Beseda s glavnoi "Ad Marginem" Aleksandrom Ivanovym i vedushchim redaktorom izdatelstva Mikhailom Kotominym.

European philosophical thought, he eventually turned to a more populist understanding of left-wing identity, focused on his country's "own history" and the "search for some kind of 'mental basis' in [Russia's] national culture."[49] In this respect, Ad Marginem explicitly claimed its alignment with certain values represented by Prokhanov. As stressed by Ivanov, the publication of Prokhanov's novel addressed his ambition to place more emphasis on the significance of Russian history and its specifically Russian content. Moreover, in his understanding, Russia's cultural particularism laid in the "madness" and "pathos" reflected in Prokhanov's work.[50] His promotion of Prokhanov, whom he described as "the singer of the ruined Soviet empire," also signaled Ivanov's ambition to rehabilitate the Soviet legacy. While he did not agree with Prokhanov's imperialist and revanchist discourse, Ivanov's decision to publish the novel was aimed as a gesture against what he regarded as the domination of "anticommunist drives" and the rejection of Soviet aesthetics in post-Soviet Russian literature.[51] In contrast, Ad Marginem's publishers sought to encourage others to stop thinking of the Soviet legacy as a burden and deviation away from the European canons and, instead, to consider it as a positive manifestation of Russian cultural specificity. More than that, they also put forward an idealized vision of the Soviet period as a time of high cultural literacy and struggle against capitalist "mass culture."[52]

In reaction, other publishers criticized Ad Marginem's association with Prokhanov as a clear departure from intellectualism, labeling it as "post-intellectualism."[53] Conversely, amid the ensuing scandal

[49] Ivanov and Kotomin, "Kultura dvizhetsia vzryvami." Beseda s glavnoi "Ad Marginem" Aleksandrom Ivanovym i vedushchim redaktorom izdatelstva Mikhailom Kotominym.

[50] Ivanov, "Prokhanov kak pevets ruinirovannoi sovetskoi imperii."

[51] On post-Soviet literature's attitude toward the Soviet legacy, see for instance Hélène Mélat, "Du traumatisme à l'évasion: Les premiers pas de la littérature postsoviétique (1992–2005)," *La revue russe* 26, no. 1 (2005): 9–24; Teresa Polowy, "Twenty Years Later: Russian Literature and Literary Studies since 1991," *Canadian Slavonic Papers/Revue Canadienne des Slavistes* 53, no. 2/4 (2011): 527–44.

[52] Ivanov and Kotomin, "'Kultura Dvizhetsia Vzryvami'. Beseda s Glavnoi 'Ad Marginem' Aleksandrom Ivanovym i Vedushchim Redaktorom Izdatelstva Mikhailom Kotominym."

[53] Aleksandr Ageev, "Golod 72. Prakticheskaia gastroenterologiia chteniia," *Russkii zhurnal*, April 17, 2002, https://web.archive.org/web/20050219000911/http:/geksogen.ru/r42.html.

surrounding the release of Prokhanov's novel, Ad Marginem aimed to challenge the literary establishment by branding Prokhanov as a "new wave" author.

4.2 A Changing System of Value Attribution within the Literary Field

4.2.1 Ad Marginem's Populist "Coup" against the Literary Establishment

Since its foundation in 1993, Ad Marginem had acquired a reputation as an avant-garde publisher, committed to editing innovative works "at the edge" (as expressed by the name "Ad Marginem"). In the 1990s, the publishers' conception of artistic and intellectual marginality led to their publication of works by European postmodern philosophers. By turning to Prokhanov, however, they sought to perform a revision of their understanding of the "avant-garde" and to spark off a scandal on the literary scene. Indeed, the publication of Prokhanov's novel was an unprecedented event in the post-Soviet field of publishing. Earlier, the publishing house Limbus-Press had reportedly bought the rights for some of Prokhanov's novels but had soon abandoned the idea of publishing them owing to a fear that "the intelligentsia would turn away" from them.[54] By contrast, as Ivanov stated in an interview, he aimed to depart from the "hysteria" of the "liberal criticism of Prokhanov" and to reject what he regarded as the "politically correct norms" ruling the "community in [the] social sciences" (*gumanitarnoe soobshchestvo*).[55] The purposely scandalous nature of Ad Marginem's decision to publish the novel was emphasized by the design of the book's cover, which pictured a man in a suit with Lenin's skull as his face.[56]

Paradoxically, Ad Marginem's established status as an avant-garde publisher allowed it to bear the responsibility for their rejection of

[54] This is reported by Lev Pirogov, "Na komsomolskom prospekte sostaialas 'Vstrecha na Elbe,'" *Ex Libris*, November 6, 2001, https://web.archive.org/web/20050103233314/http:/www.geksogen.ru/r1.html.

[55] Ivanov and Kotomin, "'Kultura Dvizhetsia Vzryvami'. Beseda s Glavnoi 'Ad Marginem' Aleksandrom Ivanovym i Vedushchim Redaktorom Izdatelstva Mikhailom Kotominym."

[56] The cover is an allusion to one of the characters planning to resurrect Lenin.

dominant standards. As explained by Bourdieu, avant-garde producers can "afford the audacious imposture of refusing all refusals by recuperating, in parody or sublimation, the very objects refused by the lower-degree aestheticism."[57] Ad Marginem's publication of Prokhanov, indeed, challenged what Bourdieu has described as the rules of the "sacred sphere of culture," which is based on the "denial of lower, coarse, vulgar, venal [and] servile ... enjoyment."[58] In contrast to accusations of "bad taste" and "poor style" that were commonly formulated by the intellectual elite against Prokhanov, Ad Marginem provided Prokhanov's work with a new public image by including it within a corpus of "new wave" literature alongside other writers published by them and acclaimed by liberal critics such as Sorokin and Kracht. As Ivanov claimed:

> I see a certain clear tendency, a new wave, to which Prokhanov obviously belongs. It unites the son of a billionaire—[Christian] Kracht, a poor student from Kharkov—Mikhail Elizarov, and Prokhanov. It is a new space that cannot be explained by using old formulas.[59]

Ivanov defended Prokhanov's style, which, according to him, departed from the classic "concept of taste."[60] He claimed to regard Prokhanov as a "writer who restored some archaic structures and epic," whom he compared with the medieval German epic poem "The Song of the Nibelungs" and with Homer's poetry.[61] Ivanov also argued that Prokhanov's combination of "hyper-Soviet" and "futurist" features shared similarities with the work of the avant-garde writers David Burliuk and Velimir Khlebnikov.[62]

[57] Pierre Bourdieu, *Distinction: A Social Critique of the Judgement of Taste*, 1 (London: Routledge, 2010), 118.

[58] Bourdieu, *Distinction*, 42.

[59] Ivanov and Kotomin, "'Kultura Dvizhetsia Vzryvami'. Beseda s Glavnoi 'Ad Marginem' Aleksandrom Ivanovym i Vedushchim Redaktorom Izdatelstva Mikhailom Kotominym."

[60] Ivanov and Kotomin, "'Kultura Dvizhetsia Vzryvami'. Beseda s Glavnoi 'Ad Marginem' Aleksandrom Ivanovym i Vedushchim Redaktorom Izdatelstva Mikhailom Kotominym."

[61] Ivanov and Kotomin, "'Kultura Dvizhetsia Vzryvami'. Beseda s Glavnoi 'Ad Marginem' Aleksandrom Ivanovym i Vedushchim Redaktorom Izdatelstva Mikhailom Kotominym."

[62] Ivanov and Kotomin, "'Kultura Dvizhetsia Vzryvami'. Beseda s Glavnoi 'Ad Marginem' Aleksandrom Ivanovym i Vedushchim Redaktorom Izdatelstva Mikhailom Kotominym."

By legitimizing Prokhanov in literary terms, Ad Marginem sought to wage a cultural war against the cultural establishment. Ivanov ridiculed his colleagues in the publishing field, whom he described as elitist and out of touch with Russian reality:

> It's okay to be left-wing and have a credit card. The problem is that in Russia, in 80% of the cities there are no ATMs. Therefore, a left-wing person cannot travel here with a credit card ... It is impossible to maintain the energy of your zealotry when you have one hundred thousand dollars on your credit card. At some point, you will want to eat fresh oysters on the Mediterranean Sea.[63]

In contrast, he described himself as a representative of a poor, yet creative and independent, publishing house:

> We are very poor. This poverty, in principle, is our greatest asset ... We of course, hate poverty, but also greatly appreciate it. There is no master above us. Nobody drives us ... We are happy people, for we have created a space of inalienable creative work.[64]

In addition to Ad Marginem's challenge to the establishment, the organizing committee of the National Bestseller Prize also chose to reward Prokhanov as part of a broader attempt to offer an alternative, profane method of literary prestige attribution promoting popular bestsellers over elite literature.

4.2.2 *The National Bestseller Prize's Promotion of Commercial Bestsellers over Elite Literature*

In 2002, shortly after its publication, *Mister Hexogen* was awarded the National Bestseller Prize. This prize, founded in 2001 and funded by private sponsors from the banking and financial industries, contributed to the proliferation of competitive book competitions, which already numbered around 300 in total.[65] As expressed by the motto

[63] Ivanov and Kotomin, "'Kultura Dvizhetsia Vzryvami'. Beseda s Glavnoi 'Ad Marginem' Aleksandrom Ivanovym i Vedushchim Redaktorom Izdatelstva Mikhailom Kotominym."

[64] Ivanov and Kotomin, "'Kultura Dvizhetsia Vzryvami'. Beseda s Glavnoi 'Ad Marginem' Aleksandrom Ivanovym i Vedushchim Redaktorom Izdatelstva Mikhailom Kotominym."

[65] Karlheinz Kasper, "Russische Literaturpreise 2002 Im Widerstreit Der Ideologien," *Osteuropa* 53, no. 6 (2003): 839. Funders of the Prize included the United Financial Group, Ingosstrakh, Regionsnab, and the Eurofinance Bank.

of the award, "Wake up famous," the prize was primarily aimed at promoting new entrants to the literary scene rather than established authors.[66] This alternative literary competition allowed Prokhanov to jettison his reputation as an illegitimate outsider and access public fame and prestige.

Run by a jury from diverse professional backgrounds, the prize offered a new type of selection procedure that abided by criteria other than purely aesthetic and literary judgment.

First, the prize was primarily market-oriented. As described by the rules of the competition, it sought to "reveal the market potential" of a literary work.[67] On top of the $10,000 reward for its recipient, the prize provided for the publication of 50,000 copies of the book and, therefore, aimed to ensure that the winner reached a wide readership. As emphasized by the eligibility criteria, which allowed for the selection of works of "other qualities [than artistic],"[68] the prospect of market sales extended beyond mere artistic concerns. One of the six writers competing with Prokhanov in the final round, Olga Slavnikova, even claimed that the commercial potential of works selected prevailed over their literary merits:

> The criterion of "artistry" is not the exclusive criterion for this award. Here, the idea of a "best seller" matters.[69]

A second distinguishing feature of the prize was the mixed professional backgrounds of the jury, which included both professional literary critics and outsiders to the literary scene. While the chairman of the prize, Viktor Toporov, qualified as an expert in the literary field, as a professional literary critic and the editor-in-chief of the publishing house Limbus-Press since 2000, the members of the three selection committees (the list of nominees shortlisting the candidates, the grand jury, and the small jury) came from a wide range of professional backgrounds.[70] In 2002, Prokhanov's novel was shortlisted for

[66] The rules of the competition are detailed on the National Bestseller Prize's website. See "Polozhenie o premii," natsbest.ru, www.natsbest.ru/polozhenie-o-premii/.

[67] "Polozhenie o premii." [68] "Polozhenie o premii."

[69] Olga Slavnikovaia, "Ia—odinokii chelovek v literature," interview by Oleg Proskurin, *Russkii Zhurnal*, May 28, 2002.

[70] Members of the list of nominees, of the grand jury, and of the small jury, are selected by the prize's organizing committee.

the competition by two members of the list of nominees: Igor Zotov, a renowned literary critic, deputy editor-in-chief of the newspaper *Nezavisimaia gazeta*, and editor-in-chief of its literary section, and Oleg Pashchenko, a member of the regional parliament of Krasnoiarsk, in Siberia. Prokhanov subsequently received sixteen votes from the fifty-five members of the grand jury. Finally, the members of the last small jury included the writer Leonid Iuzefovich, the critics Vladimir Bondarenko and Mikhail Trofimenkov, the economist and member of the State Duma Irina Khakamada, the actress Julia Aug, and the musician Sergei Shnurov. In the last round, Prokhanov won the votes of the two critics Bondarenko and Trofimenkov and arrived in an *ex aequo* position with the writer Irina Derezhkina. Prokhanov was finally chosen as the laureate by the chairman of the jury, the banker Vladimir Kogan.

On top of its professional diversity, the jury was also politically diverse, since Bondarenko, a long-time friend of Prokhanov and deputy editor-in-chief of *Zavtra*, sat with Khakamada, one of the leaders of the liberal party the Union of Right Forces. The jury's pluralistic composition has been hailed as a welcome alternative to other types of book prizes, as it included individuals who were both promoters and detractors of Prokhanov's ideas.[71]

The rehabilitation of Prokhanov's work on the cultural scene, therefore, took place in the context of an important change in the method for symbolic value attribution on the literary scene. From the perspective of Bourdieu's sociology, the nonprofessional character of the book competition undermined the role of the aesthetic "'pure' gaze," which Bourdieu holds as the organizing principle of "an autonomous field of artistic production, that is, a field capable of imposing its own norms on both the production and the consumption of its products."[72] By including the values and judgments of actors outside the literary field in its selection process, the National Bestseller Prize, indeed,

71 See Lev Danilkin, "Uroki 'Astorii,'" *Vedomosti*, June 3, 2002, https://web.archive.org/web/20060529204238/http:/geksogen.ru/r63.html; Nikolai Aleksandrov, "'Gospodin Geksogen' podelilsia s Gospodinom Limonovym," Gazeta.ru, June 3, 2002, https://web.archive.org/web/20060529204255/http:/geksogen.ru/r65.html; Oleg Proskurin, "Natsionalnyi Bestseller-2001, ili apofeoz Prokhanova," *Russkii zhurnal*, June 4, 2002, https://web.archive.org/web/20071103114237/http:/www.geksogen.ru/r72.html.

72 Bourdieu, *Distinction*, 36.

compromised the autonomy of aesthetic judgment with other concerns such as commercial interests. While Prokhanov had been isolated from the literary scene throughout the 1990s, this new selection procedure, which emphasized Prokhanov's market potential and antielite symbol, allowed him to move from the margins to the mainstream of the cultural scene. Indeed, the evolution of the media debate over *Mister Hexogen* between 2001 and 2002 promoted Prokhanov to the center stage of the public sphere.

4.3 The Collapse of Consensus among Intellectual Elites and the Legitimation of Prokhanov's Hawkish Ideas

4.3.1 New Value Uncertainty about the Distinction between Legitimate and Transgressive Public Discourse

The association of Prokhanov's work with Ad Marginem's intellectual avant-garde identity significantly changed its symbolic value. In Bourdieu's words, it revised "the code into which it [was] encoded."[73] As put by Ivanov, the "legalized Prokhanov"[74] unsettled the habitual schemes of perception of Prokhanov's prose and caused a major scandal. As sociologists Damien de Blic and Cyril Lemieux have shown, scandals, as they evolve into a controversy, signify a "public break with unanimity" in previously consensual communities.[75] Indeed, the evolution of the debate about *Mister Hexogen* from a scandal to a controversy effectively undermined the formerly unified judgment on Prokhanov.

Mister Hexogen was published in two editions, the first in 2001 and the second in 2002, with a total print-run of 110,000 copies. The novel's literary success and the media coverage of the award ceremony of the National Bestseller Prize provoked a heated discussion among literary critics. Many critics and writers voiced their outrage and indignation against Prokhanov's work:

[73] Bourdieu, *Distinction*, 35.

[74] Ivanov and Kotomin, "'Kultura Dvizhetsia Vzryvami'. Beseda s Glavnoi 'Ad Marginem' Aleksandrom Ivanovym i Vedushchim Redaktorom Izdatelstva Mikhailom Kotominym."

[75] Damien de Blic and Cyril Lemieux, "The Scandal as Test: Elements of Pragmatic Sociology," *Politix* 71, no. 3 (2005): 15.

- "The idea of the book is disgusting to me from the very beginning. They tell me that this is a super-novel, and I see that this is a cheap pamphlet" (Piotr Aleshkovskii).[76]
- "Prokhanov is absolutely outside of literature, it is a bunch of vulgarity and bad taste" (Olga Slavnikova).[77]
- "[The style of the novel] would be amusing, if it were not for the monotonous, boring creeping narration, the tortured intonation of the stylized Russian classics and its sickening vulgarity" (Nikolai Aleksandrov).[78]
- "It is ridiculous to talk seriously about Prokhanov" (Aleksandr Ageev).[79]

By disqualifying Prokhanov from the legitimate realm of literature, these reviewers perceived the publication of his novel as nothing short of scandalous. They held Prokhanov as an outsider whose exclusion was based on a set of beliefs and norms established and shared by the community of literary critics.

However, shortly after the publication of the first edition, a series of other established literary critics reacted in the opposite direction by praising its literary qualities. Among the enthusiastic critics, some sought to relate Prokhanov's style to notorious names of Russian and Western literature. Lev Danilkin highlighted resemblances with "Maiakovsky's metaphors" and portrayed Prokhanov as "the Dante of the liberal nightmare."[80] According to Dmitrii Olshanskii, the novel contained descriptions of natural landscapes that were reminiscent of Ivan Turgenev. He further claimed that Prokhanov was a "mystical writer and [was] in many respects related to Russian symbolism," as found in the work of the poets Andrei Belii and Fiodor Sologub. Olshanskii also contended that the "psychedelic," "acidic," and

[76] Petr Aleshkovskii, "Esli skrestit Zhirinovskogo s Glazunovym," *Vremia MN*, April 12, 2002, https://web.archive.org/web/20050218173528/http:/geksogen.ru/r31.html.

[77] Slavnikovaia, "Ia—odinokii chelovek v literature."

[78] Nikolai Aleksandrov, "Beda, chto skuchen tvoi roman: Geksogennyi nadezhdy patrioticheskoi belletristiki," Gazeta.ru, April 9, 2002, https://web.archive.org/web/20050218090239/http:/geksogen.ru/r23.html.

[79] Ageev, "Golod 72. Prakticheskaia gastroenterologiia chteniia."

[80] Lev Danilkin, "Tovarishch Dante: 'Gospodin Geksogen' Aleksandr Prokhanov," Afisha.ru, March 2002, https://web.archive.org/web/20050218001108/http:/geksogen.ru/r11.html.

"secretive atmosphere" of the novel established "unexpected literary connections" with the "extreme 'left' American prose." He concluded that Prokhanov could be held as the "conservative and reactionary" Russian counterpart of William Burroughs and Hunter S. Thompson.[81]

The collapse of consensus in the literary community toward Prokhanov was even more strongly accentuated during a second moment of the polemic, which took place in June 2002 after the National Bestseller Prize's jury decided to give the award to Prokhanov. One of the members of the final small jury, the renowned liberal critic Mikhail Trofimenkov, also advocated comparing Prokhanov with Andrei Belyi, William Burroughs, and Hunter S. Thompson. He argued:

> I have to mention the literary associations, which arose when I read the novel *Mister Hexogen*, with its suffocating atmosphere of provocation, conspiracy, with its dancing masks, hectic and hopeless search for a bomb, with its fear of mysterious and ubiquitous strangers. It evokes another great novel, which opened and presaged the Russian 20th century. Of course, I mean Andrei Belyi's "Petersburg."[82]

Trofimenkov's vote in favor of Prokhanov's novel exacerbated the emerging polarization within the community of literary critics. While one camp regarded the event as "the most scandalous literary prize of the decade,"[83] the other group hailed the jury's decision and added their voices to the first group of positive reviewers to claim that:

- "Prokhanov is a great writer"[84] (Viacheslav Kuritsyn).
- "Of course, there are lengths and a lot of cheap symbolism in the novel. At some points, it is boring to read all this, but in general the novel is extraordinary. Especially against the dull background of current literature"[85] (Mikhail Zolotonosov).

[81] Dmitrii Olshanskii, "Ot Geksogena do galliutsinogena," *Vremia MN*, April 5, 2002, https://web.archive.org/web/20050218090249/http:/geksogen.ru/r16.html.

[82] Mikhail Trofimenkov, "Roman meniaet chitatelskoe zrenie," *Zavtra*, June 2002, https://web.archive.org/web/20050211181402/http:/geksogen.ru/r93.html.

[83] This statement is from the editor-in-chief of the literary newspaper *Knizhnoe Obozrenie*. See Aleksandr Gavrilov, "Radi krasno-korichnevogo slovtsa," Grani.ru, June 4, 2002, https://graniru.org/Culture/m.750.html; see also Galina Iuzefovich, "S parokhoda sovremennosti," *Ezhenedelnyi zhurnal*, June 11, 2002, https://web.archive.org/web/20060529204740/http:/geksogen.ru/r95.html.

[84] Viacheslav Kuritsyn, "Geksogen bez ssylok," *Russkii zhurnal*, June 10, 2002, https://web.archive.org/web/20050211182431/http:/geksogen.ru/r82.html.

[85] Zolotonosov, "Operatsiia 'Prokhanov.'"

The critic Mikhail Zolotonosov further claimed that Prokhanov's ability to capture the "moods and fantasies circulating in the society" bore comparison with Dostoevskii. In his view, *Mister Hexogen* should be considered the "*Demons* of our days" to the extent that it provided an "attempt to logically interpret the chaos of reality by 'reordering' it with a superlogical explanation."[86] Finally, Ivan Kulikov regarded Prokhanov's novel as the direct heir of "the early 1970s techno-engineering fantasies, from which Prokhanov emerged and to which he remains faithful." He argued that the novel resembled "science-fiction movies" by the American Ed Wood and qualified as some of "the most radical technofuturistic fiction."[87]

On top of being affiliated with literary classics, Prokhanov's novel was also included in the body of Russian postmodern contemporary literature. Russian postmodernism has been authoritatively theorized by the scholar Mikhail Epstein. Building on Jean Baudrillard's definition of postmodernism as a "simulation" of reality, Epstein identifies the origins of Russian postmodernism in Soviet socialist realism.[88] According to Epstein, several features of socialist realism characterize it as an "essentially postmodern trend," such as the creation of an alternative "hyperreality" and the reproduction of an eclectic mixture of stylistic devices (combining realism, classicism, romanticism).[89] Furthermore, Epstein distinguishes a "second wave of postmodernism" in the Soviet conceptual art of the 1970s, which relied on linguistic and semiotic games to dissolve signs as "independent reality" and treat them as "objects of irony and aesthetic play."[90] Whereas the word "postmodernism" rarely featured in discussions of literature in the late 1980s, it was widely used in the 1990s to describe the overall "fashion" and "atmosphere" of post-Soviet artistic production.[91] When he resumed his literary activities at the end of the 1990s, therefore, Prokhanov faced a new context in which

86 Zolotonosov, "Operatsiia 'Prokhanov.'"

87 Ivan Kulikov, "Mutant chetyrekh," *Nezavisimaia gazeta*, March 29, 2002, www.ng.ru/neiro/2002-03-28/4_prohanov.html.

88 Epstein, "Origins and Meaning of Russian Postmodernism," 205.

89 For the full list of the postmodern features of socialist realism, see Epstein, "Origins and Meaning of Russian Postmodernism," 206.

90 Major conceptualist writers include Vladimir Sorokin, Dmitrii Prigov, and Lev Rubinstein. See Epstein, "Origins and Meaning of Russian Postmodernism," 208.

91 Epstein, "Origins and Meaning of Russian Postmodernism," 208.

"postmodernism" had become the defining genre of post-Soviet literature. In this environment, Prokhanov's style was reconsidered from the standpoint of Russian postmodernism and described as being similar to other major postmodern writers such as Sorokin, Pelevin, and Erofeev. The critic Anna Starobinets described *Mister Hexogen* as "an astonishing combination of Soviet aesthetics and trendy postmodernist tendencies."[92] Lev Danilkin stated that Prokhanov's novel could be mistaken for "an unknown text by Pelevin."[93] Finally, Trofimenkov claimed that Prokhanov's anticonformist rejection of "accepted criteria of 'good literary taste' and 'political correctness'" was similar to other works by contemporary Russian writers such Limonov, Pelevin, and Sorokin.[94] Russian and Western scholars have also identified in Prokhanov's novel aspects that fitted with their interpretation of post-Soviet postmodernism. Mark Lipovestkii and Aleksandr Etkind have suggested thinking of Prokhanov as combining postmodernism and sots-realism.[95] Anna Razuvalova claimed that both Prokhanov and the postmodern writer Viktor Pelevin spread the view that Russian politics has a "virtual nature."[96] Such parallels between Prokhanov and Russian postmodernism legitimized Prokhanov's self-conception as an avant-garde writer.[97]

The wide spectrum of literary references – including both classics and postmodernists – that critics used to draw comparisons with Prokhanov's novel highlights the multifaceted nature of his writing. Prokhanov's ambiguous style directly contributed to multiple interpretations of his

92 Anna Starobinets, "The Real Russia," *New Statesman* 16, no. 742 (February 3, 2003): xvi–xvii.
93 Danilkin, "Tovarishch Dante: 'Gospodin Geksogen' Aleksandr Prokhanov."
94 Trofimenkov, "Roman meniaet chitatelskoe zrenie."
95 Mark Lipovetskii and Aleksandr Etkind, "Vozvrashchenie tritona: Sovetskaia katastrofa i postsovetskii Roman," *Novoe literaturnoe obozrenie*, no. 6 (2008): 174–206.
96 Anna Razuvalova, "The Plot Device of Conspiracy in Nikolay Burlyaev's Film Lermontov and A Director's Diary: On the 'Ethnography of the Emotions' of the National-Conservative Community," *Forum for Anthropology and Culture*, no. 12 (2016): 155.
97 As Boris Noordenbos reported from an interview with Prokhanov, "[w]hen I interviewed him in 2009, Prokhanov proclaimed that he did not see any contradiction between the profile of Ad Marginem and his own aesthetic orientation. His political views were ultraconservative, but his aesthetics, he emphasized, had always had an avant-garde impetus." Boris Noordenbos, *Post-Soviet Literature and the Search for a Russian Identity*, Studies in European Culture and History (New York: Palgrave Macmillan, 2016), 7.

literary genre and artistic qualities. *Mister Hexogen*'s use of diverse types of language – irony, conspiracy theories, ideological discourse – and its saturation with metaphorical and hyperbolic stylistic figures indeed cast doubt on the truth value of its statements.

The "epistemological uncertainty" conveyed by Prokhanov's language has led liberal-inclined critics to offer conflicting interpretations of the political aspects of *Mister Hexogen.*[98] Some critics have dismissed Prokhanov's political views as irrelevant for his appreciation as a writer. Trofimenkov, for instance, has claimed that "it would be unfair to stick regular political labels on the writer."[99] Others have instead argued about the political implications of his novel while drawing divergent conclusions. Andrei Nemzer has described the novel as a "mocking and hysterical anti-state pamphlet,"[100] whereas Mikhail Ryklin has instead perceived it as a plea in favor of strong state "Russian fascism."[101] Nemzer has also stated that *Mister Hexogen* is "saturated with animal anti-Semitism."[102] This aspect has been further emphasized by Igor Chubarov, who has argued that the novel included anti-Semitism "not as some kind of personal ideological choice of the author, but as a layer of the undivided unconscious, which Prokhanov presents as something taken for granted, as a kind of 'general Russian feeling.'"[103] However, such claims have been denied by Viacheslav Kuritsyn, who has contended that "GG [*Gospodin Geksogen* (i.e., *Mister Hexogen*)] is not an anti-Semitic novel,"[104] and Joseph Backstein, who has declared that he "did not find anti-Semitism in it."[105]

This one-year controversy therefore resulted in the public display of a new value uncertainty about the definition of the boundaries

[98] The formula "epistemological uncertainty" was applied to Prokhanov's writing by Keith Livers. Livers, "Tower or the Labyrinth," 497.

[99] Trofimenkov, "Roman meniaet chitatelskoe zrenie."

[100] Andrei Nemzer, "Geksogen s vami," *Vremia novostei*, June 3, 2002, https://web.archive.org/web/20060529204319/http:/geksogen.ru/r69.html.

[101] "K publikatsii knigi 'Gospodin Geksogen' A. Prokhanova v izdatelstve Ad Marginem: Obsuzhdenie v sektore 'analticheskoi antropologii' IF RAN."

[102] Nemzer, "Geksogen s vami."

[103] "K publikatsii knigi 'Gospodin Geksogen' A. Prokhanova v izdatelstve Ad Marginem: Obsuzhdenie v sektore 'analticheskoi antropologii' IF RAN."

[104] Kuritsyn, "Geksogen bez ssylok."

[105] "K publikatsii knigi 'Gospodin Geksogen' A. Prokhanova v izdatelstve Ad Marginem: Obsuzhdenie v sektore 'analticheskoi antropologii' IF RAN."

between legitimate and transgressive public discourse. The identification of Prokhanov as a vulgar writer and his exclusion from legitimate literature was indeed constitutive of the established value system defining culture in the 1990s.[106] While the early scandal triggered by the publication of *Mister Hexogen* corresponded to normative judgments that had prevailed during the 1990s, its transformation into a controversy disclosed the loss of efficiency of the former norms, values, and categories of judgments.

This new dissension was clearly displayed during the roundtable composed of fifteen leading intellectuals held in June 2002 on the *Mister Hexogen* affair at the Institute of Philosophy of the Russian Academy of Sciences.[107] That this discussion of Prokhanov's work took place in such a prestigious intellectual institution in itself marked a clear evolution from the cultural paradigm of the 1990s. As researcher Mikhail Ryklin, the leader of the discussion, pointed out:

> This is perhaps the first instance when literature of such a level as *Mr. Hexogen* is discussed in this audience.[108]

Ryklin stressed that the discussion aimed to address issues such as why Prokhanov's discourse had become central, how his publisher Ad Marginem could claim intellectual continuity with their earlier philosophical publications, or how Prokhanov's work differed from other classic types of subversive literature such as Marquis de Sade's. While the discussion could have paved the way for a new literary consensus on these questions, it in fact further demonstrated the major value uncertainty prevailing in the ranks of the cultural and intellectual elite. Ryklin's dismissive descriptions of Prokhanov's prose as "grotesque," "miserable," "pornographic," and racist were strongly countered by Keti Chukhrukidze, who claimed that the success of Prokhanov's novel was entirely "justified." She contended that Prokhanov's use of "anti-Caucasian and anti-Semitic" myths and images was characteristic of

[106] As argued by Bourdieu, the determination of tastes is intimately based on the negation of other tastes. Bourdieu, *Distinction*, 111.

[107] The roundtable's participants included M. Ryklin, O. Aronson, I. Bakstein, S. Zemlianoi, V. Malakhov, O. Nikiforov, K. Chukhrukidze, I. Chubarov, B. Skuratov, I. Okuneva, E. Lavut, A. Paramonov, N. Pirtskhalava, S. Ofertas, and A. Smirnov.

[108] "K publikatsii knigi 'Gospodin Geksogen' A. Prokhanova v izdatelstve Ad Marginem: Obsuzhdenie v sektore 'analticheskoi antropologii' IF RAN."

Russian literature's populist tendency to identify with "the humiliated majority."[109] A participant in the discussion questioned whether the behavior of Ad Marginem violated "unwritten norms of decency and political correctness," while another replied by pointing to the absence of such norms:

> [A basic model or norm for political correctness] has not been developed in the "new order" (whether "pre-," "pro-" or "anti-" Putin) and yet could not be inherited directly from the Soviet era. Hence the actual situation: there is no norm, that is, *anything goes*.[110]

In place of the opposition between the "liberals" and the "national-patriots" that dominated the 1990s, the debate over *Mister Hexogen* revealed the rise of a new polarization between "liberals" and "pseudo-liberals." Indeed, liberal critics took particular issue with the attitude of Prokhanov's publishers, which they perceived as an attack on the liberal identity, rather than with Prokhanov himself:

- "One thing scares me in this story: the link between left-wing esthetes and ultra-left opposition" (Piotr Aleshkovskii).[111]
- "I am not ashamed of Prokhanov. He is incorrigible … I am ashamed of the educated, well-known party-goers who want to make candy out of shit" (Bakhyt Kenzheev).[112]

This new polarization materialized inside the publishing house Ad Marginem when Vladimir Sorokin and other writers decided to end their contract with them in protest at their decision to publish Prokhanov. Similarly, Ryklin, who had been a former associate of the editors, stated that he would not "cooperate with this publishing house under any circumstances after the publication of Prokhanov."[113]

109 "K publikatsii knigi 'Gospodin Geksogen' A. Prokhanova v izdatelstve Ad Marginem: Obsuzhdenie v sektore 'analticheskoi antropologii' IF RAN."
110 "K publikatsii knigi 'Gospodin Geksogen' A. Prokhanova v izdatelstve Ad Marginem: Obsuzhdenie v sektore 'analticheskoi antropologii' IF RAN."
111 Petr Aleshkovskii, "Vpechatleniia nedeli," *Obshchaia gazeta*, April 2002, https://web.archive.org/web/20050218173354/http:/geksogen.ru/r27.html.
112 Bakhyt Kenzheev, "Lobstery s Borneo, ili khoroshii pisatel Prokhanov," *Russkii zhurnal*, June 14, 2002, https://web.archive.org/web/20060507143317/http:/geksogen.ru/r104.html.
113 "K publikatsii knigi 'Gospodin Geksogen' A. Prokhanova v izdatelstve Ad Marginem: Obsuzhdenie v sektore 'analticheskoi antropologii' IF RAN."

One of the immediate consequences of this controversy was the intellectual legitimization of Prokhanov in the public sphere and, more generally, the rise of some of his ideas as a new cultural mainstream.

4.3.2 Prokhanov's Ideas as a New Mainstream

The success of Prokhanov, generated by his novel being released by a renowned publisher and being awarded a literary prize, together with its substantial print-run and the year-long media debate over the work, moved him from the margins to the center of the cultural scene.

During the roundtable discussion held at the Institute of Philosophy, Ryklin raised concerns over the broader development of a discursive field where Prokhanov had become a "quasi mass media figure." He voiced concerns over the demarginalization of Prokhanov's discourse:

> Nothing new has happened to his discourse; there was only a new positioning of this type of consciousness, its demarginalization. What is the reason for this? The final answer is difficult to give. When I occasionally read his rather harsh, quite vivid newspaper journalism with elements of racism and anti-Semitism, I always correlated it with a very narrow circle of people for whom he might be a cult figure ... Now it cannot be ignored, because, just like mercury, it fills all the voids. A few years ago, this situation was simply impossible to imagine.[114]

That Prokhanov was able to become a new, fashionable phenomenon testified to the fact that the aggressive nature of his rhetoric had become commonplace and, to some extent, had ceased to be compromising in the public sphere. In this sense, Prokhanov's intellectual legitimization heralded the advent of a new cultural environment characterized by the dispersion of hawkish conservatism as an increasingly hegemonic ideology. First, beyond Prokhanov's personal rehabilitation in the public sphere, the *Mister Hexogen* affair helped to demarginalize the wider national-conservative movement he represented. Upon receiving the National Bestseller Prize, Prokhanov announced that he aimed to donate the $10,000 monetary award to the foundation working for the liberation of his friend Eduard Limonov, the leader of the National Bolshevik Party who had been

[114] "K publikatsii knigi 'Gospodin Geksogen' A. Prokhanova v izdatelstve Ad Marginem: Obsuzhdenie v sektore 'analticheskoi antropologii' IF RAN."

detained in prison since 2001.[115] Prokhanov thereby politicized the award ceremony by using the benefits of recognition and publicity that had been granted to him as a resource to promote the larger national-conservative community. More generally, both partisans and opponents of Prokhanov's ideas regarded the success and media coverage of *Mister Hexogen* as a step toward the broader trivialization and legalization of extreme-right ideas. Prokhanov's close friend, the conservative literary critic Vladimir Bondarenko, who was a member of the National Bestseller Prize's final jury, hailed Prokhanov's success as a victory for the entire "Russian traditional forces."[116] Other writers close to Prokhanov's ideas, such as the younger author Zakhar Prilepin, also viewed the publication of *Mister Hexogen* as a landmark event in providing them with access to the literary establishment. In 2011, when Prilepin himself received the National Bestseller Prize, he paid tribute to Prokhanov's earlier breakthrough:

> [*Mister Hexogen*] "cracked" the literary situation. At that time, literature was dominated by the liberal public opinion, which did not let "rascals" like me into the bookshelves. Thanks to Prokhanov, I ... and other writers with left-wing views, were handed the keys to literature.[117]

At the other end of the political spectrum, the liberal political scientist Andrei Kolesnikov also considered the *Mister Hexogen* controversy as representing the opening of a growing dispersion of "far-right, ultra-conservative ideas":

> [The ideology of national-patriots] is becoming part of the literary and intellectual mainstream. And therefore, it's becoming harmless to the authorities. Imperial ultra-conservatism, all the complexes of unsatisfied nationalism and anti-Semitism are turning into some kind of intellectual game ... Ultraconservatism has become respectable – a sort of salon philosophy.[118]

115 The government accused Limonov of preparing an armed invasion of Kazakhstan. He was convicted for purchasing arms.

116 Bondarenko, "Prokhanovskii proryv."

117 Zakhar Prilepin, "Grekh zhalovatsia," *Rossiiskaia gazeta*, June 6, 2011, https://rg.ru/2011/06/06/reg-privolzhe/prilepin.html. Here, "left-wing" is used as an antiliberal term, associated with the Soviet ideals of statism, collectivism, and economic planning.

118 Andrei Kolesnikov, "Kapituliatsiia pered Istoriei," *Izvestiia*, April 23, 2002, https://web.archive.org/web/20050219000850/http:/geksogen.ru/r44.html.

Indeed, Prokhanov significantly enlarged his audience beyond the social and ideological community that regularly read his newspaper *Zavtra*. In particular, critics among the literary community worried about Prokhanov's new popularity as the "idol of the golden youth."[119] The literary scholar Ilia Kukulin stressed that Prokhanov's novel had appealed "to a relatively significant number of young readers, who on other occasions shared 'Western' aesthetic views."[120] As a matter of fact, interest in Prokhanov became a new fashion in media outlets aimed at a young, Westernized, and liberal readership, such as the magazines *Rolling Stone* and *Playboy*. As Prokhanov recounted:

> After the novel *Mister Hexogen*, I broke into the operational space ... Literary fame came to me to a certain extent. I received prizes, became fashionable. Young people, magazines like *Playboy*, *Rolling Stone* became interested in me and I read there about myself that Prokhanov is a cool dinosaur.[121]

Among literary critics, the polarization of those against and in favor of Prokhanov cut across a clear generational divide. Leading representatives of the younger generation of literary critics, born in the 1970s, supported Prokhanov against the majority of the older generation. Lev Danilkin (born in 1974), an influential and central figure of his generation, perfectly illustrates the appeal of Prokhanov to the younger generation of intellectuals. During the controversy, Danilkin emerged as one of Prokhanov's most vocal and enthusiastic defenders. In 2007, he authored the first biography of Prokhanov, which was also published by Ad Marginem.[122] In the prologue, Danilkin describes the transformation of his attitude toward Prokhanov, from a general contempt to his attraction to Prokhanov's "eccentricity":

> Like "everyone," deep down, I related to the novelist Prokhanov with deep skepticism ... At the same time, in a paradoxical way, he inspired a feeling of sympathy ... In Russia, there are not that many characters that are

119 Proskurin, "Natsionalnyi Bestseller-2001, ili apofeoz Prokhanova."
120 Ilya Kukulin, "Excerpts from 'The Legitimization of Ultra-Right Discourse in Contemporary Russian Literature,'" in *Late and Post Soviet Literature: A Reader*, ed. Mark Lipovetsky and Lisa Ryoko Wakamiya (Brighton: Academic Studies Press, 2014), 338.
121 Aleksandr Prokhanov, "Khozhdenie v Ogon," *Zavtra*, December 10, 2011, http://zavtra.ru/blogs/hozhdenie-v-ogon.
122 Lev Danilkin, *Chelovek s iaitsom, zhizn i mnenie Aleksandra Prokhanova* (Moscow: Ad Marginem, 2007).

completely eligible for the world catalogue of eccentrics of all times and nations. Prokhanov belongs to them without a doubt.[123]

Dmitri Olshanskii (1978–), also a prominent representative of the younger generation of journalists and literary critics, provides a more radical example of a shift of attitudes toward Prokhanov and his ideas. In a 2002 article entitled "How I Became a Black-Hundred," Olshanskii rejected his former "liberal" views and adherence to the "canons of the 1990s."[124] Judging them "incompatible with good literature," he referred instead to Prokhanov being awarded the National Bestseller Prize as a sign that the "time [had] come for the recognition of violent, incorrect and nationally-minded authors."[125]

This generational conflict also denoted diverging attitudes toward the Soviet literary legacy. While the older generation dismissed Prokhanov's prose as an instance of "standard Soviet literature [*sovpisovskaia*] of the 1970s,"[126] their younger counterparts hailed Prokhanov's "hyper-Sovietness" as an interesting literary feature.[127]

Beyond the year-long debate, the *Mister Hexogen* controversy permanently established Prokhanov on the cultural scene. His new status as a successful and award-winning writer gave him access to a wide range of mass media. From 2003, he started appearing as a regular guest on a progovernmental sociopolitical TV talk show run by Vladimir Solovev, one of the most popular Kremlin propagandists. Subsequently, in 2007, Prokhanov was offered a seat as a permanent guest on the weekly "Special Opinion" section of the liberally oriented radio station Ekho Moskvy.

Moreover, as the political authorities increasingly relied on conservatism as an ideological platform, the dissolution of the controversial character of Prokhanov's ideas and their extremist political content resulted in his evolution from a staunch opponent to a proregime ideologue during Putin's second term.

123 Danilkin, *Chelovek s iaitsom*, 12.

124 The Black Hundred was a Russian ultranationalist movement formed at the beginning of the twentieth century. Dmitrii Olshanskii, "Kak ia stal Chernosotentsiem," *Novaia gazeta*, 2002, www.ng.ru/ng_exlibris/2002-04-11/2_black.html.

125 Olshanskii, "Kak ia stal Chernosotentsiem."

126 Aleshkovskii, "Vpechatleniia nedeli."

127 Ivanov and Kotomin, "'Kultura Dvizhetsia Vzryvami'. Beseda s Glavnoi 'Ad Marginem' Aleksandrom Ivanovym i Vedushchim Redaktorom Izdatelstva Mikhailom Kotominym."

4.4 Conclusion

The evolution of the reception of *Mister Hexogen*, from a scandalous text to a national bestseller, highlights the role of the controversy that surrounded the publication of the novel in reconfiguring the symbolic boundaries between transgressive and legitimate discourse in the Russian public sphere. The controversy extended beyond pure aesthetic concerns, as the ambiguous nature of the novel, at once a fantasy fiction and an aggressively antiliberal political satire, contributed to the propagation of the extremist political views promoted by Prokhanov, such as conspiracy theories, the rejection of liberalism, and a thirst for Russia's great power status based on the promotion of technological modernity and a messianic religious understanding of Russia's history. While staying outside party and electoral politics, Prokhanov was able to use literature as a medium for the recognition and legitimation of his ideas. By doing so, he successfully resumed the Soviet writers' practice of doing "politics by culture," which relied on literature to affect the evolution of the norms and rules of public sociopolitical debates.[128] His discourse gained legitimacy and public visibility in the new cultural and political context brought about by Vladimir Putin's presidency. His ascension was supported by actors from various political, intellectual, journalistic, and commercial backgrounds, as the ideas and symbols carried by his novel met their ambition to sponsor and marketize a national popular culture based on the rejection of Western values and of the heritage of the 1990s.

Prokhanov's particular success among the youth was paired with the rise of a new generation of conservative intellectuals, the "Young Conservatives," who built on their elders' modernist conservatism to theorize a full-fledged ideology, called "dynamic conservatism."

[128] On Soviet intellectuals' practice of "politics by culture," see Yitzhak M. Brudny, *Reinventing Russia: Russian Nationalism and the Soviet State, 1953–1991*, Russian Research Center Studies 91 (Cambridge, MA: Harvard University Press, 1998), 13.

5 *The Rise of the Next-Generation Hawks in the 2000s*

We do not believe that there was a certain "golden age" in the past of Russia that deserves blind worship and to which we must to return. Rather, we strive to reconstruct Russia as it could have been if it had not been prevented from developing its national-state tradition … Our task is to reconstruct the normal future of Russia.

Vitalii Averianov, "Posle sobornykh slushanii opponenty zabespokoilis," 2007

As demonstrated in previous chapters, by the end of the 1990s, certain hawkish ideas had permeated official discourse, and the antiliberal coalition represented by *Zavtra* had evolved from radical opposition to competition with Boris Yeltsin's attempt to build an official form of state patriotism. Moreover, the advent of Vladimir Putin's presidency introduced a political context favorable to the rejection of the political legacy of the 1990s and the dispersion of conservatism in Russian politics.

In the early 2000s, a new generation of hawks, born in or close to the 1970s, entered the Russian public sphere. In 2005, seventy of these "Young Conservatives" (*mladokonservatory*) collectively authored the "Russian Doctrine,"[1] a document setting out a full-fledged ideology of conservative modernization, which they called "dynamic conservatism." Advocating authoritarian economic and technological development based on Russia's traditional historical and religious values, the Russian Doctrine's detailed policy program was widely promoted in a range of intellectual, political, economic, and religious milieus.

Like the older generation of hawks, the Young Conservatives were bound by their shared interpretations of common experiences that shaped their worldview as a generational and ideological group – the

[1] For simplified reading, inverted commas are no longer used in the rest of the chapter for the terms Young Conservatives, Young Conservatism, dynamic conservatism, and the Russian Doctrine.

collapse of the Soviet Union, the failures of post-Soviet democracy, and Western hegemony in the international order. Despite certain ideological differences among the group's members, they were nevertheless able to establish themselves as an intellectual movement united by an ambition of gaining hegemony over the more liberal groups prevailing in policymaking circles. Their efforts to disseminate their ideas and garner support from various economic, political, and religious actors demonstrated their ability in attracting new resources and audiences to inform and influence policies. In contrast to the older generation's amateurish intellectual style, the Young Conservatives engaged in a new form of ideological entrepreneurship based on their training as social scientists and their professionalization as public intellectuals.

This chapter investigates the conditions that led to the rise of the Young Conservatives and their role in normalizing hawkish ideas – to which they have given intellectual legitimacy, doctrinal foundations, and institutional representation in the public sphere. As Chapter 4 has illustrated the significant shift in the attitudes of liberal intellectual elites toward Prokhanov's work, this chapter demonstrates that support from prominent liberal figures influential in ruling circles, such as Gleb Pavlovskii, was crucial for the Young Conservatives' emergence as notable media intellectuals.

The sources used in this chapter include publications by Young Conservatives in the period from 1995 to 2007 and interviews with some of their leading members in Moscow in 2019: Vitalii Averianov, Mikhail Remizov, Egor Kholmogorov, Boris Mezhuev, Konstantin Krylov, and Dmitrii Volodikhin.

5.1 A New Generation of Russian Hawks

5.1.1 The Young Conservatives: Generational Continuity and Evolution

As highlighted by researcher Aleksandr Pavlov, the term "Young Conservatives" was first coined by a journalist in 2003 before later being used by members of the group themselves.[2] Prominent Young

[2] Alexander Pavlov, "The Great Expectations of Russian Young Conservatism," in *Contemporary Russian Conservatism. Problems, Paradoxes, and Perspectives*, ed. Mikhail Suslov and Dmitry Uzlaner (Leiden, Boston, MA: Brill, 2020), 166.

Conservatives include Vitalii Averianov (1973–), Egor Kholmogorov (1975–), Konstantin Krylov (1967–2020), Boris Mezhuev (1970–), and Mikhail Remizov (1978–).

As per Karl Mannheim's theory, the Young Conservatives are "sociologically significant" as an intellectual generation to the extent that their shared experiences have helped form their ideas in similar ways.[3] The first element in the consolidation of the Young Conservatives as a generation is the similarity of their biographical trajectories. In addition to being part of the same age group, approximately born in the 1970s, most Young Conservatives originate from the Muscovite urban social classes, with some affiliated to the upper-class intelligentsia.[4] Mezhuev, for example, is the son of the philosopher Vadim Mezhuev (1933–2019), who was a chief researcher at the Academy of Sciences' Institute of Philosophy. Krylov's mother was a director in a research institute at the KGB's First Chief Directorate.[5] Kholmogorov's education in Moscow's secondary School No. 57, one of the most prestigious Russian schools, similarly indicates his membership in the intellectual establishment.[6]

Furthermore, the Young Conservatives share similar academic backgrounds in the social sciences, with most of them attending Moscow's State University to study philosophy (Averianov, Krylov, Remizov, Mezhuev) or history (Kholmogorov) in the 1990s and early 2000s. Their initial connections were formed in this academic setting, exemplified by Krylov and Kholmogorov's meeting at a philosophy seminar taught by Aleksei Boldyrev, a specialist in the history of Russian philosophy.[7]

[3] Karl Mannheim, "The Sociological Problem of Generations," in *Essays on the Sociology of Knowledge* (London: Routledge & Kegan Paul, 1972), 304.

[4] Averianov, Kholmogorov, Krylov and Mezhuev were born in Moscow. Remizov, however, was born in Voronezh.

[5] Konstantin Krylov, "Vseobshchii sinopsis ili sistema mnenii," krylov.livejournal.com, 2021, https://krylov.livejournal.com/2853229.html?thread=143227757#t143227757.

[6] Some of Kholmogorov's classmates included other prominent members of cultural and intellectual elites such as the film director Pavel Badrin (1975–) and the designer Artemii Lebedev (1975–). See the school's alumni directory: www.sch57.ru/people/alumni/#y1992.

[7] Later on, Boldyrev wrote scholarly articles on the Young Conservatives. See Aleksei Boldyrev, "Russkaia Doktrina," in *Russkaia filosofiia: Entsiklopediia* (Moscow: Mir filosofii Moskva, 2019), 595–96; Aleksei Boldyrev, "Averianov," in *Russkaia filosofiia*, 9–10.

As evidenced by their earlier works, their common interests as students included themes such as Russian religious philosophy, Russian nationalism, political conservatism, and the concept of tradition. In 1997, Mezhuev completed his PhD on the social and cultural origins of the work of the nineteenth-century religious philosopher Vladimir Soloviev. His previous publications included articles such as "The 'Russian Idea' in the Face of the Challenge of Modernity" and "The Concept of 'National Interest' in Russian Sociopolitical Life."[8] Both Krylov and Averianov contributed to the journal *Volshebnaia gora* (The Magic Mountain), which focused on philosophical and metaphysical discussions concerning tradition. Averianov's 2000 PhD dissertation addressed "the problem of tradition in the twentieth-century Russian philosophy of the Russian diaspora,"[9] and in 2004 Remizov defended his thesis on "the criticism of universalism in the philosophy of the French 'New Right.'"[10]

On top of their common academic pursuits, some Young Conservatives were actively involved in Orthodox religious organizations. Following his studies at Moscow State University, Kholmogorov studied at the Russian Orthodox University of Saint John the Divine and later worked at an Orthodox bookstore.[11] In 1998–99, Averianov served as the editor-in-chief of *Pravoslavnoe knizhnoe Obozrenie* (The Orthodox Book Review), published by the Russian Orthodox Church's Publishing Committee.

Moreover, Young Conservatives shared a common experience of disillusionment with post-Soviet democracy. Instead of viewing the collapse of the Soviet Union as progress toward more freedom, they bound by a negative emotional experience of loss and failure. As put by Remizov:

[8] Boris Mezhuev, "'Russkaia Ideia' pered vyzovom sovremennosti," *Vestnik moskovskogo universiteta* 6 (1993): 29–34; Boris Mezhuev, "Poniatie 'natsionalnii interes' v rossiiskoi obshchestvenno-politicheskoi zhizni," *Polis* 1 (1997): 5–31.

[9] See the profile page of Averianov's dissertation in DisserCat, the Russian dissertations directory: www.dissercat.com/content/problema-traditsii-v-russkoi-filosofii-xx-veka-russkoe-zarubezhe.

[10] See the profile page of Remizov's dissertation in DisserCat: www.dissercat.com/content/kritika-universalizma-v-filosofii-frantsuzskikh-novykh-pravykh.

[11] Egor Kholmogorov, "Eto bylo vremia, kogda liudi sogrevali drug druga," *Vzgliad*, September 22, 2015.

> Modern Russian conservatism was undoubtedly born as a reaction to the destruction and disintegration of the Soviet empire ... The commonality of the experience of loss is of great emotional significance.[12]

A pivotal moment in shaping their political views was their disappointment with Yeltsin's regime after witnessing the constitutional crisis and repression of the opposition in October 1993.[13] The 1998 economic crisis and the 1999 NATO bombing of Serbia without a UN mandate and despite Russia's opposition at the Security Council were additional key turning points in the formation of their conservative stance. Krylov and Kholmogorov were notably involved in the demonstrations in front of the American embassy to denounce NATO's intervention. As Krylov argued, these events constituted a historical and "emotional" starting point for the formation of a "new conservatism."[14]

Another unifying factor among the Young Conservatives was their acknowledgment of the older generation of hawks as pioneering figures. They have frequently paid tribute to the work of Aleksandr Dugin and Aleksandr Prokhanov for their role as nonconformist Soviet thinkers and disseminators of an important corpus of conservative thought including Eurasianism, Orthodox traditionalism, and the European New Right's anti-universalism.[15] Furthermore, both generations embraced common ideas, emphasizing the importance of restoring Russia's civilizational independence and asserting its status as great power status in contrast to what they perceived as the "degenerate" West.[16] They also shared the goal of designing a new state ideology that would base Russia's modernization path on its traditional, country-specific values, which they viewed as distinct from the

[12] Mikhail Remizov, "Konservatizm segodnia: Analiticheskii obzor," APN.ru, January 30, 2006, https://apn-nn.com/analytic/konservatizm-segodnya-analiticheskiy-obzor.

[13] Kholmogorov, "Eto bylo vremia, kogda liudi sogrevali drug druga."

[14] Konstantin Krylov, "'Kontrreformatsiia': Predystoriia i Posleslovie," politconservatism.ru, September 10, 2015, https://politconservatism.ru/experiences/kontrreformatsiya-predystoriya-i-posleslovie.

[15] Averianov has been an active commentator on Dugin's work and has hailed him as being among the "brightest Russian 'traditionalists.'" See Vitalii Averianov, "Metafizika nichego: Ob opyte sviashchennogo pisaniia bezdny G. Dzhemalia," metacultura.ru, 1999, http://averianov.net/sii/482/?h=670.

[16] See, for instance, Vitalii Averianov, "Segodnia russkoi tserkvi 'bolshe vsekh nado,'" *NG religii*, October 11, 2000, http://averianov.net/sii/479/?h=670.

Western liberal model of modernization. All these themes were clearly articulated in the early writings of the Young Conservatives, including Krylov's 2001 book *Features of the National Behavior*,[17] Averianov's 2003 *The Nature of Russian Expansion*,[18] and Kholmogorov's 2004 *The Restoration of the Future*.[19]

While maintaining certain elements of continuity with the older generation of hawks, the Young Conservatives were also linked by their efforts to formulate a second-generation conservatism that would mark an evolution from the national-patriotic ideology of the 1990s. Their very use of the term "conservatism" as their ideological self-definition marked their ambition to aim for more respectability and normalization, in contrast to the previous labels that were associated with the older generation's political extremism, marginality, and eclecticism. As put by Krylov:

> Compared with the eclectic and ridiculous "red–brown" idol of the nineties, [conservatism] gave the impression of being strong and beautiful.[20]

As Krylov further explained, his generation's attraction to conservatism emerged in response to what they perceived as the exhaustion and sterility of the bipolar ideological confrontation that had prevailed in the 1990s between Yeltsin's regime and the national-patriotic opposition:

> Talk about "conservatism" began in the very late 1990s, when the decline of ideologies born in the White House [the Russian Federation's Government House] became apparent—that is, the "democratic" model of 1991 and the "red–brown" model of 1993. This was completely inevitable, since both ideologies were associated with Yeltsin and Yeltsinism, either positively or negatively. Yeltsin's time was drawing to a close, and everyone felt it.[21]

Averianov also emphasized that the label "Young Conservatives" was meant as an identity marker signifying that they were a "truly

[17] Mikhail Alekseev and Konstantin Krylov, *Osobennosti natsionalnogo povedeniia* (Moscow: Art-Biznes-Tsentr, 2001).
[18] Vitalii Averianov, *Priroda russkoi ekspansii* (Moscow: Lenta-Press, 2003).
[19] Egor Kholmogorov, *Russkii proekt: Restavratsiia budushchego* (Moscow: Eksmo, 2005).
[20] Krylov, "'Kontrreformatsiia': Predystoriia i posleslovie."
[21] Krylov, "'Kontrreformatsiia': Predystoriia i posleslovie."

new generation," different from their elders' "national-patriotic movement."[22] The semantic reflections that affected their decision to present themselves as "Young Conservatives" show that they aspired to a standardized ideological label that could compare with other types of political thought overseas. Indeed, the Young Conservatives' knowledge of European languages and their use of Western academic references such as Daniel Bell, Talcott Parsons, Edward Shils, and Samuel Huntington positioned their discourse in dialogue with Western sociologists, political scientists, and ideologues.

Beyond their intention of earning themselves a new reputation, Young Conservatives also opposed some of the key components of their elders' worldview, notably rejecting their nostalgia for the past and the ambition of restoring the Soviet Union. Instead, the Young Conservatives emphasized that they did not "feel any sympathy for the recent past, whether Soviet or post-Soviet,"[23] but instead were driven by their ambition of shaping and orienting their country's future. This difference was clearly spelled out at a joint meeting of the younger and older generations of conservative thinkers held in April 2004 at the Central House of Writers in Moscow, during which Remizov underscored the constructive and future-oriented dimension of the Young Conservatives' discourse:

> [The "new conservatism"] does not set as its goal the restoration or the preservation of tradition, but the reconstruction of tradition.[24]

In setting out to achieve this goal, Young Conservatives put forward a commitment to political realism and pragmatism in opposition to what they perceived as their elders' phantasmagorical discourse. In an interview, a Young Conservative distinguished their generation's focus on the technical aspects of modernization from Dugin's metaphysical perspectives and Prokhanov's idealistic vision of a new Soviet empire, which he characterized as somewhat fantastical.[25]

Moreover, instead of the first-generation hawks' attachment to the Soviet supraethnic, imperial understanding of Russian national identity, Young Conservatives shared a concern for the reestablishment

[22] See Averianov's footnote 1 in "Novye konservatory: Budushchee Rossii?," *Moskovskii vestnik* 4 (2004), http://averianov.net/sii/458/?h=670.
[23] Krylov, "'Kontrreformatsiia': Predystoriia i posleslovie."
[24] "Novye konservatory: Budushchee Rossii?"
[25] Author interview, Moscow, 2019.

of the significance and the centrality of its ethnic, rather than civic, dimension. In particular, Krylov intervened early on in the post-Soviet debate about the definition of "Russianness." In opposition to the term *rossiiane*, officially sanctioned by the 1993 Constitution to designate the citizens of the multiethnic Russian Federation, he advocated the use of the ethnic term for Russians (*russkie*).[26]

However, two distinct definitions of "Russianness" can be identified within the ranks of the Young Conservatives, resulting in divergent attitudes toward the older generation. On the one hand, Krylov, Remizov, and Mezhuev promoted a secular type of Russian nationalism, paired with an isolationist foreign policy focused on the preservation of Russia's national authenticity. This group built on the work of Vadim Tsymburskii (1957–2009), who belonged to the older generation but was not part of the national-patriotic bloc.[27] As explained by the scholar Mikhail Suslov, Tsymburskii saw Russia's communist experience as yet another attempt to be part of the West and instead argued for Russia's deliverance from its "rapture of Europe."[28] He viewed Russia as an "island," a "state-continent" separate from Europe that should primarily be protective of its borders and concerned with the cultivation of its civilizational core.[29]

On the other hand, Averianov and Kholmogorov advocated an Orthodox imperialism that evolved in a more incremental way from the national-patriotic language of the 1990s. While both expressed strong critiques of the Soviet system and emphasized the need to cleanse modern conservatism from any Soviet nostalgia,[30] they

26 As reported by Krylov, Prokhanov had refused to publish this article in *Zavtra* at the time. See Konstantin Krylov, "Rossiiane i russkie," *Traditio*, https://traditio.wiki/krylov/rossian.html.

27 Tsymburskii's essay "Ostrov Rossiia" (Russia as an Island), which was issued in the journal *Polis* in 1993, was the first book published by the Institute for National Strategy led by Remizov in 2004. In 2011, Mezhuev published a monograph on Tsymburskii: Boris Mezhuev, *Politicheskaia kritika Vadima Tsymburskogo* (Moscow: Evropa, 2011).

28 Mikhail Suslov, "Russian Conservatism as an Ideology: The Logic of Isolationism," in *Contemporary Russian Conservatism: Problems, Paradoxes, and Perspectives*, ed. Mikhail Suslov and Dmitry Uzlaner (Leiden: Brill, 2020), 95.

29 Suslov, "Russian Conservatism as an Ideology."

30 See Vitalii Averianov, "Konservatizm: Ochishchenie ot illiuzii (programma kluba konservativnykh analitikov)," *Zolotoi lev* 11–12 (2000). For his part, Kholmogorov expressed his rejection of the Soviet legacy by being a member of the noncanonical Russian Orthodox Autonomous Church, which had stood against the Russian Orthodox Church's policy of loyalty to the Soviet regime.

nevertheless built, at least in part, on the ideas of Father Dmitrii Dudko (1922–2004) and Metropolitan Ioann Snychev (1927–95), the leading religious figures of the national-patriotic bloc of the 1990s.[31] Both were advocates of a political and imperialist understanding of Russian Orthodoxy against the "apoliticality" of the official line of the post-Soviet Church.[32] Averianov and Kholmogorov expressed similar views in their essays, promoting the role of Orthodoxy as the founding, sacred source of Russia's statehood, great power status (*derzhavnost*), and messianism.[33]

Beyond these elements of ideological diversity, the Young Conservatives remained bound by what a member of the group has termed a "generational sympathy."[34] Moreover, their unity was forged through their collective opposition to the regime's "liberal–conservative" synthesis.

5.1.2 Opposition to the Regime's "Liberal–Conservative" Synthesis

Vladimir Putin's reaction against members of Yeltsin's entourage continued throughout his first presidential mandate, thereby opening up a policy environment more favorable to the circulation of conservative ideas. In 2003, Mikhail Khodorkovskii, the owner of the oil company Yukos, was arrested, and his company's assets were transferred to state-owned companies.[35] Putin also dismissed some of the key representatives of Yeltsin's former ruling elite, such as Aleksandr Voloshin, who was replaced as chief of the presidential administration in 2003

[31] Averianov paid tribute to them in several articles. See, for instance, Vitalii Averianov, "Neoborimaia krotost: Ob o. Dimitrii Dudko," *Pravoslavnoe knizhnoe obozrenie*, December 1998, http://averianov.net/sii/538/?h=670;%20 http://averianov.net/sii/483/?h=670 and Vitalii Averianov, "Rossiia: Ne ot mira sego," *Zavtra* 425 (January 8, 2002), http://averianov.net/sii/?h=478.

[32] Konstantin Kostiuk, "Tri portreta: Sotsialno-eticheskie vozzreniia v russkoi pravoslavnoi tserkvi kontsa XX veka," *Kontinent* 113 (2002), https://magazines.gorky.media/continent/2002/113/tri-portreta.html. On Dmitrii Dudko, see Oliver Bullough, *The Last Man in Russia: The Struggle to Save a Dying Nation* (New York: Basic Books, 2013).

[33] Averianov, *Priroda russkoi ekspansii*, which includes a preface by Dmitrii Dudko; Kholmogorov, *Russkii proekt: Restavratsiia budushchego*.

[34] Author interview, Moscow, 2019.

[35] For a detailed analysis of the Yukos Affair, see Richard Sakwa, *Putin and the Oligarch: The Khodorkovsky–Yukos Affair* (London: I.B. Tauris, 2014).

by Dmitrii Medvedev, and Mikhail Kasianov, who quit his position as prime minister in 2004.

The Young Conservatives enthusiastically commented on what they perceived as Putin's efforts to combat the "strongholds of the liberal opposition" and the symbols of the "old Yeltsin guard."[36] However, they also sought to dissociate themselves from what they saw as the regime's attempt to establish a consensual "liberal–conservative" synthesis as a means to consolidate the power of the presidency and discard opposition. As put by Remizov, Young Conservatism was constructed in opposition to the "conservatism of the status quo" associated with the "period of Putin's assertion in power."[37] Similarly, Averianov stressed the distinction between the authorities' instrumental use of conservatism as a "political technology" and a "serious conservative ideology" coming "from below."[38] The ambivalent attitude of Young Conservatives toward the regime was thus characteristic of Russian conservative thought, which, as shown by Paul Robinson, has historically been supportive of strong state power while being at odds with state policies.[39] This was well spelled out by Krylov:

> The Young Conservatives sincerely wanted to be loyal to the Russian state and its higher institutions. This totally coexisted with a critical attitude towards the Russian elites and even the demands for their "change."[40]

In particular, Young Conservatives opposed Putin's continued commitment to Russia's integration into the global economy and close links with the West. In the aftermath of September 11, they disapproved of Putin's decision to provide full support and operational assistance to US counterterrorist operations in Afghanistan and, subsequently, to engage in the NATO–Russia partnership agreement in 2002.[41] In reaction to the US invasion of Iraq in 2003, Mezhuev asserted his conception of Russia's foreign policy as a civilizational counterbalance

[36] Vitalii Averianov, "Gensek Vladimir Groznyi," APN.ru, August 20, 2004, http://averianov.net/sii/463/?h=670.
[37] Remizov, "Konservatizm segodnia: Analiticheskii obzor."
[38] Vitalii Averianov, "Tretii polius," *Ekspert* 10, no. 317 (2002), http://averianov.net/sii/532/?h=478.
[39] See Paul Robinson, *Russian Conservatism* (Ithaca, NY: Northern Illinois University Press, an imprint of Cornell University Press, 2019), 19.
[40] Krylov, "'Kontrreformatsiia': Predystoriia i posleslovie."
[41] On Russia's support to US counterterrorist operations, see Richard Sakwa, *Putin: Russia's Choice* (London: Routledge, 2004), 216.

to the American-led global war on terror.[42] Likewise, diverging from the regime's official foreign policy at the time, Averianov's articles recommended the adoption of an expansionist and imperialist approach aimed at Russia's reunification with Ukraine and Belarus.[43]

The regime's economic policies were another key bone of contention with the Young Conservatives, who opposed its adhesion to the principles of globalization, especially as the authorities implemented a series of reforms in preparation of the country's future accession to the World Trade Organization (WTO). In addition, in contrast to the neoliberal approach that guided the regime's welfare reforms and use of administrative methods such as new public management, the Young Conservatives advocated state-led economic modernization based on protectionism and autarky.[44]

The Young Conservatives' critique of the regime more specifically opposed what they identified as the "liberal lobby" and its influence on policy decisions.[45] One of their central targets was the "Seraphim Club" (Serafimovskii Klub), which was created in 2003 by journalists from the economic newspaper *Ekspert* (Aleksandr Privalov, Mikhail Leontev, Valerii Fadeev, and Maksim Sokolov) and two movie directors (Sergei Selianov and Aleksei Balabanov). The club's programmatic memorandum, entitled "From the Politics of Fear to a Politics of Growth," was published in January 2003 by *Vedomosti*, a major liberal-inclined business newspaper. The memorandum exemplified the attempt to build a liberal–conservative union based on the "synthesis of Russia and Freedom," which it defined as the consolidation of the post-1991 liberal reforms with the promotion of Russian patriotism.[46] As the historian Mikhail

[42] See, for instance, Boris Mezhuev, "Amerikanskii fundamentalizm i Russkaia 'Konservativnaia Revoliutsiia,'" *Logos* 1 (2003), https://magazines.gorky.media/logos/2003/1/amerikanskij-fundamentalizm-i-russkaya-8220-konservativnaya-revolyucziya-8221.html; Mezhuev, "Konflikt vneshnepoliticheskikh ideologii," APN.ru, October 8, 2004, www.apn.ru/index.php?newsid=1130.

[43] Vitalii Averianov, "Vse my nemnogo 'Ukraina,'" APN.ru, December 2, 2004, http://averianov.net/sii/459/?h=670.

[44] Katharina Bluhm and Mihai Varga, eds., *New Conservatives in Russia and East Central Europe* (Abingdon: Routledge, 2019), 9.

[45] Arkadii Maler, "Nasledniki vekhovskoi traditsii," politconservatism.ru, September 3, 2015, https://politconservatism.ru/thinking/nasledniki-vekhovskoy-traditsii.

[46] Sergei Prozorov, "Russian Conservatism in the Putin Presidency: The Dispersion of a Hegemonic Discourse," *Journal of Political Ideologies* 10, no. 2 (2005): 127.

Diunov has highlighted, unlike the liberal-conservatives' acceptance of the general direction of Russia's development since 1991, Young Conservatives rejected the political legacy of the 1990s in its entirety.[47]

In particular, Young Conservatives challenged a key idea promoted by more liberal groups, arguing that, with the development of economic globalization, state authority would eventually leave the way to transnational corporations. This notion was advanced by Sergei Chernyshev (1952–), a prominent figure in leading liberal intellectual institutions, who served as the director of the Institute of Corporate Entrepreneurship at the Higher School of Economics from 1998 to 2004. In an article entitled "Instead of a Manifesto: Entrepreneur; A New Word; A New Estate; A New Craft," published in 2000, Chernyshev built on the ideas of theoreticians of the postindustrial society such as Daniel Bell to argue that industrial economic sectors would be superseded by a new information economy increasingly developing beyond the control of the state.[48] Averianov responded to Chernyshev's essay as representative of a broader liberal elite ideology with an article published in 2001, entitled "Corporatism: The New Mythology," in which he defended the primacy of the "old" and "eternal" myths of the Russian civilization – specifically the "myth of the Family," the "myth of the Empire," and the "myth of the Church" – against the "new myths" of corporatism and the "religion" of "linear progress."[49] In contrast to a purely traditionalist worldview, however, Averianov advocated the need to "embed" Russia's civilizational myths "into modernity" in a novel way:

> We say "yes" to new technologies but we say "no" to the new order, we say "yes" to the new policy of old Russia but we say "no" to the new myths designed to bury our tradition.[50]

The Young Conservatives therefore built on their generational unity and their common opposition to liberal groups to organize themselves collectively as a new intellectual movement.

47 Mikhail Diunov, "Mladokonservatizm: Ego istoriia ego znachenie," *Russkii zhurnal*, December 5, 2009, www.russ.ru/pole/Mladokonservatizm.-Ego-istoriya-ego-znachenie.

48 Sergei Chernyshev, "Vmesto manifesta: Predpinimatel; Novoe slovo; Novoe soslovie; Novoe remeslo," *Russkii zhurnal*, September 11, 2000, http://old.russ.ru/ist_sovr/ckp/20000904_I.html.

49 Vitalii Averianov, "Korporatizm: Novaia mifologiia," *Filosofskaia gazeta*, 2001, http://averianov.net/sii/535/?h=670.

50 Averianov, "Korporatizm: Novaia mifologiia."

5.2 The Establishment of Young Conservatism in the Public Sphere

5.2.1 The Rise of Young Conservatives as Media Intellectuals

Unlike the older generation's founding experiences of political protest and opposition, Young Conservatives sought to become part of the intellectual establishment. In their view, their ascension in the public sphere should form part of a metapolitical strategy of influence, whereby they could shape policy decisions through the circulation of their ideas. In contrast to the revolutionary attitude of the National-Bolshevik Party or the electoral politics practiced by Gennadii Ziuganov, therefore, Young Conservatives were closer to Prokhanov's continuation of the Soviet intellectuals' practice of "politics by culture." However, the Young Conservatives more explicitly sought to replicate the European New Right's use of Antonio Gramsci's theory of cultural hegemony. Remizov, who devoted a chapter of his PhD thesis to this topic, presented its adoption in the Russian context as one of the main characteristic features of the new conservatism:

> We should not appeal to power, but produce it ourselves by filling the vacuum of social space. In particular, [this should be done] by transforming the context, the language of political action, creating acceptable and authoritative standards for the society and models of cultural self-identity.[51]

Kholmogorov has further theorized the Russian equivalent of Gramsci's cultural hegemony under the name *smyslokratiia* (sense-cracy). This neologism for the "power of meanings" conveyed the Young Conservatives' belief in their capacity to become an influential intellectual elite able to shape and transform social reality through their ideas.[52]

With this objective in sight, Young Conservatives endeavored to establish themselves as professional public intellectuals. Thus, alongside their publications in ideological newspapers, they also published in academic journals and mainstream media platforms. Averianov's list of publications in the 1990s and early 2000s illustrates this mix of ideological, scholarly, and journalistic discourse. His articles were

[51] "Novye konservatory: Budushchee Rossii?"
[52] Egor Kholmogorov, "'Kontrreformatsiia': Zhizn bez maiatnika," politconservatism.ru, September 10, 2015, https://politconservatism.ru/thinking/kontrreformatsiya-zhizn-bez-mayatnika.

published by the major outlets of the older national-patriot generation such as *Zavtra*, *Volshebnaia gora*, and *Moskva*; scientific philosophical journals such as *Voprosy literatury*, *Obshchestvennie nauki i Sovremennost*, and *Istoriia filosofii*; and major media that provided opinion pieces and analyses such as *Ekspert* and *Russkii zhurnal*.

Another crucial factor in the rise of the Young Conservatives as public intellectuals was their use of the internet as a new forum for sociopolitical discussion. Toward the end of the 1990s, the internet became the preferred medium of communication invested by media moguls. Gleb Pavlovskii (1951–), a former liberal dissident during the Soviet period who became a close adviser to Yeltsin's ruling circles, was one of the pioneering developers of the internet as a platform for intellectual debates.[53] In 1997, he launched two internet newspapers, *Russkii zhurnal* (The Russian Journal) and the website Polit.ru, with the aim of providing the online version of the Russian journalistic tradition of "thick journals," where intense sociopolitical and literary debates were held.[54] However, in contrast to the print press environment, where hawkish outlets such as *Zavtra* were seen as outsiders, online media became places for publication and debate among a community of intellectuals spanning a large ideological spectrum. The opening up of these new online publishing platforms facilitated to the dissemination of diverse political ideas. During an interview, one of Pavlovskii's former employees explained the ideological plurality of *Russkii zhurnal*'s editorial line by describing Pavlovskii as "genetically dissident, [someone] who always tried to give a platform for those who are officially considered marginal."[55] Stanislas Belkovskii (1971–), who was a consultant to members of Yeltsin's entourage such as the businessman and newspaper tycoon Boris Berezovskii, also played a key role in the development of an open-to-all political internet outlet, the Agency of Political News (APN) (Agentstvo politicheskikh novostei), which he created in 1999.

[53] In 1995, Pavlovskii created the Foundation of Effective Politics (FEP) with Marat Gelman (1960–) and Maksim Meier (1967–) to offer communication and consulting services for the political elite. The FEP was the major orchestrator of Yeltsin's campaign during the presidential election in 1996. See Sergei Domushchii, "Naklikali pobedu: Kak FEP igral na vyborakh v 90-kh i vyigryval," *Secretmag*, November 15, 2019, https://secretmag.ru/stories/naklikali-pobedu-kak-fep-igral-na-vyborakh-v-90-kh-i-vyigryval.htm?fbclid=IwAR2_uo0m8g6DebDFVlNbtxtmLF9B7ff6z8tkEeJ7h2VCRJ1alUBOngZCRsg.

[54] Domushchii, "Naklikali pobedu." [55] Author interview, Moscow, 2019.

As emphasized by a Young Conservative, the advent of the internet significantly enhanced their public presence by granting them access to a deliberative space free from censorship.[56] This new opportunity, for instance, prompted Krylov to establish his own website, "Traditio," where he could publish written materials that had previously been difficult to place in other outlets.[57] The internet also provided Krylov and Kholmogorov – both of whom mentioned the weight of economic hardship on their decision to abandon their ambitions of pursuing a PhD and an academic career – with a new source of revenue. Being among the pioneering users of the Russian web allowed them to profit out of their technical and practical knowledge of the internet. The creation and management of websites was one of the typical ways this generation of intellectuals was able to earn money.[58]

The internet also enabled the Young Conservatives to organize their first collective actions. In 1998, Krylov and Kholmogorov became associates and coeditors of the website Russiandoctrine.ru, which, in Krylov's words, became "one of the first Russian nationalist projects of the Runet [Russian internet]."[59] As further argued by the historian Mikhail Diunov, the creation of the site represented a significant challenge to the generally liberal orientation that dominated political discussions on the internet:

> The site immediately caused a stir, since there had not been any political sites of this kind on the Russian network until that moment. Krylov and Kholmogorov's works were published there, while the main trend of the Russian Internet was liberalism with varying degrees of radicalism.[60]

The first Russian social networking service, "Live Journal" (Zhivoi zhurnal), created in 1999, became another important public forum in which the Young Conservatives were able to enter into public debates with a mass audience and acquire fame as opinion-makers. In interviews, Young Conservatives described how they gained recognition as prominent public figures, with people actively discussing, criticizing,

56 Author interview, Moscow, 2019.
57 Such as his article "Rossiiane i russkie," which he had written in 1993. Krylov, "Rossiiane i russkie."
58 Kholmogorov managed the activities of the Russian Orthodox Autonomous Church's website "Tserkovnost." Averianov worked on the creation of the Orthodox informational portal "pravoslavie.ru," launched in 2000.
59 Konstantin Krylov, "Obo mne," https://krylov.cc/about.php?id=72.
60 Diunov, "Mladokonservatizm: Ego istoriia ego znachenie."

or praising him.[61] In addition to serving as a vehicle of public recognition, Live Journal also provided a place to aggregate likeminded people. As reported by Pavel Sviatenkov, one of the members of the Young Conservatives, Live Journal played an instrumental role in him becoming acquainted with Krylov and Kholmogorov, enabling their creation of a community of thinkers:

> For me it all began with the Live Journal. It was there, in the communal kitchen of Russian intellectuals of the early 2000s, that the first ideological circles arose, and from which the Young Conservative movement emerged. After the collapse of the Soviet Union, social ties collapsed, and it was the Internet that created them all over again. It was there that the conversation arose, the consolidation around the LJ [Live Journal] of Krylov and Kholmogorov … It was a kind of Masonic lodge—a closed prestigious community where everyone knew one another and it was possible to become acquainted with many influential people simply by scribbling a couple of lines in one's diary.[62]

The Young Conservatives' combination of learned discourse, scholarly references, and polemical style formed a new type of intellectual with tools that differed from the older generation's use of radical rhetoric. Pavlovskii's *Russkii zhurnal* and Belkovskii's APN became their main publication platforms. Through these online publications, their discourse was able to reach a large audience among the intellectual, cultural, and political elite. In 2003, *Russkii zhurnal*'s publication of Krylov's article "Rus and Nerus," which reproduced the controversial theses of his previously self-published article "Civic Russians [*rossiiane*] and Ethnic Russians [*russkie*]," testified to his discourse gaining legitimacy in the informational space.[63] In addition to greater media outreach and the legitimation of their discourse, online media also provided important career opportunities to the Young Conservatives. In 2003, for example, Mikhail Remizov became the head of the politics department of *Russkii zhurnal*, and he was subsequently recruited as editor-in-chief of APN in 2004.

[61] Author interviews, Moscow, 2019.
[62] Quoted in Katharina Bluhm, "Postmodernity and Modernity as Political Terms," in *Contemporary Russian Conservatism*, ed. Mikhail Suslov and Dmitry Uzlaner (Leiden: Brill, 2020), 160.
[63] Konstantin Krylov, "Rus i Nerus," *Russkii zhurnal*, October 7, 2003, http://old.russ.ru/politics/20031007-kryl.html.

5.2.2 *The Birth of Young Conservatism as an Intellectual Movement*

In line with their ambition to gain influence through the pursuit of cultural hegemony, the Young Conservatives invested in a set of media and intellectual organizations to build their identity as an intellectual movement in the public sphere. As the editor-in-chief of the politics section of *Russkii zhurnal*, Remizov laid out the foundations of this group-building by organizing the Conservative Press Club (Konservativnii press-klub),[64] which was explicitly pitted as a counterreaction to the Seraphim Club.[65] The Conservative Press Club held its first two meetings in the office of *Russkii zhurnal* in 2003 before moving in 2004 to the hotel of Saint Danilov Monastery with Belkovskii's financial support.[66] Subsequently, Belkovskii provided an institutional environment to the Young Conservatives with the creation of the Institute of National Strategy (INS) and the launch of a new version of APN, which had a majority of Young Conservatives on its editorial board. Headed by Remizov, the INS eventually became the organizational basis for the group. Likewise, APN was directed by Young Conservatives, with Mezhuev as its editor-in-chief from 2005 to 2007, followed by Krylov from 2007 to 2020. APN became a central and permanent intellectual platform for the Young Conservatives, where they published the programmatic works that established the theoretical underpinnings of their movement. As put by Nataliia Androsenko, a scholar closely associated with the Young Conservatives, APN became a symbolic marker of the group's identity:

> For the next two years [2004–6], APN was the most important intellectual platform for Young Conservatism ... For every conservative or nationally oriented intellectual, it became an obligatory "matter of honor" to publish on APN.[67]

[64] Remizov, "Konservatizm segodnia: Analiticheskii obzor."
[65] Remizov, "Konservatizm segodnia: Analiticheskii obzor."
[66] Viktor Militarev, "Doklad 'Kontrreformatsiia' v moei lichnoi istorii," politconservatism.ru, September 4, 2015, https://politconservatism.ru/thinking/doklad-kontrreformatsiya-v-moey-lichnoy-istorii.
[67] Nataliia Androsenko, "Publitsistika Mladokonservatorov v sovremennom kommunikativnom prostranstve Rossii," *Kommunikologiia* 4, no. 1 (2016): 160–72.

While APN represented the more secular, nationalist-inclined wing of the Young Conservatives, the Orthodox, imperialist-inclined wing was actively involved in 2004 in the creation of the internet portal Pravaia.ru, which became one of the major forums of Orthodox conservatism.

By 2005, the Young Conservatives were able to formally establish themselves as an intellectual group in the public sphere and to assemble their ideas into collective doctrinal documents. The institutionalization of the movement was led by Kholmogorov, who created the "Conservative Meeting" (Konservativnoe Soveshchanie) to hold weekly group discussions and prepare a group manifesto, entitled "Counter-Reformation," which was published in March 2005 on the website Pravaia.ru.[68] While taking part in the Conservative Meeting, Averianov also organized a parallel organization, the Center for Dynamic Conservatism (Tsentr Dinamicheskogo Konservatizma), which issued the Russian Doctrine in the fall of 2005.[69]

Both projects involved Young Conservatives with the aim of substantiating scattered ideas and formalizing them into a group manifesto able to influence the course of politics. In contrast to single-authored articles, the Counter-Reformation and the Russian Doctrine were collaborative doctrinal works intended to affirm each individual's membership in a broader intellectual movement. As put by Pavel Sviatenkov, their individual commitment to joining forces displayed the greater authority and significance that they had acquired as a group:

> It was obvious to me that, together, the members of the Conservative Meeting had more weight and social capital than separately. At that time, these intellectuals ... meant more together than separately.[70]

Likewise, the authors of the Russian Doctrine emphasized its "congregational" aspect, moving away from the principle of individual authorship:

[68] The text was reproduced here: "Kontrreformatsiia," *Russkii Obozrevatel*, www.rus-obr.ru/ru-club/4066.

[69] The Russian Doctrine was first published as a print brochure. The text can be accessed at: "Tezisy Russkoi Doktriny," November 2005, http://averianov.net/sii/510/?h=604.

[70] Pavel Sviatenkov, "Veselaia semeika," politconservatism.ru, September 25, 2015, https://politconservatism.ru/thinking/veselaya-semeyka.

The team worked according to the network principle: each [author] took part in the creation of the document, members of the editorial board actively helped each other in determining the ideological vectors and the crystallization of the spiritual, cultural and political meaning of the Doctrine ... Therefore, it was decided to abandon the exact indication of the authorship of certain chapters and paragraphs–"authorship" in the Doctrine spread throughout the text and sometimes simply cannot be clearly defined. The effect of congregational work arose, which in itself is a unique result.[71]

The social practice of intellectual reunions and discussions fostered the Young Conservatives' sense of group belonging. Their enthusiasm for the creation of a social venue to exchange ideas among themselves was indeed foundational in prompting their move from individual publications to collective writing. Sviatenkov, for instance, emphasized his primary interest in the habits and practice of an intellectual society over its actual theoretical task:

For me, the Conservative Meeting, as our own little Masonic lodge, was more important than the report that it was preparing.[72]

The Young Conservatives' formation as a public group was spurred by the immediate political context of the year 2004–2005. Indeed, the testimonies of the Counter-Reformation's signatories reveal that the document was written in reaction to the Orange Revolution – a series of protests that occurred in Ukraine from November 2004 to January 2005 to contest the results of the presidential election favoring the pro-Russia candidate, Viktor Yanukovych. The protests succeeded in calling for a second run-off vote, which resulted in the victory of the other candidate, Viktor Yushchenko. The Young Conservatives perceived the revolution as an operation orchestrated by Western forces to overthrow the pro-Russian regime, potentially posing a threat to the stability of the Russian state if similar scenarios were to be replicated domestically.[73] As put by Arkadii Maler, one of the Counter-Reformation signatories:

71 "Sergievskii proekt," rusdoctrina.ru, www.rusdoctrina.ru/page95505.html.
72 Sviatenkov, "Veselaia semeika."
73 For an exposition of this narrative on the Orange Revolution, see Vladimir Golyshev, "Adresaty nashego doklada nakhodilis v Kremle i na staroi ploshchadi," politconservatism.ru, September 7, 2015, https://politconservatism.ru/thinking/adresaty-nashego-doklada-nakhodilis-v-kremle-i-na-staroy-ploshchadi.

The original reason for writing the Counter-Reformation report was the so-called Orange revolution in Ukraine at the end of 2004 and the desire to stop a similar revolution in Russia.[74]

According to Kholmogorov, the Orange Revolution provided an opportunity for the Young Conservatives' discourse to gain greater political resonance in Russian politics:

I had the feeling of a certain window of opportunity for the Russian conservatives, which made it possible to speak out at least as a little noticeable social force. The Orange Revolution really strained the Kremlin and we started to see that we could be at least noticed, if not heard.[75]

In the meantime, the Young Conservatives' doctrinal work also reacted to the particular political climate within Russia. They coalesced around a shared critique of the reforms initiated by the regime, particularly sparked by the monetization of pension benefits. Adopted in the spring of 2005, this policy aimed to replace social benefits in kind with direct cash payment and was met with a wave of mass demonstrations. As mentioned by Kholmogorov, the Young Conservatives sought to use the opportunity provided by this specific context to propose a "systemic answer" to what they identified as a broader "political vice" associated with reform practices.[76]

The Young Conservatives therefore positioned themselves as an alternative to both the regime's political reformism and the threat of a proliberal domestic revolution. Moreover, as they attributed the path of reforms to the influence of the "liberal lobby" within the ruling elite under the leadership of Pavlovskii,[77] they sought to replicate a central gathering place akin to Pavlovskii's methods of influence.[78] In addition to their shared core of beliefs, the publication of the Russian Doctrine and the Counter-Reformation thus highlighted the Young Conservatives' shared objective of becoming an alternative to the liberal intellectual elite. In a 2009 statement reflecting on the history of their movement, Remizov indeed stressed that the significance of the Young Conservatives as a "social phenomenon" was

[74] Maler, "Nasledniki vekhovskoi traditsii."
[75] Kholmogorov, "'Kontrreformatsiia': Zhizn bez maiatnika."
[76] Kholmogorov, "'Kontrreformatsiia': Zhizn bez maiatnika."
[77] Maler, "Nasledniki vekhovskoi traditsii."
[78] Kholmogorov, "'Kontrreformatsiia': Zhizn bez maiatnika."

not to achieve intellectual hegemony but to "form a fraction of the politicized intelligentsia, different from the liberal one."[79] External analysts also identified the publication of the Young Conservatives' collective manifestos as the public birth of a new political generation. Aleksandr Tsipko, a liberal-conservative political scientist, described the Russian Doctrine as:

> a significant turning point in the political and spiritual life of Russia, the emergence of a whole generation of young people who are looking for the meaning of their lives in building a new, sovereign Russia.[80]

He further added:

> We are witnessing the emergence of a Russian conservative elite, which we did not have in the late 1980s and early 1990s, when the fate of the country was being decided.[81]

As highlighted by Remizov, the Counter-Reformation and the Russian Doctrine defined the social and conceptual significance of Young Conservatism by delineating the distinctions between what they considered as "ideologically ours" and what they saw as "ideologically foreign."[82] Both documents, despite some nuanced differences, converged in establishing fundamental tenets of Young Conservatism. These included a forward-looking perspective focused on Russia's development and autonomy as a distinct civilization, countering globalism with prioritizing geopolitical sovereignty. They advocated for economic protectionism, fostering the nationalization of natural resources, state corporatism, and social solidarity. Other important themes included promoting ethnic Russian demographics and restraining migration, affirming the legitimacy and indivisibility of the Russian state as the successor of both the Russian Empire and the Soviet Union, endorsing strong autocratic state authority and bolstering religious traditionalism by granting religions with greater influence in cultural and political realms. Additionally, they embraced

[79] "Sovremennyi konservatizm v Rossii: Neklassicheskoe mirovozzrenie; Stenogramma ekspertnoi vstrechi," dynacon.ru, May 20, 2009, www.dynacon.ru/content/articles_idk/337.

[80] Aleksandr Tsipko, "V ozhidanii Gagarina," *Literaturnaia gazeta* 1 (2006), www.rusdoctrina.ru/page95540.html.

[81] Tsipko, "V ozhidanii Gagarina."

[82] Remizov, "Konservatizm segodnia: Analiticheskii obzor."

the principle of *smyslrokatiia*, which champions the political influence of intellectual elites.

Despite their common core principles, the documents also underscored the existence of two distinct ideological currents within the group: secular nationalism and Orthodox imperialism. A major source of difference between the documents lay in their organizational basis. While the Counter-Reformation arose organically from the Young Conservatives, the Russian Doctrine was developed within the structure of the Russian Entrepreneur Foundation, a charitable organization created by Orthodox businessman Sergei Pisarev (1960–). As part of its ambition of funding ideological and political projects, Pisarev's foundation had been publishing the newspaper *Russian Entrepreneur* since 2001 to provide a media platform for the Orthodox business community. The Russian Doctrine project came about as the natural outcome of the growth of this community.

As a result, the Counter-Reformation and the Russian Doctrine went through different writing processes. Whereas the Counter-Reformation's thirteen signatories were mainly Young Conservatives, the Russian Doctrine was written by an editorial board of nine members that sought the advice of more than thirty "experts" and twenty "consultants."[83] Moreover, while the same names cut across the signatory lists of the two documents, the authors played different roles in creating the texts and oriented their content in different directions.[84] The Counter-Reformation fell mainly under the intellectual leadership of Krylov's secular nationalism. As acknowledged by Kholmogorov, the Counter-Reformation was predominantly guided by the intellectual leadership of Krylov.[85] Ilia Brazhnikov, an Orthodox conservative who was involved in both projects, recounted his diminished bargaining power in the editing process of the Counter-Reformation compared to the secular line advocated by Krylov:

> If we talk about my personal participation, I represented the "Orthodox" wing in the Conservative Meeting. Consequently, "my" stylistic and verbal

[83] "Avtorskii kollektiv," rusdoctrina.ru, www.rusdoctrina.ru/page95506.html.

[84] Authors who participated in the Counter-Reformation and the Russian Doctrine include Averianov, Krylove, Remizov, Sviatenkov, Kholmogorov, Maler, Mezhuev, Ilia Brazhnikov, Mikhail Golovanov, Vladimir Golyshev, and Kirill Frolov.

[85] Kholmogorov, "'Kontrreformatsiia': Zhizn bez maiatnika."

layer in the report is everything that concerns "Tradition," "the Eastern Christian civilization" and the role of the "Orthodox Church." In the draft, which was twice as long as the final text, it was a solid piece. In the latest edition—it represented one scanty paragraph, and [Russian Orthodoxy]—one phrase.[86]

In contrast, the Russian Doctrine was significantly influenced by Averianov's leadership. Unlike Krylov, who strongly rejected the intellectual legacy of the older generation of conservatives, Averianov adopted a conciliatory approach toward them, inspiring the Russian Doctrine's goal of uniting Russia's diverse "public patriotic forces."[87] Averianov emphasized that the Russian Doctrine aimed to unify rather than divide, seeking to bridge generational and ideological gaps among conservatives:

> We tried to switch our patriotic tradition from the state of long disputes, monographs and collections of articles into the state of a conciliar [*sobornii*] work.[88]

In this declaration, Averianov resumed the older generation's use of the Orthodox concepts of conciliarity (*sobornost*) and community (*sobor*) as unifying concepts to transcend divisions within the national-patriotic ranks.

Moreover, while both documents advocated a dynamic understanding of tradition based on the principle of organic change,[89] the Russian Doctrine, the most thoroughly organized and theorized project, was more specifically tailored to Averianov's Orthodox conception of dynamic conservatism.

[86] Ilia Brazhnikov, "Vopreki nazvaniiu doklad nes v sebe dukh istinnoi reformatsii," politconservatism.ru, September 2, 2015, https://politconservatism.ru/prognosis/vopreki-nazvaniyu-doklad-nyes-v-sebe-dukh-istinnoy-reformatsii.Brazhnikov, "Vopreki nazvaniiu doklad nes v sebe dukh istinnoi reformatsii."
[87] "Tezisy Russkoi Doktriny."
[88] Vitalii Averianov, "Posle sobornykh slushanii opponenty zabespokoilis," Narodnoe Radio, August 4, 2007, http://averianov.net/sii/493/?h=674.
[89] The Counter-Reformation defined its conception of organic change as follows: "The most avant-garde and bold solution to a particular problem should be presented as a restoration of an old custom or an institution verified by experience, following a precedent or extending a longstanding and respected tradition." See "Kontrreformatsiia." Organic change is a central concept in the history of Russian conservative thought, see Robinson, *Russian Conservatism*, 9; Suslov and Uzlaner, *Contemporary Russian Conservatism*, 37.

5.3 The Russian Doctrine: Professionalized Ideological Entrepreneurship

5.3.1 Averianov: Leading Theorizer of the Combination of Tradition and Modernity

Averianov is the leading theorizer of the ideology termed "dynamic conservatism," advocated by the Russian Doctrine, which combines Orthodox traditionalism with a sovereigntist program of authoritarian technological and economic modernization. This ideology was constructed as a means of enabling the younger generation to affiliate with the older generation's modernist conservatism while simultaneously distinguishing themselves from it.

After completing his PhD dissertation on "the problem of tradition in twentieth-century Russian philosophy," which he defended in 2000, Averianov proceeded to develop a conservative worldview grounded on an Orthodox understanding of tradition in two long scholarly articles. In "Tradition and Traditionalism in Scientific and Social Thought in Russia (1960s–1990s)," published in *Obshchestvennie nauki i sovremennost* (Social Sciences and Modernity), Averianov addressed the issue of tradition from the perspective of modernization and developmental theories.[90] In the second article, "Tradition as Continuity and Service," published in the journal *Chelovek* (Human Being), Averianov provided his definition of tradition from the standpoint of an "Orthodox traditionalist."[91] In this case, he positioned himself in debates that were then taking place within the Orthodox Church. As put by the sociologist Aleksandr Agadjanian, starting from 2000, tradition had become the central concept on which the Orthodox Church based its doctrinal production and contribution to the public debate. However, the church's first major post-Soviet doctrinal document engaging with societal issues, the 2000 "Basis of the Social Concept of the Russian Orthodox Church," focused on what Agadjanian calls the "more secular" sense of tradition as a vehicle

[90] Vitalii Averianov, "Traditsiia i traditsionalizm v nauchnoi i obshchestvennoi mysli Rossii (60-e – 90-e gg. XX veka)," *Obshchestvennie nauki i sovremennost* 1 (2000): 68–77.

[91] Vitalii Averianov, "Traditsiia kak preemstvennost i sluzhenie," *Chelovek* 2 (2000): 38–51.

of moral values rather than its religious sense as the "ecclesiastic canonical tradition."[92]

By contrast, Averianov sought to extricate the concept of tradition from its "modern widespread understanding" and restore the relevance of the theological concept of "Holy Tradition" in Russia's sociopolitical debates.[93] In doing so, Averianov partly built on the critique of modern society by Western traditionalist philosophers, referring to René Guénon's opus *Symbols of Sacred Science* (1964) to blame the pluralism and moral relativism of the "open society" on its loss of contact with "its inner sacred tradition" and "the idea of Tradition with a capital letter."[94] In line with this, Averianov advocated a multifaceted conception of tradition that includes (1) tradition as an order of inheritance, which ensures the reproduction of "the essence of the inherited" through a set of rules and obligations, (2) tradition as a process of inheritance, which ensures the "adequate renewal of the content embedded in [the sociocultural inheritance]," and (3) a traditional system, which corresponds to the entire society and culture, forming "the complete tradition as a whole" and perpetuating it through traditional ideology, institutions, and organizations. However, Averianov departed from European traditionalism by adding a fourth aspect to tradition, which he called "tradition as a sacred hearth (*ochag*)" and which he grounded in Russian Orthodox theology. In his view, this fourth aspect of tradition is a God-driven "Revelation" without which tradition would turn into an "inert stranglehold."[95] Here, Averianov opposed the European traditionalist conception of sacred tradition as fundamentally esoteric. Instead, he built on the teachings of the early Christian theologians Saint Basil the Great and Saint Dionysius the Areopagite to argue that the mysterious, transcendental meaning of tradition is not encrypted in "esoteric darkness" but rather is characteristic of its "internal apophaticity" (i.e., its divine nature), which is silent and inaccessible to external consciousness. Averianov's argument against European traditionalist esotericism also applied to its Russian promoters among the older generation of conservatives and,

92 Alexander Agadjanian, "Tradition, Morality and Community: Elaborating Orthodox Identity in Putin's Russia," *Religion, State and Society* 45, no. 1 (2017): 41.
93 Averianov, "Traditsiia kak preemstvennost i sluzhenie."
94 Averianov, "Traditsiia kak preemstvennost i sluzhenie."
95 Averianov, "Traditsiia kak preemstvennost i sluzhenie."

in particular, to Dugin. According to Averianov, in Dugin's theory, the "principle of 'esotericism' stands above the principle of 'traditionalism,'" and "sacred traditions turn out to be tools in the hands of secret occult forces."[96] Moreover, while Dugin emphasized the existence of a primordial sacred tradition common to all societies, Averianov viewed "Sacred Tradition" as culturally, nationally, and religiously entrenched in Russian Orthodoxy.[97] Averianov further stressed the gap between his conception of "spontaneous Russian traditionalism" and what he perceived as Dugin's "fake Orthodox traditionalism."[98] He pejoratively portrayed Dugin's traditionalism as a "fashionable" and "postmodern" posture against the "neoliberal" ideological environment of the 1990s and denounced its instrumental and contextual character.[99]

Another important difference between Averianov's traditionalism and the European-inspired traditionalism of Dugin was its relationship to modernity. While Guénon and Dugin radically opposed the "ideology of modernism" as shaped by the post-Reformation Western *logos*, Averianov offered a more nuanced perspective, establishing a distinction between destructive innovations and innovations that can be "understood as a kind of divine action."[100] Most importantly, Averianov highlighted the "dynamic" nature of traditionalism, which posits that tradition can rely on its evolutionary and adaptive properties to maintain its "active position in a changing world":

> Unlike the ideology of fundamentalism, which is fixed at a specific stage in the formation of a given civilization, the traditionalism of a complete tradition should be dynamic in nature. It should be tuned to an active position in a changing world and strive to develop its maximum ability to adapt.[101]

Instead of the antimodern character of Dugin's traditionalism, Averianov was closer to the Orthodox modernism that was advocated

96 Averianov, "Traditsiia i traditsionalizm v nauchnoi i obshchestvennoi mysli Rossii (60-e – 90-e gg. XX veka)."
97 Averianov, "Traditsiia i traditsionalizm v nauchnoi i obshchestvennoi mysli Rossii (60-e – 90-e gg. XX veka)."
98 Vitalii Averianov, "Raznye konservatizmy, raznye traditsionalizmy," pravoslavie.ru, September 4, 2001, http://averianov.net/sii/475/?h=670.
99 Averianov, "Raznye konservatizmy, raznye traditsionalizmy."
100 Averianov, "Traditsiia kak preemstvennost i sluzhenie."
101 Averianov, "Traditsiia kak preemstvennost i sluzhenie."

by Russian cosmists at the end of the nineteenth century and beginning of the twentieth.[102] Indeed, as demonstrated by his article "Civilization in the Labyrinths of Cosmism," published in 2003, Averianov was acquainted with the work of Nikolai Fedorov, Vladimir Vernadskii, Konstantin Tsiolkosvkii, and Aleksandr Chizhevskii.[103] He hailed Fedorov as a "great reformer of Christianity" and argued that Russian cosmism's "synthesis of positive science and religious philosophy" set the preconditions that allowed for the major Soviet technological breakthroughs.

Averianov has particularly stressed the central influence of the Orthodox émigré theologian Vladimir Lossky (1903–58) on his conception of tradition. First, Averianov built on Lossky's neopatristic approach to theology, focused on the teaching of early Christian authors. As explained by the scholar Andrey Shishkov, this emphasis represented a conservative reaction against the nineteenth-century Orthodox theological tradition, which they claimed had been influenced by Western philosophy and viewed as being prone to "pseudomorphosis" (heterodoxy, distortion, and perversion).[104]

Alongside this rigorist approach to Orthodox theology, Averianov credited Lossky with originating a "dynamic" concept of tradition aimed at adapting past heritage to present times. Averianov viewed this "dynamic" aspect of tradition as facilitating the "full-fledged creativity" of new interpretations within church traditionalism.[105] This interpretation enabled Averianov to develop an ideology centered on the Orthodox tradition's dynamic role in influencing and guiding secular culture and societal orientations.

Averianov formulated this ideology in a series of three articles published on the religion page of *Nezavisimaia gazeta*'s website during 2000–2001. This move away from academic journals to a mainstream media platform expressed his intention to popularize his theoretical

102 On Russian cosmism's Orthodox modernism, see Boris Knorre, "Fedorovskoe religiozno-filosofskoe dvizhenie kak primer religioznogo modernizma," *Russian Review* 10 (2006).

103 Vitalii Averianov, "Tsivilizatsiia v labirintakh kosmizma," *Ekspert* 5 (2003), http://averianov.net/sii/528/?h=478.

104 Andrey Shishkov, "Eastern Orthodoxy, Conservatism, and (Neo)Palamite Tradition in Post-Soviet Russia," in *Contemporary Russian Conservatism: Problems, Paradoxes, and Perspectives*, ed. Mikhail Suslov and Dmitry Uzlaner, 332–33.

105 Averianov, "Raznye konservatizmy, raznye traditsionalizmy."

ideas to a broader readership. In the article "On the 'Synthesis' of Orthodox Ideology," he introduced the term "dynamic conservatism" for the first time, defining it as the ideology he advocated:

> Dynamic conservatism [is] the infinite ability and readiness of a tradition that has only one source of origin (God) to renew its manifestations.[106]

He also spelled out his vision of the balance between tradition and modernity:

> Tradition does not avoid innovations and does not fight against them, but presupposes the determination of clear boundaries within which the effect of innovation is possible and beyond which it cannot go.[107]

Dynamic conservatism assumed a clear political role for the Orthodox Church. In his article "Today, the Russian Church Is Needed More than Anything Else," Averianov argued that the church and the church tradition "established the sole correct direction in blending the eternal and the temporal, in creating new forms of inheritance from the past."[108] However, departing from traditional religious conservatism, Averianov advocated for a "reconciliation" between the "ecclesiastical way of life" and the realities of the modern world.[109] He further proposed utilizing modernity and modernism as "instruments" in the service of the Orthodox Church:

> What is relevant for the Church is not to conform to the demands of modern institutions, but for modern tools and methods to align with its spiritual needs. Orthodoxy should equip itself with the entire arsenal of weapons of the modern liberal civilization, putting its powerful and effective technology at its service.[110]

Averianov's politicization of Orthodoxy was strongly rejected by other leading religious thinkers, such as the historian Aleksandr Krylezhev (1957–) and scholar of Christian theology Konstantin Kostiuk (1967–). Krylezhev deplored the work of Averianov, claiming that he represented "the newest type of 'Orthodox thinkers' and

106 Vitalii Averianov, "O 'sinteze' pravoslavnoi ideologii," *NG religii*, March 7, 2000, http://averianov.net/sii/479/?h=639.
107 Averianov, "O 'sinteze' pravoslavnoi ideologii."
108 Averianov, "Segodnia russkoi tserkvi 'Bolshe vsekh nado.'"
109 Averianov, "Segodnia russkoi tserkvi 'bolshe vsekh nado.'"
110 Averianov, "O 'Sinteze' pravoslavnoi ideologii."

modern theo-ideologists ... who borrow the concept of Tradition in its theological sense and transfer it to society."[111] Kostiuk similarly denounced Averianov's transformation of "values dear to a Christian: tradition, morality, religiosity, collegiality" into the "simple set of values of 'dynamic conservatism': authoritarianism, syncretism, imperialism, nationalism, militarism, isolationism."[112]

Averianov's theorization of "dynamic conservatism" was thoroughly developed in the Russian Doctrine, published in 2005.[113]

5.3.2 Russian Doctrine: A Policy Program Based on Dynamic Conservatism

The Russian Doctrine formulates a complete program of modernization policies relying on dynamic conservatism's mixed approach to tradition and innovation, covering six areas – "A Spiritual and Political Nation," "The Russian Soul," "The Russian State," "The Russian Economy," "The Russian Society," and "Paths toward Transformation."

The doctrine advocates for a traditionalist agenda, emphasizing the "rebirth and new ascent of the Russian civilization" as an alternative to what the perceived crisis and decline of the "liberal paradigm" and the "liberal world order."[114] The authors propose a cyclical economic vision, suggesting that the cycle of integration and globalization started in the 1980s was to be substituted with a cycle of "disintegration and restoration of a new balance of nations and civilizations."[115] This perspective, which reproduces the long wave theory of Soviet economist Nikolai Kondratiev (1892–1938), highlights several trends exhausting the neoliberal model of economic globalization: the emergence of "independent emission centers with stable currency sovereignty," such as the euro and the Chinese yuan, challenging the international dollar standard, and, most importantly, China's industrial and economic rise

111 Aleksandr Kyrlezhev, "Tupiki provintsialnogo myshleniia," *Nezavisimaia gazeta*, October 18, 2000, www.ng.ru/ideas/2000-10-18/8_tupik.html.
112 Quoted in Averianov, "Segodnia russkoi tserkvi 'bolshe vsekh nado.'"
113 The doctrine was first published as a brochure by the Center of Dynamic Conservatism and was later issued in a book edition of more than 800 pages. See *Russkaia Doktrina* (Moscow: Iauza-Press, 2007).
114 "Tezisy Russkoi Doktriny." 115 "Tezisy Russkoi Doktriny."

confronting Western dominance.[116] The authors argue that "around 2010 and maybe even earlier, the Western powers will abandon the course of globalization due to their inability to compete with China."[117]

In response to this analysis, the authors call for Russia's withdrawal from global economic integration processes and for the adoption of a political agenda based on the development of its "Tradition-Civilization." They define "Tradition-Civilization" as a "single complex of a human community," where the "traditional core" and the "civilization shell" continuously interact and renew each other through a blend of "spiritual, intellectual and humanitarian mechanisms" alongside "technological, social and economic mechanisms."[118] Achieving "harmony within Tradition-Civilization," they assert, represents the "historical ideal and task of the ideology of dynamic conservatism."[119]

The doctrine's traditionalist agenda includes several key points. First, it assumes a continuist vision of Russia's history, rejecting the idea of a historical and legal break with the Russian Empire in 1917 and with the Soviet Union in 1991. Consequently, contemporary Russia is seen as the direct heir to the medieval Muscovy, founded at the end of Mongol rule in 1480. As further put by the doctrine, the preservation of Russia's original sovereignty and its "political and cultural constants" necessitates distancing the country from Western influences.[120] In particular, in opposition to the Western Roman legal culture, the doctrine posits that the Russian legal tradition is based on a "synthesis of Roman and Byzantine law."[121] The authors therefore declare that adhesion to what they perceive as Western-inspired legal principles, such as the "principle of separation of powers" and the "supremacy of human rights," is "non-binding" and "debatable."[122] Instead, they put forward the concepts of "spiritual sovereignty" and "social truth" as the Russian state's authentic "supervalues."[123] The doctrine elaborates on "spiritual sovereignty"[124] to assert that

116 "Tezisy Russkoi Doktriny." 117 "Tezisy Russkoi Doktriny."

118 "Osnovnye poniatiia i terminy Russkoi Doktriny," rusdoctrina.ru, www.rusdoctrina.ru/page95513.html.

119 "Osnovnye poniatiia i terminy Russkoi Doktriny."

120 "Tezisy Russkoi Doktriny." 121 "Tezisy Russkoi Doktriny."

122 "Tezisy Russkoi Doktriny." 123 "Tezisy Russkoi Doktriny."

124 On the concept of "spiritual security" as a component of Russia's national security, see Julie Fedor, "Chapter 7: Securitizing the Russian Soul," in *Russia and the Cult of State Security: The Chekist Tradition, from Lenin to Putin* (London: Routledge, 2013), 2, footnote 8.

Russia's national sovereignty relies as much on the protection of its physical territory as on the preservation of its authentic self, its "otherness," and "civilizational independence."[125]

Aligned with Averianov's worldview, the doctrine adopts an imperialist rather than ethnonationalist vision of Russia's national identity. The authors view the concept of nation-state as dangerous and conducive to the fragmentation of Russia's territory.[126] Instead, they advocate for the imperial nature of the Russian state, where the Russian ethnic core, which they refer to as the "Great Russians" (Velikorossy), defines the ethnocultural character of the Russian state and civilization while interacting with "the ethnic minorities" within a "supranational alliance."[127] In this context, the term Russian (*russkii*), as used in the title of the doctrine (Russkaia Doktrina), is intended not in a narrow ethnic sense but rather as an expression of Russianness (*russkost*) that encompasses the supranational alliance of all the Russian peoples in "service of Russia" (*sluzheniia Rossii*). As Averianov explained:

> For us, the concept of "Russianness" (*russkost*) is, above all, a civilizational attribute linked to a great culture, a great state and a huge historical space. Everything that is part of this space, that has entered the flesh and blood of our civilization and that has grown into the rhythm of the nation's and the country's life, is considered Russian (*russkii*).[128]

However, the doctrine clearly outlines the allegedly "state-building" (*gosudarstvoobrazuiushchii*) role of the "Great Russians" and assumes that Russia's national identity is grounded in Orthodoxy. In the words of the doctrine's authors, Orthodoxy "performs the function of maintaining national identity" and should be regarded as the "force identical to the entire national-state tradition in Russia."[129] As a result, the doctrine presses for the desecularization of the Russian state and the transition to a confessional regime enacting the "union of the state with the Church."

125 "Tezisy Russkoi Doktriny."
126 See the entry "natsionalizm" in "Osnovnye poniatiia i terminy Russkoi Doktriny."
127 "Tezisy Russkoi Doktriny."
128 Vitalii Averianov, "Russkaia Doktrina: Eto sobiraiushchii, a ne razdeliaiushchii dokument," Interfaks-Religiia, August 20, 2007, http://averianov.net/sii/491/?h=635.
129 "Tezisy Russkoi Doktriny."

Furthermore, the doctrine advocates a theocratic vision of the Russian state, suggesting that its sovereignty is founded on its eschatological mission as the world's *katechon*. Scholar Victor Shnirelman emphasizes that the doctrine draws on Metropolitan Ioann's identification of the Christian concept of *katechon*, defined by the Apostle Paul in the Bible as the force that restrains the advent of the Antichrist, aligning this concept with Russia's world mission and great power status.[130] The doctrine also upholds the messianic vision of Russia as the "Third Rome," heir to the Christian *katechonic* early Roman and Byzantine empires. In this view, Russia assumes the role of the world's savior, offering an alternative to both the "new paganism of the West" and the "new barbarism of the South." Unlike the Western-centric nature of the post–Cold War order, the doctrine's geopolitics pictures Russia as the leader of an alternative globalization based on a multipolar world and on the development of regional partnerships. Accordingly, Russia would become the initiator of a Eurasian alliance including Iran, India, and China, based on a collective security treaty and economic and cultural cooperation.

The doctrine's traditionalism is coupled with an ambitious modernizing program of economic, social, and technological development. The authors challenge the common perception of "conservative reforms" as a "logical contradiction." Instead, they contrast dynamic conservatism with "classic conservatism," arguing that Orthodox traditionalism can harmoniously be integrated with modernizing policies:

> Contrary to the popular opinion of the intelligentsia, the Orthodox tradition has consistently demonstrated examples of socioeconomic, political and cultural modernization without compromising its doctrinal foundations. The Russian faith has always embraced the goal of building an earthly social system that does not provide an escape from the world but rather aims to transform it and establish a world power (by building a spiritual and political stronghold against destructive forces).

As Averianov later explained, the doctrine's authors were not driven by a reactionary attitude seeking to preserve a fixed past tradition. Instead, they aimed to guide Russia's development according to an

130 Victor Shnirelman, "Russian Neoconservatism and Apocalyptic Imperialism," in *Contemporary Russian Conservatism: Problems, Paradoxes, and Perspectives*, ed. Mikhail Suslov and Dmitry Uzlaner, 364.

ideal of tradition that has manifested in various forms throughout Russian history:

> We do not consider ourselves fundamentalists; we do not believe that there was a certain "golden age" in the past of Russia that deserves blind worship and to which we must return. Rather, we strive to reconstruct Russia as it could have been if it had not been prevented from developing its national-state tradition ... Our task is to reconstruct the normal future of Russia.[131]

The doctrine therefore portrays itself as an "ideology of national development and growth."[132] A dedicated chapter addresses economic issues, contrasting itself with the liberal economic model by advocating a developmental economy set on achieving "social truth." As the authors explain, social truth, along with spiritual sovereignty, is the "highest spiritual and political ideal of Russia."[133] It is based on a range of values such as "harmony of the social strata," "protection of the poorest and the weakest," "subordination of the goals of economy and politics to the goals of the society," and the "disclosure of the creative potential of the people and the individual."[134]

As noted by Katharina Bluhm, the authors do not call for a return to a Soviet-type planned economy, or to the ancestral ideal of the "community-romance."[135] They accept the market economy and private property but advocate strong state economic models, such as Japan in the 1950s, France and Italy in the 1960s, South Korea and Taiwan in the 1980s, and China in the 2000s. The doctrine opposes Russia's membership in the WTO and the "open economy" model, pleading instead for a "transition towards a reasonable protectionism."[136] Key policy recommendations include combating capital flight, promoting domestic investments through by revising the credit system, and stimulating internal demand through wage increases and social policy reforms.

Moreover, the authors envision a uniquely Russian archetype of the businessman, referred to as the "house-builder" (*domostroitel*). Unlike the Western *Homo economicus*, driven by consumption and

131 Averianov, "Posle sobornykh slushanii opponenty zabespokoilis."
132 See "velikii perelom" in "Osnovnye poniatiia i terminy Russkoi Doktriny."
133 "Tezisy Russkoi Doktriny."
134 "Osnovnye poniatiia i terminy Russkoi Doktriny."
135 Bluhm and Varga, *New Conservatives in Russia and East Central Europe*, 12.
136 "Tezisy Russkoi Doktriny."

personal enrichment, the house-builder views economy and finance as tools for social service and solidarity.[137] The doctrine also calls for significant state investments in innovation, education, research, and "breakthrough strategic scientific projects" to transition from an oil-dependent economy to a leading producer of technologies. The authors foresee a new "era of supermodernity," termed the "cognitive era," succeeding postindustrialism. In this vision, technological progress and human enhancement are religiously anchored, with the expansion of "human capabilities" allowing individuals to "develop the enormous creative possibilities inherently placed in them by God."[138]

To undertake these reforms, the doctrine outlines a series of concrete transformative measures, including the "large-scale rotation of elites" and "significant repressions."[139] While citing Stalin and Ivan the Terrible as examples of authoritarian leadership, the authors advocate for measures they describes as less severe, defining "repressions" as primarily involving "loss of status" and "confiscation of property."[140] Additionally, they recommend the implementation of a new "Law on Mass Media" with rigid controls and censorship mechanisms. They argue that high-level state committees composed of intellectual elites should determine the country's policy agenda.[141] For instance, the State Committee for the Vitality of the People would focus on "restoring demographic well-being," beginning with a proposed five-year state of emergency to address the issues of demography, family and marriage, birth, and medical care of the younger generation.[142]

In conclusion, the Russian Doctrine formulates an authoritarian and religiously grounded vision of Russia's path to modernization. Initially seen as a pivotal moment in the emergence of Young Conservatism as a public movement upon its publication in the autumn of 2005, it subsequently gained traction beyond their ranks, influencing broader intellectual, political, religious, and economic circles.

137 See "domostroitel" in "Osnovnye poniatiia i terminy Russkoi Doktriny."
138 See "kognitivnaia epokha" in "Osnovnye poniatiia i terminy Russkoi Doktriny."
139 "Tezisy Russkoi Doktriny."
140 "Tezisy Russkoi Doktriny."
141 "Tezisy Russkoi Doktriny."
142 "Tezisy Russkoi Doktriny."

5.3.3 *The Public Career of the Russian Doctrine*

The Russian Doctrine gained prominence as a public document through a strategic promotion effort orchestrated by its authors to highlight the emergence of a new "ideological and political force."[143]

Unlike the Counter-Reformation, which primarily targeted government officials, the Russian Doctrine aimed at a diverse audience encompassing intellectual, academic, political, administrative, religious, and economic circles.[144] Specifically, the doctrine was directed toward what Averianov termed "healthy business circles," seen as pivotal agents for fostering societal change.[145] This outreach was supported by the organizational infrastructure and financial backing of the Russian Entrepreneur Foundation, which provided substantial resources. This support facilitated the establishment of the "Center for Dynamic Conservatism" to further institutionalize their initiative.

The public launch of the doctrine leveraged the Russian Entrepreneur Foundation's existing networks and connections with ruling elites.[146] The first major public presentation of the doctrine occurred at the "Russian Week" hosted by the Foundation on the Greek island of Corfu in October 2005.[147] This event was supported by the Russian Federal Agency for Military–Technical Cooperation and the Russian embassy in Greece, attracting prominent figures, such as Vitalii Tretiakov, a notable political scientist and media personality; Aleksandr Tsipko, a columnist for *Literaturnaia gazeta*; Valerii Fedorov, the head of the Russian Public Opinion Research Center (VTsIOM); Sergei Pykhtin, a member of the State Duma; and Vasilii Likhachev, a member of the Federation Council, the Federal Assembly's upper house; among others.[148]

According to reports in *Russkii kurier* and *Vremia novostei*, participants expressed some reservations regarding the doctrine's

143 "Tezisy Russkoi Doktriny."

144 See Averianov's description of the doctrine's expected audience in Vitalii Averianov, "Obrashchenie k 'reshitelnomu menshinstvu,'" APN.ru, June 2005, http://averianov.net/sii/450/?h=670.

145 Averianov, "Obrashchenie k 'reshitelnomu menshinstvu.'"

146 Andrei Kobiakov, "Doktrina: Sobornyi trud," *Zavtra* 39 (September 2007).

147 "Vsia khronika."

148 Nikolai Poroskov, "Novye odissei," *Vremia novostei* 198 (October 25, 2005).

"mysticism," "monarchism," and "utopianism."[149] However, the doctrine's authors objective was largely achieved as the document was widely recognized as a significant political event that elevated their visibility in the public sphere. Federation Council member Likhachev purportedly committed to supporting the doctrine's promotion within government bodies.[150]

An immediate outcome of this event was the publication of excerpts from the doctrine in the November 2005 issue of *Politicheskii klass* magazine. Subsequent public presentations of the Russian Doctrine quickly followed.[151] Networking initiatives included the Saint Petersburg Patriotic Forum, which was attended by representatives from Orthodox academic institutions, Orthodox clergy, and conservative public figures.[152] Notably, on December 1, 2005, the doctrine was extensively discussed during a conference organized by the Union of Writers of Russia, of which many doctrine authors were members. This union, a gathering place for conservative writers and publicists, bridged generational gaps among conservatives. Leading national-patriotic figures – such as Valentin Rasputin, the village prose writer; Stanislas Kuniaev, the editor-in-chief of *Nash Sovremennik*; and Sergei Baburin, one of the leaders of the Rodina party and the vice-speaker of the State Duma – attended this meeting and expressed enthusiasm for the doctrine.[153] Valerii Ganichev, chairman of the union, praised it as an "extraordinarily important and significant document."[154] The meeting was also attended by Metropolitan Kirill Gundiaev, who became patriarch of the Russian Orthodox Church in 2009.[155] In his speech, Metropolitan Kirill endorsed the doctrine, suggesting its practical use in national dialogues on Russia's fundamental values.[156]

Throughout 2006, the doctrine and its authors garnered increased attention amid the regime's efforts to solidify its conservative agenda.

149 Sergei Frolov, "Stanet li 'doktrina' panatseei?," *Russkii kurer*, October 24, 2005; Poroskov, "Novye odissei."
150 Poroskov, "Novye odissei."
151 See "Iz ZhZh-dnevnika Egora Kholmogorova." 152 "Vsia khronika."
153 "Iz ZhZh-dnevnika Egora Kholmogorova."
154 Vitalii Averianov, "Nuzhno stat zavisimymi ot budushchego Rossii," APN.ru, December 7, 2005.
155 Metropolitan Kirill entertained close ties with the Union of Writers' chairman Valerii Ganichev, who was the deputy head of the World Russian People's Council, a public organization headed by the Orthodox Church's patriarch.
156 "Razgovor po sushchestvu," Portal "Mir Rossii," December 30, 2005, www.rusdoctrina.ru/page95545.html.

This period followed the 2004 Ukrainian Orange Revolution and the 2005 mass protests against benefit monetization, prompting the Kremlin to launch an ideological counterresponse aimed at preempting domestic revolutions.[157] Central to this conservative shift was Vladislav Surkov, deputy head of the presidential administration and chief ideologue of United Russia.

In the first half of 2006, Surkov theorized the concept of "sovereign democracy" as Russia's model of government.[158] This concept emphasized bolstering state authority to safeguard against internal destabilization akin to color revolutions and to assert Russia's great power status within the global economy.[159] The regime's conservative turn was underscored in May 2006 during Putin's annual address. Previously, in 2005, Putin had emphasized Russia's development as a free and democratic state, aligning with European cultural ideals and prioritizing liberalization and foreign investment in the economy.[160] However, by 2006, Putin's discourse reflected a significant shift toward state-led economic and technological development. He announced a comprehensive investment program in technological innovation and outlined "national projects" in healthcare, education, agriculture, and housing funded through federal budgets.[161] This address marked a turning point for conservative intellectuals, as noted by Prokhanov:

> The presidential message surprised many patriots. Putin, whom we all considered a neoliberal, a Westerner, almost a satellite of the United States, proclaimed a course towards Russia's development and sovereignty.[162]

157 For a detailed examination of the 2005 protests, see Samuel A. Greene, *Moscow in Movement: Power and Opposition in Putin's Russia* (Stanford: Stanford University Press, 2014), 146.

158 Vladislav Surkov, "Nasha rossiiskaia model demokratii nazyvaetsia 'suverennoi demokratiei,'" Edinaia Rossiia, June 28, 2006, https://web.archive.org/web/20080430012854/http://www.edinros.ru/news.html?id=114108.

159 See Clémentine Fauconnier, *Entre le marteau et l'enclume: La fabrication d'une hégémonie partisane dans la Russie de Poutine* (Villeneuve-d'Ascq: Presses Universitaires du Septentrion, 2019), 116.

160 Vladimir Putin, "Annual Address to the Federal Assembly of the Russian Federation," Website of the President of Russia, April 25, 2005, http://en.kremlin.ru/events/president/transcripts/22931.

161 Vladimir Putin, "Annual Address to the Federal Assembly," Website of the President of Russia, May 10, 2006, http://en.kremlin.ru/events/president/transcripts/23577.

162 Sergei Glazev and Aleksandr Prokhanov, "Eto: Nashi idei," *Zavtra* 26 (2006).

To the authors of the Russian Doctrine, Putin's rhetorical shift signaled the dissemination of their ideas within the upper echelons of power. Averianov interpreted Putin's introduction of "national projects" as the inception of a "new course" that diverged from liberal doctrines advocating maximum economic openness.[163]

Following Putin's 2006 address, the doctrine's authors further solidified their position within public discourse. Averianov participated in a roundtable at the Moscow mayor's office, bringing together notable political and intellectual figures to discuss Putin's speech. Likewise, Andrei Kobiakov appeared on the sociopolitical TV program *National Interest*, hosted by Dmitrii Kisilev on Rossia 1, a prominent progovernmental media platform, marking a pivotal moment in the public promotion of the Russian Doctrine. Kobiakov joined popular public experts such as Tretiakov, Tsipko, and Valerii Fadeev, editor-in-chief of *Ekspert* magazine.[164] Moreover, during the broadcast, the journalist Kisilev described Putin's discourse as an "unusually ideologized address" and stressed its proximity to the ideas of the Russian Doctrine:

> Last week, Vladimir Putin put forwards the key elements of a national doctrine. A group of Russian intellectuals have proposed their own version, much more extensive and detailed. The goals are the same—a strong and prosperous Russia. The intonation is also close.[165]

Furthermore, Fadeev, who spearheaded the publication of an economic doctrine titled "Return to Leadership" for the ruling party United Russia, acknowledged that his work aligned perfectly with the economic section of the Russian Doctrine.[166]

The doctrine's authors consolidated their influence in the media and public discourse by establishing a website dedicated to discussions and analyses of the Russian Doctrine, rusdoctrina.ru. In 2007, an updated and revised edition of the Russian Doctrine was published as a book by the prominent publishing house Iauza-Press. Initially printed in April with 5,000 copies, it was reissued with an additional 5,000 copies in September.[167] The book's release was accompa-

[163] Averianov, "Konservatizm v otdelno vziatoi strane." [164] "Vsia khronika."
[165] "RTR programma 'Natsionalnyi interes,'" May 14, 2006, www.rusdoctrina.ru/page95537.html.
[166] "RTR programma 'Natsionalnyi interes.'" [167] "Vsia khronika."

nied by a series of public presentations and conferences. For example, Averianov delivered lectures on the doctrine at the Moscow City Pedagogical University (MGPU) and the Russian State University for the Humanities (RGGU) in April and May.

The doctrine delivered its most concrete outputs in key strategic conservative institutions: the Rodina party and the Russian Orthodox Church. Following a meeting with Rodina party leadership in February 2006, the authors of the doctrine were enlisted to draft a programmatic document focusing on demographic and migration issues. Led by Averianov, a team of experts produced the manifesto titled "Saving, Developing and Multiplying the Nation," which heavily drew upon the ideas articulated in the Russian Doctrine. This document, edited by Rodina's leader Dmitrii Rogozin, was endorsed by the party as a cornerstone of its political agenda.[168] In preparation for the parliamentary elections of 2007, Rogozin intensified his collaboration with the authors of the Russian Doctrine. During the founding congress of his new party, Great Russia (Velikaia Rossiia), held in May 2007, the Russian Doctrine was formally declared as the party's ideological bedrock, with copies distributed to all eighty delegates present at the congress.[169]

The Russian Doctrine's authors also established close ties with the Russian Orthodox Church. Significant Orthodox figures hailed the doctrine as a pivotal document. In March 2006, a statement from the Moscow Theological Academy underscored the shared concerns between the church and the doctrine regarding the "decline of Russia" and the endorsement of initiatives aimed at its restoration.[170] While theologians expressed reservations about aspects of the doctrine, such as its assertive stance against the West and its departure from "universal human values," the communiqué recommended leveraging the Russian Doctrine as a foundation for dialogue among all "patriotic forces."[171]

As previously noted, similar sentiments were expressed by Metropolitan Kirill during the Union of Writers meeting in

[168] "Sberezhenie, razvitie i preumnozhenie natsii," 2006, http://averianov.net/doc/618/?h=635.

[169] "Vsia khronika." Eventually, the party was denied registration by the Federal Registration Service and was therefore not allowed to compete in the elections.

[170] Moskovskaia dukhovnaia akademiia, "O Russkoi Doktrine," www.rusdoctrina.ru/page95538.html.

[171] Moskovskaia dukhovnaia akademiia, "O Russkoi Doktrine."

December 2005. Kirill's suggestion to utilize the Russian Doctrine as a platform for a national dialogue on Russia's fundamental values was concretely realized in 2007 through the framework of the World Russian People's Council (Vsemirnyi Russkii Narodnyi Sobor, VRNS). Headed by the patriarch of the Orthodox Church, the VRNS is a public organization established in 1993 with the goal of contributing to the "spiritual, cultural, social, and economic revival of Russia and the Russian [*russkii*] people."[172] According to Averianov, during 2006–2007, the VRNS emerged as "a leading force of a new ideological community," fostering collaboration between the authors of the Russian Doctrine and Orthodox authorities.[173] At its annual congress in 2007, attended by a broad audience of religious and intellectual political figures, the Russian Doctrine was presented by Averianov and Kobiakov. In June of that year, the VRNS Bureau conducted a dedicated discussion on the Russian Doctrine and formally endorsed it in a subsequent public statement:

> The World Russian People's Council discusses and regards the initiative under the general title "Russian Doctrine" as a national program aimed at strengthening statehood, enhancing the welfare of Russian citizens and bolstering our country's position on the global stage.[174]

Two months later, in August 2007, another VRNS council session focusing on the Russian Doctrine took place at the Department for the Church's External Relations. During this gathering, the VRNS Bureau underscored the alignment between its principles and those articulated in the Russian Doctrine:

> Participants in the session affirm that the Russian Doctrine embodies the Council's repeated assertion that traditional moral and spiritual values should form the foundation of the country's social, political, and economic development.[175]

172 On the objectives and mission of the VRNS, see point 2.1 of its founding charter: "O sobore: Ustav."

173 Vitalii Averianov, "Mezhdu tsarstvom i diktaturoi: Sravnivaia 'Proekt Rossiia' i Russkuiu Doktrinu," KM.ru, August 30, 2007, http://averianov.net/sii/490/?h=674.

174 "Vsemirnyi russkii narodnyi sobor rassmatrivaet 'Russkuiu Doktrinu' v kachestve natsionalnogo proekta," June 28, 2007, www.rusdoctrina.ru/page95531.html.

175 "Itogovyi protokol sobornykh slushanii vsemirnogo russkogo narodnogo sobora po teme 'Russkai Doktrina,'" rusdoctrina.ru, n.d., www.rusdoctrina.ru/page95520.html.

Importantly, the bureau announced the initiation of an official collaboration with the authors of the Russian Doctrine. The VRNS tasked them with drafting a doctrine on "Russia's Youth" for presentation at the 2008 annual congress, and with delivering a "Program of medium-term transformations of Russia" at the Ekaterinburg branch congress in July 2008.[176] These announcements garnered extensive media coverage and were generally perceived as marking a conservative shift in the Orthodox Church's identity. A journalist from *Moskovskii Komsomolets*, for instance, characterized the VRNS session on the Russian Doctrine as the first significant church deliberation on the "potential transition from a secular state to a confessional state."[177] Analysts notably highlighted Metropolitan Kirill's political evolution. While in the 1990s Kirill faced criticism from Orthodox fundamentalists for his advocacy of religious pluralism and ecumenism, his outspoken endorsement of the Russian Doctrine indicated a shift toward more radical anti-Western and antiglobalist perspectives.[178] According to a reporter from *Nezavisimaia gazeta*:

> One thing is certain: thanks to Metropolitan Kirill's actions, in the eyes of Russian liberals, the ROC [Russian Orthodox Church] has solidified its positions as a conservative institution.[179]

Finally, the Russian Doctrine garnered support within broader conservative intellectual circles, where it was celebrated as a unifying manifesto. In this regard, the doctrine achieved its stated goal of serving as a platform for uniting diverse conservative viewpoints across generational lines. In 2007, Averianov characterized the doctrine's reception among conservatives as follows:

> The Doctrine possesses a rather unique potential for integration. Both during its development and thereafter, individuals from various shades of

[176] "Itogovyi protokol sobornykh slushanii vsemirnogo russkogo narodnogo sobora po teme 'Russkai Doktrina.'"

[177] Sergei Bychkov, "V Rossii postroiat suverennuiu teokratiiu?," *Moskovskii komsomolets*, September 12, 2007, www.rusdoctrina.ru/page95794.html.

[178] See Kostiuk, "Tri portreta: Sotsialno-eticheskie vozzreniia v russkoi pravoslavnoi tserkvi kontsa XX veka;" Aleksandr Soldatov, "Atomnoe pravoslavie," *Ogonek* 37 (September 2007), www.rusdoctrina.ru/page95795.html; Aleksei Makarkin, "Pravoslavnyi stalinizm," *Ezhednevnyi zhurnal*, September 5, 2007, www.rusdoctrina.ru/page95797.html.

[179] Pavel Krug, "Komu liazhet na stol 'Russkaia Doktrina'?," *Nezavisimaia gazeta*, September 5, 2007, www.rusdoctrina.ru/page95798.html.

patriotic orientations have found common ground within it. They view it as a reason not so much to argue as to help each other.[180]

Indeed, prominent figures from the older national-patriotic generation have praised the doctrine for its ability to synthesize diverse perspectives within the entire conservative community. During the Union of Writers gathering, Baburin, for example, remarked:

> [A]ny writer who is in this room can find in the text of the "Russian Doctrine" what he has previously written or spoken.[181]

Similarly, Dugin highlighted the doctrine's broad and inclusive appeal.[182]

Kalashnikov, one of the three main authors of the doctrine and a frequent *Zavtra* contributor, played a key intermediary role in fostering the circulation between the doctrine's ideas and *Zavtra*'s editorial board. A lengthy interview with Kobiakov was featured in *Zavtra* in 2007, setting the first steps of interaction and exchange between these two communities of conservative thinkers.[183] Prokhanov himself has endorsed the Russian Doctrine as an effort to solidify "Putin's new course."[184] He viewed the doctrine in a similar vein to his own work following Putin's 2006 speech, where he sought to articulate the ideological framework underpinning what he perceived as the regime's trajectory toward restoring Russia as an empire. Prokhanov's essay titled *The Symphony of the Fifth Empire*, published in 2006, portrayed Putin as a providential leader whose actions would lead to the restoration of the Russian "Fifth Empire."[185] The authors of the Russian Doctrine welcomed Prokhanov's "Fifth Empire" theory positively. Averianov, for example, positioned both projects within the same "new patriotic wave," characterizing them as contributing to a "polyphonic environment of social thought" unified by a similar agenda.[186]

180 Averianov, "Russkaia Doktrina: Eto sobiraiushchii, a ne razdeliaiushchii dokument."
181 "Razgovor po sushchestvu."
182 "Radio 'Svoboda,'" August 20, 2007, www.rusdoctrina.ru/page95813.html.
183 Kobiakov, "Doktrina: Sobornyi trud." 184 "Radio 'Svoboda.'"
185 Aleksandr Prokhanov, *Simfoniia "Piatoy imperii"* (Moscow: Eksmo, 2007).
186 Averianov, "Mezhdu tsarstvom i diktaturoi: Sravnivaia 'Proekt Rossiia' i Russkuiu Doktrinu."

Therefore, the Russian Doctrine emerged as a pivotal document that united key conservative political, religious, and media institutions, defining a shared agenda spanning different generations.

5.4 Conclusion

This chapter has disclosed the social and doctrinal processes through which dynamic conservatism consolidated as a fully theorized and publicly circulating ideological label. It has illustrated how the formation of this ideology corresponded with the rise of a cohort of young conservative intellectuals intent on redefining modern Russian conservatism. This process of shaping ideological identity was influenced by the group's interactive social dynamics and doctrinal distinctions from older generations of hawkish thinkers and competing ideological factions.

Furthermore, the chapter has highlighted the successful establishment of the Young Conservatives as a new segment of the intellectual elite, contributing to policy discourse. The Russian Doctrine, published in 2005, promoted dynamic conservatism as a comprehensive ideology that systematically integrated conservative traditionalism with technological modernity. The doctrine's trajectory in the public sphere, along with its endorsement by key political and religious conservative entities, underscored dynamic conservatism's capacity to compete operationally with alternative sociopolitical theories of modernization.

6 *Inside the Regime's Market for Ideology (2005–2012)*

Around 2005, the Kremlin actively appeared on the market [of ideas]. [Vladislav] Surkov started buying ideas, buying resources ...

A completely new type of division emerged, between those who received money from the government and those who did not, those who went to the service of the regime, no matter from which side and with what kind ideology, and those who did not.

A., political consultant, interview, Moscow, 2019

As outlined in preceding chapters, by 2005, conservative thinkers spanning different generational cohorts had gained legitimacy within Russia's intellectual elite. From 2005 onward, these ideologues began establishing ties with the political circles. Notably, the ruling party, United Russia, increasingly relied on them to bolster social and ideological backing against challenges posed by liberal and nationalist opposition groups.

Following the cycle of protests and shifts in elite leadership during the winter of 2011–12, a think tank encompassing both older and younger generations of hawkish conservatives – the Izborskii Klub – formalized transactional mechanisms between intellectual and political spheres. This institutionalization solidified ideology production as a strategic asset patronized by members of the ruling elite. The Izborskii Klub convened individuals with diverse ideological leanings, from Marxism–Leninism to monarchism, under a broad "state-patriotic" (*gosudarstvenno-patrioticheskii*) ideology integrating traditional values with advanced economic and technological modernization.[1] Initially comprising twenty-five members, the club has since expanded into the largest coalition of conservative figures, comprising approximately sixty members from varied professional backgrounds including

[1] See the "About Us" section of the Izborskii Klub's website: "O klube," Izborskii Klub, https://izborsk-club.ru/about.

intellectuals, politicians, economists, journalists, entrepreneurs, clerics, and members of the security forces.

This chapter demonstrates that, while the regime selectively adopted some of the hawks' ideas over the years 2005–12, it remained committed to the principle of "managed pluralism." Originally coined by Harley Balzer to describe the mix of authoritarian and liberal principles during Putin's first term, this phrase has been adopted by other scholars to describe the regime's approach to fostering and restricting pluralism in certain policy sectors based on its perception of acceptability.[2] This chapter shows that managed pluralism also applies to the field of ideological production, as the regime did not seek to endorse a single state ideology but rather aimed to amplify certain idea networks over others in response to changing strategic environments.

Analysis of the career paths of conservative ideologues from 2005 to 2013 is based on publications and materials archives on their websites such as the website of the Institute of Dynamic Conservatism[3] and the website of the Izborskii Klub.[4] All the routine activities of the club are registered in the monthly journal of the club, *Izborskii Klub: Russkie strategii*, under the section "Chronology of the Club's Events" (*Khronologiia meropriiatii kluba*).[5] In addition, the chapter is based on interviews conducted with representatives of political elites involved during the period studied, as well as with the Izborskii Klub's leadership – its chairman, Aleksandr Prokhanov, and its two deputy chairmen, Vitalii Averianov and Aleksandr Nagornii – and with several other members of the club.[6] Finally, biographical details of the club's members provided on their profile page of the club's website were used to undertake a prosopographic analysis of their identity as a group. However, these details were not systematically verified, they are presented here as provided by the site. Annex 2 identifies the professional occupation of each of the twenty-five founding

2 Harley Balzer, "Managed Pluralism: Vladimir Putin's Emerging Regime," *Post-Soviet Affairs* 19, no. 3 (2003): 189–227; Damian Strycharz, "More than Putin: Managed Pluralism in Russia's Foreign Policy," *International Affairs* 100, no. 2 (2024): 655–74.

3 See the section "Materials of the IDK Website (2009–12)" (Materialy saita IDK [2009–2012]): www.dynacon.ru/arh_idk.

4 https://izborsk-club.ru.

5 See the list of the journal's issues for the year 2013: https://izborsk-club.ru/magazine#2013.

6 See the list of interviews in Annex 1.

members of the club and details their connection to specific social milieus: universities, the media, partisan organizations, state institutions, and religious organizations. Annex 3 also uses biographical data to rank each of the additional members who joined in the 2013–12 period according to the type of resource they have brought to the club – such as financing, public outreach, analytical expertise, advocacy, and relations with the political establishment.

6.1 Ideology in Transaction between Intellectual and Political Elites

6.1.1 The Ruling Party's Outsourcing of Ideological Production to Russian Hawks

Following the Ukrainian Orange Revolution in 2004 and the 2005 demonstrations against the monetization of pensioners' benefits, the ruling elites started to organize an ideological counterreaction against the spread of antiregime criticism.

Although the leaders of the presidential party, United Russia, had previously emphasized their lack of interest in ideology, in 2005 they created a think tank called "The Center of Social-Conservative Politics" (Tsentr sotsialno-konservativnoi politiki) with the aim of influencing a debate on the party's ideological identity. These efforts led to the creation of an internal party think tank, the Center for Social-Conservative Politics (Tsentr sotsialno-konservativnoi politiki), and two discussion clubs, the "Social-Conservative Club" (Sotsialno-konservativnii klub) and the liberal-conservative "4th November Club" (Klub 4 noiabria). As shown by Clémentine Fauconnier and Marlène Laruelle, these clubs testified to the emergence of two rival, albeit nonofficial, party wings, the "social conservative" and the "liberal conservative" currents, which mostly argued over the degree of state involvement in the economy.[7] Both currents concurred, in 2006, on the party's self-identification as a "conservative party," whereby

[7] Marlène Laruelle, "Inside and around the Kremlin's Black Box: The New Nationalist Think Tanks in Russia," Institute for Security and Development Policy (2009): 25–31; Clémentine Fauconnier, *Entre le marteau et l'enclume: La fabrication d'une hégémonie partisane dans la Russie de Poutine* (Villeneuve-d'Ascq: Presses Universitaires du Septentrion, 2019), 124.

conservatism was broadly understood as a centrist ideology aimed at the protection and stabilization of the existing order.[8]

In parallel, the party increasingly solicited outside conservative ideologues, including both the national-patriots and the Young Conservatives, as providers of ideological resources for selected purposes. Vladislav Surkov, the deputy head of the presidential administration, played an instrumental role as the main orchestrator of the use of these ideologues for the party's needs. Surkov was primarily concerned with the ideological indoctrination of the youth. In 2005, he founded two mass patriotic youth movements, "Nashi" (Ours) and "Molodaia Gvardiia" (The Young Guard). In an interview, a former employee of the Foundation for Effective Politics (FEP) working closely with Surkov at the time, explained that these youth movements sought to fight a "propaganda battle" against the threat of an orange revolution by training the youth in countering street protests.[9] As shown by Véra Nikolski, Nashi and Molodaia Gvardiia partnered with Aleksandr Dugin's Eurasian Youth Union (Evraziiskii soiuz molodozhi), using it as their main "ideological reservoir."[10] In an interview, a department head of Molodaia Gvardiia in 2006–2009 also reported that the organization had invited Dugin and Prokhanov, along with other experts and political scientists, to speak as guest lecturers.[11] Surkov's engineering of ideological production for the regime also appealed to the younger generation of conservative ideologues. As explained in an interview by a Young Conservative, Surkov ordered a condensed version of the Russian Doctrine, published in 2007 under the title "Time to Spread Your Wings" (*Pora raspravit krylia*).[12] Despite the author considering this version of the Russian Doctrine too lenient, they acknowledged that this commissioned work proved the regime's alignment with its ideas to a certain extent and its intention to foster cooperation.[13]

In 2007, the relationship between the ruling elite and the Young Conservatives became even more cooperative as the regime sought

[8] On United Russia's definition of conservatism, see Fauconnier, 127.
[9] Author interview, Moscow, 2019.
[10] Véra Nikolski, *National-bolchevisme et néo-eurasisme dans la Russie contemporaine: La carrière militante d'une idéologie* (Paris: Mare & Martin, 2013), 353.
[11] Author interview, Moscow, 2019.
[12] Author interview, Moscow, 2019.
[13] Author interview, Moscow, 2019.

to address the rise of interethnic tensions and of antistate nationalist movements. Indeed, in 2006, the murder of ethnic Russians by Chechens in the town of Kondopoga spilled over into a series of clashes between ethnic groups as well as mass meetings against the government held by Russian nationalist groups to call for the eviction of illegal migrants. The standoff between Russian nationalist movements and the political authorities reached a peak in November 2006, when Moscow's mayor decided to ban the Russian March led by the Movement against Illegal Immigration (Dvizhenie protiv nelegalnoi immigratsii or DPNI). It was against this backdrop that Ivan Demidov, one of the leaders of Molodaia Gvardiia responsible for ideology and political work and an adviser to the party's Central Election Commission, launched a reflection process on the theme of Russian nationalism inside the party. This initiative, called the "Russian Project," using the ethnic word for Russian (*russkii*), resulted in the creation of the "Russian Club" (Russkii Klub), headed by Young Conservative Egor Kholmogorov.[14]

Over the period from 2007 to 2008, the Russian Club held regular meetings attended by leading Young Conservatives, such as Mikhail Remizov, Konstantin Krylov, Boris Mezhuev, Vitalii Averianov, and Pavel Sviatenkov. The club played a crucial role in shaping the party's policy agenda concerning Russia's national identity, contributing to documents such as the "Concept of the State National Policy"[15] and the "Law on Naturalization and Citizenship."[16] Additionally, it aimed to counteract the rise of antiregime Russian nationalism while formulating an authorized vision of Russian nationalism. As Demidov clarified during an interview in 2007, the objective was to strategically leverage nationalist sentiments in anticipation of the 2008 presidential elections:

> The appearance of the Russian Project in the pre-election political year is a reaction to efforts by opposition forces to make a populist use of Russian themes.[17]

[14] Ivan Demidov, "Russkii proekt vo vsemirnoi pautine," Sostav.ru, www.sostav.ru/news/2007/05/18/27.

[15] "Russkie v natsionalnoi politike RF," *Russkii obozrevatel*, July 19, 2007, www.rus-obr.ru/ru-club/85.

[16] "Migratsiia i derussifikatsiia v sovremennoi Rossii," *Russkii obozrevatel*, August 2, 2007, www.rus-obr.ru/ru-club/86.

[17] Demidov, "Russkii proekt vo vsemirnoi pautine."

Young Conservatives perceived the establishment of the Russian Club as a progression from their previous "Conservative Meeting," marking a step forward in their access to the political elite. As put by one of them, the Russian Club was a reiteration of the methodology that they had employed to write the "Counter-Reformation" manifesto in 2005, albeit now supported by the party's resources.[18] The primary objective of the Russian Club was to advocate for collaboration between nationalists and the regime, emphasizing the incorporation of nationalist themes into the government's agenda.[19] They criticized nationalist tactics involving street protests, advocating instead for "constructive dialogue with the current political elite" aimed at preserving and strengthening "Russia as a state of the Russian people and the Russian nation."[20] Ideas from the Russian Club were circulated to the highest level of the party's leadership through the intermediary of Demidov. As he explained:

> As the project leader, I was invited to the working group of the presidium of the General Council of United Russia to prepare proposals on national policy and interfaith dialogue.[21]

Demidov's ability to promote the Russian Club's ideas within the party increased after he assumed leadership of the ideological department of the party's political department in February 2008.

However, the delegation of idea generation to external ideologues eventually sparked concerns within the party. A participant in the Russian Club argued that the personal objections of Iurii Shuvalov, director of United Russia's Center for Social-Conservative Policy, who felt that ideology was being usurped from him, led to the termination of the club.[22] Laruelle's analysis, however, highlights that Shuvalov considered the Russian Club's emphasis on the ethnic dimension of Russian national identity too radical, pushing instead for the party's line to return to a supranational understanding of the Russian idea.[23]

18 Author interview, Moscow, 2019.
19 "Krizis russkogo natsionalizma," *Russkii obozrevatel*, October 11, 2007, www.rus-obr.ru/ru-club/91.
20 "Zakat zapada i natsionalizm slobod," *Russkii obozrevatel*, October 25, 2007, www.rus-obr.ru/ru-club/92.
21 Demidov, "Russkii proekt vo vsemirnoi pautine."
22 Author interview, Moscow, 2019.
23 Laruelle, "Inside and around the Kremlin's Black Box," 36.

Meanwhile, the party's reliance on outside ideologues as sources of policy ideas caused divisions among the hawks, dividing those willing to collaborate from those who opposed such alliances.

6.1.2 In or Out of the Regime's Market for Ideology: A Career Path for Ideologues

The regime's strategy of engaging hawkish ideologues was accompanied by a system of resource allocation that included media visibility, honorific status attribution, and financial support. These mechanisms of promotion and demotion of the public profiles of ideologues created new delineations among them, based on their inclination for cooperation or dissent.

In 2005, the establishment of the Civic Chamber (Obshchestvennaia palata), a consultative body comprising representatives from civil society tasked with reviewing proposed legislation, provided a platform for bestowing official recognition and symbolic honors on public figures approved by the government. The initial composition of the Civic Chamber in 2006, consisting of forty-two members personally appointed by Putin, notably included three influential figures from the 1990s generation of national-patriotic ideologues: Leonid Borodin, editor-in-chief of the journal *Moskva*; Valerii Ganichev, chairman of the Union of Writers of Russia; and Pavel Gusev, editor-in-chief of the newspaper *Moskovskii komsomolets*.[24]

Meanwhile, other prominent national-patriotic ideologues such as Dugin and Prokhanov gained increased visibility as they expressed support for Putin's regime. In 2008, Dugin was appointed as a professor of philosophy at Moscow State University, a role that, according to Demidov, acknowledged him as a "recognized and respected political expert" within the ranks of the presidential party.[25] Nikolski further noted that Dugin became a frequent guest on major sociopolitical TV talk shows and an authorized commentator during election broadcasts.[26] In contrast, Eduard Limonov, Dugin's former ally in founding

[24] The list of members was published on the Civic Chamber's website: https://old.oprf.ru/about/chambermembers/members2006.

[25] Cited in Nikolski, *National-bolchevisme et néo-eurasisme dans la Russie contemporaine*, 317.

[26] Nikolski, *National-bolchevisme et néo-eurasisme dans la Russie contemporaine*, 317.

the National Bolshevik Party, maintained his commitment to radical antiregime opposition. Limonov and his party members faced physical confrontations by pro-Kremlin youth organizations like Nashi, culminating in the banning of his party on April 19, 2007.[27]

Prokhanov's increased presence in the mass media also exemplifies the state's cooptation of proregime ideologues. Beginning in 2003, Prokhanov became a regular guest on the sociopolitical TV talk show hosted by the renowned pro-Kremlin journalist Vladimir Solovev. By 2007, he had been invited to serve as a permanent guest on the weekly "Special Opinion" segment of Ekho Moskvy radio.

Beyond his media appearances, Prokhanov's growing influence in the public sphere was tangibly illustrated by his initiative, in 2007, to erect a monument near Pskov known as the Sacred Hill (Sviashchennii Kholm).[28] Described by Prokhanov as "the spiritual center of Russia," the "Sacred Hill" was constructed using earth fragments gathered from across Russia, symbolizing the reunification of Russia's fragmented history.[29] Prokhanov emphasized that this project embodied his commitment to merging spirituality with modern technology, evident in the placement of an Orthodox cross atop a hill constructed using advanced techniques.[30] In realizing this endeavor, Prokhanov demonstrated his ability to garner support from influential figures across military, political, religious, cultural, and academic circles.[31] As he explained, the local branch of United Russia provided financial and organizational assistance for the "Sacred Hill" project.[32]

27 Nikolski, *National-bolchevisme et néo-eurasisme dans la Russie contemporaine*, 342–43.

28 See Edith Clowes, "Provinces, Piety, and Promotional Putinism: Mapping Aleksandr Prokhanov's Counter-Utopian Russia," in *The Post-Soviet Politics of Utopia: Language, Fiction and Fantasy in Modern Russia*, ed. Mikhail Suslov and Per-Arne Bodin (London: I. B. Tauris, 2020), 46–47 and Victoria Donovan, "Militarized Memory," in *Russia's Regional Identities: The Power of the Provinces*, ed. Edith W. Clowes, Gisela Erbslöh, and Ani Kokobobo (London: Routledge, 2018), 76.

29 Aleksandr Prokhanov, "S kholma vidna vsia Rossiia," *Zavtra*, October 2, 2007, http://zavtra.ru/blogs/2007-10-0311.

30 Prokhanov, "S kholma vidna vsia Rossiia."

31 Including the military general Gennadii Troshev, the movie director Nikita Mikhalkov, the Archimandrite Tikhon Shevkunov, the director of the federal state enterprise Admiralty Shipyards, the commander of Pskov's airborne division, and rectors of local universities. See Prokhanov, "S kholma vidna vsia Rossiia."

32 Prokhanov, "S kholma vidna vsia Rossiia."

Its inauguration ceremony, attended by Pskov's administrative officials and blessed by the regional Orthodox bishop, underscored Prokhanov's role in shaping Russian identity and its representation within Russian territory.[33]

The allocation of state resources to proregime ideologues, particularly through financial support, introduced new divisions within intellectual circles. According to a former employee of FEP:

> Just around 2005, the Kremlin actively appeared on the market [of ideas]. Surkov started buying ideas, buying resources ... Before, there were just ideological differences. Some were liberals, other conservatives, the third socialists, something like that. A completely new type of division emerged, between those who received money from the government and those who did not, those who went to the service of the regime, no matter from which side and with what kind ideology, and those who did not. For instance, many oppositionists, especially nationalists, were sympathetic to Dugin. But when he began to work with Surkov, they all turned away from him.[34]

Specifically, the presidential party's approach to Young Conservatives led to fragmentation within the group. Between 2005 and 2007, existing ideological rifts within the group – pitting secular nationalists against Orthodox imperialists – evolved into a political divide centered on attitudes toward cooperation with the regime. This divide became pronounced during the 2006 "Russian March," which occurred amid escalating interethnic tensions and was banned by city authorities as an extremist and xenophobic gathering. While nationalist factions associated with DPNI continued to participate, maintaining their antigovernment stance, Orthodox organizations and leaders like Sergei Baburin and Dmitrii Rogozin withdrew and held a separate meeting. Among Young Conservatives, Orthodox imperialists such as Averianov criticized the agitational shift toward ethnic nationalism, viewing it as a destabilizing force threatening the Russian state.[35] Averianov contrasted this with the "national-patriotic platform," rooted in Russian civilization and Orthodox faith, advocating for a strong authoritarian state.[36] Meanwhile, nationalists joined forces with liberal

33 "V pskovskoi oblasti osviatili krest 'Sviashchennogo Kholma,'" *Regnum*, September 27, 2007, https://regnum.ru/news/economy/891482.html.

34 Author interview, Moscow, 2019.

35 Vitalii Averianov, "Rassypavshaiasia matreshka," RPmonitor, December 2006, http://averianov.net/sii/526/?h=630.

36 Averianov, "Rassypavshaiasia matreshka."

opposition factions in forming a collective antigovernment opposition, as evidenced by Yabloko's public support for the 2006 Russian March in defense of assembly freedoms.[37]

In this evolving landscape, the original unity forged by the threat of the Orange Revolution among Young Conservatives began to dissipate.[38] Instead, as put by Arkadii Maler, some members embraced a "national orangeism," aligning with oppositional liberal forces critical of the government's policies and treatment of ethnic Russians.[39] Others, like Kholmogorov, Averianov, and Maler, sought cooperation with political authorities to bolster state power.[40]

The establishment of the "Russian Club" by United Russia delineated clear distinctions between the two groups. According to one of the club's participants, the funding of its meetings by United Russia played a pivotal role in attracting attendees, as many were still grappling with the lingering economic challenges from the post-Soviet era and came for practical reasons.[41] As they further added, the Russian Club also served to legitimize a specific circle of intellectuals, whom they described as individuals willing to align their ideas and beliefs with the regime's needs for self-preservation, contrasting them with antigovernment nationalists, whom they characterized as radicals.[42] They acknowledged that their own decision to align closer with Kremlin circles had transformed them into a "guardian" (*okhranitel*), dedicated to preserving the regime. In contrast, figures like Pavel Sviatenkov, a prominent member of the Young Conservatives in the early 2000s, criticized the evolution of these guardians into state contractors devoid of intellectual autonomy:

> Being the heir of the 1990s, the political power decided not to engage in dialogue with public intellectuals, but simply to buy them. And in the most unacceptable format—without maintaining autonomy.[43]

37 "Moskovskoe 'Iabloko' podderzhalo provedenie 'Russkogo Marsha,'" Radio sbododa, November 1, 2006, www.svoboda.org/a/269476.html.

38 Arkadii Maler, "Traektorii mladokonservatizma," *Russkii zhurnal*, May 15, 2009, http://russ.ru/Mestnyj-vzglyad/Traektorii-mladokonservatizma.

39 Mikhail Diunov, "Mladokonservatizm: Ego istoriia ego znachenie," *Russkii zhurnal*, December 5, 2009, www.russ.ru/pole/Mladokonservatizm.-Ego-istoriya-ego-znachenie.

40 Diunov, "Mladokonservatizm." 41 Author interview, Moscow, 2019.

42 Author interview, Moscow, 2019.

43 Pavel Sviatenkov, "Veselaia semeika," Politconservatism.ru, September 25, 2015, https://politconservatism.ru/thinking/veselaya-semeyka.

The state's cooptation of some conservative ideologues led to what Laruelle describes as the "etatization" of their beliefs. She notes that conservative intellectuals have been able to "feed [their] ideological products to the Kremlin" through an interactive process with the regime.[44] While Laruelle's analysis focuses on Putin's conservative shift in 2012, the groundwork for the regime's adoption of key hawkish ideas was already being laid during 2007–2008.

By the end of Putin's second term, three significant developments in his policies and discourse underscored this shift. First, the Kremlin embraced protectionist measures and state investment policies advocated by modernist conservatives, diverging from free-market principles. Sergei Glazev, a leader of the Rodina party, noted in 2007 that "almost all of [Rodina's] program requirements are being implemented today, although three years ago they were rejected by the ruling party."[45] He detailed specific measures adopted by the regime that aligned with Rodina's agenda, such as the creation of a development bank, using the stabilization fund for development, and initiating a proactive demographic policy.

Second, Putin promoted the concept of "spiritual security," a core idea in the Russian Doctrine. Russia's 2000 National Security Concept had already highlighted the country's "spiritual renewal" and society's "spiritual and moral development" as national interests.[46] In 2007, Putin further linked the country's security to its spiritual identity. During his Annual Address to the Federal Assembly, he stated that the "spiritual unity of the people" was "as important a factor for development as political and economic stability."[47] In the same year, at the annual press conference, Putin identified Russia's traditional religions and its nuclear arsenal as the two main pillars of national security:

[44] Marlène Laruelle, "Making Sense of Russia's Illiberalism," *Journal of Democracy* 31, no. 3 (2020): 119.

[45] Sergei Glazev, "Nasledie 'Rodiny,'" APN.ru, September 4, 2007, www.apn.ru/index.php?newsid=17727.

[46] "National Security Concept of the Russian Federation," Website of the Ministry of Foreign Affairs of the Russian Federation, January 10, 2000, www.mid.ru/foreign_policy/official_documents/-/asset_publisher/CptICkB6BZ29/content/id/589768.

[47] Vladimir Putin, "Presidential Address to the Federal Assembly," Website of the President of Russia, April 26, 2007, http://en.kremlin.ru/events/president/transcripts/24203.

Both the traditional faiths of the Russian Federation and Russia's nuclear shield are two things that strengthen Russian statehood and create the necessary conditions for ensuring the country's internal and external security.[48]

Finally, Putin enacted a clear anti-Western stance in foreign policy during the 2007 Munich Security Conference, where he criticized the post–Cold War world order and its US-centric unipolarity.[49]

Despite the etatization of some of their beliefs and the state's cooptation of their career, proregime conservative ideologues maintained a critical view of what they perceived as the regime's instrumental use of their ideas according to the context and to its needs. Ilia Brazhnikov, one of the Young Conservatives who chose to cooperate with the regime, similarly highlighted the superficial nature of the regime's conservative rhetoric:

The authorities only adopted a conservative and protectionist rhetoric. After the Munich speech, it experienced some discursive evolution. In essence and in terms of personalities, the power remained the same as it was.[50]

During an interview, a political consultant, who was involved in delivering policy advice to ruling circles as an employee of Pavlovskii's FEP in 2004–2009, also reported the sense of disillusionment felt by many intellectuals following their cooperation with the regime: "We wanted to influence decisions, and they wanted to use us for propaganda purposes."[51]

6.1.3 *Hawks' Lobbying for the Etatization of Their Ideas*

Despite their privileged status gained through cooperation with the regime, hawkish ideologues faced limited autonomy and influence.

[48] "Transcript of Press Conference with the Russian and Foreign Media," Website of the President of Russia, February 1, 2007, http://en.kremlin.ru/events/president/transcripts/24026.

[49] "Speech and the Following Discussion at the Munich Conference on Security Policy," Website of the President of Russia, February 10, 2007, http://en.kremlin.ru/events/president/transcripts/24034.

[50] Ilia Brazhnikov, "Vopreki nazvaniiu doklad nes v sebe dukh istinnoi reformatsii," Politconservatism.ru, September 2, 2015, https://politconservatism.ru/prognosis/vopreki-nazvaniyu-doklad-nyes-v-sebe-dukh-istinnoy-reformatsii.

[51] Author interview, Moscow, 2019.

By the end of Putin's second term, they were profoundly disillusioned with the party system, particularly after their main partisan organization, Rodina, was denied registration for the 2007 legislative elections. Sergei Glazev, one of Rodina's founding leaders, exemplified the choice to forgo political autonomy in favor of policy influence. In 2008, Glazev chose to work with the regime as deputy secretary general of the Eurasian Economic Community,[52] viewing it as the only viable option to promote his ideas:

> The Rodina People's Patriotic Union was perceived by the ruling party as a threat to its serene reign ... The authorities could not like this, since they want to have a monopoly on [the socioeconomic development of the country]. Therefore, it swallowed up our bloc, destroying its organizational component and "digesting" the ideological one ... In general, work in the State Duma has lost any significant meaning. If you want to achieve the adoption of any bill, then you need, firstly, to convince the government of this and, secondly, to join the party in power. Being in the parliamentary opposition, you simply waste time and opportunities to implement your ideas.[53]

Despite the conservative consolidation of the regime during Putin's second term, the ruling elites maintained ideological diversity. Political analysts often characterize the primary divide within the "Putin Court" as between the *siloviki*, originating from the security services, and the "liberals."[54] Although both factions endorsed strong executive power, the *siloviki* favored full state control over the economy, whereas the liberals advocated for a business environment based on entrepreneurial freedom and the rule of law.[55]

The beginning of Dmitrii Medvedev's presidency in 2008, with Putin serving as prime minister, bolstered the liberal faction. Medvedev was committed to democratization and economic modernization, aiming to limit authoritarian state power and strengthen the rule of

52 The Eurasian Economic Community (EAEC) was a regional organization established in 2000 by Russia, Belarus, Kazakhstan, Kyrgyzstan, and Tajikistan. In 2015, the EAEC was terminated and replaced by the Eurasian Economic Union, which includes Armenia, Belarus, Kazakhstan, Kyrgyzstan, and Russia.

53 Glazev, "Nasledie 'Rodiny.'"

54 See, for instance, Olga Kryshtanovskaya and Stephen White, "Inside the Putin Court: A Research Note," *Europe-Asia Studies* 57, no. 7 (2005): 1065–75.

55 Kryshtanovskaya and White, "Inside the Putin Court," 1071.

law. His vision was outlined in his programmatic article published in September 2009, "Russia, Forward!" In the article, Medvedev criticized the outdated "semi-Soviet social sphere" and the "paternalistic attitudes" that fostered the belief that "all problems should be solved by the government."[56] He called for the improvement of Russia's democratic institutions and advocated for a competitive economy based on individual freedom and responsibility. Medvedev also emphasized that Russia's modernization should involve the "harmonization" of its relations with Western democracies through the "rapprochement and interpenetration of [their] cultures and economies."[57] In line with Western liberal modernization theories, Medvedev believed that technological advancements would drive Russia's economic and political liberalization:

> The growth of modern information technologies, something we will do our best to facilitate, gives us unprecedented opportunities for the realization of fundamental political freedoms, such as freedom of speech and assembly.[58]

Medvedev's reformist approach to policymaking, which was critical of central state power, fostered the emergence of new expert groups outside state institutions. Scholar Ilia Kukulin contends that Medvedev's modernization program ignited a debate across "most groups of the political spectrum" regarding the definition of "modernization."[59] This "battle of modernities" resulted in the creation of "rival lobbies," each vying to position themselves as "advisers" to the president, who assumed an "arbiter" role.[60]

The foundation of the Institute of Dynamic Conservatism (Institut Dinamicheskogo Konservatizma, IDK) in 2009 by the lead authors of the Russian Doctrine, Averianov and Kobiakov, positioned itself within the growing landscape of think tanks and expert groups aiming to influence ruling elites with their ideas and concepts. As Averianov explained, this initiative implements the concept of a "thinking

56 "Dmitry Medvedev's Article, Go Russia!" Website of the President of Russia, September 10, 2009, http://en.kremlin.ru/events/president/news/5413.
57 "Dmitry Medvedev's Article, Go Russia!"
58 "Dmitry Medvedev's Article, Go Russia!"
59 Ilia Kukulin, "Sentimentalnaia tekhnologiia: Pamiat o 1960-kh v diskussiiakh o modernizatsii 2009–2010 godov," *Neprikosnovennyi zapas* 6 (2010).
60 Kukulin, "Sentimentalnaia tekhnologiia: Pamiat o 1960-kh v diskussiiakh o modernizatsii 2009–2010 godov."

corporation" (*mysliashchaia korporatsiia*), an idea originally proposed by Glazev.[61]

With the IDK, hawkish ideologues developed the organizational apparatus and habits of a think tank aimed at contributing to the government's agenda. Such practices included holding "expert meetings," "seminars," and "roundtables" addressing concrete policy areas such as innovation politics, the global economic crisis, energy policy, and Russia's entry into the World Trade Organization.[62] The institute also produced analytical documents (*doklady*), forecasts, and group memoranda. Shortly after its founding, the IDK demonstrated its influence at the highest levels of political decision-making. At Medvedev's personal request, Maksim Kalashnikov, a key IDK member, was convened for a meeting with the head of the presidential administration, Sergei Sobianin, to present policy recommendations on Russia's technological development. Later on, Kalashnikov also met with Surkov, who was at the time Sobianin's deputy in charge of domestic affairs. Following these meetings, Kalashnikov's proposals were forwarded to the Russian Academy of Sciences for further examination.[63]

Within the environment of think tanks, the IDK positioned itself as a conservative counterbalance to the Institute of Contemporary Development (Institut sovremennogo razvitiia, INSOR), led by liberal economist Igor Iurgens and officially associated with Medvedev.[64] As Edwin Bacon has highlighted, INSOR's reports focused on modernization and advocated for Russia's full integration into the West through extensive democratization reforms and cooperation with Western powers, including NATO membership.[65] The IDK sought to

[61] Averianov, "Mysliashchaia korporatsiia," *Moskovskie novosti*, October 14, 2007.

[62] See, for instance: "Realnyie innovatsii i ikh imitatsii v Rossii," dynacon.ru, June 10, 2009, www.dynacon.ru/content/articles_idk/331; "Rossiia i mirovoi krizis: Prognozy i stsenarii," dynacon.ru, August 27, 2009; "Antikrizisnye mery i energetike: Vopros natsionalnogo budushchego," dynacon.ru, October 5, 2009, www.dynacon.ru/content/articles_idk/353; "Memorandum, priniatyi uchastnikami ekspertnoi vtrechi 'kto i zachem vtiagivaet Rossiiu v VTO,'" dynacon.ru, February 22, 2011, www.dynacon.ru/content/articles_idk/499.

[63] Robert Coalson, "Kalashnikov in the Kremlin," Radio Free Europe, December 9, 2009, www.rferl.org/a/1899581.html.

[64] Medvedev is the chair of the Institute's board of trustees. See: http://insor-russia.ru/en/about_us.

[65] Edwin Bacon, "Policy Change and the Narratives of Russia's Think Tanks," *Palgrave Communications* 4, no. 1 (2018): 4.

challenge INSOR's influence over Medvedev's vision of economic and technological development based on market economy. Specifically, the IDK criticized Medvedev's plan to emulate Silicon Valley by establishing high-tech business hubs like the Skolkovo Innovation Center near Moscow.[66] Instead, the IDK promoted a modernist conservative vision of Russia's development, rooted in the Russian Doctrine, which emphasized the integration of Orthodox religion and technological modernity as an "imperial, authoritarian, and not liberal-democratic" alternative to the "ideology of Skolkovo":

> The purpose of the ideology and reform agenda that we propose is the formation of a centaur from Orthodoxy and an innovative economy, from high spirituality and high technology. This centaur will represent the face of Russia in the twenty-first century.[67]

The IDK explicitly aimed to engage directly with political authorities. The core members of IDK – Averianov, Kobiakov, Kalashnikov, Demurin, and Kholmogorov – articulated their stance toward the regime in a 2010 programmatic text coauthored with Vladimir Khomiakov, leader of the Orthodox social movement "People's Council" (Narodnyi Sobor), titled "We Believe in Russia" (My verim v Rossiiu). This text underscored the divide between pro-state conservative ideologues and oppositional nationalists. They identified "Russian national democrats" alongside "pro-Western liberals" and "transnational forces opposed to the traditional values of Russian civilization" as their three primary political opponents.[68] The authors pragmatically justified their decision to collaborate with elite groups they identified as "objectively interested in preserving Russian statehood"[69] on the basis of strategic alignment with shared interests.[70]

The publication of this programmatic text, characterizing anti-regime ethnic nationalism as a destabilizing force, disrupted IDK's association with Krylov. This rupture was clearly manifest during a

[66] See for instance: Vitalii Averianov, "Dvusmyslennost prezidentskogo poslaniia," *Russkii obozrevatel*, December 1, 2010, http://averianov.net/sii/438/?h=619.

[67] Vitalii Averianov, "Nuzhnye drugie liudi," *Zavtra*, July 14, 2010, https://zavtra.ru/blogs/2010-07-1431.

[68] "My verim v Rossiiu," in *My verim v Rossiiu: Ot Russkoi Doktriny k Izborskomu Klubu* (Moscow: Russkaia tsivilizatsiia, 2019): 390.

[69] "My verim v Rossiiu," 725. [70] "My verim v Rossiiu," 732.

roundtable organized by IDK in March 2011. The seminar aimed to gather a spectrum of conservative thinkers – from "national-imperial" to "national-democratic" inclinations – to deliberate on Russia's future path: whether toward a national state, an empire, or potential collapse.[71]

Participants included representatives from the older generation of national-patriots such as Prokhanov, Young Conservatives like Averianov, Remizov, and Kholmogorov, and nationalist figures such as Krylov. Tensions escalated during the discussion when philosopher Petr Kalitin characterized Krylov's nationalism as defeatist, drawing parallels with Yeltsin's instrumental use of Russian nationalism to gain power, which ultimately contributed to the collapse of the Soviet state.[72] Krylov vehemently objected to this comparison, leading to a heated exchange and his eventual departure from the seminar, as well as his exclusion from future IDK events. In a subsequent article, titled "Old Patriotism" ("Staropatriotizm"), Krylov deepened the rift, criticizing what he perceived as the ideological backwardness of the "Old Patriots," including Prokhanov and Averianov. He portrayed their alliance with the regime against nationalism as a submissive and opportunistic quest for proximity to the ruling elite.[73]

Thus, at this juncture, attitudes toward the regime supplanted generational dynamics as the primary organizing principle shaping divisions among conservative intellectuals. Notably, the IDK forged closer ties with the older generation of national-conservative intellectuals. *Zavtra*'s editor-in-chief, Aleksandr Nagornii, described the IDK as a "leading hub of intellectual creativity within the sphere of Russian public thought."[74] In April 2011, the IDK hosted a roundtable to deliberate on the "methods and scenarios for the self-organization of Russian patriotic forces" in anticipation of the 2012 presidential elections, thereby launching the reflection process that ultimately led to the creation of the Izborskii Klub.[75]

71 "Russkoe zavtra: Natsionalnoe gosudarstvo, imperiia ili rasseiane? Stenogramma kruglogo stola," dynacon.ru, March 22, 2011, www.dynacon.ru/content/articles_idk/512.

72 "Russkoe zavtra: Natsionalnoe gosudarstvo, imperiia ili rasseiane? Stenogramma kruglogo stola."

73 Konstantin Krylov, "Staropatriotizm," APN.ru, June 9, 2011, www.apn.ru/index.php?newsid=24317.

74 Averianov, "Nuzhnye drugie liudi."

75 "Puti i stsenarii samoorganizatsii russkikh patrioticheskih sil v 2011–2012 gg.," dynacon.ru, April 28, 2011, www.dynacon.ru/content/articles_idk/520.

Besides sharing a strategic commitment to collaboration with authorities, the IDK's dedication to forming a "non-partisan social coalition" of "like-minded individuals" "beyond the party system" echoed a foundational tenet of early 1990s national-patriotic platforms.[76] In contrast, Krylov turned to oppositional party politics with the creation of the National-Democratic Party (Natsionalno-demokraticheskoi partii).

6.2 The Izborskii Klub: The Institutionalization of the Russian Hawks' Idea Network

6.2.1 Ideological Polarization in Russian Politics in 2011–2012

In the winter of 2011–12, mass demonstrations triggered by election fraud and the rejection of Putin's candidacy for a third presidential term led to an unprecedented degree of polarization between the liberals and *siloviki* within the ruling elite. The "castling" move, whereby Putin was nominated as the party's candidate for the 2012 presidential elections, provoked the disappointment of those who had expected Medvedev to run for a second term.[77] Moreover, the extension of the presidential term to six years solidified Putin's personal, authoritarian grip on Russian politics.[78] According to a survey by the Levada Center, Putin's popularity declined significantly, from 49 percent in June 2008 to 27 percent in October 2011.[79]

The December 2011 legislative elections saw United Russia lose its constitutional majority due to a protest vote, receiving only 49.3 percent of the vote.[80] Widespread reports of fraud during the elections sparked the largest demonstrations since the 1990s, rallying under the slogan "For Fair Elections." The protests drew tens of thousands in Moscow, with around 80,000 participants on Bolotnaia Square on December 10 and 100,000 on Sakharov Prospekt on December 24.[81]

76 "My verim v Rossiiu," 728.
77 Sakwa, *Putin Redux: Power and Contradiction in Contemporary Russia* (Abingdon; Burlington, VT: Routledge, 2014), 113.
78 Sakwa, *Putin Redux*, 113.
79 Cited in Fauconnier, *Entre le marteau et l'enclume*, 212.
80 Sakwa, *Putin Redux*, 118.
81 For a detailed study of the Bolotnaia protests, see Samuel A. Greene, *Moscow in Movement: Power and Opposition in Putin's Russia* (Stanford: Stanford University Press, 2014), 202–13.

Rather than a simple standoff between protesters and the regime, the demonstrations revealed internal divisions within the ruling elite. Alexei Kudrin, a prominent liberal figure who had served as finance minister since 2000, openly criticized the "castling" maneuver and was subsequently dismissed in September 2011 after Putin's nomination. Kudrin later played an active role in the December protests, advocating for fair elections.[82] Surkov, who also supported Medvedev's reelection bid and expressed sympathy for the protesters, was demoted from his position as first deputy head of the presidential administration to deputy prime minister.[83] By contrast, the *siloviki* took on new responsibilities, as exemplified by the appointment of Sergei Ivanov, a former Soviet KGB officer and minister of defense, as head of the presidential administration in December 2011.

As Sakwa argues, the breakdown of Putin's previous ideological consensus, referred to as the "Putin majority," prompted him to pivot his 2012 presidential campaign toward the most conservative and anti-Western segments of the electorate. Concurrently, as the popularity of the presidential party waned and Surkov's influence diminished, Putin increasingly relied on nonparty actors to mobilize ideological and social support for his candidacy. This shift toward direct engagement with civil society actors was underscored by the appointment of Viacheslav Volodin as Surkov's successor as first deputy head of the administration. Volodin, previously overseeing the All-Russian Popular Front (Obshcherossiiskii narodnyi front, ONF), had mobilized support for United Russia's legislative campaigns through major civil society organizations such as the Union of Pensioners, the Union of Industrialists and Entrepreneurs, and the association "Women of Russia."[84] Another signal for this move was Putin's gathering of a dozen political analysts in February 2012 to discuss his presidential campaign. Participants included leaders from established political research institutes, alongside conservative thinkers like Remizov, Kholmogorov, and the Orthodox monarchist Nataliia Narochnitskaia.[85]

[82] Sakwa, *Putin Redux*, 120. [83] Sakwa, *Putin Redux*, 131.

[84] Dmitrii Orlov, "ONF i vyzov razvitiia," *Nezavisimaia gazeta*, May 12, 2011, www.ng.ru/politics/2011-05-12/3_kartblansh.html.

[85] "Predsedatel Pravitelstva Rossisskoi Federatsii V. V. Putin Vstretilsia s Politologami," Website of the Government of the Russian Federation, February 6, 2012, http://archive.government.ru/docs/18008.

During this period, conservative ideologues – including Prokhanov, Dugin, Kurginian, and Leontev from the older generation, and Averianov and Korovin from the younger generation – seized a significant opportunity to orchestrate a collective ideological response to the protesters. As the third wave of large-scale demonstrations unfolded on February 4 at Bolotnaia Square, they convened a parallel gathering at Poklonnaia Hill, drawing approximately 140,000 participants united under the banner of an "anti-Orange coalition," expressing their opposition to calls for liberalizing reforms.

Importantly, their actions and rhetoric contributed directly to the growing ideological divide within the Russian political landscape. As articulated by journalist Mikhail Leontev in his public call to join the Poklonnaia Hill gathering, these parallel events crystallized distinct identity boundaries between two opposing groups – "us" (*nashi*) and "them."[86] Prokhanov coined the terms "Poklonobortsy" ("Fighters of Poklonnaia") and "Bolotokhodtsy" ("Bolotnaia-goers") to solidify a geographical and conceptual divide, marking distinct social and ideological groups.[87]

Although key figures of the anti-Orange coalition – such as Dugin, Prokhanov, and Kurginian – had ceased to convene as a unified group, the resurgence of their leadership and the collective fervor sparked by renewed street protests revived their former group dynamics and demonstrated their ability to rekindle a sense of collective identity. This historical reunion laid the groundwork for the group's decision to institutionalize themselves into a formal structure. In September 2012, under the joint leadership of Prokhanov and Averianov, the participants of Poklonnaia Hill transformed their contextual mobilization into a permanent institution known as the Izborskii Klub, which emerged as the preeminent organization representing conservative ideologues.

The establishment of the Izborskii Klub also enacted the division between oppositional and loyalist factions within the ranks of the Young Conservatives. Averianov's active involvement at Poklonnaia stood in contrast to Krylov's participation in the Bolotnaia protests,

86 Mikhail Leontev, "O mitinge na poklonnoi," *Zavtra*, February 3, 2012, https://zavtra.ru/blogs/o-mitinge-na-poklonnoj.

87 Aleksandr Prokhanov, "Poklonobortsy vs Bolotokhodtsy," *Zavtra*, February 16, 2012, https://zavtra.ru/blogs/poklonobortsyi-vs-bolotohodtsyi.

further solidifying the "national-orangeist" alliance between nationalist forces and advocates for liberal-democratic reforms.[88]

The Izborskii Klub therefore provided a structured framework to address the evolving dynamics that emerged from this cycle of protests and elite rotation – the ruling elite's demand for legitimizing ideological resources and the conservative ideologues' resumption of collective public actions.

6.2.2 *An Interelite, Intergenerational, Interideological Think Tank*

The Izborskii Klub institutionalized the existence of an idea network, centered on a modernist conservative agenda, and stretching across political and intellectual elites.

The club's connections with political elites were initially facilitated by its ties to key figures elevated to influential positions following the December 2011 elite rotation. Sergei Glazev, one of the club's founding members, became an adviser to the president on the development of Eurasian economic integration. Dmitrii Rogozin, a long-time acquaintance of Prokhanov and of *Zavtra*'s board, was appointed deputy prime minister in charge of the defense industry.[89] Additionally, in an interview, an Izborskii Klub member mentioned the new deputy head of the presidential administration, Viacheslav Volodin, as one of the club's supporters within the ruling elite.[90] Vladimir Medinskii, appointed minister of culture in 2012, also demonstrated his personal support of the club by attending its inauguration ceremony in Pskov on September 8, 2012. Funded by the regional administration, the ceremony was also attended by Andrei Turchak, who was at the time the governor of Pskov and later became the secretary of the general council of United Russia.[91] According to

[88] For more details on the national-democrat alliance, see Marlène Laruelle, "Alexei Navalny and Challenges in Reconciling 'Nationalism' and 'Liberalism,'" *Post-Soviet Affairs* 30, no. 4 (July 4, 2014): 276–97.

[89] On the relations between Prokhanov and Rogozin, see Marlène Laruelle, "The Izborsky Club, or the New Conservative Avant-Garde in Russia," *Russian Review* 75 (October 2016): 634.

[90] Author interview, Moscow, 2019.

[91] On the regional administration's funding of the Izborskii Klub ceremony, see Andrei Kolesnikov, "Maskonskoe lozhe," gazeta.ru, September 11, 2012, www.gazeta.ru/column/kolesnikov/4764101.shtml?updated.

the Izborskii Klub's website, Turchak played an "important role" in the creation of the club.[92]

On the intellectual side, Prokhanov was clearly the leading organizer of the Izborskii Klub. The choice of Izborsk, a fortress-city near Pskov, as the founding location and name of the club was rooted in Prokhanov's longstanding connections with the region, dating back to the 1960s, when he had joined a community of architects working on the restoration of Pskov's churches. In 2007, Prokhanov further established Pskov as the geographic and "spiritual" center of his ideological projects with the creation of the "Sacred Hill." On the day of the Izborskii Klub's inauguration, this incremental evolution of Prokhanov's past projects was put forward.[93]

Continuity with Prokhanov's previous initiatives was also one of the key selection criteria for the club's founding members. This ideological and personal proximity was primarily based on shared experiences and involvement in common actions. This highlights the foundational role of the late Soviet and immediate post-Soviet coalitions as an enduring binding experience central to the Izborskii Klub's concept of "like-minded person" (*edinomyshlennik*). Dugin also underscored that the Izborskii Klub was composed of "patriots" united by their past militant backgrounds, reactivated by the favorable context of the regime's conservative turn:

> It seems to me that the Izborskii Klub is the last call. The last call from us, patriots, calling to join the battle that we have been waging for a long time: each of us has behind them years of selfless labor for the good of the patriotic idea, for the good of our country. For the first time, we find ourselves in new historical conditions, when we can really influence something and change a lot.[94]

92 "O klube."
93 "Nachalo," dynacon.ru, September 2012, www.dynacon.ru/content/articles/886.
94 "Zasedanie kluba na 'Energomashe,'" Izborskii Klub, September 21, 2012, https://izborsk-club.ru/889. In resuming his collaboration with Prokhanov, Dugin contrasted with Sergei Kurginian, who maintained a firm oppositional stance against the regime, thereby rejecting the Izborskii Klub's principle of cooperating with the authorities. Furthermore, interviews with members of the Izborskii Klub revealed additional factors contributing to Kurginian's exclusion from the club, including his ongoing personal conflict with Dugin and his preference for individual actions over collective work.

Table 6.1 *Distribution of the Izborskii Klub's founding members (2012) by generational group*

Generational group	Izborskii Klub's founding members (2012)
G1: born before 1955	8
G2: born 1955–70	14
G3: born after 1970	3

Source: Individual Izborskii Klub members' pages, available at https://izborsk-club.ru/members

Indeed, most of the Izborskii Klub's founding members were tied to one of the two key rallying organizations of the 1990s national-patriotic coalition: Prokhanov's newspaper *Zavtra* and the Union of Writers of Russia.[95]

A novel feature of the club, however, was its intergenerational dimension, exemplified by the association of Prokhanov, the club's chairman, with Averianov, the deputy chairman and a leading figure of the Young Conservatives. In this respect, the club clearly built on the meetings initiated by Averianov's IDK and the older generation of national-patriotic conservatives. Beyond Averianov, the Izborskii Klub incorporated the most active members of the IDK, including Kobiakov and Kalashnikov.

As shown in Table 6.1 below, three generational groups can be identified in the early composition of the club:

The first generational group consists of the club's "tutelary figures," who have led prestigious carriers in their fields and received official state honors. Notable members include writer Iurii Poliakov (1954–), recipient of several state orders; historian Andrei Fursov (1951–), a department head in the Russian Academy of Sciences; historian Nataliia Narochnitskaia (1948–), appointed by President Putin as executive director of the Paris-based European Institute for Democracy and Cooperation, one of two Russian-funded nongovernmental organizations abroad; and Colonel-General Leonid Ivashov (1943–), who concluded his military career in 2001 as head of the main directorate of international military cooperation at the Ministry of Defense.

[95] See Annex 2.

The second generational group, forming the core of the club, comprises individuals at the peak of their careers, holding influential positions with access to the highest echelons of the ruling elite. This group is dominated by economists such as Sergei Glazev (1961–), a personal adviser to the president, and media personalities Mikhail Deliagin (1968–) and Mikhail Khazin (1962–). Other leading figures include philosopher and university professor Aleksandr Dugin (1962–); journalist Mikhail Leontev (1958–), regarded as "President [Putin]'s favorite journalist";[96] and Orthodox Metropolitan Tikhon (Shevkunov), known as Putin's personal confessor.[97]

Finally, the third group is composed of young emerging leaders and opinion-makers, such as Valerii Korovin (1977–), a discipline of Dugin and deputy head of the International Eurasian Movement, and Nikolai Starikov (1970–), a well-known essayist and blogger whose books have reached significant circulation, with 20,000 copies sold in 2011 for his essay on the nationalization of the ruble and in 2012 for his essay on Stalin.

Another defining features of the Izborskii Klub is its ideological diversity. The club's website describes its ideological program as a "synthesis" of the "various views of Russian statesmen (from socialists and Soviet patriots to monarchists and Orthodox conservatives)."[98] The "Declaration of Ulianovsk," one of the founding manifestos of the club, published in January 2013, also underlines the transideological character of the group:

> We, figures of various professions with different convictions, rallied in the Izborskii Klub, appeal to all patriots of Russia, regardless of their ideological orientations.[99]

By uniting conservative ideologues with a broad spectrum of views, the club aimed to address the conservatives' historical inability to

[96] Andreas Umland, "Vers une société incivile? Contextualisation du déclin des partis politiques d'extrême droite en Russie post-soviétique," in *Le rouge et le noir : Extrême droite et nationalisme en Russie* (Paris: CNRS Éditions, 2016), 22.

[97] Ilia Zhegulev, "Samye vliiatelnye v RPTs—o glvanykh deistvuiushchikh litsakh Russkoi Pravoslavnoi Tserkvi," Meduza, November 26, 2015, https://meduza.io/feature/2015/11/26/samye-vliyatelnye-v-rpts.

[98] "O klube."

[99] "Ulianovskaia Deklaratsiia Izborskogo Kluba," *Izborskii Klub: Russkie strategii* 3 (2013): 46.

maintain cohesion as a group. This unity was particularly challenged by two longstanding controversies within conservative ranks: the debate between proponents and critics of technological modernity, and the dispute between Soviet imperialists and Orthodox conservatives, commonly referred to as the "Reds and Whites."[100]

Regarding the first issue, the club includes a wide range of perspectives, from Dugin's and Korovin's rejection of technological modernity to Kalashnikov's futurism and skepticism toward traditionalism. On the second issue, the club comprises Orthodox traditionalists such as Averianov, Narochnitskaia, Dugin, and Korovin, Marxist ideologues like Sergei Cherniakhovskii, and Soviet imperialists like Prokhanov.

The cohesion of the club, despite these ideological cleavages, primarily stemmed from its members' alignment within the new ideological landscape shaped by the 2011–12 protests, distinguishing between regime loyalists and oppositionists. Moreover, they shared a mutual interest in forging a network bridging intellectual and political divides aimed to bolster their influence over policy decisions. In leveraging Putin's conservative shift, Izborskii Klub members strategically played down and resolved internal disagreements, prioritizing a synthesis of ideologies over strict ideological consistency. This approach drew criticism from both communists and monarchists alike.[101] Consequently, the club's divergence from other communist and monarchist factions performatively marked the boundaries of a distinct group identity committed to coalition-building, in contrast to those deemed "irreconcilable." As articulated by Averianov:

> The fact that the club seems red to someone and white to someone else is an indirect confirmation that the "red–white" synthesis, at least within the club itself, is not some kind of illusion, but that it is happening in reality.[102]

[100] On this divide within the Izborskii Klub, see also Laruelle, "Izborsky Club, or the New Conservative Avant-Garde in Russia," 635.

[101] Averianov mentioned the criticism raised by the Russian Communist Workers' Party in his article "Izborskii Klub i Glavnyi Vopros Epokhi," *Izborskii Klub: Russkie strategii* 6 (2013): 20. The monarchist historian Piotr Multatuli fiercely condemned the Izborskii Klub's ideology, which he named "Prokhanovism" and denounced as "extremely dangerous" and "militantly anti-Orthodox." Petr Multatuli, "'Rediska naoborot': Kuda vedet Izborskii Klub?" religare.ru, January 29, 2013, www.religare.ru/2_99349.html.

[102] Averianov, "Izborskii Klub i glavnyi vopros epokhi," 19.

To foster group cohesion, the club has actively undertaken what sociologists refer to as "framing activities," molding the group's collective ideological identity to accommodate diverse perspectives.[103] In this effort, the club authored two foundational programmatic documents aimed at solidifying adherence to an ideological synthesis. The first document, titled "Strategy of the 'Big Breakthrough'" (Strategiia "Bolshogo ryvka"), preached both advanced technological progress and the preservation of spiritual values.[104] The second document, "Beyond the 'Reds' and 'Whites'" (Po tu storonu "krasnykh" i "belykh"), promoted the "reconciliation" and "unification" of "patriotic statesmen," advocating for a "strategic alliance" between the Soviet ideal of "social justice" and Orthodox "traditionalist values."[105]

One of the key rhetorical strategies used in these documents to justify the ideological coalition of diverging views was to insist on the urgency of addressing a "wartime" context, asserting that Russia faces an imminent existential crisis.[106] The "Strategy of the 'Big Breakthrough'" is portrayed as a "mobilization ideology" and a "practical mechanism of crisis management" designed to address a "context of global systemic crisis."[107] According to the document, three critical factors – the global financial crisis of 2008, escalating economic competition between China and the United States, and the looming threat of climate change and ecological disasters – could precipitate a "world war" and push Russia into catastrophic scenarios: "disintegration," "absorption by competitors," or "a revolution led by a counter-elite."[108] To avoid such scenarios, the document advocates for the adoption of a "national strategy for a Big Breakthrough" resting on both "spiritual mobilization" and accelerated technological

103 David A. Snow, "Framing and Social Movements," in *The Wiley-Blackwell Encyclopedia of Social and Political Movements* (John Wiley & Sons, Ltd, 2013).
104 "Strategiia 'Bolchogo Ryvka,'" Izborskii Klub, January 30, 2013, https://izborsk-club.ru/975.
105 "'Krasno-belyi' Soiuz—budushchee Rossii," *Izborskii Klub: Russkie strategii* 3 (2013): 38.
106 "Zasedanie kluba na 'Energomashe,'" Izborskii Klub, September 21, 2012, https://izborsk-club.ru/889.
107 "Mobilizatsionnyi proekt—Osnovnaia predposylka strategii 'Bolshogo Ryvka,'" dynacon.ru, 2013, www.dynacon.ru/content/articles/976.
108 "Mobilizatsionnyi proekt—Osnovnaia predposylka strategii 'Bolshogo Ryvka.'"

development as the only path to ensure Russia's "national survival."[109] A similar argument is advanced in the club's reports devoted to the dispute between Reds and Whites. The unification of Reds and Whites is put forward as a necessary coalition to prevent the "dismemberment of [the] state."[110] Furthermore, they argue that this coalition is justified because Reds and Whites share a common historical adversary, the "liberal project." According to their viewpoint, this liberal project prevailed over "traditional Russia" during the February 1917 revolution and contributed to the collapse of the Soviet Union in 1991.[111] The Red–White reconciliation, therefore, is framed as a militant "front" against the country's "liberal-globalizing" enemies:

> To avert impending catastrophe, we call on all statesmen who value the future of Russia to act as a united patriotic, imperial front opposing the liberal-globalizing ideology and its proponents, who serve the interests of our geopolitical enemies.[112]

The Izborskii Klub's production of a wartime narrative as the basis for the group's transideological unity was paired with the promotion of the concrete military dimension of this mobilization. For instance, the club's second meeting was hosted in the factory of a major Russian rocket engine manufacturer.[113] In this respect, the Izborskii Klub reproduced the type of militaristic discourse promoted by the antiliberal coalition in the late Soviet Union, which portrayed the Russian army as the natural carrier of their ideals. The club's "Manifesto of the Founding Fathers" defined the development of "Russian weaponry" and of "Russia's defense and industrial complex" as the realization of the country's "religious mission."[114]

Another strategic framing tactic employed by the club to solidify its commitment to an ideological synthesis involved conducting meetings at locations symbolizing the historical confrontation between Reds and Whites, to reinvest them with a renewed cohesive narrative.

109 "Mobilizatsionnyi proekt—Osnovnaia predposylka strategii 'Bolshogo Ryvka.'"
110 "Ulianovskaia deklaratsiia Izborskogo Kluba," *Izborskii Klub: Russkie strategii* 3 (2013): 46.
111 "Ulianovskaia deklaratsiia Izborskogo Kluba."
112 "Ulianovskaia deklaratsiia Izborskogo Kluba."
113 "Manifest ottsov-osnovatelei," dynacon.ru, September 8, 2012, www.dynacon.ru/content/articles/887.
114 "Manifest ottsov-osnovatelei."

For instance, in November 2012 in Ekaterinburg, Prokhanov advocated for the synthesis of Orthodox traditionalism and Soviet industrialism, participating in a religious ceremony at the Church on Blood and visiting the Snezhinsk nuclear center.[115] He remarked:

> The Church on Blood and the nuclear center in Snezhinsk are symbols of the Russian history over the past hundred years ... It's a story in which two eras, two empires—white and red—converged in a bloody conflict. And this conflict of minds and theories, of execution ditches and construction pits, is coming to an end.[116]

Similarly, in December 2012, the Izborskii Klub's roundtable addressing the division between "Red" and "White" Russia was held in Ulianovsk, Lenin's birthplace, in the prerevolutionary building of the Assembly of the Nobles, and in the presence of the Orthodox bishop Innokenty (Iakovlev).[117] On the same day, the military dimension of this coalition was underscored by another roundtable on the "reconciliation of Russian statesmen in the twenty-first century," held at the Aviastar aircraft factory.[118]

Individually, members of the Izborskii Klub have framed their allegiance to the group's ideological synthesis on varying grounds, either as a firm endorsement or a strategic stance vis-à-vis alternative positions. Prokhanov and Averianov, for instance, have embraced the fusion of Reds and Whites as a principled commitment to what they perceive as a coherent ideological agenda. They draw on the theoretical frameworks of Father Dmitrii Dudko and Metropolitan Ioann Snychev, who conceptualized the "reconciliation" between Nicholas II and Stalin, positing Stalin's elevation to a status akin to Nicholas II as the leader and guardian of the Russian Empire following the Soviet victory in 1945.[119] In contrast, figures like Dugin and Cherniakhovskii

[115] The Church on Blood in Honor of All Saints was built on the site of the Ipatiev House, where Nicholas II and his family had been assassinated by the Bolsheviks.

[116] Aleksandr Prokhanov, "Prekrashchenie gubitelnoi raspri," *Izborskii Klub: Russkie strategii* 3 (2013): 17.

[117] "Dve traditsii gosudarstvennosti: Put k primireniiu," *Izborskii Klub: Russkie strategii* 3 (2013): 22.

[118] "'Krasno-belyi' soiuz- budushchee Rossii."

[119] Vitalii Averianov, "Izborskii Klub i glavnyi vopros epokhi," *Izborskii Klub: Russkie strategii* 6 (2013): 18–28. Prokhanov mentioned Snychev and Dudko during a roundtable in Ulianovsk. See "XXI vek: Bratanie krasnykh i belykh," Izborskii Klub, December 21, 2012, https://izborsk-club.ru/898.

view the Red–White synthesis as a historical alliance formed after 1991 against liberalism and capitalism. For them, this synthesis represents a pragmatic alignment of shared priorities and objectives. Cherniakhovskii articulated this perspective clearly:

> The issue of reconciliation between "Reds" and "Whites" is not a question of abandoning one's historical preferences and beliefs—despite the difference that separates monarchists and communists. It is a question of the unity of those who believe that Russia should be sovereign, and that power in it should be capable and strong, against all those who try to subordinate Russia to the dictates of international structures, deprive it of sovereignty and turn its economy into a colonial appendage of economic imperialism of other powers ... What really matters is not to merge and form an ideological synthesis, which is unreachable and would lead to clashing and opposing positions, but a political union in which each side does not abandon its principles, values and symbols, but unites around common political goals, in confronting threats to the country and its opponents.[120]

Likewise, in an interview, another club member rationalized their commitment to transcending the divide between communism and monarchism as primarily based on their common opposition against liberalism.[121]

In addition to their shared situational position and interest in an ideological coalition, the cohesion of the Izborskii Klub members relied on the interpersonal relations they had built in the past or cultivated through their group activities. For instance, during an interview, a member mentioned their strong personal sympathy for Prokhanov as being more significant than their differing perspectives on technological modernity.[122] Likewise, another member emphasized that they had developed an excellent rapport with Cherniakhovskii regardless of some of their ideological divergences.[123]

The club also mitigated its internal inconsistencies by focusing on its collective opposition to liberal idea networks.

[120] Sergei Cherniakhovskii, "Izborsk i Ulianovsk," APN.ru, January 21, 2013, www.apn.ru/publications/article28236.htm.
[121] Author interview, Moscow, 2019. [122] Author interview, Moscow, 2019.
[123] Author interview, Moscow, 2019.

6.2.3 The Izborskii Klub's Competition with Liberal Idea Networks

The establishment of the Izborskii Klub was facilitated by a propitious political climate. Following his reelection as president in May 2012, Putin implemented a pronounced conservative turn.[124] This shift was evident in the enactment of several laws aimed at protecting Russia's "traditional values," notably the law against "the promotion of non-traditional sexual identities" and the law against "obstruction of the exercise of the right of the liberty of conscience and religious liberty," commonly called the "antigay law" and the "antiblasphemy law," respectively, which were passed by the Duma in June 2013.[125]

However, despite this conservative reaction, Putin's mode of governance, based on various networks of influence and managed pluralism, maintained a competitive environment for the provision of ideological resources in which the Izborskii Klub was rivaled by platforms based on other networks and sets of ideas. A central part of the framing processes used by the Izborskii Klub's leaders to fix their public identity, therefore, involved defining themselves and positioning their organization in relation to other entities.

First, among conservative elites, the Izborskii Klub's major competitor was the Institute of Socio-economic and Political Research (Institut sotsialno-ekonomicheskikh i politicheskikh issledovanii, ISEPI), established concurrently and overseen by Dmitrii Badovskii, deputy head of the presidential administration's domestic politics department. The ISEPI functioned primarily as an analytical center promoting Russian conservative thought through the publication of a quarterly journal, *Tetradi po konservatizmu* (Notes on Conservatism).[126] In contrast to

124 An extensive body of literature addresses the regime's 2012 conservative turn. See, for instance: Andrei Tsygankov, "Crafting the State-Civilization: Vladimir Putin's Turn to Distinct Values," *Problems of Post-Communism* 63, no. 3 (May 3, 2016): 146–58; Katharina Bluhm and Mihai Varga, eds., *New Conservatives in Russia and East Central Europe* (Abingdon: Routledge, 2019); Mikhail Suslov and Dmitry Uzlaner, eds., *Contemporary Russian Conservatism: Problems, Paradoxes, and Perspectives* (Boston, MA: Brill, 2020).

125 Daniel Weiss, "The New Russian Legislation on Blasphemy and Swearing: The Parliamentary Debates," *Zeitschrift für Slavische Philologie* 72, no. 2 (2016): 289–321.

126 See the list of issues here: http://isepr.ru/almanah.

the Izborskii Klub, which was dominated by the older generation of national-patriotic ideologues advocating an imperial understanding of Russian statehood and national identity, ISEPI's editorial board predominantly comprised Young Conservatives inclined toward secular nationalism such as Remizov and Mezhuev. Moreover, as highlighted by Katharina Bluhm, ISEPI operated under the auspices of a public official, thereby being integrated into the governmental structure.[127] The Izborskii Klub, therefore, positioned itself between what one of the members of the club's leadership described in an interview as the radical oppositionists, represented by Krylov's National-Democratic Party, and the pragmatic experts working directly for the administration.[128]

In contrast, the Izborskii Klub endeavor to assert its organizational autonomy at the intersection of intellectual and political spheres. While a large number of the club's founding members had been involved in partisan politics in the 2000s, their transition to the "club" format was partly motivated by disillusionment with the Russian electoral system, in which their parties had encountered administrative barriers impeding their participation in the elections. In an interview, a club member revealed that their experience in electoral politics had led them to realize that gaining a position as a deputy was not contingent on winning elections but on adhering to directives from the presidential administration, discouraging the expression of dissenting ideas.[129] While adopting the club format signaled their decision not to directly compete against the ruling party, it also emerged as an alternative model for organizing political and ideological coalitions outside the constraints imposed by the regime's control over the party system.

Membership in the Izborskii Klub represented a definitive commitment to legitimizing and sustaining Putin's political system. However, the club aimed to exert ideological influence and negotiate greater scope for action within decision-making circles. Dugin articulated this strategic shift in the inaugural issue of the Izborskii Klub's journal, highlighting the club's backing of Putin as a strategy to protect him from adversaries perceived as more detrimental and to supplement

[127] Katharina Bluhm, "Russia's Conservative Counter-Movement: Genesis, Actors, and Core Concepts," in *New Conservatives in Russia and East Central Europe*, ed. Katharina Bluhm and Mihai Varga (Abingdon: Routledge, 2019), 35.

[128] Author interview, Moscow, 2019.

[129] Author interview, Moscow, 2019.

with their own agenda what they perceived as Putin's lack of a unified ideological framework:

> On the one hand, Putin embodies a reactionary force that opposes Westernizing liberal destructive tendencies ... But on the other hand, Putin does not have a comprehensive internal vision to consistently implement patriotic reforms ... The Izborskii Klub emerged at the beginning of Putin's third term precisely as an initiative to develop a national idea ... encompassing of strategies, values, goals and historical frameworks to unite the society and the state against internal and external threats.[130]

The club's website's "About Us" section explicitly contrasted its "state-patriotic" stance with that of the "liberal community," positioning itself as an alternative to numerous liberal-oriented clubs and venues.[131] In this regard, the Izborskii Klub aimed to step into the role formerly held by prominent consultancy groups that advised the government, such as Gleb Pavlovskii's FEP, Igor Iurgens's INSOR, and the Valdai Club.[132] The club aimed to occupy the space vacated by Pavlovskii's move to the opposition and the waning influence of Iurgens's liberal network by adopting a similar organizational model.[133] This goal was clearly expressed in the club's stated mission: "To create and present analytical reports to the authorities and Russian society aimed at shaping an updated, patriotically oriented state policy across all spheres of national life."[134]

To establish itself as a credible rival, the Izborskii Klub adopted certain symbolic and organizational features similar to those of its counterparts. For example, its name, "Izborskii Klub," mirrors that of the Valdai Club, which similarly derived its name from the location of its inaugural meeting near Lake Valdai. The ability of the Izborskii Klub to gain recognition as the conservative counterpart of major liberal centers is evidenced by the reaction of Iurgens, the director of INSOR

130 Aleksandr Dugin, "Russkii otvet na vyzov zapada," *Izborskii Klub: Russkie strategii* 1 (2013): 75.
131 "O klube."
132 The Valdai Club is a think tank managed by a consortium of foreign policy expert centers (the Council on Foreign and Defense Policy, the Russian International Affairs Council, the Moscow State Institute of International Affairs Relations, and the Higher School of Economics), which organizes an annual international forum, attended by the Russian president, to discuss domestic and global issues.
133 Dugin, "Russkii otvet na vyzov zapada," 74.
134 "O klube."

and a member of the Valdai Club, who perceived the emergence of the club as a threat.[135] Journalistic accounts covering the founding of the Izborskii Klub have similarly portrayed it as a direct competitor to the Valdai Club:

> Conservative patriots hope that in the future their recommendations will fall on the table of the country's leadership and will not be rejected, and that the President will regularly meet with members of the Izborskii Klub, just like he meets with members of the Valdai Club, which is considered liberal. The Kremlin is not yet going to equate these two clubs in importance, sources in the presidential administration told *Kommersant*: first, I would like to see what the Izborskii alternative can offer.[136]

Critics have gone as far as labeling the Izborskii Klub as the new "official think-tank," although the actual cooperation between the club and ruling circles is more nuanced, as will be explored in detail in the subsequent chapter.[137] The following section delves into how the Izborskii Klub has mobilized its resources and influence to position itself as an ideological entrepreneur, aiming to strategically influence political decision-making and media narratives.

6.3 The Izborskii Klub as an Entrepreneur of Capital for Policy Influence

6.3.1 The Club's Strategy of Resource Aggregation through Various Memberships

On top of their belonging to preconstituted networks and generational groups, the Izborskii Klub's members have been recruited on the basis of their capacity to bring resources and capital contributing to the club's objectives. Positioned as an intermediary between intellectual conservative circles and the ruling elites, the club sought to gather members with significant legitimacy and recognition in both environments.

[135] Aleksandra Samarina, "Apostoly konservativnogo patriotizma," *Nezavisimaia gazeta*, September 10, 2012, www.ng.ru/politics/2012-09-10/1_apostoly.html.

[136] "Antivaldaiskaia vozvyshennost," *Kommersant*, September 10, 2012, www.kommersant.ru/doc/2019043.

[137] Ivan Preobrazhenskii, "Imperiia bet po liberalam," September 10, 2012, www.rosbalt.ru/blogs/2012/09/10/1032462.html.

Analysis of the members' biographies, networks, and activities allows for identification of key characteristics of the initial group composing the club in 2012–13. Annex 2 ranks the Izborskii Klub's founding members into nine professional categories: economists (six members), philosophers (four), journalists (four), historians (three), writers (two), political scientists (two), businessmen (one), politicians (one), the military (one), and the clergy (one).[138] Moreover, the table shows that one of their common central assets is their membership in diverse social milieus: universities, the media, political parties, state institutions, and religious organizations. Their connections to diverse networks allow them to combine three important resources that were arguably decisive in their inclusion as founding members:

- Substantial intellectual capital, characterized by advanced academic qualifications (fourteen members hold either a "Candidate of Sciences" or "Doctor of Sciences" degree), affiliations with the Russian Academy of Sciences, publications in scientific journals, and teaching roles in prominent universities.
- Established public reputation and visibility: Nearly all founding members are prolific authors of articles, essays, and novels. They regularly contribute to a wide array of newspapers and journals, they appear frequently on major television and radio channels, and some host renowned programs such as the sociopolitical program *Odnako* on the TV channel *Pervii Kanal.*
- Legitimacy within ruling elites: A majority of founding members have held or currently hold roles in state institutions, providing expertise, consulting services, or receiving prestigious state honors.

In addition to this initial wave of recruitment, from 2012 to 2021 the club's membership grew from twenty-five to sixty-one. Compared to the founding group, the additional members did not necessarily belong to preconstituted networks but rather seem to have been brought in for their individual capital and resources. A member of the club's leadership noted that, after the club stabilized around thirty members, other recruits were assimilated into the existing core without introducing new ideological perspectives.[139] According to another founding member, a common pathway to membership involved

[138] The rest of this section is based on the information displayed in Annex 2.
[139] Author interview, Moscow, 2019.

producing substantial and intellectually engaging work, alongside active participation in club events as an expert.[140]

Annex 3 offers a concise overview of the professional and biographical backgrounds of members admitted during the period spanning 2012–21. The table delineates five types of resources possessed by these new members: analytical expertise, advocacy skills, public outreach capabilities, financial resources, and connections within the political sphere.

Recruitment based on competencies in analytical expertise, advocacy, or public outreach typically served as entry strategies for younger members joining the club. For instance, Dmitrii Egorchenkov (1980–), who initially served as an affiliated expert from 2016 to 2018, ascended to full membership shortly after assuming in 2017 the role of director of the Institute for Strategic Studies and Forecasts at the People's Friendship University of Russia (RUDN), a position that endowed him with robust analytical resources and regular media access. Similarly, Mikhail Kildiashov (1986–), a poet and essayist, progressed from chairing the club's Orenburg branch to becoming a permanent member in 2019. His advancement paralleled his active engagement in advocacy as secretary of the Union of Writers of Russia and member of the Civic Chamber of the Orenburg region.

The addition of younger members underscored the Izborskii Klub's capacity to attract new competencies, while simultaneously demonstrating its appeal through the inclusion of established figures possessing resources such as public acclaim, financial capital, and connections with influential political circles. This is exemplified by the membership of Nobel laureate physician Zhores Alferov (1930–), renowned filmmaker Karen Shakhnazarov (1952–), and Viacheslav Shtyrov (1953–), former deputy chairman of the Federation Council from 2010 to 2014, the upper house of the Russian Federal Assembly.

The trajectory of Oleg Rozanov (1969–) within the club further highlights the increasing significance of financial resources in shaping the club's hierarchy, surpassing the influence of personal connections. A businessman based in Briansk, Rozanov joined the Izborskii Klub in 2013 and subsequently established and led an informational and analytical center within the club known as Kope Peresveta. His appointment as the club's executive secretary overseeing regional and

[140] Author interview, Moscow, 2019.

Table 6.2 ***Distribution of the Izborskii Klub's founding members (2012) and added members (2012–21) by generational group***

Generation	Founding members (2012)	Added members (2012–21)	Total
G1: born before 1955	8	14	22
G2: born 1955–70	14	11	25
G3: born after 1970	3	11	14

Source: Individual Izborskii Klub members' pages, available at https://izborsk-club.ru/members

international activities in 2015 was accompanied by his substantial contributions of financial and organizational resources, providing for the establishment of an office in a prestigious business complex on Ilinka Street in central Moscow, a short distance from the Kremlin.[141]

In addition to the club's initial ideological diversity, the expansion of its membership introduced generational and professional diversity. As illustrated in Table 6.2 below, while the club initially consisted of only three members from the third generation (born after 1970), eleven individuals from this younger cohort were welcomed into the club between 2012 and 2021.

The intergenerational composition of the Izborskii Klub distinguished it from the traditional division between Young Conservatives and the older generation of national-patriots that characterized earlier conservative coalitions. This made the Izborskii Klub unique compared to other organizations, such as ISEPI, which was predominantly led by Young Conservatives.

Additionally, the influx of new members introduced professional diversity to the club. Table 6.3 below highlights the primary professional activity of each member, listed in decreasing order of representation within the club. This table indicates that, between 2012 and 2021, the club integrated three new professional categories: politicians (who became the second most significant group within the club), natural scientists, and managers.

The heterogeneous distribution of the club's members across various professional fields results in significant variations in their modes

141 "Oleg Rozanov (biografiia)," Izborskii Klub, https://izborsk-club.ru/10982.

Table 6.3 *Distribution of the Izborskii Klub's founding members (2012) and added members (2012–21) by professional activity*

Professional activity	Founding members (2012)	Added members (2012–21)	Total
Social scientists (university professors, researchers, publicists)	15	10	25
Politicians		9	9
Artists (writers, film directors, actors, graphists)	2	6	8
Journalists	4	1	5
Businessmen	2	3	5
Clerics	1	2	3
Natural scientists (university professors, researchers)		2	2
Managers		2	2
Security forces (army, police)	1	1	2
Total	25	36	61

Source: Individual Izborskii Klub members' pages, available at https://izborsk-club.ru/members

of discourse production and legitimation. Notably, there is a substantial gap between scientific-rational and dogmatic-militant discourses. The former is advocated by members such as Nobel laureate physician Zhores Alferov and Georgii Malinetskii, a mathematician and department head at the Academy of Sciences. In contrast, the dogmatic-militant discourse is represented by radical ideologues like Valerii Korovin and Nikolai Starikov, as well as religious figures such as Mufti Albir Krganov and Metropolitan Tikhon (Shevkunov).[142]

There are distinct variations in the status of Izborskii Klub members within each professional sector, ranging from highly established individuals to those in more marginal positions.[143] Among academic scholars, for instance, the club includes both a Nobel Prize–winning physician and young professors at the start of their careers, such as Georgii Filimonov (1980–). In the political arena, the club's

[142] See Annex 3.

[143] For the professional and biographical details of members mentioned in this paragraph, refer to Annexes 2 and 3.

membership spans local politicians like Viktor Grinkevich, an MP in the regional parliament of Briansk, and Iurii Lastochkin, the former mayor of Rybinsk who was convicted of embezzlement and sentenced to prison in 2015, as well as prominent figures like Murat Ziazikov, deputy plenipotentiary representative of the president of the Russian Federation in the Central Federal District, and Viacheslav Shtyrov, former deputy chairman of the Federation Council. In literature, the club features notable figures such as Zakhar Prilepin, a recipient of numerous Russian and international literary prizes, alongside Mikhail Kildiashov, a poet from Orenburg. Within the Orthodox Church, the club includes influential clerics like Metropolitan Tikhon (Shevkunov), rumored to be Putin's personal confessor, and Bishop Augustine (Anisimov) of the local Gorodets diocese.

The expansion of the club's membership to encompass a diverse array of professional backgrounds and statuses indicates its capacity to foster a type of sociability and a sense of "like-mindedness" that extends beyond the original interpersonal network of its founding members. The club's broad appeal demonstrates that affiliation with it offers significant benefits, attracting both young, emerging public figures and well-established, high-ranking officials. The following section will elucidate the club's appeal by examining how access to and use of the club's collective capital enables its members to influence the public sphere as a collective ideological force.

6.3.2 *The Use of the Club's Capital as a Collective Ideological Entrepreneur*

An overview of the Izborskii Klub's activities during its inaugural year, 2012–13, reveals that the club successfully positioned itself in the public sphere as a collective ideological entrepreneur.[144] This position was supported by the production of four types of group capital: providing a social venue for group consolidation, professionalizing the group's ideological discourse, contributing to public events that shape the country's policy agenda, and disseminating the group's ideas within domestic and international elite networks.

[144] This part is based on the list of activities published at the end of each monthly Izborskii Klub journal in the year 2013. The full list of the club's issues in 2013 is accessible here: https://izborsk-club.ru/magazine#2013.

The primary advantage offered by the club is the increased visibility and coherence of the group it represents. Crucially, the club provides a material and institutional venue for group sociability. The club's two offices in Moscow offer distinct environments for social interaction. The office in a business center on Ilinka Street, close to the Kremlin, reinforces the club's identity as a political power hub. This office features a meeting room for members and guests, a secretariat office, and Rozanov's private office, highlighting the professional and established status of the organization. In contrast, the club's second office, near the Smolenskaia metro station, resembles a private apartment, offering a different ambiance for the group's activities. During an interview held in this office, a member highlighted its convivial nature, intended for more informal, friendlier meetings.[145] These two offices tangibly embody and reinforce the group's identity, both as a social group of peers and as an advocacy group. Besides purveying a venue for the group's sociability, the offices enabled the club to hold roundtables that established the group's priorities and interests. In this regard, the club served as a platform to frame a collective discourse more elaborately and visibly, contrasting with the former fragmentation of smaller group initiatives. The publication of the club's monthly journal, *Izborskii Klub: Russkie strategii* (Izborskii Klub: Russian Strategies), offers a concrete materialization of the group's existence and agenda. Furthermore, the Izborskii Klub strengthened the group's collective identity through practices of loyalty, where members act together, appear in public together, and commit to common causes. In 2013, the club organized seven group trips across the country, visiting Sverdlovsk, Briansk, Belgorod, Iakutia, Dagestan, Volgograd, and Kursk. Other group-building activities included symbolic ceremonies that established the club's identity and history, such as the public presentation of the first issue of *Izborskii Klub: Russkie strategii* at the Russian Academy of Sciences, the celebration of the club's anniversary in November 2013 at the Olimpiiskii business center, and the launch of a book series named after the Izborskii Klub by the publisher Knizhnyi Mir. Participation in these activities has provided various ways for members to self-identify with the club. While some may base their membership on adherence to the group's ideological

[145] Author interview, Moscow, 2019.

platform, others may affiliate through the social and ritual markers of the group's identity in the public sphere.

The second significant asset provided by the club is the professionalization of ideological discourse. Presented as a "club of experts" in the "About Us" section of its website, the Izborskii Klub aims to transform the ideologues' past reputation as extremist thinkers, integrating them into the legitimate, established sphere of expert discourse. This shift marks a significant change in their strategy for public communication. Previously, conservative ideologues often engaged in polemical and pamphleteering discourse to oppose what they criticized as an elitist and technocratic liberal intelligentsia. However, through the Izborskii Klub, they have sought to position themselves as credible rivals to liberal experts by adopting a similarly authoritative rhetorical style. To this end, the club emphasizes its respectability and competence in producing technical knowledge. The club actively produces long analytical reports, termed *ekspertnye doklady* ("expert reports"), on various policy areas. In 2013, the club's journal featured reports on topics including military reforms, information wars, scientific innovations, cybersecurity, Eurasian integration, food security, and agricultural policy. These reports frame the group's ideological views – militaristic, imperialist, anti-Western – with sophisticated analytical designs, incorporating charts, graphics, and statistics. Moreover, the club seeks to position itself as a bridge between ideological production and external technical expertise. For example, in January 2013, the club hosted a roundtable discussion on the "problems and prospects of the Russian space industry" at the office of the Rosobshchemash Corporation, an aircraft and spacecraft factory, featuring participation from leading specialists in the domestic space industry.[146]

The professionalization of its ideological discourse enabled the Izborskii Klub to reach new audiences and contribute to official expertise aimed at shaping the country's policy agenda. The club's reports, targeted at policymakers, frame ideological claims and worldviews as pragmatic and beneficial policy choices. The club's ability to present its reports at high-level forums of experts

[146] "Khronologiia meropriiatii kluba," *Izborskii Klub: Russkie strategii* 2 (2013): 109.

and policymakers demonstrates its success in being recognized as a legitimate producer of expert discourse. For instance, in May 2013, several Izborskii Klub members participated in the annual Moscow Economic Forum, an expert conference aimed at developing government recommendations,[147] where they advocated against the "neoliberal approach to economic and social issues"[148] and held a session dedicated to presenting their founding report, "Strategy of the 'Big Breakthrough.'"[149] Similarly, in December 2013, Izborskii Klub members lectured on digital and information wars during a conference coorganized with the Center for Military and Political Research of MGIMO, one of Russia's most prestigious universities.[150] Notably, in 2013, Izborskii Klub representatives were invited to the annual forum of the Valdai Club, thereby gaining recognition and influence among their central competitors.[151] Additionally, in June 2013, their participation in the Congress of the ONF club demonstrated their integration into the nonparty mechanisms established by the government to involve civil society in providing ideas and support for the regime. The club has also established its own venues for circulating its ideas within ruling circles by including high-ranking officials among its members and through advocacy efforts aimed at policymakers. For example, in December 2013, following a roundtable on new history textbooks used in schools, the club summarized its views in a resolution sent to the president of Russia, the head of the Russian Historical Society, and the chairman of the State Duma.[152]

Finally, the Izborskii Klub has developed connections with a network of domestic and international ruling elites. In particular, the club has leveraged Prokhanov's longstanding connections with the political establishment, dating back to his career as a Soviet journalist for *Literaturnaia gazeta*. During the club's regional trips in 2013, they

147 See the "About Us" page of the forum: https://me-forum.ru/about.
148 "Izborskii Klub prinial uchastie v I Moskovskom Ekonomicheskom Forume," dynacon.ru, May 2013, www.dynacon.ru/content/articles/1111.
149 "Izborskii Klub prinial uchastie v I Moskovskom Ekonomicheskom Forume."
150 "Konferentsiia v MGIMO," dynacon.ru, December 2013, www.dynacon.ru/content/articles/2376.
151 "Khronologiia meropriiatii kluba," *Izborskii Klub: Russkie strategii* 8 (2013): 117.
152 "Khronologiia meropriiatii kluba," *Izborskii Klub: Russkie strategii* 1 (2014): 108.

met with governors and held conferences attended by local political, religious, intellectual, and economic elites. For instance, in April 2013, the club organized a meeting in Sverdlovsk on "reindustrialization," which included the plenipotentiary representative of the president in the Urals Federal District, a local bishop, and the rector of the Ural Institute of Business.[153] This meeting was followed by a roundtable at the Ural Mining and Metallurgical Company, hosted by CEO Andrei Kozitsyn.[154] In August 2013, the club met with the president of the Republic of Sakha (Iakutia) and held a conference featuring the head of the republic's Federation of Trade Unions, the minister of culture, the chairman of the Civic Chamber, and regional writers and historians. They also met with representatives of the Lena United River Shipping Company to discuss the "Arctic vector of the development of Russian civilization."[155] Other regional meetings in Briansk, Belgorod, Dagestan, Volgograd, and Kursk followed a similar format, and some resulted in the establishment of local branches of the Izborskii Klub. In an interview, a club member explained that these branches often received support from an entrepreneur who assumed primary financial responsibilities, viewing the club as a strategic avenue to acquire administrative resources and lobby their interests to the political establishment.[156]

Beyond Russian domestic politics, the club has established relations with prominent leaders in the Middle East. In 2013, the club scheduled a trip to Syria, where Prokhanov, Leontev, and Shevchenko met with President Bashar al-Assad, and a trip to Qatar, where Prokhanov and Sultanov met with Khaled Mashal, the then-leader of Hamas.[157] Additionally, in June 2013, the club held a meeting in Moscow with then-Iranian president Mahmoud Ahmadinejad.[158]

153 "Reindustrializatsiia: Chelovek truda," dynacon.ru, April 2013, www.dynacon.ru/content/articles/1294.
154 "Natsionalnaia model ekonomiki," dynacon.ru, April 2013, www.dynacon.ru/content/articles/1295.
155 See the summary of this trip in "Khronologiia meropriiatii kluba," *Izborskii Klub: Russkie strategii* 7 (2013): 108–9.
156 Author interview, Moscow, 2019.
157 Aleksandr Prokhanov, "Nash desant v Damask," dynacon.ru, July 2013, www.dynacon.ru/content/articles/1463. On the meeting with Hamas, see "Khronologiia meropriiatii Kluba," 2014.
158 "Akhmadinezhad v Izborskom Klube," *Izborskii Klub: Russkie strategii* 6 (2013): 2.

By the conclusion of 2013, the Izborskii Klub had firmly established itself as a collective ideological force in the public sphere. The dissemination and application of its ideas as resources for political action will be analyzed in the next chapter.

6.4 Conclusion

This chapter has illustrated that hawkish ideologues have increasingly been sought out by the ruling party to provide ideological backing for the regime amid mounting criticism from liberal and nationalist opposition factions. During the winter of 2011–12, protests and shifts in elite leadership underscored ongoing challenges to Russia's authoritarian political structure. The subsequent establishment of the Izborskii Klub formalized an interelite network bridging hawkish ideologues with conservative members of the ruling establishment. Despite the regime's authoritarian tendencies, the club emerged as an alternative to traditional party politics, offering a platform for an ideological coalition aimed at shaping policy directions. The club has introduced a new approach for the hawks to engage in public discourse, acting as a collective ideological entrepreneur involved in national political discussions through participation in forums, advisory bodies, and media platforms. The forthcoming chapter will delve into how the club's ideas circulated within ruling circles and influenced concrete policy decisions.

7 *Competing for Russia's Grand Strategy (2012–2022)*

We, who belong to another independent civilization, ... are developing and choosing an alternative path of development, alien to globalism ... But by defending our civilization, we are making a global cause, asserting a global alternative.

Izborskii Klub report, "Sviashchennaia istoriia: Zdes i seichas," 2018

From 2012 to 2022, the Izborskii Klub sought to use its influence to encourage the Russian regime to adopt a state ideology drawing on both religious conservatism and technological modernity. As the club viewed it, ideology was a crucial strategic resource in the pursuit of Russia's grand strategy leading to the reassertion of its imperial nature through military and cultural confrontation with the West.

Following the Arab Spring and the 2011–12 demonstrations in Moscow, the perception of liberal values as a threat to the country's security and their association with Western influence became dominant in Russian political and military circles. In this context, the Izborskii Klub's activities have been promoted by the regime through different types of state-sponsorship practices: symbolic support from high-ranking officials, financial support from the presidential administration, and partnership agreements between the club and the government. The hawks' ideas have been used in official policy documents and in Putin's speeches to justify Russia's revisionist and expansionist foreign policy, which culminated in the annexation of Crimea in 2014 and the invasion of Ukraine in 2022.

A few scholars have examined the circulation of conservative intellectuals' ideas and narratives in the views expressed in official documents.[1] However, this chapter departs from mere discourse

[1] Luke March, "Nationalism for Export? The Domestic and Foreign-Policy Implications of the New 'Russian Idea,'" *Europe-Asia Studies* 64, no. 3 (2012): 401–25; Mikhail Suslov, "Geographical Metanarratives in Russia

analysis by examining the evolution of the social and material interactions between the Izborskii Klub and policymaking elites.[2] In doing this, the chapter is based on a review of all the activities recorded in the "Chronology" section of each monthly issue of the Izborskii Klub's journal from 2013 to 2021, as well as on interviews held with Izborskii Klub members.[3]

Much like other authoritarian states, the Russian regime has sought to accommodate domestic ideological polarization between different schools of strategic thought. Indeed, analysts of domestic foreign policy debates in China and Iran have underlined the persistence of a competitive space where rival groups confront and contest each other's policy positions according to their divergent identifications of the country's threats and priorities.[4] Likewise, despite the centralized and patrimonial nature of the political system under Putin's rule, research on the Russian think tank industry has emphasized the existence of a moderately competitive space for the public promotion of policy ideas.[5] As evidence for this, scholars have pointed to the diversity of

and the European East: Contemporary Pan-Slavism," *Eurasian Geography and Economics* 53, no. 5 (2012): 575–95; Maria Engström, "Contemporary Russian Messianism and New Russian Foreign Policy," *Contemporary Security Policy* 35, no. 3 (2014): 356–79; Marlène Laruelle, "Russia as a 'Divided Nation,' from Compatriots to Crimea: A Contribution to the Discussion on Nationalism and Foreign Policy," *Problems of Post-Communism* 62, no. 2 (2015): 88–97; Edith Clowes, "Provinces, Piety, and Promotional Putinism: Mapping Aleksandr Prokhanov's Counter-Utopian Russia," in *The Post-Soviet Politics of Utopia: Language, Fiction and Fantasy in Modern Russia*, ed. Mikhail Suslov and Per-Arne Bodin (London: I. B. Tauris, 2020), 262.

2 Two other studies address the influence of the Izborskii Klub by looking at the club's connections within the presidential administration, but they only cover the first period of the club's activities until 2016 and 2018. See Marlène Laruelle, "The Izborsky Club, or the New Conservative Avant-Garde in Russia," *Russian Review* 75 (2016): 626–44; Edwin Bacon, "Policy Change and the Narratives of Russia's Think Tanks," *Palgrave Communications* 4, no. 1 (2018): 94.

3 The full list of Izborskii Klub journal issues is accessible on the club's website: https://izborsk-club.ru/magazine.

4 On Iran, see Wendy Ramadan-Alban and Thierry Balzacq, "Pivotal Powers: Iran," in *Comparative Grand Strategy: A Framework and Cases*, ed. Thierry Balzacq, Peter Dombrowski, and Simon Reich (Oxford: Oxford University Press, 2019). On China, see Zhu Xufeng, "The Influence of Think Tanks in the Chinese Policy Process: Different Ways and Mechanisms," *Asian Survey* 49, no. 2 (2009): 337.

5 Alexander Graef, "Influential or Irrelevant? The Role of Foreign Policy Think Tanks in Russia," in *Russia's Foreign Policy: The Internal–International Link*

"ideological niches," "policy positions," and "narratives" represented in the think tank landscape.[6]

Analysis of the distribution of state-sponsored resources shows that the Russian regime promoted and demoted the Izborskii Klub depending on how doing so contributed to the regime's strategies of action in certain policy areas in specific contexts. While the club rose, from 2012 to 2014, as an hegemonic think tank recognized as a contributor to Russia's strategic objectives, the collapse of consensus between the club's agenda and the Kremlin on Russian policy toward the conflict in Donbass led to the club's relegation to a subordinate strategic subculture. Starting from around 2016, the hawks' policy influence was challenged by more liberal-inclined groups, committed to delivering economic growth through the normalization of Russia's relation with the West. Although liberals regained influence over economic policies, hawkish groups retained sway in specific sectors such as education, indicating the regime's continued strategy of maintaining a certain degree of pluralism across different policy niches. Moreover, the Izborskii Klub compensated for the reduction of state resources over time by forming a lobby group – funded by Orthodox entrepreneurs – maintaining constant contact with domestic and international policy networks to advocate its vision of a grand strategy for Russia.

The fluctuating state support for the Izborskii Klub highlights the inconsistencies and variations in the ruling elites' sponsorship of ideological production, thereby challenging the perception of the Russian regime as undergoing a linear process of ideological radicalization. These shifts in the respective power of elite networks challenge views of strategic culture as a monolithic culture guiding institutional choices. This chapter accordingly puts forward a more sociologically grounded view of strategic culture as a competitive space where various strategic subcultures supported by rival domestic groups contend

(Milan: Ledizioni LediPublishing, 2021), 13–14; Alexander Graef and Anton Barbashin, "Thinking Foreign Policy in Russia: Think Tanks and Grand Narratives," Atlantic Council, November 12, 2019, www.atlanticcouncil.org/in-depth-research-reports/report/thinking-foreign-policy-in-russia-think-tanks-and-grand-narratives. Bacon, "Policy Change and the Narratives of Russia's Think Tanks."

[6] Bacon, "Policy Change and the Narratives of Russia's Think Tanks," 2; Laruelle, "Izborsky Club, or the New Conservative Avant-Garde in Russia," 644; Graef and Barbashin, "Thinking Foreign Policy in Russia: Think Tanks and Grand Narratives."

for influence over policymakers' perceptions and decisions.[7] The chapter eventually demonstrates that, until around 2020, the Kremlin merely selectively and contextually endorsed the hawks' ideology. Instead of fixing a state ideology, the regime relied on preserving ideological competition within elite groups to ensure a flexible course of action and a variety of sources of social support through changing strategic environments.

7.1 The Hawks' Contribution to the Regime's Strategic Objectives (2012–2014)

7.1.1 The Rise of the Izborskii Klub as an Hegemonic State-Sponsored Think Tank

Compared with other think tanks focused on delivering expertise on domestic or foreign policies, the Izborskii Klub aimed more generally at the production of a state ideology, which, in its view, should serve as a strategic resource to legitimize Russia's authoritarian state power and its distinction from the West. More particularly, the Izborskii Klub advocated ideological resources as a substitute for the so-called administrative resources – such as electoral fraud, pressure on voters, and barriers to the registration of independent political parties – that have been used by the regime to make sure that the presidential party wins elections.[8] This argument gained a wider audience among ruling circles in the post-2012 political context, marked by widespread reproval of the ruling party's corrupt practices. Following the Bolotnaia street protests in response to electoral fraud, Putin's return to power in 2012 was accompanied by the regime's conservative ideological consolidation to justify Russia's distinct path in opposition to Western liberal democracies. Domestically, Putin's conservative agenda was laid out in his annual address to the Federal Assembly in 2012, which emphasized the role

[7] On the concept of "strategic subculture," see Alan Bloomfield, "Time to Move On: Reconceptualizing the Strategic Culture Debate," *Contemporary Security Policy* 33, no. 3 (2012): 437.

[8] See Aleksandr Prokhanov, "Ot partii vlasti: K partii russkoi mechty," *Zavtra*, September 24, 2018, https://zavtra.ru/blogs/ot_partii_vlasti_-_k_partii_russkoj_mechti.

of "spiritual" and "traditional values" as an answer to the country's "demographic and moral crisis."[9] The concepts of "tradition" and "traditional values," used in formulas such as "the tradition of a strong state," "traditional family," "traditional sexuality," and "traditional religions," became central norms used in Putin's and other high-ranking officials' discourse to justify policy decisions.[10] Putin also put forth a conservative foreign policy and development strategy for Russia based on the conservation of its traditional identity and values as a distinct civilization. At the 2013 annual Valdai forum, Putin affirmed Russia's "desire for independence and sovereignty in spiritual, ideological and foreign policy spheres" and rejected attempts to implement "western-style liberalism" and "a standardised model of a unipolar world."[11]

The Izborskii Klub hailed the regime's conservative turn as a "signal" granting recognition to its long-standing advocacy of a state ideology.[12] The club's vice-chairman, Aleksandr Nagornii, wrote that Putin had "turned to the circle of ideas, values and concepts that have been nurtured for many years by Russian patriot-sovereigntists [*patriot-derzhavniki*] including the newspaper *Zavtra* and the Izborskii Klub, Aleksandr Prokhanov and his associates."[13]

[9] Vladimir Putin, "Presidential Address to the Federal Assembly," Website of the President of Russia, December 12, 2012, http://en.kremlin.ru/events/president/news/17118. The social and cultural conservative agenda pushed for by this discourse was followed by the implementation of concrete repressive policies such as the "antigay law" and the "antiblasphemy law."

[10] See, for instance, the "State Conception of the Family Policy of the Russian Federation," which declared that the state would prioritize "the promotion of the well-being of families and of traditional family values." "Kontseptsiia gosudarstvennoi semeinoi politiki do 2025 goda," *Rossiiskaia gazeta*, August 29, 2014, https://rg.ru/2014/08/29/semya-site-dok.html.

[11] Vladimir Putin, "Meeting of the Valdai International Discussion Club," Website of the President of Russia, September 19, 2013, http://en.kremlin.ru/events/president/news/19243. On Putin's conceptualization of Russia as a distinct civilization, see Andrei Tsygankov, "Crafting the State-Civilization: Vladimir Putin's Turn to Distinct Values," *Problems of Post-Communism* 63, no. 3 (May 3, 2016): 146–58.

[12] See Aleksandr Notin, "Valdaiskii signal," *Izborskii Klub: Russkie strategii* 3 (2014).

[13] Aleksandr Nagornii, "Ot Miunkhena k Valdaiu," Izborskii Klub, October 3, 2013, https://izborsk-club.ru/1897. See also Aleksandr Prokhanov, "Gosudarstvu byt!" Izborskii Klub, December 23, 2013, https://izborsk-club.ru/2384.

At the beginning of Putin's third term, therefore, the Izborskii Klub was well positioned to become an influential producer of ideological resources for the regime's foreign and security policies. The most important marker of the club's status as a state-sponsored organization is its connections with insiders within the presidential administration and the government, who serve as bridges between the club and policy circles. The participation of the culture minister, Vladimir Medinskii, and of the governor of Pskov, Andrei Turchak, in the inauguration ceremony is a typical symbolic practice explicitly establishing the political support enjoyed by the club within ruling circles.

Other dominant state-sponsored think tanks rely on similar informal state sponsorship – for example, the Council on Foreign and Defense Policy (SVOP), which was founded by the academic Sergei Karaganov and former members of the Soviet military and intelligence services in 1991, and the Valdai Club. Neither structure receives direct funding from the presidential administration but they are deemed state-sponsored to the extent that they have established personal and business relations with high-ranking members of the government and/or major state-owned companies.[14] Some of the Izborskii Klub's members and supporters are also members of the SVOP, thereby showing that the club is well established in high-level foreign policy networks. This overlap appears, for instance, with Dmitrii Rogozin, former deputy prime minister in charge of the defense industry (2011–18) and director general of Russia's space agency Roscosmos, who is a member of the SVOP and an informal supporter of the Izborskii Klub.[15] Likewise, according to Marlène Laruelle, the Izborskii Klub member Leonid Ivashov, a retired colonel-general, is an "influential mediator between nationalist circles and the military."[16]

Other key intermediaries between the club and defense policy circles include the retired major-general Aleksandr Vladimirov, president of

[14] Graef and Barbashin, "Thinking Foreign Policy in Russia."

[15] See Laruelle, "Izborsky Club, or the New Conservative Avant-Garde in Russia," 634. As evidence of Rogozin and Prokhanov's links, see Prokhanov's 2012 interview of Rogozin: Aleksandr Prokhanov, "Russkii OPK: Sol Soli Zemli," *Zavtra*, February 22, 2012, https://zavtra.ru/blogs/russkij-opk-sol-soli-zemli.

[16] Laruelle, "Izborsky Club, or the New Conservative Avant-Garde in Russia," 632.

the College of Military Experts, who has contributed to the development of major official documents and legislation such as Russia's military doctrines and security strategies.[17] He has been regularly involved with the Izborskii Klub as an expert on military issues, in particular for the publication of the club's 2013 report on the military reform.[18] As Averianov notes, this report was directly presented to Minister of Defense Sergei Shoigu.[19] The Izborskii Klub member Sergei Glazev, Putin's former adviser on Eurasian economic integration (2012–19), also enjoyed direct personal access to the president and the presidential administration.[20]

Finally, Prokhanov, as a well-known journalist and writer with close ties to the former Soviet military–industrial complex, also maintained important connections with high-ranking officials in the defense industry. These continued relations are evidenced by the hosting of the Izborskii Klub's meetings in the offices of some of the most important strategic defense companies, such as the aircraft factory Aviastar and the rocket engine manufacturer Energomash. And on his eightieth birthday, in 2018, Prokhanov received personal congratulations from President Putin; the president of the Republic of Belarus, Aleksandr Lukashenko; Minister of Defense Sergei Shoigu; the director of the Foreign Intelligence Services, Sergei Naryshkin; and the head of the presidential administration, Anton Voino.[21]

The Izborskii Klub's main argument – that their hawkish ideology is a strategic resource ensuring the sovereignty of the state – became dominant in Russia's strategic thinking circles. In fact, the Izborskii Klub's entry into the Russian think tank industry was met with the decline of its major liberal adversary, Igor Iurgens's Institute of Contemporary Development (INSOR), which had enjoyed a special status during

17 Vladimirov's continued influence in policy circles is demonstrated by his appointment in 2015 as deputy minister of education and science. See his biography here: "Reziume: Vladimirov Aleksandr Ivanovich," Kadet.Ru, www.kadet.ru/lichno/vlad_v/vlad_in1.htm.

18 "Voennaia reforma kak sostavnaia chast kontseptsii bezopasnosti RF: Sistemno-dinamicheskaia otsenka," Izborskii Klub, February 6, 2013, https://izborsk-club.ru/994.

19 Vitalii Averianov, "Izborskii Klub provodit psikhoterapiiu," Izborskii Klub, June 4, 2013, https://izborsk-club.ru/1317.

20 Graef and Barbashin, "Thinking Foreign Policy in Russia."

21 See the Izborskii Klub's journal, issue no. 2 (2018): 111.

Medvedev's presidential term.[22] Using the Eastview Russian Central Newspapers database to review the number of mentions that INSOR and the Izborskii Klub have received in the Russian press, Edwin Bacon shows that INSOR peaked at around 300 mentions per year in 2011, a figure that declined to fifty mentions per year in 2013.[23] In comparison, mentions of Prokhanov's Izborskii Klub and the newspaper *Zavtra* reached around 150 per year during the first half of Putin's third term.[24]

Beyond the media space, anti-Western, antiliberal, national-patriotic ideas became increasingly prominent in expert foreign policy discourse and led to important agenda shifts in some of the main state-sponsored think tanks.[25] In particular, the Valdai Club underwent important management and organizational changes and became the main conceptualizer, along with SVOP, of Russia's "pivot to the East" and integration within a "Greater Eurasia" as an alternative to the "Union of Europe" that it had earlier advocated.[26] As a consequence, the Izborskii Klub set up cooperative relations with the Valdai Club, which it had initially identified as a rival liberal counterpart. Beginning in 2012, Prokhanov participated in Valdai's annual forum, thereby joining one of the most influential platforms for expert foreign policy debates attended by the Russian president and other senior government officials. The Russian Institute for Strategic Studies (RISI), which is directly funded by the presidential administration, embraced an even more radical program under the leadership of Lieutenant General Reshetnikov, an Orthodox Christian conservative, who appointed the monarchist historian Petr Multatuli as head of its analysis and assessment department.[27]

22 Iurgens himself attributed his institute's marginalization to the victory of conservative "interest groups" over the liberal "coalition for the future," which he had sought to build as a support group of Medvedev's presidency. See Igor Iurgens, "My proigrali okhraniteliam," *The New Times*, March 5, 2012, https://newtimes.ru/articles/detail/50506.

23 Bacon, "Policy Change and the Narratives of Russia's Think Tanks," 5.

24 Bacon, "Policy Change and the Narratives of Russia's Think Tanks," 5.

25 Graef, "Influential or Irrelevant?" 30.

26 The concept of the "Union of Europe" was coined by Karaganov. It advocated the establishment of "areas of cooperation and co-development" and the creation of a "common strategic space" between the European Union and Russia. See Sergei Karaganov, "Soiuz Evropy: Poslednii shans?" *Rossiia v globalnoi politike*, July 9, 2010, https://globalaffairs.ru/articles/soyuz-evropy-poslednij-shans.

27 Graef and Barbashin, "Thinking Foreign Policy in Russia."

In this environment, the Russian International Affairs Council (RIAC), a think tank established by President Medvedev in 2010 under the patronage of the Ministry of Foreign Affairs, remained the only influential state-sponsored think tank supporting cooperation rather than confrontation with the West.

Paralleling these moves in the think tank industry in the post-2012 context, major policy documents reconfigured the definition of Russia's security to include a strong ideological dimension to Russia's confrontation with the West. As highlighted by Engström, the 2013 Foreign Policy Concept advances the need for Russia to formulate an "ideological offensive" against the West's "soft power."[28] Likewise, the 2014 Military Doctrine brought to the fore the existence of threats characterized by the "integrated" use of military force and "other non-military measures implemented with the widespread use of the protest potential of the population."[29] Indeed, in the aftermath of the colored revolutions, the Arab Spring, and the Bolotnaia demonstrations, the Russian military's threat narrative perceived popular uprisings as techniques used by outside forces to instigate chaos and fulfill their interests.[30] This threat narrative on colored revolutions echoed Prokhanov's theory of the "organizational weapon," which he had developed in the 1990s to account for the fall of the Soviet Union. This theory claims that a society can control another society externally by a "system of economic, ideological, psychological and perhaps even parapsychological sources of influence."[31] In this context, Russia's foreign and security policies emphasized the need to confront the "Western offensive against Russia" that was being waged in the media and cyberspace and to "invest in 'patriotic upbringing' at home."[32] The Izborskii Klub's provision of patriotic, anti-Western discourse therefore acquired a positive strategic role for the country's security. The club produced analytical reports on some of the key

[28] Engström, "Contemporary Russian Messianism and New Russian Foreign Policy," 362.
[29] Cited in Tracey German, "Harnessing Protest Potential: Russian Strategic Culture and the Colored Revolutions," *Contemporary Security Policy* 41, no. 4 (2020): 556.
[30] German, "Harnessing Protest Potential," 554.
[31] See Leonid Shebarshin and Aleksandr Prokhanov, "Shef razvedki v gostiakh u 'Dnia,'" *Zavtra*, August 1991.
[32] Alexander D. Chekov et al., "War of the Future: A View from Russia," *Survival* 61, no. 6 (2019): 40.

issues of concern for the Russian military, such as security in the information and cyber spaces.[33] In 2014, the language of the Izborskii Klub was directly deployed by the Russian president to legitimize Russia's annexation of Crimea.

7.1.2 A Provider of Ideological Legitimation for Russia's Annexation of Crimea

Following the Maidan Revolution in Ukraine that deposed President Viktor Yanukovych in February 2014, Russia seized control of the Crimean Peninsula through a conjuncture of military, political, informational, and psychological measures that scholars have identified as "hybrid warfare."[34] The Izborskii Klub played an instrumental role in providing narratives and actions in support of Russia's annexation of Crimea. On February 13, the club issued a memorandum that described the Maidan protests as a "civilization aggression" instigated by the United States with the aim of "turning Ukraine into an anti-Russian state."[35] On March 18 and December 4, during his speeches to the Federal Assembly justifying the annexation of Crimea, Putin put forward the same narrative. He portrayed the ouster of the pro-Russian Ukrainian president Viktor Yanukovych as a "coup" orchestrated by Ukrainian politicians "disciplined" by "foreign sponsors."[36] He further argued that the 2004 Ukrainian Orange Revolution and the Maidan Revolution were led by "our Western partners" and directed against Russia.[37] The language Putin used to claim Crimea's Russian identity almost exactly mirrored Prokhanov's own argumentation, which he had developed in an article published a few days before Putin's speech. Prokhanov referred to the baptism of Prince

[33] See, for instance, the report "Russia: The Military Vector," published in issue 2 of the Izborskii Klub's journal (2013) and the reports "Network Wars" and "Digital Wars of the 21st Century," published in issue 10 (2013).

[34] Maria Snegovaya, "Putin's Information Warfare in Ukraine: Soviet Origins of Russia's Hybrid Warfare," Russia Report 1 (Washington, DC: Institute for the Study of War, 2015).

[35] "Spasti Ukrainu!" Izborskii Klub, February 13, 2014, https://izborsk-club.ru/2602.

[36] Vladimir Putin, "Address by President of the Russian Federation," Website of the President of Russia, March 18, 2014, http://en.kremlin.ru/events/president/news/20603.

[37] Putin, "Address by President of the Russian Federation," March 18, 2014.

Vladimir in the Crimean church of Chersonesus, and the subsequent Christianization of Kievan Rus, to argue that Crimea constituted the spiritual and political center of Russia.[38] Putin developed a similar line of argument, thereby endorsing one of the major theses of the hawks' ideology, according to which Orthodox Christianity had played a key role in the construction of the Russian state:

> Christianity was a powerful spiritual unifying force that helped involve various tribes and tribal unions of the vast Eastern Slavic world in the creation of a Russian nation and Russian state. It was thanks to this spiritual unity that our forefathers for the first time and forevermore saw themselves as a united nation. All of this allows us to say that Crimea, the ancient Korsun or Chersonesus, and Sevastopol have invaluable civilisational and even sacral importance for Russia, like the Temple Mount in Jerusalem for the followers of Islam and Judaism.[39]

Putin's discourse sanctioned several other essential arguments that had been promoted by the hawks since the 1990s. In particular, by describing Crimea as a "historically Russian land" and its annexation as a form of reparation for the "outrageous historical injustice" caused by the collapse of the Soviet Union, Putin officially acknowledged the well-established national-conservative view that Russia is a "divided nation."[40] According to Laruelle, those making this argument claim that the collapse of the Soviet Union created a gap between Russia's "territorial body" and its "cultural body" and hence call for the protection of Russian minorities abroad and for the reintegration of Belarus, part of Ukraine, and northern Kazakhstan into Russian territory.[41] Putin put forward the same narrative:

> Millions of people went to bed in one country and awoke in different ones, overnight becoming ethnic minorities in former Union republics, while the Russian nation became one of the biggest, if not the biggest ethnic group in the world to be divided by borders.[42]

38 Aleksandr Prokhanov, "Krymskoe vino pobedy," *Zavtra*, March 13, 2014, https://zavtra.ru/blogs/kryimskoe-vino-pobedyi.
39 Vladimir Putin, "Presidential Address to the Federal Assembly," Website of the President of Russia, December 4, 2014, http://en.kremlin.ru/events/president/news/47173.
40 Putin, "Address by President of the Russian Federation," March 2014.
41 Laruelle, "Russia as a 'Divided Nation,'" 90–91.
42 Putin, "Address by President of the Russian Federation," March 2014.

Putin also embraced the hawkish narrative condemning the Kosovo crisis, NATO's bombing campaign against Serbia, and US intervention in Iraq, Afghanistan, and Libya as a series of manifestations of the United States' unilateral affirmation of its supremacy in violation of international law.[43] In Putin's view, the crisis in Ukraine resulted from the same patterns of unlawful American interference:

> Our western partners, led by the United States of America, prefer not to be guided by international law in their practical policies, but by the rule of the gun. They have come to believe in their exclusivity and exceptionalism, that they can decide the destinies of the world, that only they can ever be right.[44]

The Izborskii Klub widely hailed its convergence of views with the president on this set of arguments in a report entitled "Putin in the Mirror of the Izborskii Klub."[45]

In addition to discourse production, the Izborskii Klub was involved in concrete actions with the aim of legitimizing the annexation of Crimea. Ahead of the Crimean status referendum on March 16, the club held a "rally of solidarity with the people of Crimea" in the Russian city of Briansk that was reportedly attended by 5,000 people.[46] Furthermore, the club set up a "fund for assistance for the population of Crimea and all of Ukraine."[47] Izborskii Klub members were also involved in legitimation actions in Crimea in and around the March 16 referendum on its reunification with Russia. The writer Nikolai Starikov, for instance, participated in a conference in the city of Simferopol, during which he claimed that the results of the referendum were "a completely legitimate basis for the proclamation of the independence of Crimea and Sevastopol from Ukraine and their subsequent entry into the Russian Federation."[48] The Izborskii Klub's active contribution to Russia's annexation of Crimea was officially acknowledged by the government of the new Republic of Crimea. Dmitrii Polonskii, deputy chairman of Crimea's Council of Ministers and minister of internal policy, information, and

43 This represents a significant shift from Putin's support and assistance to the US intervention in Afghanistan in 2001.
44 Putin, "Address by President of the Russian Federation," March 2014.
45 See issues no 2 and 3 (2014).
46 Izborskii Klub's journal, issue no. 4 (2014): 104.
47 Izborskii Klub's journal, issue no. 4 (2014): 105.
48 Izborskii Klub's journal, issue no. 4 (2014): 105.

communications, conveyed his "gratitude" to Prokhanov and the Izborskii Klub for their "consistent position on our Crimean issue," adding that their opinion "played a significant role in the events of the Crimean Spring."[49]

The Russian military also lent official recognition to the Izborskii Klub's strategic role in the country's security by naming the aircraft bomber Tupolev Tu-95, a strategic missile carrier, after the city of Izborsk and decorating it with the club's logo, thereby reviving the Soviet tradition of placing national emblems on military aircraft.[50] The aircraft was presented during a ceremony in August 2014 at the Engels Air Force Base, one of Russia's two most important operational airbases, a few kilometers from the city of Saratov. The ceremony was attended by high-ranking military, political, and even Orthodox officials, such as the commander of the long-range aviation division of Russia's Aerospace Forces, the governor of the Saratov region, and a regional bishop.[51] At the end of August 2014, the Izborskii Klub built on these connections to the military and political establishment to perform a ritual dedicated to the "symbolic reunification of the Crimean lands [with Russia]."[52] The club hosted a ceremony in the city of Izborsk, attended by the commander of the Izborskii Tupolev and the governor of Pskov, during which they reactivated the meaning of the "Sacred Hill" monument by scattering over it pieces of soil over it that they had collected from Crimean sites of strategic military importance.

During the period surrounding Russia's annexation of Crimea, from February to August 2014, the Izborskii Klub therefore became an hegemonic ideological group officially recognized as a contributor to the realization and legitimation of Russia's strategic goals. However, following the club's involvement in the conflict in eastern Ukraine, the state reduced the level of support it provided to the organization, leading to its relegation to the rank of a subordinate strategic subculture.

[49] Quoted in Izborskii Klub's journal, issue no. 7 (2014): 16.
[50] Laruelle, "Izborsky Club, or the New Conservative Avant-Garde," 626.
[51] Aleksandr Prokhanov, "Strategicheskii bombardirovshchik 'Izborskii Klub,'" *Zavtra*, August 21, 2014, https://zavtra.ru/blogs/strategicheskij-bombardirovschik-izborskij-klub.
[52] Izborskii Klub's journal, issue no. 8 (2014): 117.

7.2 The Regime's Commitment to Managed Ideological Pluralism (2014–2016)

7.2.1 Novorossiia and the Collapse of Consensus between the Regime and the Hawks

In the period since the annexation of Crimea, the Izborskii Klub has been a key supporter of the separatist insurgent groups in the Donetsk and Luhansk territories of the eastern Ukrainian region of Donbass. The club played an instrumental role in legitimating the insurgency by becoming one of the most active theorizers and propagators of the concept of "Novorossiia" (New Russia). This term was first used at the end of the eighteenth century to designate the Russian Empire's new territories on the north of the Black Sea, including Donbass, which were acquired from wars with the Ottoman Empire.[53] In the spring of 2014, the term Novorossiia was reactivated by Donbass insurgents and their supporters as a way to justify their claims for independence from Ukraine.

A diverse range of ideological groups was involved in the new mythmaking around Novorossiia, ranging from Orthodox monarchist groups envisioning Donbass as part of historical imperial Orthodox Russia, to nationalist and neo-Nazi groups, using the Donbass insurgency to call for a generalized uprising against the Ukrainian and Russian regimes.[54] For the Izborskii Klub, Novorossiia provided an opportunity to put into practice their ideology of dynamic conservatism as the "basis for the emerging state on the southwestern borders of the Russian Federation."[55] In the club's "The Ideology of Novorossiia" report, Prokhanov and Kalashnikov portrayed the industrial and technological resources of the Donbass region as providing the ideal testing ground to develop their technocratic, futuristic ideals.[56] Prokhanov further alluded to the dual technological and spiritual dimensions of Novorossiia – as the heir of "a powerful technosphere inherited from the Soviet times" and of "primordial mystical

[53] Marlène Laruelle, "The Three Colors of Novorossiya, or the Russian Nationalist Mythmaking of the Ukrainian Crisis," *Post-Soviet Affairs* 32, no. 1 (2016): 56–65.
[54] Laruelle, "Three Colors of Novorossiya," 62–65.
[55] Izborskii Klub's journal, issue no. 5 (2014): 7.
[56] See issue 5 of the Izborskii Klub's journal (2014): 4 and issue no. 5 (2014): 27.

forces" that arose from its historical origins in the "mysterious depths of the ancient Slavs" – to conclude that the territory combined "technocratic cosmism with the mystical secret of the origin of the human race."[57] This narrative was combined with the promotion of Novorossiia as the perfect site for the implementation of the club's ideals of social justice based on economic nationalization and collectivism. Dugin stressed that the "social meaning of the Novorossiia project" was "the overthrow of the oligarchy, the nationalization of large private monopolies and the transfer of industrial facilities from private hands to the people themselves."[58]

Finally, Novorossiia was also portrayed as the affirmation of the different components of the Izborskii Klub's definition of the spiritual and cultural foundations of Russian civilization. For Prokhanov, Novorossiia was part of the Russian "multinational sovereign state in which all languages, all beliefs, all talents and national cultures form a flourishing synthesis."[59] Leonid Ivashov and Vitalii Averianov further emphasized the "Orthodox-Slavic" dimension of Novorossiia and its belonging to the "East Slavic brotherhood of the Great Russians," which is constitutive of the larger civilizational ensemble that they refer to as "Russia-Eurasia" or "the great Russian civilization."[60] They further contrasted this ethnic, cultural, and religious determination of Novorossiia with pejorative descriptions of Ukraine as a "limitroph" defined by its "absence of a clear cultural and civilization self-identification,"[61] and of Ukraine's Catholic tradition as a secret cult "sponsored by Western intelligence services."[62] The state project of Novorossiia, therefore, allowed the Izborskii Klub to hold together the eclectic technocratic, socialist, Orthodox monarchist and Eurasianist components of its ideological coalition. In that sense, the "Novorossiia myth-making" can be compared with the events of October 1993, since both moments generated a rallying effervescence that allowed the eclectic group of antiliberal hawks to unite their ideological positions in opposition to a common enemy.[63]

[57] Izborskii Klub's journal, issue no. 5 (2014): 4.
[58] Izborskii Klub's journal, issue no. 5 (2014): 13.
[59] Izborskii Klub's journal, issue no. 5 (2014): 4.
[60] Izborskii Klub's journal, issue no. 5 (2014): 10–11, 18.
[61] Izborskii Klub's journal, issue no. 5 (2014): 11.
[62] Izborskii Klub's journal, issue no. 5 (2014): 18.
[63] Laruelle, "Three Colors of Novorossiya," 70.

As one of the most vocal champions of the Novorossiia cause, the Izborskii Klub increasingly diverged from the direction of Russia's official foreign policy. Within the think tank industry, Reshetnikov's RISI was the only other institute that actively supported the Donbass insurgency. In April 2014, Putin himself publicly mentioned the term "Novorossiia":

> I would like to remind you that what was called Novorossiya (New Russia) back in the tsarist days—Kharkov, Lugansk, Donetsk, Kherson, Nikolayev and Odessa—were not part of Ukraine back then.[64]

However, in the following months, Putin explicitly distinguished the Russian state's official position from the Novorossiia campaign led by Russian ideologues and battlefield insurgents. In May 2014, the Russian regime failed to recognize the validity of the referenda held in Luhansk and Donetsk and the republics' subsequent proclamation of independence from Ukraine. Instead, the Kremlin reportedly called for the insurgents to restrain their effort to seize control of eastern Ukrainian territory.[65] In August 2014, in a statement that addressed the "Novorossiia militia," Putin called for a humanitarian corridor to be opened for "Ukrainian service members who have been surrounded" and for negotiations between the Ukrainian authorities and "Donbass representatives."[66] As stressed by Laruelle, this latter terminology "unassumingly" avoided the word "Novorossiia" and showed the president's disengagement from militant narratives.[67] Mikhail Suslov has further highlighted the spread of a popular internet meme conveying the idea that Putin was "ditching" Novorossiia.[68]

In contrast, over the summer of 2014, the Izborskii Klub became increasingly involved in supporting the separatists not only through its ideological legitimation of Novorossiia but also through direct assistance to the Donbass political and military leadership.

[64] Vladimir Putin, "Direct Line with Vladimir Putin," Website of the President of Russia, April 17, 2014, http://en.kremlin.ru/events/president/news/20796.

[65] International Crisis Group, "Rebels without a Cause: Russia's Proxies in Eastern Ukraine," Europe & Central Asia 254 (July 2019).

[66] Vladimir Putin, "President of Russia Vladimir Putin Addressed Novorossiia Militia," Website of the President of Russia, August 29, 2014, http://en.kremlin.ru/events/president/transcripts/46506.

[67] Laruelle, "Three Colors of Novorossiya," 57.

[68] Mikhail Suslov, "The Production of 'Novorossiya': A Territorial Brand in Public Debates," *Europe-Asia Studies* 69, no. 2 (February 7, 2017): 104.

The Eurasianist Union of Youth, led by Izborskii Klub member Valerii Korovin, recruited and sent numerous volunteers to join the fighting on the ground.[69] Izborskii Klub members themselves did not travel to Donbass at that time but closely liaised with the local leaders to provide them with policy advice and organizational support. The club had particularly strong connections with the three founding figures of the Donetsk People's Republic (DPR): Governor Pavel Gubarev, Prime Minister Aleksandr Borodai, and Minister of Defense Igor Girkin-Strelkov. Prokhanov reported that all of them had previously contributed to his newspaper *Zavtra*.[70] In addition, Aleksandr Borodai is the son of the philosopher Iurii Borodai (1934–2006), who was a close friend of Prokhanov and a regular columnist for *Zavtra* in the 1990s. Aleksandr Borodai was also well acquainted with the Izborskii Klub member Mikhail Leontev, a journalist and head of the oil company Rosneft's analytical department, which had employed him as a press officer.[71] The Izborskii Klub members' close working relations with the leadership of the DPR was reflected in their contribution to the wording of the new state's constitution.[72] The club further increased its influence with the creation of a local branch in Donetsk, headed by Pavel Gubarev. Throughout the summer, this local branch of the Izborskii Klub organized working groups and meetings to deliver policy recommendations such as the creation of a "textbook on the history of Novorossiia" and on the "economic and political system of the newly built Novorossiia."[73]

In the fall of 2014, the Novorossiia campaign was decisively halted by the Russian regime, which covertly organized the ousting of Gubarev, Girkin-Strelkov, and Borodai and their replacement by a new government headed by Aleksandr Zakharchenko. As experts have argued, this new leadership served as a proxy for the Kremlin, which provided it with political and military support in exchange for their dependence on Moscow.[74] The Kremlin's more direct control of the

[69] Laruelle, "Three Colors of Novorossiya," 59.
[70] Quoted in Laruelle, "Three Colors of Novorossiya," 58.
[71] Laruelle, "Three Colors of Novorossiya," 59.
[72] Laruelle, "Three Colors of Novorossiya," 59.
[73] Izborskii Klub's journal, issue no. 7 (2014): 117.
[74] Laruelle, "Three Colors of Novorossiya," 59; Tatyana Malyarenko and Stefan Wolff, "The Logic of Competitive Influence-Seeking: Russia, Ukraine, and the Conflict in Donbas," *Post-Soviet Affairs* 34, no. 4 (July 2018): 191–212.

Donbass region eliminated the Izborskii Klub's influence over politics on the ground. Russia's foreign policy officially dismissed narratives on Novorossiia with the signing of the Minsk Protocol on September 5, 2014, in which Russia, Ukraine, and the separatist republics agreed to reintegrate the Donbass into Ukraine with a special status of local autonomy in certain areas of the Donetsk and Luhansk regions.

The Kremlin's choice to favor diplomacy over the use of force represents a key tipping point in the relation between the political and the ideological fields. It clearly showed that, despite the transactions occurring between them, the rules and interests guiding political decision-making are defined in interaction with other fields of forces, such as the military and economics. Indeed, as argued by an expert report, the Russian president's rejection of intensive military involvement in the Donbass was presumably inspired by the rising costs of the conflict due to Western sanctions and the weakening of the separatist movement on the ground.[75]

Following this collapse of strategic consensus with the Kremlin, the Izborskii Klub lost access to some of its key state-sponsored resources. In particular, Dugin's role as a leading ideologist of Novorossiia and promoter of insurgent fighting against Ukraine led to his dismissal as professor and head of the Department of Sociology and International Relations of the Faculty of Sociology of Moscow's State University.[76] Dugin's position on Novorossiia had mostly raised concerns due to its domestic consequences in Russia.[77] Indeed, in May 2014, Dugin had called for the extension of the Novorossiia movement inside Russia:

> The new party of Pavel Gubarev embodies the way to a Russian future, the path to the New Russia. Novorossiia here has both a direct and a metaphorical sense. Russia itself should be reborn, become another, cleanse, wake up, come back to its Russian, Eurasian identity. In freeing Novorossiia from Kiev's junta, the Russian heroes free Russia itself from the leftovers of the 1990s, the oligarchic system, Western influence, and spiritual and moral decadence.[78]

Dugin further called for the launch of a "Russian revolution" against what he condemned as the influence of "Atlanticism," Western values,

[75] International Crisis Group, "Rebels without a Cause."
[76] "Rektor MGU uvolil Aleksandra Dugina," lenta.ru, June 27, 2014, https://lenta.ru/news/2014/06/27/dugin.
[77] Laruelle, "Three Colors of Novorossiya," 66.
[78] Quoted in Laruelle, "Three Colors of Novorossiya," 66.

and the oligarchy.[79] While Dugin stressed that this revolution should be "for Russia and Putin," his discourse was still likely to have been perceived as too radically critical of the regime.

In addition to this episode, relations between the Izborskii Klub and the presidential administration became increasingly antagonistic as club members criticized the management of the conflict in Donbass by Vladislav Surkov, the president's adviser on Ukraine, and instead argued in favor of a "Stalinian" answer to the crisis.[80] As advocated by Nagornii, instead of diplomatic negotiations, the "Stalinian recipe" would involve a "total military operation" relying on the intervention of a "liberation army" manned with volunteers from Russia's private military corporations and supported by missile strikes against strategic targets.[81] By the end of 2014, the club's commitment to a full-scale military confrontation with the West had widened the gap with the more nuanced attitude voiced by Putin. Despite his criticism of the West's sanctions as the latest act in a "policy of containment" firmly entrenched in history, Putin maintained that "under no conditions will we curtail our relations with Europe or America."[82] In contrast, in September and November 2014, the Izborskii Klub published two reports, entitled "Prevent War—Win the War"[83] and "Cold War 2.0,"[84] that affirmed the "inevitable nature of the strategic confrontation between the West and Russia" and called for the mobilization of "all available resources for the needs of the country's development and the creation of asymmetric means of deterring the enemy in the course of a tough confrontation."[85] Moreover, in view of their focus on Russia's challenges in its competition for growth and development against the West, Izborskii Klub members resumed their critique of the regime's economic policies. In December 2014, Averianov

79 Izborskii Klub's journal, issue no. 5 (2014): 14.
80 Valerii Korovin, "O Surkove i ego agenture," Izborskii Klub, March 31, 2014, https://izborsk-club.ru/2905.
81 Aleksandr Nagornii, "Stalinskii retsept," Izborskii Klub, June 25, 2014, https://izborsk-club.ru/3409.
82 Putin, "Presidential Address to the Federal Assembly," December 4, 2014.
83 "Predotvratit voinu: Pobedit v voine," Izborskii Klub, September 30, 2014, https://izborsk-club.ru/3963.
84 Vladimir Ovchinskii and Elena Larina, "Kholodnaia voina 2.0," Izborskii Klub, November 11, 2014, https://izborsk-club.ru/4224.
85 "Novaia staraia kholodnaia voina: Zakliuchenie," dynacon.ru, http://dynacon.ru/content/articles/4409/#a6.

denounced Putin's continued commitment to a "neoliberal" economic program and claimed that, despite the "Crimean enthusiasm," the regime had ceased to be in tune with the club's conservatism:

> "Crimean enthusiasm" cannot last long ... Sometimes there is a feeling that the President is only covering up the ongoing economic course with populist stuffing of the right ideas: about the massive development of infrastructure projects, deoffshorization, strengthening of the welfare state, etc.[86]

Although it was demoted from its position as an hegemonic ideological group toward the end of 2014, the club was however nonetheless retained as a strategic subculture in specific policy niches such as patriotic education and Russia's soft power in the post-Soviet space.

7.2.2 *The Izborskii Klub as a Subordinate Strategic Subculture*

The second half of Putin's third term, from 2015 to 2018, was characterized by increased competition between the different strategic subcultures represented in the think tank industry, which resulted in diminished visibility for the Izborskii Klub's imperialist discourse.

The last official state subvention for the club was granted in December 2015, when the club received 10 million rubles (around €150,000 at the time) from the presidential administration, which was one of the largest grants delivered to civil society organizations that year.[87] The grant provided support for the development of the club's work on the concept of the "Russian world," a central issue for Russian strategic thinking about the definition of an expanded Russian civilization beyond the limits of the Russian territory.[88] From January to August 2016, the club ran nine roundtables dedicated to this issue in different Russian cities. The grant led to the club's deployment in Moldova, where it created a local subdivision in April 2016. The inaugural conference was held on the theme of

86 Vitalii Averianov, "Putin slishkom tiazhelo rasstaetsia s sastarelymi illiuziiami," Izborskii Klub, December 20, 2014, https://izborsk-club.ru/4397.
87 "Granty ot Putina dadut za propagandu russkogo mira i borbu s pedofilami," rbc.ru, December 8, 2015, www.rbc.ru/politics/08/12/2015/5666f9cf9a7947d88622c924.
88 For a definition of the "Russian world," see Marlène Laruelle, "The 'Russian World': Russia's Soft Power and Geopolitical Imagination," Center on Global Interests, 2015, 6.

the two countries' "common ties" as part of the same "Russian world."[89] In September 2016, the club eventually published "The Russian World Doctrine." The document offered a "new offensive strategy" aimed at "the reconstruction of the Russian state of the imperial type," which involved "the formation of Russia's spheres of interests" to compete with the West in the Balkans and Black Sea region, the protection of ethnic Russians' political and cultural rights in Ukraine, and the development of cooperation mechanisms with "compatriots" overseas.[90]

Toward the end of 2016, however, the Izborskii Klub's imperialist agenda had clearly lost ground within the policy circles of the presidential administration. Major changes in state-sponsorship practices during this period demonstrate that the Kremlin was seeking to downplay the conservative-authoritarian repertoire and promote liberal-democratic groups as a counterbalance. An important signal of this was sent by the change of management of the presidential administration after the September 2016 legislative elections. Viacheslav Volodin, a proponent of radical anti-Western conservative rhetoric and an informal supporter of the Izborskii Klub, was moved from the key executive position of first deputy chief of staff of the presidential administration, which is in charge of supervising domestic politics, to the less influential role of chairman of the State Duma.[91] His successor, Sergei Kirienko, a prime minister during the 1998 economic crisis, member of the party "Union of Right Forces" in 1999, and former head of the state nuclear energy corporation Rosatom (2005–16), was more associated with the liberal, technocratic elites.[92] As highlighted by the Russian journalist Andrey Perstev, this change of management at such a high-level position reflected the growing "battle for

[89] Izborskii Klub's journal, issue no. 5 (2016): 14.

[90] Vitalii Averianov, "Doktrina russkogo mira," Izborskii Klub, September 26, 2016, https://izborsk-club.ru/10269.

[91] As mentioned in Chapter 5, during an interview, an Izborskii Klub member referred to Volodin as one of the "patrons" of the club. On Volodin as a proponent of traditional Orthodox values, see also Mikhail Zygar, *All the Kremlin's Men: Inside the Court of Vladimir Putin* (New York: PublicAffairs, 2016), 248–50.

[92] "Russia's Technocrat-in-Chief: How Sergey Kiriyenko Transformed the Kremlin's Domestic Policy and Quietly Gained Influence within the Putin Administration," meduza.io, October 11, 2019, https://meduza.io/en/feature/2019/10/11/russia-s-technocrat-in-chief.

influence" between factions within the political elite respectively represented by Volodin and Kirienko.[93]

These shifts of power in the presidential administration had direct consequences for the think tank industry. In 2016, the presidential administration reorganized its funding scheme for civil society organizations, with future funding to be delivered through a unique entity, the Russian Presidential Grant Fund, which was placed under Kirienko's direct supervision. In 2017–19, the top ten recipients of the fund were involved in work with children or people with special needs, while projects with a "more patriotic orientation," such as those involved in the "preservation of historical memory" or "public diplomacy and compatriots," were in a clear minority.[94] Indeed, following the implementation of this new competitive scheme, each of the three applications for funding from the Izborskii Klub was rejected.[95]

Reductions in funding for the hawks was also paired with their exclusion from the management of state-sponsored think tanks. At RISI, Reshetnikov was replaced in 2016 by Mikhail Fradkov, the former director of the Foreign Intelligence Services (2007–16), who dissolved most of RISI's management and discarded his predecessor's Orthodox monarchist agenda.[96] In contrast, the Center for Strategic Research (CSR), which had been put on hold in the period 2011–16, emerged as the dominant policy platform after it was placed under the leadership of Aleksei Kudrin, former finance minister (2000–11) and a leading figure of the liberal political elite. In May 2016, Kudrin was appointed by presidential decree as a cochair of the presidential working group on economic affairs, which established a direct link between the presidential administration and the CSR, leading the latter to assume the status of the most influential expert platform.[97] With a focus on socioeconomic issues and normalization of relations with the

93 Andrey Pertsev, "Volodin vs. Kiriyenko: The Battle for Influence in Russia's Power Vertical," *Carnegie Moscow Center*, June 16, 2017, https://carnegiemoscow.org/commentary/71280.

94 Marlène Laruelle and Laura Howells, "Ideological or Pragmatic? A Data-Driven Analysis of the Russian Presidential Grant Fund," *Russian Politics* 5, no. 1 (2020): 42–45.

95 The club applied in 2018, in 2019, and in 2020. All the applications are recorded on the website: https://xn--80afcdbalict6afooklqi5o.xn--p1ai/public/application/cards.

96 Graef and Barbashin, "Thinking Foreign Policy in Russia."

97 Graef, "Influential or Irrelevant?" 26.

West as a necessary condition for reaching GDP growth targets, the CSR's agenda neatly contrasted with the Izborskii Klub's concerns with Russia's imperial expansion and confrontation with the West.

However, the 2016 reshuffle of the ruling elites left room for a conservative agenda in the education sector. The new minister of education, Olga Vasileva, a historian specializing in relations between the state and the Russian Orthodox Church, had put forward a conservative agenda as part of her previous work in the presidential administration dealing with the governmental commissions for religious associations and with the preparation of a school curriculum on "patriotic history."[98] From 2016 to 2018, the Izborskii Klub closely collaborated with her ministry on the implementation of the state program entitled "Patriotic Education of Citizens of the Russian Federation 2016–2020."[99] The program's objectives included "improvement of the methods of work on patriotic education of citizens," "military-patriotic education of children and youth," and "development of the volunteer movement as an important element of the system of patriotic education of youth." In 2017, after a meeting between Prokhanov, Rozanov, and Olga Vasileva, the Izborskii Klub was granted the task of drafting patriotic education programs for secondary schools.[100] The club also set up cooperation agreements on the implementation of the state program of patriotic education, with regional administrations in Saint Petersburg and in the Khanty-Mansiiskii district.[101]

7.3 A Strategic Subculture Maintained through a Conservative Lobby Group (2018–2022)

7.3.1 The Izborskii Klub's Expansion of Regional and International Policy Networks

Although the Izborskii Klub had lost hegemony over expert foreign policy debates toward the end of Putin's third term, it remained active

[98] "Kto takaia Olga Vasileva: Chto izvestno o novom ministre obrazovaniia," tass.ru, August 19, 2016, https://tass.ru/politika/3551544.

[99] "Pravitelstvo Rossiiskoi Federatsii: Postanovlenie ot 30 dekabria 2015 goda n 1493; O gosudarstvennoi programme 'Patrioticheskoe vospitanie grazhdan Rossiiskoi Federatsii na 2016–2020 gody,'" https://docs.cntd.ru/document/420327349?marker=6560IO.

[100] Izborskii Klub's journal, issues no. 7 (2017): 113 and no. 5 (2018): 101.

[101] Izborskii Klub's journal, issues no. 6 (2018): 105 and no. 7 (2018): 130.

as a strategic subculture through moving the focus of its strategy from federal elites to Russian regional elites and international policy circles.

Using similar processes to those in the Donbass, the club established offices throughout the country in order to liaise with the local leadership and contribute policy advice.[102] The club aimed to become involved in ideology-drafting for regional governors in the same way as it had worked on the concept of Novorossiia. As a club member explained in an interview, these "provincial ideologies" were designed to narrate the origin and history of each Russian province. They were intended to serve as a "new language" for governors, enabling them to frame their policies as a continuation of the "grand narrative of Russian history."[103] From the summer of 2014 until the end of 2016, the chronology of the club's journal reported sixteen trips to different regional administrative centers by Prokhanov either individually or as head of a delegation composed of other Izborskii Klub members. On each of these visits, the club met with the corresponding regional governor or head of state. By the end of 2016, the visits had led to the establishment of eight regional branches of the Izborskii Klub, in Kursk, Orel, Iaroslavl, Kurgan, Krasnodar, Zikhiia-Izbora, Groznyi, and Sevastopol (in Crimea). The creation of local subdivisions allowed the club to involve regional governors and local elites in roundtables on themes dear to its ideological agenda such as "Orthodoxy as a stimulus for national development" in Kursk, "spiritual mobilization" in Orel, "the imperialism of modern Russia" in the Chechen Republic, and "Russian world: prayers and strategies" in Iaroslavl. In 2017–18, the club sustained and expanded its regional strategy in other territories, such as Tatarstan and in the Mari El Republic.

As a club member explained, most of the club's regional branches were financially sponsored by local entrepreneurs who perceived the club as a provider of administrative resources that would allow them to "lobby their interest" to the political establishment in Moscow through the club's supposed connections with decision-makers within the presidential administration.[104] Although the club member described this perception as an "illusion," stressing that the club was

[102] The information below is based on a review of the club's activities available on the club's journal's "Khronologiia" pages.
[103] Author interview, Moscow, 2019. [104] Author interview, Moscow, 2019.

primarily a "group of intellectuals," the club's legitimacy in the eyes of regional elites arguably built on the reputation it had acquired during the first years of its operation as a state-sponsored think tank close to the presidential administration.

The Izborskii Klub used the same strategy in the post-Soviet space, with a focus on eastern Ukraine, the Baltics, and Moldova. First, despite the signing of the Minsk Protocol, the club continued its active campaign for Novorossiia. Inside Russia, the club organized actions in support of the insurgency, such as a rally on Poklonnaia Gora and celebrations of the deeds and victories of Donbass military commanders.[105] In the fall of 2014, members of the Izborskii Klub went on a fieldtrip to Donbass, during which they met with both the former leaders of the DPR – Gubarev, Girkin-Strelkov – and the newly elected government, including Prime Minister Aleksandr Zakharchenko and First Deputy Prime Minister Andrei Purgin.[106] Subsequently, Izborskii Klub members regularly traveled to Donbass to maintain contact with politicians and militias on the ground and attend conferences and book presentations organized by their local branch. In May 2015, for instance, the Izborskii Klub of Novorossiia hosted a presentation of Korovin's book, *The End of the Ukraine Project*, in Donetsk.

The club also developed strong connections with Zakharchenko through the intermediary of its member Zakhar Prilepin, a famous writer. Over the years 2015–18, Prilepin collected and personally delivered humanitarian aid for the Donbass population and enrolled in the ranks of the DPR Armed Forces. In February 2017, he was decorated by Zakharchenko with the shoulder straps of a major of the Armed Forces of the DPR and promoted to the rank of political instructor and deputy commander of a battalion.[107] The club was therefore able to maintain activities on the ground and keep regular contacts with the Donbass leadership.

In the Baltics, the Izborskii Klub's agenda was overseen by Aleksandr Gaponenko (1954–), who created a regional branch of the club in

105 See Victoria Donovan, "Militarized Memory," in *Russia's Regional Identities: The Power of the Provinces*, ed. Edith W. Clowes, Gisela Erbslöh, and Ani Kokobobo, 1st ed., Routledge Contemporary Russia and Eastern Europe Series 80 (London: Routledge, 2018), 77.

106 All of Prokhanov's interviews with them were published in issue no. 11–12 of the Izborskii Klub's journal (2014).

107 Izborskii Klub's journal, issue no. 2 (2017): 121.

Riga in 2015. A former associate professor in economics at the Riga Higher Military-Political School in the 1980s, Gaponenko has been a champion of the rights of ethnic Russian communities in the Baltics since the fall of the Soviet Union. As reported by his biographical page on the club's website, he has organized a referendum for granting the Russian language the status of a state language in Latvia.[108] Over the years 2016–18, the Izborskii Klub in Moscow held joint conferences with the regional branch in Riga to organize publications and actions to promote the "divided nation" narrative.[109]

The Izborskii Klub's influence in the post-Soviet space proved particularly fruitful in Moldova, where its regional branch was set up in 2016 under the patronage of the leader of the Moldovan Socialist Party, Igor Dodon, who became the president of the Republic of Moldova after the December 2016 elections. The Izborskii Klub was therefore able to reproduce a similar scenario to that in Donbass, where its regional subdivision became a key platform to connect directly with the ruling elites and provide them with policy advice. In an interview, a member of the club's leadership referred to Dodon as the club's "close friend" and "ally."[110] Before the elections, the Moldovan Izborskii Klub had set up a clearly pro-Russian agenda with a sharp critique of Moldova's relations with the European Union. The club's conferences, attended by local politicians, Moldovan Orthodox clerics, and Izborskii Klub members from Moscow, focused on themes such as "Moldova and Russia: common history, common values, common vision of the future" and "European integration and its negative consequences for the former countries of the Soviet bloc." In December 2016, as first deputy chairman of the Izborskii Klub, Rozanov attended the inauguration ceremony of President Dodon, during which they reportedly discussed the "prospects for cooperation between Russian and Moldova" and the continued cooperation between the Izborskii Klub and its division in Moldova.[111]

108 See "Aleksandr Gaponenko," Izborskii Klub, https://izborsk-club.ru/11358.

109 In 2018, Gaponenko's activism in social networks led to his arrest by the Latvian authorities on charges of "attempting to overthrow the government," "inciting ethnic hatred," and "acting in favor of a foreign state." The Izborskii Klub published a public appeal and organized an international picketing in Estonia, Moldova, and Moscow to ask for his release. He was eventually discharged. See issue 8 of the Izborskii Klub's journal (2018): 130.

110 Author interview, Moscow, 2019.

111 Izborskii Klub's journal, issue no. 1 (2017): 121.

To date, the Izborskii Klub has not set up offices in other post-Soviet countries. However, the club has entertained connections with Tajikistan, where Prokhanov was able to witness the antiterrorist exercises of the Collective Security Treaty Organization in 2017, and with Azerbaijan, where Prokhanov personally met with President Ilham Aliyev during a visit in 2017. The Izborskii Klub has therefore been practicing informal diplomacy and soft power in the post-Soviet space through its own resources and networks of partners.

The club also connected with a network of policymakers globally to form a worldwide ideological axis based on a rejection of the United States' dominance of the international order. In 2015, the club's members put forward this agenda by attending two ceremonies dedicated to the commemoration of the casualties of NATO and US military operations. The first was held in Serbia on the sixteenth anniversary of NATO's bombing of Yugoslavia during the Kosovo War of 1999. The second was held in Japan on the seventieth anniversary of the nuclear bombing of Hiroshima and Nagasaki. On this occasion, Izborskii Klub members met with the mayor of Hiroshima and set up a permanent bilateral forum with Japanese historians and political scientists to work on Russian–Japanese relations.[112]

The club's other key international partners include China, Iran, and North Korea. The Izborskii Klub initiated relations with China during a trip by Prokhanov to Shanghai in April 2014, during which he delivered a speech on the rapprochement between Russia and China. In July 2014, an official meeting was hosted by the Chinese embassy in Moscow between Izborskii Klub members and the Chinese ambassador. In the following years, the Izborskii Klub held joint conferences with two well-established Chinese think tanks. In 2015, it partnered with the state Institute for Social Development of Europe and Asia to host a conference in Beijing entitled "China and Russia in a Changing World." As highlighted by Averianov's speech at the conference, a chief aspect of the Izborskii Klub's interest in China is its search for a "Russian idea" that would draw inspiration from the concept of the "Chinese dream" put forward by Xi Jinping as a national model of development based on the "synthesis of conservatism and

[112] Izborskii Klub's journal, issue no. 8 (2015): 102.

progressivism" as an alternative to the "individualism" and "atomization" associated with the "American dream."[113]

In 2017, the Izborskii Klub also held a working meeting in Moscow with another important Chinese think tank, the Institute of Financial Research of the Renmin University of China. Izborskii Klub members Sergei Glazev and Iurii Tavrovskii have proved to be major assets in the club's relations with China. As the adviser to the Russian president on Eurasian economic integration, Glazev has held regular meetings with his counterparts in China on issues of Russian–Chinese cooperation and Eurasian integration. Tavrovskii, meanwhile, has gained recognition as a journalist and author of popular essays on China and Russian–Chinese relations.[114] In 2019, he was awarded the National Prize for merit in literature by a panel of high-ranking Chinese officials, including a member of the Politburo of the Central Committee of the Communist Party, the head of the Propaganda Department, and the press minister.[115]

The Izborskii Klub has found other important international partners in Iran and North Korea, where the club has emphasized the countries' common situation with Russia as the targets of American sanctions and as the sites of an alternative to "Americanism" and "globalism."[116] As mentioned in the preceding chapter, the foundation of the club was shortly followed, in 2013, by the organization of a meeting with then-Iranian president Mahmoud Ahmadinejad (2005–13), a personal friend of Prokhanov. In the aftermath of the election of President Hassan Rouhani in 2013, the club maintained contacts with the Iranian authorities by holding talks with the Iranian ambassador in Moscow and organizing a series of meetings

[113] Vitalii Averianov, "Doklad v Pekine," Izborskii Klub, May 20, 2015, https://izborsk-club.ru/5604.

[114] See, for instance, Iurii Tavrovskii, *Si Tszinpin: Po stupeniam kitaiskoi mechty* (Moscow: Eksmo, 2015); Iurii Tavrovskii, *Novyi shelkovyip put: Glavnyi proekt XXI veka* (Moscow: Eksmo, 2017); Iurii Tavrovskii, *Si Tszinpin: Novaia epokha* (Moscow: Eksmo, 2018).

[115] This prize was established by the Chinese government in 2005 to reward foreign authors for their contribution to the popularization of Chinese literature and culture abroad. See Izborskii Klub's journal, issue no. 10 (2019): 133.

[116] See Prokhanov's comments on his trips to North Korea (April 2014) and Iran (December 2014) respectively in the Izborskii Klub's journal, issues no. 5 (2014): 133 and no. 11–12 (2014): 122.

in Iran between Prokhanov and political and religious officials. In 2016, club members traveled to Tehran to hold a joint conference with the Institute of Political and International Studies of the Iranian Ministry of Foreign Affairs on the theme "Iran and Russia in a changing world," which reportedly led to their signature of strategic cooperation agreements.[117]

Similar working meetings have also been held with the embassy and political leaders of North Korea in Moscow and Pyongyang.[118] In 2016, the North Korean government showed its support of the Izborskii Klub's work by granting Prokhanov the International Kim Il-sung Prize, which is conferred for contribution to the study and propagation of the Juche idea, the regime's national ideology.

At the level of national politics, the club's leadership brought dynamic conservatism to the fore of its agenda in order to challenge the hegemony of liberal groups in domains where it was the most established, i.e., economic, scientific, and technological policies.

7.3.2 A Private Lobby Group Focused on Russia's Economic and Technological Modernization

In the few studies on Russia's think tanks that mention the Izborskii Klub, the club's focus on Russia's domestic modernization has often been neglected. However, Russia's economic, scientific, and technological development has been a founding and enduring concern for the Izborskii Klub, a concern that became its trademark in the years 2018–21. Indeed, the club sought to challenge the influence of liberal groups, especially Kudrin's CSR, over the definition of Russia's path toward growth and development.[119] The Izborskii Klub's economists have consistently advocated a socialist and collectivist economic

[117] Izborskii Klub's journal, issue no. 2 (2016): 108.

[118] Prokhanov went on two working trips to North Korea, in 2014 and 2017. On the last one, he met with the chairman of the Presidium of the Supreme People's Assembly and the deputy chairman of the Central Committee of the Workers' Party. See Izborskii Klub's journal, issue no. 2 (2017): 121.

[119] Irina Busygina and Mikhail Filippov, "The Limits of Conservative Influence on Economic Policy in Russia," in *New Conservatives in Russia and East Central Europe*, ed. Katharina Bluhm and Mihai Varga, Routledge Contemporary Russia and Eastern Europe Series 85 (Abingdon: Routledge, 2019), 158.

doctrine, pressing for Eurasian economic integration, the nationalization of industries, expansionary monetary policies, and protectionist mechanisms against importations and capital flight.[120]

By contrast, in 2016–18 a more liberal, Western-inspired, and market-driven approach to science and technology increasingly prevailed in the Russian president's agenda. The Izborskii Klub strongly disapproved of the politics of the main institutions responsible for implementing science and technology policies at the time, such as the Presidential Council for Science and the Federal Agency for Scientific Organizations (FANO), created in 2013. They denounced FANO on the grounds that it was dominated by "liberal financiers oriented towards ... property privatization," leading research to be tailored to the demands of the market rather than the needs of the state.[121] Putin's annual address to the Federal Assembly of March 2018, which set out his program for the presidential elections to follow a few weeks later, further established a vision of science and technology that stood in sharp contrast to the Izborskii Klub's model of development. The word "tradition" was mentioned only once, with the words "breakthrough" (*proryv*) and "change" (*izmenenie*) becoming the new mantra of the government.

At this time, Putin's discourse was generally supportive of a liberal and progressive conception of technological modernization based on foreign standards, private entrepreneurship, partnerships with the West, and globalization. He described Russia as a "land of opportunity," stressing the need to "expand freedom in all spheres," to "open the country to the world and to new ideas and initiatives," to "get rid of anything that stands in the way of our development and prevents people from unleashing their potential," to "gradually reduce the [state's] share in the economy," and finally to "eliminate all barriers for the development and wide use of robotic equipment, artificial intelligence, unmanned vehicles, e-commerce and Big Data processing technology."[122] He also portrayed great power competition almost

120 Anders Åslund, "Sergey Glazyev and the Revival of Soviet Economics," *Post-Soviet Affairs* 29, no. 5 (2013): 375–86.

121 Aleksandr Nagornii, "Akademiki trepeshchut pered vlastiu," Izborskii Klub, December 1, 2016, https://izborsk-club.ru/11258.

122 Vladimir Putin, "Presidential Address to the Federal Assembly," Website of the President of Russia, March 1, 2018, http://en.kremlin.ru/events/president/news/56957.

exclusively in technological terms, unlike the civilizational approach to global competition he had advocated in his address of March 2014.

While economic and technological modernization has been a constant theme for the Izborskii Klub since its creation, the prioritization of this issue also followed from the club's efforts to secure new funding sources from private entrepreneurs. In 2019, the club received financial support from Sergei Pisarev, a monarchist Orthodox entrepreneur involved in real estate, retail, and hotel industries, who had already funded the Russian Doctrine in 2005.[123] The Izborskii Klub's appeal to Pisarev's financial sponsorship, therefore, introduced a new capitalist element into its ideological synthesis, which already combined monarchism and Sovietism.

The club's campaign for this integrated vision of Russia's grand strategy, promoted under the slogan of the "Russian Dream," resulted in the formation of an influential lobby group comprising conservative religious, economic, and political elites.

7.3.3 *The Club's Campaign for Russia's Grand Strategy*

In October 2018, an Izborskii Klub roundtable entitled "In Search of the Russian Dream and the Image of the Future" established the focus of the club's agenda for the following years as the promotion of a "new technocratic mythology of development."[124] With this goal in mind, the club has aimed to offer an alternative to the liberal theory of modernization. To do that, the club has promoted Russian cosmism as the philosophical basis for Russia's model of development, based on the "combination of ultramodern science … with spiritual enlightenment."[125] Averianov reasserted the view that the convergence of the Soviet Union with Western institutions was to blame for the Soviet elite's failure to carry out "a long-term mobilization strategy to implement the ideals of … Russian cosmic thinkers Fedorov, Tsiolkovskii, Vernadskii."[126]

123 Izborskii Klub's journal, issue no. 5–6 (2019): 143.
124 "Stenogramma kruglogo stola Izborskogo Kluba 'V poiskakh russkoi mechty i obraza budushchego,'" Izborskii Klub, October 10, 2018, https://izborsk-club.ru/15978.
125 "Stenogramma kruglogo stola Izborskogo Kluba 'V poiskakh russkoi mechty i obraza budushchego.'"
126 "Stenogramma kruglogo stola Izborskogo Kluba 'V poiskakh russkoi mechty i obraza budushchego.'"

The Izborskii Klub further spelled out its conception of Russian cosmism as a strategic alternative for development in a series of reports. The report "Sacred History," published in December 2018, argues that Russian cosmism offers an "ideological synthesis" combining "Orthodox ethics with the values and conquests of Soviet modernity." According to this "technocratic traditionalism," developments and innovations in science and technology can be "organically combined" with conservative cultural, moral, and religious values.[127] In a subsequent report, "Transhuman vs. Human," published in October 2020, technocratic traditionalism is positioned within contemporary ideological debates as an alternative to the dichotomy between "technocracy" and "ecological apocalypticism."[128]

On the one hand, the Izborskii Klub seeks to distinguish Russian cosmism from Western transhumanism. Because they converge on key ideas – such as the achievement of immortality, the colonization of space, human enhancement – several transhumanist thinkers have identified Russian cosmism as an avant-garde type of transhumanism.[129] By contrast, the Izborskii Klub has stressed their incompatibility by arguing that transhumanism is a "natural outcome" of "Western-European atheistic evolutionism," whereas Russian cosmism is deeply anchored in Christian religious philosophy and anthropology.[130] In the club's view, transhumanism is a symptom of the "spiritual degradation" of humanity and will lead to the "de-humanization of a person" and its reduction to "a machine of computer technology."[131] In contrast, the report defines Russian cosmism as the "highest, most conscious form of Christianity" that seeks a "synthesis of modern science and patristic theology."[132] Moreover, the authors view Western transhumanist entrepreneurs such as Elon Musk as driven

127 "Sviashchennaia istoriia: Zdes i seichas," Izborskii Klub, December 30, 2018, https://izborsk-club.ru/16343.

128 "Russkii kovcheg: Alternativnaia strategiia mirovogo razvitiia"; "Transchelovek protiv cheloveka," Izborskii Klub, October 31, 2020, https://izborsk-club.ru/20212.

129 See, for instance, Giulio Prisco's reference to Federov in Giulio Prisco, "Maximum Jailbreak, and the Legacy of Stephen Hawking," turingchurch.net, October 22, 2018, https://turingchurch.net/maximum-jailbreak-and-the-legacy-of-stephen-hawking-3a5773b9e6df.

130 "Transchelovek protiv cheloveka."

131 "Transchelovek protiv cheloveka."

132 "Transchelovek protiv cheloveka."

by capitalist, elitist business interests. Instead, they contend, Russian cosmism is turned toward the achievement of the world's "Common Cause," where the technological achievement of resurrecting the ancestors serves the moral transformation of humanity and its "spiritual enlightenment."[133]

On the other hand, the Izborskii Klub also takes issue with ecological and conservative critics of technological progress. It describes the concept of "limits to growth," developed by the Club of Rome's 1972 report, as a typically "Western idea" that relies on the "deeply pessimistic" view of "Earth of a closed system" with limited natural resources.[134] Furthermore, it also denounces the "theory of sustainable development" as a "project for artificial population reduction imposed on almost the whole world by the UN conference in Rio de Janeiro in 1992."[135] Instead, it puts forward Russian cosmism's beliefs in the extraterritorial expansion of humanity and in man's ability to control natural processes.

Specifically, for Russia, the club advocates a series of ambitious scientific and technological projects to better exploit the country's natural resources, such as drilling in the Arctic to seek oil and natural gas reserves and modernizing the exploitation of Russia's fertile soils. In addition, the club envisages Russia as the leader of technological solutions to natural resource scarcity, such as industries to convert Arctic ice into fresh water for global consumption.[136] The Izborskii Klub, therefore, explicitly differentiates itself from bioconservatives, who perceive technology as a source of moral alienation or social inequality. In contrast, Izborskii Klub authors have embraced a firm techno-enthusiasm/-optimism by defending an "ideology of development" based on "wise technologies" and the ethics of "Christian anthropology."[137]

133 "Russkii kovcheg: Alternativnaia strategiia mirovogo razvitiia."
134 "Russkii kovcheg: Alternativnaia strategiia mirovogo razvitiia."
135 "Russkii kovcheg: Alternativnaia strategiia mirovogo razvitiia."
136 "Russkii kovcheg: Alternativnaia strategiia mirovogo razvitiia."
137 "Transchelovek protiv cheloveka." By contrast, other contemporary Russian artists and thinkers have advocated a more liberal, universalist understanding of Russian cosmism as part of a dialogue with Western modernity. See Marina Simakova, Anton Vidokle, and Arseny Zhilyaev, "Cosmic Doubts," in *Art without Death: Conversations on Russian Cosmism*, ed. Bart de Baere and E-Flux Journal (Berlin: Sternberg Press, 2017), 109–29.

The "technocratic traditionalism" synthesis worked out by the club in 2018–20 served to complete its vision of the grand strategy that Russia should pursue to achieve its national and international goals. The club's major policy goal then became the government's adoption of this long-term strategic developmental plan, for which it campaigned under the name "Russian Dream."[138]

The concept of the Russian Dream was largely informed by the club's interaction with its Chinese counterparts. Prokhanov played a particularly important role in developing the Izborskii Klub's equivalent to the Chinese dream. In numerous articles, he has praised the realization of a Russian Dream blending industrial and technological achievements with Orthodox spirituality in service of an imperial authoritarian state.[139] At the regional level, Prokhanov produced an inventory of each region's spiritual and technological resources, heritage, and patrimony that formed their particular regional "Dream" and contributed to the broader "Russian Dream."[140] At the national level, he identified the Russian Dream with the major "geostrategic projects" initiated by the government such as the exploration of the Arctic to enrich Russia with hydrocarbon deposits and the construction of the Northern Sea shipping route.[141] As Averianov further argued, the Russian Dream includes a messianic aspect and should be offered worldwide as an alternative to the American Dream through the development of projects such as exploration of space, the regulation of nature, and the search for immortality.[142]

The Izborskii Klub's campaign for the Russian Dream was originally launched on mass media and eventually gained access to policy circles. During the initial phase, in 2018, Prokhanov was employed by the state-owned news TV channel Rossiia 24 to tour the country and report on each region's religious, industrial, and economic sites and their contribution to the Russian Dream. In the fall of 2018, weekly

138 See the Izborskii Klub's journal, issue no. 9 (2019), devoted to the concept of the "Russian Dream."

139 See, for instance, Aleksandr Prokhanov, "Putin—Russkii mechtatel," *Zavtra*, January 2019.

140 See, for instance, his description of the Russian Dream in Iamal, Arkhangelsk, and the Caucasus regions in Aleksandr Prokhanov, "Mechta neiziasnimaia," Izborskii Klub, December 27, 2018, https://izborsk-club.ru/16324.

141 Prokhanov, "Putin: Russkii mechtatel."

142 Vitalii Averianov, "Nevidimaia os mira: Nam nuzhen orden mechtanostsev," Izborskii Klub, January 3, 2020, https://izborsk-club.ru/18514.

episodes of his TV reportage, entitled *In Search of the Russian Dream*, were broadcast on Rossiia 24.[143] On each of his visits to the regions, Prokhanov met with the governor or head of state and subsequently maintained regular contact with them. Prokhanov's TV reportage in the Sverdlovsk region, the fifth most populated Russian region, was praised by the governor, Evgenii Kuivashev, and led to his establishment of working relations with the Izborskii Klub. In February 2019, the governor expressed support for the club's creation of a regional branch of the "Academy of the Russian Dream" based in Ekaterinburg, Sverdlovsk's administrative center.[144]

Similar public support for the development of a regional branch of the Academy of the Russian Dream was voiced by the governor of Belgorod, Evgenii Savchenko.[145] Prokhanov's TV reportage also brought about recognition for the concept of the Russian Dream from federal political elites. In July 2019, Prokhanov was invited to the State Duma to show and discuss his documentary film *Russia: A Nation of Dreams*, produced by Rossiia 24. The audience included the chairman of the State Duma, Viacheslav Volodin, and the leaders of the main parliamentary groups.[146]

In 2020–21, the Izborskii Klub's cooperation with the monarchist oligarch Konstantin Malofeev, the founder of one of the largest Russian investment funds, enjoying extensive connections to political and economic elites, led to a new stage in the development of the Russian Dream campaign. Malofeev has actively promoted a conservative political agenda as an organizer of meetings of far-right political parties across Russia and Europe, as founder of Orthodox charity organizations focused on the promotion of traditional values, and as one of the core sponsors of the Donbass insurgency in the summer of 2014.[147] He has cultivated close relations with Izborskii

143 "V poiskakh russkoi mechty: Gorst zemli," Izborskii Klub, September 17, 2018, https://izborsk-club.ru/15849.
144 Aleksandr Prokhanov, "Nasha rabota tolko nachinaetsia," Izborskii Klub, February 28, 2019, https://izborsk-club.ru/16571.
145 See issue 2 of the Izborskii Klub's journal (2019): 142.
146 "V gosudarstvennoi Dume predstavili dokumentalknii film 'Narod mechty,'" Website of the State Duma of the Russian Federation, July 22, 2019, http://duma.gov.ru/news/45809.
147 Malofeev was identified as one of the actors involved "in support of the destabilization of Eastern Ukraine" and was included in the list of persons subject to sanctions by the European Union in July 2014.

Klub ideologues: In 2016, Dugin was appointed the editor-in-chief of Malofeev's internet TV channel Tsargrad.[148] In 2019, Malofeev's links with the Izborskii Klub tightened further after he was appointed by Patriarch Kirill as deputy head of the World Russian People's Council (VRNS), the church's central public discussion and advocacy platform.

Malofeev's role as a leader of the VRNS provided institutional shape to the existence of an ideological interest group at the crossroads of prominent religious, economic, and intellectual elites. Shortly after his nomination, Malofeev set the VRNS agenda on writing a strategy for the development of Russia inspired by the Izborskii Klub's concept of the Russian Dream, entitled "Russian Dream: 2050." In December 2019, a press conference held by Malofeev and the Izborskii Klub leadership (including Prokhanov, Averianov, and Rozanov) officially announced their joint work on the Russian Dream.[149] This partnership provided the Russian Dream campaign with major new resources. The VRNS organized four committees composed of 100 experts dedicated to the "Russian Dream" strategy.[150]

Moreover, Malofeev's ability to access the highest level of the policymaking elite to promote ideas was demonstrated by his successful campaign for the inclusion of new constitutional amendments during the process of constitutional reform launched by Vladimir Putin in 2020. While the major aim of this reform was to suppress the presidential term limits to allow Putin to run for a third consecutive mandate, it also included a series of other amendments.[151] As acknowledged by Malofeev, the eventual adoption of amendments mentioning the Russian people's "faith in God" and enforcing a strict definition of

[148] While Dugin left this position in 2017, he has remained an active employee of Tsargrad TV. My interview with him, in 2019, was held in his personal office in the Tsargrad TV building in Moscow.

[149] "Prezentatsiia knigi 'Verouchenie russkoi mechty. Ideologiia gosudarstva rossiiskogo,'" pressmia.ru, December 16, 2019, http://pressmia.ru/pressclub/20191216/952558794.html.

[150] "Demografiia, narodosberezhenie i nravstvennost: Zamglavy VRNS Malofeev o sudbonosnoi dlia strany 'Russkoi Mechte; 2050,'" vrns.ru, https://vrns.ru/news/demografiya-narodosberezhenie-i-nravstvennost-zamglavy-vrns-malofeev-o-sudbonosnoy-dlya-strany-russk.

[151] "Obrazovana rabochaia gruppa po podgotovke predlozhenii o vnesenii popravok v konstitutsiiu," Official Website of the President of Russia, January 15, 2020, http://en.kremlin.ru/events/president/news/18089.

marriage as the union between a man and a woman matched the demands of "all traditionally minded people" that he sought to represent.[152] As he further claimed, these amendments were suggested by Patriarch Kirill during a meeting Malofeev convened with the first deputy chief of staff of the presidential administration, Kirienko.[153]

Although there is no public information available on the circulation of the VRNS's "Russian Dream: 2050" strategy to the government or the presidential administration, the evolution of the Russian Dream campaign nevertheless demonstrates the Izborskii Klub's capacity to translate its ideological theorization into policy recommendations carried by a strategic partner – the VRNS under the leadership of Malofeev.

7.4 Conclusion

This chapter has traced the career of the Izborskii Klub through an analysis of the discursive circulation of the club's ideas and the social and material interaction between the club and policy circles. It has shown that the club's ideas have contextually informed some of the regime's strategic views and policy choices, such as the threat narrative on colored revolutions and the annexation of Crimea. In this respect, despite the abolition of a state ideology in the Russian Constitution of 1991, the regime has resumed some of the Soviet state's practices of grounding policy decisions in ideological narratives. By contrast with the Soviet Union, however, the Russian state's sponsorship of ideology was not aimed at the development of a coercive ideological apparatus but rather at the conservation of "managed pluralism" to ensure a certain degree of flexibility in policy choices. Over the period 2012–21, the Izborskii Klub has fallen from a dominant to a subordinate position in the competition between the different strategic subcultures represented in the think tank industry. Instead of the club's imperialist and revisionist foreign policy, more liberal groups promoting Russia's economic development through the normalization of its relations with the West have gained influence with the presidential administration put in place in 2016.

152 Max Seddon, "The Russian Oligarch Who Wants Vladimir Putin to Be a Tsar," *Financial Times*, March 13, 2020.

153 Seddon, "Russian Oligarch."

As an alternative to state support, the club has been financed by private entrepreneurs, in particular the monarchist oligarch Malofeev, who have sustained the club's ideas as a strategic subculture among influential conservative elites across economic, political, and religious milieus. By contrast with the state's practice of ideological balancing and compromise, these private sponsors have proved their principled adherence to the club's ideology by providing important material and organizational support to advocate and implement the club's vision of Russia's grand strategy, based on Russian cosmism's blend of science and spirituality, as an alternative to the Western liberal secular model of modernity.

8 *Shaping Russia's Wartime Ideology (2022–2024)*

The activities of the forces that formed the Izborskii Klub … turned out to be largely built around preaching and apologizing for the return of the empire. All of us, one could say, acted as forecasters—some even say prophets—of this fifth empire.

In my opinion, February 22, 2022 is the moment when the fifth empire started to step on the threshold.

Vitalii Averianov, "Ukraina: Lish povod dlia velikogo sobytiia," 2022

As shown in Chapter 7, following the annexation of Crimea in 2014, the regime's engagement in diplomatic negotiations with Ukraine through the Minsk agreements explicitly diverged from the Izborskii Klub's advocacy of the full-scale invasion of Ukraine and integration of Donbass into Russia. While the Izborskii Klub was subsequently sidelined by the presidential administration's politics of ideological sponsorship, Vladimir Putin's decision to invade Ukraine on February 24, 2022, marked a pivotal shift in his strategic thinking in the direction of the Izborskii Klub's imperialist ideology.

Why did Putin authorize this move in 2022, while he restrained it in 2014? A significant challenge in understanding the factors that led to the Kremlin's decision to engage in warfare is the lack of access to Russia during 2020–22 due to Covid-related travel restrictions, which prevented the collection of first-hand fieldwork and observations in the years immediately preceding the invasion. Various changes in domestic and international environments likely contributed to creating conditions that prompted the Russian regime to abandon diplomatic negotiations and resort to an unrestrained, revisionist use of military force. The Russian army's combat training during the Syria campaign arguably bolstered confidence in its military capabilities, while the buildup of financial reserves and closer partnership with China helped support the costs for a large-scale operation and mitigate the impact of Western sanctions.[1] Domestically, the 2020 constitutional amendments lifting restrictions on presidential terms, combined with two years of Covid-related isolation from international exchanges, potentially fostered an environment more accepting of authoritarian measures. The crack-down on opposition, including Alexei Navalny's imprisonment in 2021, further consolidated internal control and reduced dissent.

While acknowledging that structural pressures exerted by the international order and material capabilities matter in strategic decision-making, the focus of this book lies in assessing the causal impact of the ideological consolidation of the Russian regime on its policy choices. Having shown that state support of the hawkish stance represented by the Izborskii Klub has waxed and waned and that it severely contracted ahead of the war, this research challenges teleological narratives describing the invasion as the fatal, predetermined outcome of Putin's ideological radicalization.[2] Instead, the concept of "managed ideological pluralism" highlights the regime's caution, at least until 2022, not to pledge allegiance to a single state ideology. Rather than centering on Putin as the unitary actor involved in grand strategizing, it suggests that the war was one of the policy outcomes made available by the mode of administering idea networks that the regime has put into place over the past decades to balance the influence among elite groups representing different strains of strategic culture.

While the leadership of the Izborskii Klub has acknowledged their lack of influence over Putin's decision to invade Ukraine, depicting it as a "revolution from above" that occurred contrary to their own expectations, they have nonetheless enthusiastically praised it as the realization of the "fifth empire" they had "prophesized."[3] This chapter

[1] For an examination of the Russian regime's engagement in successive wars from Chechnya to Ukraine and going through Syria, see Mark Galeotti, *Putin's Wars: From Chechnya to Ukraine* (Oxford: Osprey Publishing, 2022). On Putin's strategy of financial reserves accumulation, see Vladislav Zubok, "Can Putin Survive? The Lessons of the Soviet Collapse Essays," *Foreign Affairs* 101, no. 4 (2022): 84–96.

[2] See, for instance, Fiona Hill and Angela Stent, "The World Putin Wants. How Distortions about the Past Feed Delusions about the Future," *Foreign Affairs* 101 (October 2022), www.foreignaffairs.com/russian-federation/world-putin-wants-fiona-hill-angela-stent.

[3] Vitalii Averianov, "Ukraina: Lish povod dlia velikogo sobytiia," Izborskii Klub, April 4, 2022, https://izborsk-club.ru/22582.

delves into the years 2022–24 to investigate how the shifting dynamics of ideological formation and dissemination during wartime have reshaped the role of Russian hawks in the realm of ideology production. It raises the question of whether the invasion of Ukraine coincided with the evolution of the Russian political system from managed ideological pluralism to an institutionalized state ideology enforced by a coercive apparatus.

Unlike previous chapters, which have integrated sources from interviews and fieldwork observations, this chapter relies solely on discourse analysis, given the distinctive circumstances of the ongoing war. Additionally, owing to the immediacy of this context, the literature utilized predominantly comprises materials from Russian newspapers operating in exile, such as *Meduza*. These newspapers have retained access to sources linked to the presidential administration or the Kremlin, offering valuable insights into the inner workings of the Russian regime amid the wartime environment. However, it is crucial to acknowledge the inherent limitations of anonymous sourcing, which necessitate a degree of caution when interpreting data obtained from these sources.

This chapter argues that the Russian regime has restored elements reminiscent of the Soviet-style "vertical," facilitating the propagation of norms and principles through a bureaucratic chain of command. However, the regime has not completely reconstructed a cohesive institutionalized state apparatus. Its doctrinal framework remains adaptable. In addition to official state-led initiatives, the regime continued to oversee ideology formation through interactions and transactions with a variety of nonstate ideological entrepreneurs. This involvement of diverse actors across state and nonstate realms maintained a certain degree of ideological polarization within policy circles. The critical dimension of the hawkish prowar "Z-Space" advocating more radical military action and repression, and the notable instance of Wagner's mutiny in 2023, followed by the dismissal of high-ranking military officials like Commander-in-Chief of the Russian Aerospace Forces Sergei Surovikin, serve as illustrations of this dynamic. Moreover, the hawks' production of narratives justifying Russia's imperialism and war violence encountered resistance from recent intellectual emigrants, who have established organizations in exile dedicated to fostering critical thinking and dissent within intellectual circles.

8.1 Russia's Grand Strategic Shift

8.1.1 A Hegemonic Hawkish Strategic Culture

The Russian regime's foreign policy adopted a clearly revisionist stance by first recognizing the independence of the Donetsk and Luhansk People's Republics on February 22, 2022, then invading Ukraine on February 24 and eventually annexing the Donetsk, Luhansk, Zaporizhzhia, and Kherson regions on 21 September.[4]

Vladimir Putin's justification for the use of armed force and rejection of the international order was grounded in arguments that had long been championed by the most hawkish conservative elites, notably the Izborskii Klub. Ahead of the war, Putin's article "On the Historical Unity of Russians and Ukrainians," which he published in July 2021, had fully endorsed the rhetoric put forward by the Izborskii Klub since 2014, which viewed Ukraine as a failed state, artificially created by the Soviet Union, ruled by "neo-Nazis," and engaged in "Russophobic" policies.[5] In his February 21, 2022, speech recognizing the independence of the Donetsk and Lugansk People's Republics, Putin reasserted these claims and further emphasized that Ukraine was not just a "neighboring country" but an "inalienable part" of Russia's history and spiritual space.[6] On February 24, justifying the invasion, Putin claimed the military operation aimed to protect Russian people from "facing humiliation and genocide perpetrated by the Kiev regime" and to "demilitarize and denazify Ukraine."[7]

[4] For a thorough and historical exploration of Russia's evolving relations with Ukraine and the West preceding the war, see Serhii Plokhy, *The Russo-Ukrainian War: The Return of History* (New York: W. W. Norton & Company, 2023).

[5] See Vladimir Putin, "On the Historical Unity of Russians and Ukrainians," Website of the President of Russia, July 22, 2022, http://en.kremlin.ru/events/president/news/66181. For works previously published by the Izborskii Klub and voicing similar views, see, for instance, Valerii Korovin's book *Konets proekta "Ukraina"* (The End of the Project "Ukraine") (St. Petersburg: SBP, 2014) or the Izborskii Klub's report on the "Russian world": "Doktrina Russkogo Mira," Izborskii Klub, September 26, 2016, https://izborsk-club.ru/10269.

[6] Vladimir Putin, "Address by the President of the Russian Federation," Website of the President of Russia, February 21, 2022, http://en.kremlin.ru/events/president/news/67828.

[7] Vladimir Putin, "Address by the President of the Russian Federation," Website of the President of Russia, February 24, 2022, http://en.kremlin.ru/events/president/news/67843.

Second, Putin framed the military confrontation as a broader struggle against NATO and a defiance of the US-dominated world order. He leveled accusations regarding Ukraine's alleged intent to acquire nuclear arms and the purported ongoing presence of NATO military forces in Ukraine.[8] By June 2022, Putin had declared that the "era of a unipolar world order has come to an end," positioning Russia as a key player in the establishment of a new multipolar global structure.[9]

In particular, Putin's prolific use of the term "Novorossiia" to denote the Zaporizhzhia and Kherson regions signified a notable shift in his strategic discourse toward alignment with the ideas of the Izborskii Klub. Initially, as highlighted in Chapter 7, in the summer of 2014, Putin's decision to halt the "Novorossiia campaign" in favor of supporting separatist insurgency in Eastern Ukraine marked a significant departure from the Izborskii Klub's line. However, since 2022, Putin has consistently employed the term "Novorossiia" across various contexts. The normalization of this term was officially introduced by his 2021 article on the "historical unity of Russians and Ukrainians," where he underlined the significance of Novorossiia as a region historically linked to Russia, emphasizing its incorporation into the Russian Empire in the eighteenth century.[10] Following the signing of treaties on the accession of Donetsk and Lugansk People's Republics and the Zaporizhzhia and Kherson regions to Russia, Putin has repeatedly claimed the historical and cultural ties of these regions to Russia, asserting their importance for Russia's strategic interests: "by defending our compatriots in Donbass and Novorossiia, we are defending Russia itself."[11] He has often referred to Donbass

[8] Putin, "Address by the President of the Russian Federation," February 21, 2022.

[9] Vladimir Putin, "St Petersburg International Economic Forum Plenary Session," Website of the President of Russia, June 22, 2022, http://en.kremlin.ru/events/president/news/68669.

[10] Vladimir Putin, "On the Historical Unity of Russians and Ukrainians," Website of the President of Russia, July 12, 2021, http://en.kremlin.ru/events/president/news/66181.

[11] Vladimir Putin, "Signing of Treaties on Accession of Donetsk and Lugansk People's Republics and Zaporozhye and Kherson Regions to Russia," Website of the President of Russia, October 5, 2022, http://en.kremlin.ru/events/president/news/69465. See also Vladimir Putin, "Address on Day of Reunification of the Donetsk People's Republic, Lugansk People's Republic and the Zaporozhye and Kherson Regions with Russia," Website of the President of Russia, October 2, 2023, http://en.kremlin.ru/events/president/news/72403.

and Novorossiia as "liberated, historical regions"[12] and "primordial Russian lands," framing their inclusion into Russia as a rightful return home.[13] Moreover, Putin's discourse extends beyond historical theorization to administrative normalization, making integrating Donbass and Novorossiia into Russia's economic, legal, and administrative framework a priority policy objective.[14]

In addition to his confrontational foreign policy, Putin has pursued a repressive authoritarian agenda domestically, also espousing the rhetoric long advocated by the Izborskii Klub. A few weeks after the invasion, he emphasized the dichotomy between "true patriots" and "scum and traitors," calling for the expulsion of the so-called fifth column of national traitors. He stressed the urgency of "detoxifying society" through the expulsion of dissenters "like an insect in [the] mouth."[15] This rhetoric has led to the adoption of a number of repressive laws, resulting in the criminalization of antiwar protests and the banishment of critical media outlets.[16]

In this context of "wartime Putinism,"[17] the level of ideological diversity within elite circles, previously analyzed in earlier chapters as part of the regime's "managed ideological pluralism," significantly contracted. The pivotal Security Council meeting held on February 21, 2022, focused on deciding between pursuing talks with the West or recognizing the independence of the Donetsk and Lugansk People's Republics, exemplifies what could be termed a forced consensus. Initial shock and confusion were evident among several

[12] See Vladimir Putin, "Meeting with State Duma Party Leaders," Website of the President of Russia, December 19, 2023, http://en.kremlin.ru/events/president/news/73000; Vladimir Putin, "United Russia Party Congress," Website of the President of Russia, December 19, 2023, http://en.kremlin.ru/events/president/news/73013.

[13] Vladimir Putin, "Meeting with Government Members," Website of the President of Russia, August 4, 2023, http://en.kremlin.ru/events/president/news/71892.

[14] Vladimir Putin, "Security Council Meeting," Website of the President of Russia, April 13, 2023, http://en.kremlin.ru/events/president/news/70870.

[15] "Meeting on Socioeconomic Support for Regions," Website of the President of Russia, March 16, 2022, http://en.kremlin.ru/events/president/news/67996.

[16] Human Rights Watch, "Russia Criminalizes Independent War Reporting, Anti-War Protests," March 7, 2022, www.hrw.org/news/2022/03/07/russia-criminalizes-independent-war-reporting-anti-war-protests.

[17] Marlène Laruelle, "Russia's Ideological Construction in the Context of the War in Ukraine," Russie.Eurasie.Reports, Institut Français des Relations Internationales, March 2024.

attendees, including notable figures like Nikolai Patrushev, secretary of the Security Council, and Sergei Naryshkin, director of the Foreign Intelligence Service, who initially advocated for continuing diplomatic negotiations and maintaining compliance with the Minsk agreements.[18] Nonetheless, Putin's pressure to align their positions secured unequivocal support for recognition. This instance highlights the swift consolidation of elite support behind Putin's aggressive foreign policy agenda, marking a departure from previous tendencies toward managed ideological diversity.

Since the onset of the war, defections from elite circles have been exceedingly rare, although a few notable instances have occurred. One prominent defection took place in March 2022, when Anatoli Chubais, appointed as Vladimir Putin's special representative on climate issues in 2020 and a figure from the regime's liberal wing, resigned. Among other high-ranking officials, another notable resignation came from Arkadi Dvorkovitch, a former deputy prime minister who managed the Skolkovo technology investment fund.[19]

Furthermore, journalist Andrei Pertsev has argued that, despite the dominance of the "party of war," there remained a certain level of alternative policy orientations embodied by the "party of peace" and the "party of silence."[20] According to his sources, members of the "peace party" include key figures of the business and banking sectors, such as Andrei Kostin, president and chairman of VTB Bank, Herman Gref, chief executive officer (CEO) of Sberbank, and Sergei Chemezov, CEO of the state corporation Rostec. Chemezov even publicly criticized the regime's policy of total import substitution as ineffective in a column for the business newspaper RBC.[21] On the

[18] Vladimir Putin, "Security Council Meeting," Website of the President of Russia, February 22, 2022, http://en.kremlin.ru/events/president/news/67825.

[19] Benoît Vitkine, "En Russie, Anatoli Tchoubaïs, conseiller de Poutine et figure libérale, fait défection," *Le Monde*, March 24, 2022, www.lemonde.fr/international/article/2022/03/24/en-russie-anatoli-tchoubais-conseiller-de-poutine-et-figure-liberale-fait-defection_6118948_3210.html.

[20] Andrey Pertsev, "'In Public There Are Only Jingoistic Voices' How Russia's War against Ukraine Continues to Divide Putin's Elites," *Meduza*, June 17, 2022, https://meduza.io/en/feature/2022/06/17/in-public-there-are-only-jingoistic-voices.

[21] Sergei Chemezov, "'Otkuda prenebrezhenie k rossiiskomu?' Glava 'Rostekha' ob importozameshchenii," RBC, June 15, 2022, www.rbc.ru/opinions/economics/15/06/2022/62a87e589a7947cbf332c253.

other hand, the "party of silence" comprises officials who opt not to publicly comment on the war while maintaining active roles in Russia's leading economic and political institutions. Prime Minister Mikhail Mishustin, Moscow Mayor Sergei Sobianin, and Elvira Nabiullina, the governor of the Central Bank, are among the most prominent members of this group.

The significant dominance of the "party of war," however, underscores the remarkable stability and cohesion among the elite and the uniformity of their discourse. Some of the key people identified as intermediaries between Izborskii Klub and ruling circles were given more policy weight. The appointment of Vladimir Medinskii, former culture minister (2012–20) and one of the founding supporters of the Izborskii Klub, as the head of the Russian delegation for negotiations with Ukraine in February 2022, demonstrated the Kremlin's ambition to assign significant policy influence to the most conservative elite groups in the management of war-related policies. Moreover, prominent figures once considered the most "liberal," such as Dmitri Medvedev, deputy chairman of the Security Council, and Sergei Kirienko, first deputy chief of staff of the presidential administration, have emerged as some of the most outspoken propagandists of the war. Specifically, Medvedev has gained notoriety for his aggressive and hateful messages on social media platforms, where he has referred to Ukrainians as "bastards and degenerates."[22] He has further portrayed the conflict as a holy war against Satan,[23] calling for the complete annihilation of Ukraine,[24] suggesting scenarios involving a Russian nuclear strike[25] and issuing threats of military attacks against NATO countries.[26]

[22] Dmitrii Medvedev, "Menia chasto sprashivaiut…," Telegram, June 7, 2022, https://t.me/medvedev_telegram/105.

[23] Dmitrii Medvedev, "Pochemu nashe delo pravoe…," Telegram, November 4, 2022, https://t.me/medvedev_telegram/206.

[24] Dmitrii Medvedev, "WHY WILL UKRAINE DISAPPEAR? BECAUSE NOBODY NEEDS IT," X (formerly Twitter), April 8, 2023, https://x.com/MedvedevRussiaE/status/1644669039095037953.

[25] Dmitrii Medvedev, "Eshche raz o primenenii iadernogo oruzhiia…," Telegram, September 27, 2022, https://t.me/medvedev_telegram/181.

[26] Dmitrii Medvedev, "Ukrainian criminals have announced that…," X (formerly Twitter), August 29, 2023, https://x.com/MedvedevRussiaE/status/1696537158465851619.

This convergence of public "styles"[27] displayed by ruling elites indicates a departure from the recognition of diverse systems of thought, interests, and beliefs, toward the establishment of anti-Western, conservative imperialism as the prevailing hegemonic discourse. In this sense, the analytical distinction between liberal-technocratic elites and the *siloviki* (members of the security forces) has diminished significantly.

Moreover, state institutions have been involved in intense wartime state crafting, showing concerted bureaucratic efforts at increasing consistency and rigidity of the ideational underpinning of the Russian regime. A series of laws, presidential decrees, and policy documents has embedded the interests, values, and principles of Russia as a state.[28] One such example is the 2022 presidential decree titled "Fundamentals of State Policy to Preserve and Strengthen Traditional Russian Spiritual and Moral Values,"[29] which outlines a set of policy goals for ensuring national security by preserving traditional values. This decree emphasizes the importance of 17 traditional values,[30] presenting them as critical for safeguarding national sovereignty. As noted by Ben Noble, the decree operationalizes the securitization of these values by assigning a range of national security and defense state entities the responsibility for implementing the policy.[31]

The integration of traditional values into Russia's strategic culture and foreign policy goals is evidenced by two other significant documents. The first is the September 2022 presidential decree titled "On the Validation of the Concept of Russia's Humanitarian Policy

27 Andrey Pertsev, "From Kremlin Courtiers to Propaganda Serfdom," *Riddle Russia*, April 6, 2022, https://ridl.io/from-kremlin-courtiers-to-propaganda-serfdom/.

28 The Duma passed a historic total of 653 laws in 2022 Leonid Uvarchev, "Gosduma priniala v 2022 godu rekordnoe chislo zakonov — 653," *Kommersant*, December 22, 2022, www.kommersant.ru/doc/5736100.

29 "Ukaz Prezidenta Rossiiskoi Federatsii No 809," Website of the President of Russia, November 9, 2022, http://kremlin.ru/acts/bank/48502.

30 Point 5 of the decree defines traditional values as including "life, dignity, human rights and freedoms, patriotism, citizenship, service to the Fatherland and responsibility for its fate, high moral ideals, strong family, creative work, priority of the spiritual over the material, humanism, mercy, justice, collectivism, mutual assistance and mutual respect, historical memory and continuity of generations, the unity of the peoples of Russia."

31 Ben Noble, "'Traditional Values' and the Limits of Civic Unity," *Russia Post*, November 21, 2022, https://russiapost.info/politics/traditional_values.

Abroad," which outlines a comprehensive framework for Russia's role on the international scene as the guardian and protector of traditional spiritual and moral values against the perceived threat of globalization to cultural identity.[32] Moreover, the 2023 Concept of Foreign Policy also emphasizes the promotion and protection of traditional Russian spiritual and moral values as essential components of Russia's national interests.[33]

8.1.2 *The Izborskii Klub: Radical Ideologists of the War*

Izborskii Klub members have staunchly asserted their role as visionaries and ideologues of the war. A few days after the war began, Aleksandr Prokhanov was seen aboard a military aircraft flying over Ukraine, echoing his previous Soviet role as a war reporter known as the nightingale of the general staff. In an interview on February 28, 2022, for the newspaper *Komsomolskaia Pravda*, Prokhanov vividly described his experience:

> Well, here I am now, sitting in the cockpit of a Russian attack aircraft. And under my wings I see Sumy, Chernigov, the suburbs of Kiev, Mariupol, Melitopol. I am flying over the Ukrainian black soil, which Russian tanks are cutting through, correcting the monstrous violence done to Russian history in 1991. Today, this peaceful divorce, which was used to mess with our heads, which ended in such pain, such suffering, such misfortune for many of our peoples, is being overcome. Today we are again married to Ukraine. And Russians are putting bandages on that terrible cut of 1991.[34]

This rhetoric, with its fascist-like exaltation of violence as a means for regeneration, glorifies the military aggression as a necessary means for restoring national pride and unity and for addressing Prokhanov's longstanding obsession with the collapse of the Soviet Union. In further commentaries, the journalist conducting the interview depicted

[32] "Ukaz Prezidenta Rossisskoi Federatsii No 611," Website of the President of Russia, September 5, 2022, http://kremlin.ru/acts/bank/48280.

[33] "Concept of the Foreign Policy of the Russian Federation," Website of the Ministry of Foreign Affairs of the Russian Federation, March 31, 2023, https://mid.ru/en/foreign_policy/fundamental_documents/1860586/.

[34] "O Spetsoperatsii na Ukraine," *Komsomolskaia Pravda*, February 26, 2022, www.kp.ru/daily/27369.5/4551490/.

the war as a "dramatization of Prokhanov's novels," enthusiastically highlighting the parallels between the imagined narratives of Russia's imperial restoration in Prokhanov's works and the reality of Russia's invasion of Ukraine. Likewise, Vitalii Averianov has hailed February 22 as a crucial step toward the realization of Russia's envisioned "fifth empire," as articulated in the Izborskii Klub doctrinal works.[35] This concept describes a historical continuum of Russia's imperial legacy, comprising four previous empires – Kievan Rus, Muscovy, the Romanov Empire, and the USSR – and culminating in the establishment of a fifth empire. Averianov has thereby sought to underscore the revolutionary implication of the invasion of Ukraine for Russia's own historical path, framing it as a "revolution from above," steering Russia's historical trajectory away from what he characterizes as the "abnormality of the post-Soviet order" and toward the "restoration" of what he deems as "the natural order."[36] Furthermore, he has attributed a quasi-divine significance to Putin's actions, depicting them as the fulfillment of a sacred destiny: "This is not the will of an individual, it is, to put it bluntly, the will of God for Russia."[37] Such esoteric interpretations function to rationalize and legitimize the war within a broader context of historical inevitability and divine providence.

These viewpoints were consolidated into a cohesive group stance in the Izborskii Klub's manifesto released in September 2022, titled "Wartime: Disaster of Victory."[38] The document depicts the war as a defensive measure and a profound struggle for survival against a "monstruous" Western adversary intent on eradicating Russia's essence and independence. Moreover, under the rallying cry "Donbass saved Russia," the club lauds the war's historic achievement of one of their longstanding objectives: fostering ideological cohesion by uniting various factions, including monarchists and communists, under a "common cause." Lastly, the text asserts the club's role as a guiding force in shaping Russia's trajectory, steering the country toward their own vision of its destiny: "The Izborskii Klub does not have its own

[35] Vitalii Averianov, "Ukraina – Lish povod dlia velikogo sobytiia," Izborskii Klub, April 4, 2022, https://izborsk-club.ru/22582.
[36] Vitalii Averianov, "Vesna ochistitelnaia," Izborskii Klub, March 18, 2022, https://izborsk-club.ru/22500.
[37] Averianov, "Ukraina – Lish povod dlia velikogo sobytiia."
[38] Izborskii Klub's journal, issue no. 8 (2022): 2.

tank and air armies. We do not have our own intelligence services or secret services. We have a vision of Russian history, in which Russia is revealed in its tragic and sublime beauty."

In assuming roles as champions and ideological figures of the conflict, members of the club have found themselves thrust in the spotlight. The death of Dugin's daughter, Daria Dugina, in August 2022,[39] in an attack reportedly directed at her father, along with the attempted assassination of another club member, the writer Zakhar Prilepin, in May 2023,[40] highlights their perceived central role in legitimizing the war, making them notable targets.

However, despite their proclaimed position as the war's chief ideologues, members of the Izborskii Klub have expressed criticism of the regime's management of the conflict, citing various concerns.

First, they called for a more radical and comprehensive mobilization effort and a more effective execution of the war. Following the invasion, Averianov highlighted that, despite the initiated "revolutionary" changes, significant transformations were yet to materialize. He cautioned against the regime succumbing to "compromises or doubts," while also warning against the influence of what he referred to as a "hidden fifth column" within the state's elite.[41] Similarly, Prokhanov, in an analysis from July 2022, lamented the perceived detachment of Russian society from the war's realities, accusing the state leadership of viewing the conflict as a localized issue rather than a national crisis. Contrary to the regime's insistence on labeling the intervention as a "special military operation," Prokhanov boldly defined it as a "war," even advocating for its transformation into a "holy," "people's war" defending the existence of the Russian people and territories.[42] Additionally, Aleksandr Dugin, in a statement from November 2022, explicitly criticized the war's conduct, holding the "power" accountable for Russia's military retreat from the city of Kherson.[43]

39 Aleksandr Dugin, "Vragi Rossii podlo, ispodtishka ubili moiu doch," Izborskii Klub, August 22, 2022, https://izborsk-club.ru/23224.
40 Zakhar Prilepin, "Demonam soobshchaiu: Vy nikogo ne zapugaete," Izborskii Klub, May 7, 2023, https://izborsk-club.ru/24289.
41 Averianov, "Vesna ochistitelnaia."
42 Aleksandr Prokhanov, "Ei, ukhnem!" Izborskii Klub, July 28, 2022, https://izborsk-club.ru/23128.
43 Aleksandr Dugin, "Kherson – Poslednii rubezh otstupleniia," November 11, 2022, https://tsargrad.tv/articles/aleksandr-dugin-herson-poslednij-rubezh-otstuplenija_662480?fbclid=IwZXh0bgNhZW0CMTAAAR1V

Like Prokhanov, he stressed the need for the war to evolve into a full-fledged "people's war," necessitating comprehensive mobilization and militarization of the nation. In a subsequent article penned in 2024, he reiterated the imperative of imposing "total militarization" across all cultural, educational, informational, and psychological domains.[44]

As they view it, one necessary step to ensure the full mobilization of the country is the imposition of a state ideology. Izborskii Klub members have praised Putin's ideological radicalization as a significant advancement. In response to Putin's speech on the annexation of the Donetsk, Luhansk, Zaporizhzhia, and Kherson regions, Dugin acknowledged: "The President's speech directly voiced key code concepts – 'Greater Russia,' 'country-civilization,' Russian Spring, 'liberation mission,' multipolarity, 'genuine strategic sovereignty,' 'sovereign path of development,' anti-colonial movement, radical rejection of Western hegemony and claims for a unipolar world order."[45] However, they continued to advocate for an even more profound progression, which includes the formal adoption of a state ideology. As Dugin has emphasized: "A military ideology, an ideology of victory, must be established in the country. It is impossible to fight without an idea."[46]

Although the war has brought the issue of a state ideology to the forefront, it remained a contentious topic within ruling elites. As Marlène Laruelle has highlighted, the debate over abolishing Article 13 of the Constitution, which prohibits the adoption of a state ideology, unfolded at the Eleventh Saint Petersburg International Legal Forum in May 2023.[47] While the minister of justice, Konstantin Chuychenko, and other hawkish war proponents, such as Medvedev and Medinskii, called for repealing Article 13, others, such as Valerii

nobbqQLX-52LdgGMaKjI2a5H22i6awa2oDf1tyKzDt9YDQFB9O3z6bc_aem_AZbR0oFQxeBHz9tX_dqK1I_qiPDMkpOPPRFGFCWEGngL_Oeb7r2pG3EUR0pZ_hDcWiGi3CDngMpMtOMAoAalithz.

44 Aleksandr Dugin, "Rossii nuzhna totalnaia militarizatsiia," Izborskii Klub, March 11, 2024, https://izborsk-club.ru/25427.

45 Aleksandr Dugin, "Putin provozglasil Russkuiu Ideiu," Izborskii Klub, October 4, 2022, https://izborsk-club.ru/23400.

46 Dugin, "Rossii nuzhna totalnaia militarizatsiia."

47 Laruelle, "Russia's Ideological Construction in the Context of the War in Ukraine."

Zorkin, president of the Constitutional Court, upheld a legalist position, arguing against changing the constitution.[48]

In advocating for the implementation of a state ideology, members of the Izborskii Klub framed the war in Ukraine as merely a single facet of a broader systemic and global conflict against the West, encompassing military, cultural, economic, financial, and psychological dimensions. Shortly after the commencement of the war, Averianov redirected attention from Ukraine to the broader Western context, asserting the necessity to prioritize "mental warfare." He argued that such emphasis is crucial owing to the persistent and multifaceted nature of the "hybrid confrontation between Russia and the West." He emphasized that, while Ukraine serves as a "tactical platform for Western aggression," the primary battleground of this overarching struggle was not confined to Ukrainian territory. In his view, therefore, Putin's use of the term "denazification" functions effectively as an "operational-tactical, propaganda, and potentially legal concept." However, Averianov proposed expanding the scope of the identified ideological adversary to encompass a wider notion of "liberal fascism," positioning Ukraine as just one manifestation of a broader phenomenon rooted in "American and Western European liberal fascism."[49] Likewise, Dugin emphasized that the military operation targeted "not only Nazism" but also "liberalism and globalism."[50] This rhetoric brutally denies any sovereignty to Ukraine, portraying it as a mere battleground of civilizations: "Ukraine is not a country but a territory of a battle of civilizations."[51] For the Izborskii Klub, therefore, the war extends beyond a geopolitical contest for territorial acquisition; it represents a broader struggle for Russia's place in the world and the assertion of its civilizational identity. As Averianov argued, "[t]he essence of the Fifth Empire lies not so much in the return of lost lands, but in the resurgence of an independent civilization onto the world stage."[52] Beyond the Ukrainian warfront,

48 "Ministr Iustitsii nachal diskussiiu ob otmene zapreta na ideologiiu," *Vedomosti*, May 12, 2023, www.vedomosti.ru/politics/articles/2023/05/12/974675-ministr-yustitsii-nachal-diskussiyu-ob-otmene-zapreta-na-ideologiyu.

49 Averianov, "Vesna ochistitelnaia."

50 Aleksandr Dugin, "Ocherednaia oshibka Fukuiamy," Izborskii Klub, March 20, 2022, https://izborsk-club.ru/22508.

51 Dugin, "Putin provozglasil Russkuiu Ideiu."

52 Averianov, "Vesna ochistitelnaia."

Averianov underscored Russia's imperative to liberate itself from what he characterizes as its "quasi-colonial dependence" on the West.[53] In his vision, Russia should endeavor to systematically disrupt the principal "strongholds" of globalization, including the "gender agenda" and "Western environmentalism," among other things, and establish a new world order. In pursuing this objective, Russia should enhance its autonomy as an independent Eurasian civilization forging alliances with countries along a "trans-Caspian axis," including China, India, and Iran, to establish a "self-sufficient economic space."[54]

Finally, the Izborskii Klub's radical stances were paired with calls for domestic repressions, viewing the wartime context as an opportunity to instigate elite changes within Russia. These positions, which have long been part of the club's agenda, have gained momentum with Putin's adoption of rhetoric that distinguishes between patriots and a purported "fifth column" of traitors. Izborskii Klub members advocate for even more draconian and totalitarian measures, including tactics of terror, and call for violent purges. Averianov has explicitly stated that achieving "victory over the internal enemy" necessitates the "purification of the state," describing it as the "Great Cleansing of Russia" and advocating for the "purge of subversive forces in the elite of the state," regardless of the "cruelty" of such actions.[55] In November 2022, the club convened a roundtable discussion titled "The Crisis of the Elites and Mechanisms of Cadres Revolution," which resulted in the publication of an entire issue of the Izborskii Klub's journal dedicated to this theme, featuring unabashed endorsements of replicating repressive policies akin to those implemented during the eras of Ivan the Terrible and Stalin.[56] The club was particularly focused on eliminating what they identified as liberal forces within the Russian society to replace them with a "patriotic Russian intelligentsia."[57] Averianov called for a purge of "liberal fascism," targeting entities such as the Yeltsin Center and various human rights organizations, which he equated with "progressive" organizations influenced by Western ideologies.[58] Most prominently, the club underscored the necessity of a radical overhaul

[53] Averianov, "Vesna ochistitelnaia." [54] Averianov, "Vesna ochistitelnaia."
[55] Averianov, "Vesna ochistitelnaia."
[56] Izborskii Klub's journal, issue no. 4 (2023).
[57] Aleksandr Prokhanov, "Golos russkoi istorii," Izborskii Klub, March 5, 2022, https://izborsk-club.ru/22430.
[58] Averianov, "Vesna ochistitelnaia."

of economic elites, accusing them of undermining Russia's economic sovereignty by integrating it into the global economy and thus making it vulnerable to Western sanctions.[59] The club aspired to lay the groundwork for a new wartime economy, seeking to supplant what they perceived as the prevailing influence of liberal principles. As stated by Prokhanov, "our economists are ready to create a new Russian economy, restoring the industries crushed by Gaidar."[60] Sergei Glazev, one of the club's most prominent economists, particularly vehemently criticized the Central Bank, alleging that its leadership has been influenced by what he terms the "enemy's cognitive weapons," effectively causing them to act in ways that serve foreign interests rather than national ones. He contended that the Central Bank's policies were largely driven by recommendations from the International Monetary Fund, aligning with the interests of large domestic banks and financial structures that benefit from manipulating the ruble's exchange rate. More generally, Glazev denounced the presence of an "influential lobby," comprising Russia's main monetary and financial structures, which he claimed has formed around a policy agenda based on private interests rather than national ones, thereby impeding Russia's ability to develop and respond to sanctions effectively.[61]

These diverse points of criticism raised by the Izborskii Klub reflect the ambivalent attitude of the broader "Z-space," which comprises a diverse range of prowar opinion leaders and bloggers.[62] Despite its self-proclaimed patriotism, this space has emerged as a pivotal arena for political thought and dissent within contemporary Russia, advocating more radical military action and repression.[63] They have

59 Aleksandr Prokhanov, "Russkoe omovenie," Izborskii Klub, March 18, 2022, https://izborsk-club.ru/22501.

60 Prokhanov, "Golos russkoi istorii." The economist Egor Gaidar, Russia's acting prime minister in 1992, implemented a set of accelerated liberalizing economic reforms known as shock therapy. See Section 3.3.1 in Chapter 3.

61 Sergei Glazev, "Takie sobytiia, kak seichas, proiskhodiat raz v stoletie," Izborskii Klub, March 28, 2022, https://izborsk-club.ru/22542.

62 The most popular ones, such as "Wargonzo" and "Operation Z—voenkory russkoi vesny" boast over 1 million and almost 900,000 subscribers, respectively. See "Return of the Voenkor: The Military as a New Opinion Leader in Russia?," *Russia Post,* August 14, 2022, https://russiapost.info/politics/voenkor.

63 Ivan Filipov and Yevgeny Senshen, "'The Z-Space Has Unexpectedly Become a Place For Political Thought,'" *Russia Post*, November 14, 2023, https://russiapost.info/society/zchannel.

become increasingly critical of the regime's conduct of the war, especially in the context of Ukraine's successful counteroffensive in the fall of 2022 that was paired with the withdrawal of Russian troops from the Kharkov Region, the surrender of Kherson, and the failure to capture Kyiv.

The evolution of Igor Girkin-Strelkov represents a significant transformation in his role within Z circles. Recognized as one of the leading military commanders of separatist forces in Donbass in 2014, he emerged in 2022 as a prominent critic of Vladimir Putin's leadership and military strategy.[64] In April 2023 he founded the "Club of Angry Patriots" (Klub rasserzhennykh patriotov), aimed at denouncing the regime's perceived inability to achieve victory in the Ukrainian conflict. This culminated in his arrest in July 2023 on charges of extremism, followed by his conviction in January 2024 to a four-year prison sentence.

Evgenii Prigozhin, the founder of the Wagner group private military company, underwent a similar transformation from a notable figure in the war effort to a vocal critic of the Russian government's handling of the conflict. Starting from February 2023, Prigozhin publicly accused the Russian military of failing to provide sufficient ammunition to his forces, sparking a public dispute with military leaders. Subsequently, he intensified his criticism, alleging crimes committed by officials within the Ministry of Defense and accusing a Russian unit of attacking his personnel.[65] Prigozhin's disillusionment with the Kremlin's narrative of the war deepened as he rejected justifications for the conflict and accused Moscow of lying to the public.[66] Prigozhin's dramatic act of defiance against Vladimir Putin's leadership reached its climax when he spearheaded an armed rebellion on June 24, 2023. While a truce was seemingly reached through the mediation

64 "Russian Offensive Campaign Assessment," Institute for the Study of War, December 6, 2022, http://dev-isw.bivings.com/.

65 "Prigozhin Asks Prosecutors to Probe 'crime' by Top Russian Defence Officials," *Reuters*, May 31, 2023, www.reuters.com/world/europe/prigozhin-asks-prosecutors-investigate-crimes-by-top-russian-defence-officials-2023-05-31/.

66 Pjotr Sauer, "Wagner Chief Accuses Moscow of Lying to Public about Ukraine," *The Guardian*, June 23, 2023, www.theguardian.com/world/2023/jun/23/wagner-chief-accuses-moscow-of-lying-to-public-about-ukraine-yevgeny-prigozhin.

of President of Belarus Aleksandr Lukashenko,[67] Prigozhin's subsequent death in the crash of a plane carrying Wagner's entire leadership on August 23, 2023, was, according to Western intelligence, orchestrated by the Kremlin.[68]

The Izborskii Klub has maintained close ties with Prigozhin, exemplified by his attendance at Daria Dugin's funeral ceremony.[69] Both Prilepin and Dugin have expressed their admiration for Prigozhin, holding him as a "historic figure"[70] and the "leader of the war."[71] Dugin, in particular, supported Prigozhin's confrontation with the military hierarchy, viewing it as a catalyst for the "purification, enlightenment and spiritualization of society and the entire ruling class."[72] However, Dugin's support waned during the 24-hour military rebellion, which he viewed as the "first chord of a monstrous catastrophe" and an "accident of Russian statehood." In contrast, Dugin praised Putin and Lukashenko as "heroes ... who saved the country from the brink," while calling for the dismissal of lower-ranked ruling elites, blaming them for provoking the situation.[73] This attitude reflects Dugin's strategic decision to limit his agenda to advocating for elite rotation, avoiding direct criticism of the regime or calls for regime change. This cautious stance contrasts sharply with his 2014 promotion of a revolutionary Novorossiia movement within Russia, which had resulted in his dismissal from Moscow State University and exclusion from state media.

67 "Belarus Becomes Unlikely Refuge for Wagner's Boss," *Le Monde*, August 8, 2023, www.lemonde.fr/en/international/article/2023/06/26/belarus-becomes-an-unlikely-refuge-for-wagner-s-boss_6037745_4.html.

68 "How Putin's Right-Hand Man Took Out Prigozhin," *The Wall Street Journal*, December 22, 2023, www.wsj.com/world/russia/putin-patrushev-plan-prigozhin-assassination-428d5ed8.

69 "Biznesmen Prigozhin prishel na proshchanie s ubitoi Darei Duginoi s medaliu Geroia Rossii," *Daily Storm*, April 23, 2022, https://dailystorm.ru/news/biznesmen-prigozhin-nazval-ubituyu-daryu-duginu-kamnem-v-osnove-rossiyskogo-velichiya.

70 Zakhar Prilepin, "Nasha elita po-prezhnemu sostoit iz bolshikh sprutoobraznykh mafioznykh soobshchestv," Izborskii Klub, October 23, 2023, https://izborsk-club.ru/24860.

71 Aleksandr Dugin, "Faktor 'Vagnera' i tezis spravedlivosti," Izborskii Klub, April 10, 2023, https://izborsk-club.ru/24137.

72 Dugin, "Faktor 'Vagnera' i tezis spravedlivosti."

73 Aleksandr Dugin, "Posle miatezha. Tochka bifurkatsii," Izborskii Klub, June 28, 2023, https://izborsk-club.ru/24505.

Other members of the Izborskii Klub offered more radical critical perspectives on Prigozhin's actions during the military rebellion. Vladislav Shurygin condemned Prigozhin for his "immorality," labeling him a "traitor squared" for betraying both Putin and the members of his private military company. He portrayed Prigozhin as a self-serving adventurer who prioritized his ambitions over the well-being of his followers and the state's stability.[74] Prokhanov, on the other hand, described Prigozhin's rebellion as a "gas bubble" resulting from societal and state decay. He emphasized the danger and chaos during the rebellion, likening it to the collapse of Soviet state in 1991 and warning of the potential catastrophic consequences for Russia's sovereignty and stability. While the rebellion was quelled, Prokhanov asserted that it caused "enormous damage" to the "sacredness of state power," exposing significant weaknesses within the Russian state.[75]

The Izborskii Klub's combination of critical perspectives and loyalty to the regime has enabled it to significantly contribute to state-sponsored wartime ideological production, while concurrently advancing its own ideological agenda.

8.2 Wartime Transformations of the Sphere of Ideology Production

8.2.1 Restoring Elements of the Soviet Vertical

The Russian state has significantly intensified its indoctrination efforts to justify the war in Ukraine with the production of ideological and intellectual frameworks validating the invasion. According to Laruelle's report for the French Institute of International Relations (IFRI), the state's "toolkit of indoctrination" during wartime has reached a much broader segment of the population, expanding beyond the previously targeted underprivileged youth. She highlights this through the extensive state program for patriotic education, coordinated by the Ministries of Education and Defense, which, with a significantly increased budget,

74 Vladislav Shurygin, "Dvazhdy predatel," June 28, 2023, https://izborsk-club.ru/24504.

75 Aleksandr Prokhanov, "Puzyri zemli," Izborskii Klub, June 27, 2023, https://izborsk-club.ru/24498.

organized 1.5 million events in 2022 alone.[76] Moreover, educational materials tailored to the "special operation" in Ukraine were swiftly introduced, reaching 20 million schoolchildren with video messages asserting that Russia's actions are defensive, forced by Western aggression, and aimed at preventing a "genocide." These narratives are reinforced across multiple platforms, from quizzes to cartoons, and prominently feature presidential speeches as core content.[77]

These intensified indoctrination efforts were coupled with the restoration of elements reminiscent of the Soviet-era "vertical," facilitating the propagation of norms and principles through a bureaucratic chain of command. A sign of this restoration is the presidential administration's initiative to introduce deputy heads for information and political work within federal ministries, departments, and state companies, as reported by *Kommersant*. According to the newspaper's sources, this initiative aimed to create a unified "semantic and informational field" within departments, echoing Soviet practices.[78] Indeed, as stressed by Andrei Pertsev, this approach mirrors the role of the secretaries of the party cells of the Communist Party of the Soviet Union, who were working as political instructors, reinforcing the state's control over the dissemination of information and the loyalty of workers to the authorities.[79]

This vertical is coordinated at its top by the presidential administration's Department for Domestic Affairs, led by Sergei Kirienko. In this capacity, Kirienko has shifted from his previous technocratic leadership style to become the chief ideological "patron" of the state system. Under his guidance, the presidential administration recentralized ideological production within two in-house think tanks: the Institute of Socio-Economic and Political Research (ISEPI) and the Social Research Expert Institute (EISI).[80]

[76] Laruelle, "Russia's Ideological Construction in the Context of the War in Ukraine."

[77] "Deux ans de guerre en Ukraine : En Russie, la militarisation à marche forcée de l'éducation," *Le Monde*, February 23, 2024, www.lemonde.fr/international/article/2024/02/23/deux-ans-de-guerre-en-ukraine-en-russie-la-militarisation-a-marche-forcee-de-l-education_6218077_3210.html.

[78] "Oruzhie massovogo raziasneniia," *Kommersant*, April 22, 2022, www.kommersant.ru/doc/5326305.

[79] Andrey Pertsev, "Sergei Kirienko's New Sphere of Influence," *Riddle Russia*, May 18, 2022, https://ridl.io/sergei-kirienko-s-new-sphere-of-influence/.

[80] Laruelle, "Russia's Ideological Construction in the Context of the War in Ukraine."

Vladimir Putin's presidential address to the Federal Assembly on February 21, 2023, the first since the commencement of the war, underscored a more targeted approach to ideological indoctrination efforts. His call to enhance the quality of school and university textbooks, particularly prioritizing subjects like history, social science, literature, and geography, reflected a strategic focus on shaping the perceptions and beliefs of the younger generation.[81] This endeavor led to the implementation of major programs targeting school and university students.

Since September 2022, schools had already been mandated to conduct flag-raising ceremonies weekly and to deliver a class called "Conversations about Important Things." This initiative entails teachers educating schoolchildren about the nature of the "special military operation" and reinforcing the state-sanctioned narrative surrounding the conflict, portraying Ukrainian "nationalists" in a negative light. Notably, the inaugural session of these conversations was led President Putin himself on September 1, 2022, symbolizing the regime's direct involvement in shaping the ideological discourse within educational institutions.[82] Another pivotal educational policy enacted since September 2023 involves the introduction of a new textbook for the history of twentieth-century Russia, specifically tailored for the eleventh grade, marking the end of high school education. Coauthored by former culture minister Vladimir Medinskii, historian from the Academy of Sciences Aleksandr Chubarian, and the rector of the Moscow State Institute of International Relations (MGIMO), Anatolii Torkunov, the textbook serves to cement the historical narrative propagated by the current regime, aiming to shape the perceptions of future generations. As the historian Sergei Ivanov observes, the book reflects a pronounced hostility toward the West, evident from the outset, where the authors align themselves with Stalinist rhetoric against "cosmopolitanism."[83] Furthermore, the textbook asserts that, in the 1990s, Western propaganda imposed individualistic values at the expense of traditional Russian cultural values, leading to a

[81] Putin, "Address by the President of the Russian Federation," February 21, 2022.

[82] Laruelle, "Russia's Ideological Construction in the Context of the War in Ukraine."

[83] Ivanov, "What Russia's New History Textbook Reveals," *Russia Post*, August 18, 2023, https://russiapost.info/politics/new_history.

societal focus on personal success and materialism. As also stressed by Laruelle, the book depicts Ukraine's independence as an "anti-Russia project" and offers a favorable reassessment of the Soviet Union, criticizing dissident culture and the perestroika era.[84]

Furthermore, the education system has expanded its military education component, with the introduction of a new course titled "Fundamentals of Homeland Security and Defense" slated for the 2024–25 academic year. This course builds upon the foundation laid by the previous "Fundamentals of Life Safety." Designed for students starting from the fifth grade, the curriculum is structured to acquaint children with military-technical knowledge. As reported by *Meduza*, this includes an in-depth study of the specifications of military equipment such as sniper rifles, antitank grenade launchers, and the Kalashnikov assault rifle. Additionally, students will engage in drill training, familiarize themselves with general military regulations, and explore concepts such as "the essence and importance of military discipline" and "the essence of unified command."[85]

Universities are also undergoing a transformative initiative known as the Russian DNA project. Spearheaded by the presidential administration, in collaboration with the Ministry of Science and Higher Education, the Znanie (Knowledge) Society and EISI, this endeavor seeks to reshape the humanities and social sciences curricula. As Laruelle observes, the term "DNA" symbolizes the state's efforts at delineating and consolidating the core ideologemes and repertoires that constitute Russia's identity.[86] The DNA project included the introduction, starting September 1, 2023, of a new teaching module aimed at first-year students across Russian universities. Titled "Foundation of Russian Statehood," this course seeks to delineate "the specific features of the historical path of the Russian State and the distinctiveness of its political organization."[87] As highlighted by *Meduza*, the guidelines of

[84] Laruelle, "Russia's Ideological Construction in the Context of the War in Ukraine."

[85] "'Fundamentals of Homeland Security' How Russia Is Turning Schools into Training Grounds for Future Soldiers," *Meduza*, April 1, 2024, https://meduza.io/en/feature/2024/04/01/fundamentals-of-homeland-security.

[86] Laruelle, "Russia's Ideological Construction in the Context of the War in Ukraine."

[87] See the curriculum guidelines issued by the Ministry of Science and Higher Education: https://fgosvo.ru/uploadfiles/method/Ps_MON_MN_11_1516_PK_21042023.pdf

the program issued by the Minister of Science and Higher Education underscore its primary objective of fostering a heightened sense of civic responsibility and patriotism among students.[88] According to sources close to the Kremlin cited by *Meduza*, the course was essentially designed to serve as a contemporary counterpart to the "scientific communism" curriculum taught in universities during the Soviet era. A source also informed *Meduza* that policymakers in the Kremlin perceived Russia's historical challenges as stemming from its intelligentsia and, thus, the new curriculum seeks to shape a "correct intelligentsia" aligned with the regime's agenda.[89] Specifically, the emphasis is purportedly placed on students attending engineering and technical universities, with the belief that the collapse of the USSR was partly due to inadequate ideological instruction of scientific and technical workers, leading to the growth of antiestablishment sentiments among IT professionals. This assertion emphasizes a significant theme that has been highlighted throughout this book's chapters: the persistent concern among intellectual and political elites, spanning both the Soviet and post-Soviet periods, regarding combining technological modernization with the preservation of an ideologically selected set of Russian national values.

The initiation of this program underscores the significance of "curators" tasked with overseeing and executing state-driven ideological endeavors. In February 2023, Andrei Polosin assumed the primary role as the lead organizer of the DNA project. Polosin boasts an extensive career as a political strategist with close ties to Kirienko, whom he has described as his "mentor."[90] By May 2023, he left his position as the head of regional relations at the state nuclear power corporation Rosatom to assume the role of deputy rector at the Russian Presidential Academy of National Economy and Public Administration. In this capacity, he is responsible for the development of the new university curriculum.

The "Foundation of Russian Statehood" course comprises five parts: "Understanding Russia," "The Russian Civilization-State,"

88 Andrey Pertsev, "'Almost Greater than Most Countries' A Required Ideological Curriculum Is about to Be Thrust upon Russia's Colleges. Here's the Syllabus for Russia's Future 'Patriotic Intelligentsia,'" *Meduza*, May 31, 2023, https://meduza.io/en/feature/2023/05/31/almost-greater-than-most.

89 Andrey Pertsev, "An 'Experienced Strategist' The Man behind Russia's New Ideological Course for University Students," *Meduza*, June 10, 2023, https://meduza.io/en/feature/2023/06/10/an-experienced-strategist.

90 Pertsev, "An 'Experienced Strategist' The Man behind Russia's New Ideological Course for University Students."

"The Russian Worldview and Values of the Russian Civilization," "Russia's Political Order," and "Future Challenges and the Country's Development." As emphasized by Polosin, the redesign of this curriculum aligns with the ideological framework outlined in the presidential decree on traditional values.[91] Additionally, according to disclosures from *Meduza*, another source of course content draws from an article on "fundamental values perception" in Russia, coauthored by Polosin.[92] This article asserts that the Russian worldview is rooted in a "pentabase" consisting of five core entities: individual, family, society, state, and country. Furthermore, as underscored by *Kommersant*, a significant aspect of the course is the emphasis on "value constants" integral to Russia's identity, notably the enduring significance of a strong state power throughout Russian history in safeguarding national statehood.[93]

8.2.2 The Regime's Continued Transactions with Nonstate Ideological Actors

The regime's approach to ideological production does not rely solely on the reconstruction of a Soviet-like vertical. In addition to official state-led initiatives, the regime maintains a multifaceted strategy by engaging with various nonstate ideological entrepreneurs.

Among these, significant centers of idea production include the Russian Orthodox Church, led by Patriarch Kirill, who advocates a narrative emphasizing the "spiritual and moral" dimensions of the conflict and framing it as a "holy war" to safeguard the "unified spiritual space of Holy Russia," shielding the world from the "assault of globalization and the triumph of the West, which has descended into Satanism."[94] Additionally, influential figures from the

[91] "Vlasti zapustili novyi etap reformy prepodavaniia sotsiogumanitarnykh nauk v vuzakh," *Vedomosti*, March 13, 2024, www.vedomosti.ru/society/articles/2024/03/13/1024943-vlasti-zapustili-novii-etap-reformi-prepodavaniya-sotsiogumanitarnih-nauk-v-vuzah.

[92] Pertsev, "An 'Experienced Strategist' The Man behind Russia's New Ideological Course for University Students."

[93] Anna Vasileva, "Istoriia stanet tsaritsei nauk," *Kommersant*, February 2, 2023, www.kommersant.ru/doc/5798930.

[94] "Nakaz XXV Vsemirnogo russkogo naradnogo sobora 'Nastoiashchee i budushchee russkogo mira,'" *Patriarchia.ru*, March 27, 2024, www.patriarchia.ru/db/text/6116189.html.

think-tank industry, such as Sergei Karaganov, honorary chairman of the Presidium of the Council for Foreign and Defense Policy, play a prominent role as producers of narratives justifying the war. In recent years, Karaganov has portrayed Russia's invasion of Ukraine as part of a broader defensive "war against the West," advocating for extreme measures such as preemptive nuclear strikes in countries supporting Ukraine, "in retaliation" for their "past and present acts of aggression."[95] Furthermore, Karaganov has overseen, under the auspices of the Ministry of Foreign Affairs, the formulation of a foreign policy framework centered on Russia's leadership position as a civilizational pole, articulating a "world majority" against the West.[96]

Numerous other ideological centers actively promote rationales legitimizing the war. Among them is the Zinovev Club, named after the late philosopher Aleksandr Zinovev (1922–2006), who transitioned from being a Soviet dissident exiled in Europe to being a staunch critic of "Westernism" (*zapadnizm*), which he associated with the globalization under the dominance of the United States, before returning to Russia in 1999, nostalgic for the USSR.[97] His ideas have gained traction among Russia's ruling elites. In 2022, Vladimir Putin issued a presidential decree commemorating the centenary of Zinovev's birth and directing the organization of events in his honor.[98] Following Russia's invasion of Ukraine, the Zinovev Club, chaired by the widow of the philosopher, Olga Zinoveva, has been proactive in responding to this call, by organizing a series of conferences in collaboration with the state TV channel Russia Today, addressing topics such as "Why

[95] Sergei Karaganov, "A Difficult but Necessary Decision," *Russia in Global Affairs*, June 13, 2023, https://eng.globalaffairs.ru/articles/a-difficult-but-necessary-decision/.

[96] Sergei Karaganov, Dmitry Trenin, and Alexander Kramarenko, "Russia's Policy towards World Majority," *Report under the Auspices of the Ministry of Foreign Affairs of the Russian Federation*, 2023, www.mid.ru/upload/medialibrary/c98/cjmfdf73760bme0y99zqllj51zzllrvs/Russia%E2%80%99s%20Policy.pdf.

[97] For a detailed presentation of Zinovev's ideas and their appropriation in wartime Russia, see Chapter 2 in Mikhail Suslov, *Putinism – Post-Soviet Russian Regime Ideology* (London, New York: Routledge, 2024).

[98] "Putin podpisal ukaz o prazdnovanii v 2022 godu stoletiia so dnia rozhdeniia filosofa Zinoveva," *TASS*, October 1, 2021, https://tass.ru/obschestvo/12558461.

Russia is right: a holy war,"[99] "Russophobia as the new Holocaust,"[100] and "The new decolonization is de-Westernization."[101]

Various other entities are also actively engaged in ideological activities in the occupied territories of Eastern Ukraine. In May 2022, several organizations, including "Sun of the North" (Solntse Severa), the Donetsk Philosophical Society, the publishing house Russian Philosophy, the Donetsk Higher Combined Arms Command School, and the Coordination Center for Assistance to Novorossiia collaborated to organize the inaugural online "Philosophical Council" on the theme of "The Great Russian Name Correction."[102] Following the conference, a book edited by Andrei Korobov-Latyntsev, an officer of the People's Militia of the Donetsk People's Republic, was released with the intention of distribution among battalions on the front lines. The book includes chapters authored by various individuals, including one by Aleksandr Dugin titled "The Phenomenon of War: Metaphysics, Ontology, and Borders" and another titled "Ukraine as the Territory of Armageddon." Additional chapters cover topics such as "Basic Concepts of Russian Ideological Defense," "The True Objective of the SVO [Special Military Operation] and the War: The De-Westernization of Ukraine and Russia," and "The Holy War of Russia in the Eschatological Logic of History: The Ideocratic Foundations of World War III."[103] Subsequently, a similar assembly of authors convened for "philosophical councils" in December 2022 and 2023, organized by the group known as the United Movement Russian Philosophy, in collaboration with the newspaper *Zavtra*. The 2023 council, which brought together more

[99] "Zasedanie Zinoveskogo kluba. Pochemu Rossiia prava: sviashchennaia voina," *Rossiia segodnia*, July 26, 2023, https://pressria.ru/20230726/955003264.html.

[100] "Zasedanie Zinoveskogo kluba. Pochemu Rossiia prava: rusofobiia kak novii kholokost," *Rossiia segodnia*, April 22, 2022, https://pressria.ru/20220422/953612214.html.

[101] "Zasedanie Zinoveskogo kluba. Novoia dekolonizatsiia kak dezapadnizatsiia," *Rossiia segodnia*, September 26, 2023, https://pressria.ru/20230926/955466392.html.

[102] *Filosofkskii Sobor. Velikoe Russkoe Ispravlenie Imen*, May 28, 2022, www.youtube.com/watch?v=CVBMI5wvWWg.

[103] Solntse Severa, "Sbornik filosofskogo sobora 'Velikoe russkoe ispravlenie imen' za 2022 god," VK, June 4, 2022, https://vk.com/@solsevera-sbornik-filosofskogo-sobora-velikoe-russkoe-ispravlenie-imen.

than 60 speakers, aimed to delineate the Russian myths at the core of the "Russian idea."[104]

Some of the activities of these nonstate ideological groups receive direct sponsorship from the state. The Presidential Fund for Cultural Initiatives, established in 2021, has emerged as the primary source of financial support for ideological production.[105] For instance, the fund has provided backing to Sun of the North for establishing an online university with the goal of integrating residents from the occupied territories of Donbass into a "unified Russian cultural and civilizational framework."[106] This institution, named the People's University after Daria Dugina, offers lectures in philosophy, history, religious studies, and anthropology.

Furthermore, according to reports from *Meduza*, leaked documents from the presidential administration revealed the existence of 15 "autonomous nonprofit organizations" that receive substantial state funding and are involved in creating and disseminating state propaganda.[107] Notably, the Internet Development Institute and Dialog, among others, play key roles in financing and disseminating progovernment cultural content and internet propaganda. Additionally, the Integration Production Center focuses on cultivating "public opinion leaders" who endorse state-sanctioned narratives. In particular, the center provides funding for the "Russian Dream" movement, which is a derivative of the Izborskii Klub, also established by Prokhanov.

The Izborskii Klub itself has notably flourished in terms of recognition and state sponsorship. Various forms of state support have contributed to legitimizing the club's activities. First, there is symbolic recognition, evident through direct contacts and interactions between the club's leadership and ruling elites. As reported by Pertsev in November 2022, sources from the presidential administration acknowledged that figures like Dugin and Prokhanov had become

104 "Russkii mif kak osnavanie russkoi idei," November 27, 2023, https://zavtra.ru/blogs/russkij_mif_kak_osnovanie_russkoj_idei.

105 The website of the Presidential Fund can be found at: https://xn--80aeeqaabljrdbg6a3ahhcl4ay9hsa.xn--p1ai/.

106 See the presentation of this project on Sun of the North's website: https://solsevera.ru/public-university.

107 "State-Controlled 'Autonomy' How the Kremlin Uses 'Independent Organizations' to Do Its Propaganda Dirty Work," *Meduza*, February 26, 2024, https://meduza.io/en/feature/2024/02/27/state-controlled-autonomy.

"frequent visitors" to the Kremlin.[108] They had reportedly been consulting with high-ranking officials such as Kirienko and Aleksandr Kharichev, head of the Division of the Operation of the State Council, on the development of a "new ideology" and providing input on official speeches made by Kirienko and Putin. Another indication of these interactions is Prokhanov's attendance at Putin's speech in the Kremlin on the integration of the Donetsk, Luhansk, Zaporizhzhia, and Kherson regions into Russia on September 30, 2022.[109]

Several instances of recognition of honorific status were directly conferred upon Prokhanov by Putin. On October 27, 2023, during the plenary session of the Valdai International Discussion Club, Putin engaged in a dialogue with Prokhanov, expressing his familiarity with and admiration of Prokhanov's work and praising him as a "true Russian patriot in the kindest, best and broadest sense of the word."[110] On February 26, 2023, on the occasion of Prokhanov's eighty-fifth birthday, he received felicitations from Presidents Putin and Lukashenko, as well as several other political and governmental figures including Viacheslav Volodin, Naryshkin and Kirienko.[111] Subsequently, on July 10, 2023, Prokhanov was honored with the Order of Alexander Nevsky by presidential decree, recognizing his active engagement in social activities.[112]

The promotion of Izborskii Klub products as integral components of Russia's official war culture has also garnered significant forum and public visibility. Prokhanov has frequently appeared in the media, participating in extensive one-on-one interviews to discuss the war's implications for Russia's future. As an example, he participated as the main guest on Rossiia-1 TV's program *Life and Fate* on

108 Andrey Pertsev, "'Hawkish Times Need Hawkish People' How the Death of Daria Dugina Helped Her Father, Alexander Dugin, Rise from Ultraconservative Fringe Philosopher to Key Kremlin Ideologue," *Meduza*, November 3, 2022, https://meduza.io/en/feature/2022/11/03/hawkish-times-need-hawkish-people.

109 See Prokhanov's article relating his attendance of the speech: Aleksandr Prokhanov, "Za nami – Rossiia!" Izborskii Klub, October 4, 2022, https://izborsk-club.ru/23399.

110 Vladimir Putin, "Valdai International Discussion Club Meeting," Website of the President of Russia, October 31, 2022, http://en.kremlin.ru/events/president/news/69695.

111 Izborskii Klub's journal, issue no. 3 (2023): 124.

112 Izborskii Klub's journal, issue no. 7 (2023): 124.

December 7, 2022, where his prose and drawings were abundantly showcased, underscoring their importance through on-screen presentation and presenter quotations.[113] The club has also engaged in the creation and dissemination of cultural works centered around the war. On July 12, 2023, in Nizhnii Tagil, the premiere of the opera *Walking into Fire*, composed by club member Aleksandr Ageev and featuring a libretto based on Prokhanov's poetry, was displayed in the tank factory of Uralvagonzavod.[114]

The government's interest in these cultural productions was evidenced by Prokhanov meeting with Minister of Culture Olga Liubimova in February 2024.[115] Furthermore, in May 2024, Prokhanov's literary work received significant acclaim with the premiere of the blockbuster film *Callsign Passenger* (*Pozyvnoi Passazhir*), directed by Ilia Kazankov. Adapted from Prokhanov's novel *Murder of Cities* (2015), the movie chronicles the experiences of a Russian soldier fighting in Donbass. Despite its initial rejection by the Cinema Fund in 2014, the film's production with substantial state support signals a clear evolution from the state's previous detachment from the Izborskii Klub's advocacy of the Donbass conflict to a full endorsement.[116]

The cohesive and continuous alignment of views between the state and the Izborskii Klub on the war since 2022 is further evidenced by the significant financial sponsorship from the state. In October 2022, the club acknowledged that its journals were issued and printed with financial support from the Presidential Fund for Cultural Initiatives.[117] This funding has also enabled the club to run the "Russian Dream: Donbass" project, which focuses on creating cultural and educational programs aimed at promoting the concept of "Novorossiia" in the occupied territories of Ukraine. This initiative directly operationalizes the objectives outlined in Putin's discourses of integrating these territories into a "common cultural and civilizational space." Within the framework of this project, the Izborskii Klub has undertaken various

113 "Zhizn i sudba," Rossiia-1, December 7, 2022, https://smotrim.ru/video/2525882.
114 Izborskii Klub's journal, issue no. 7 (2023): 124.
115 Aleksandr Prokhanov, "Dolgozhdannii avangard," Izborskii Klub, February 1, 2024, https://izborsk-club.ru/25276.
116 "Peredelat patsifista," *Novaya gazeta*, April 7, 2024, https://novayagazeta.eu/articles/2024/04/07/peredelat-patsifista.
117 Izborskii Klub's journal, issue no. 9 (2022): 111.

activities emphasizing its role in promoting ideological narratives and bolstering support for the war effort. These include distributing literature and books to the Academy of Culture and Arts and libraries, and organizing a "cultural and educational festival" in Luhansk aimed at fostering "connections with cultural, literary, and artistic figures." Additionally, the club has provided "humanitarian aid to civilians and special equipment to fighters on the front line."[118]

The Izborskii Klub has also played a significant role in the state-led "Russia DNA" project, with its members actively contributing to the development of the course "Foundations of Russian Statehood." Averianov was included in the expert working group for this course, and he, along with other club members, participated in consultations at various universities to shape its content.[119] Within these consultations, the Izborskii Klub presented and advocated its vision of Russia's identity and political development, encapsulated in the document "Worldview of Russian Civilization: The Path to Yourself."[120] It seeks "practical applicability" by providing the ideological foundation for the development of "modern public policies," particularly in education and culture. Notably, the document seeks to pave the way for the conduct of Russia's "paradigmatic development," defined by its "own worldview tradition" independent from Western civilization. Central to this text is the assertion that, despite historical contradictions and discontinuities, the coherence of the "Russian cultural and civilizational worldview" endures. The document strives to demonstrate this internal coherence by synthesizing the intellectual efforts of "Russia's finest minds over centuries." It outlines four "axial spaces" in the Russian ideological landscape: populism, Eurasianism, the "metaphysics of unity," and Russian cosmism. The document shows a clear continuity with previous doctrinal work by the club set on promoting Russian cosmism as Russia's national idea. Indeed, as claimed by the authors, the "Russian worldview" is ultimately concerned with the integration of cultural, organic, spiritual, and technological realms. Accordingly, the overarching "Russian ideal" is the "spiritualization

[118] Izborskii Klub's journal, issue no. 5 (2023): 132–33.

[119] See, for instance, consultations convened at the National Research Nuclear University of the Moscow Engineering Physics Institute on July 27, 2023. Izborskii Klub's journal, issue no. 7 (2023): 124.

[120] Izborskii Klub's journal, issue no. 1 (2024): 6–87.

of the technosphere," which they link to Vladimir Vernadskii's theory of transformation of the biosphere into the noosphere.

The "Worldview of Russian Civilization" received significant endorsement from ruling elites responsible for education policies. As the lead organizer of the "Russian DNA" project, Polosin was pivotal in coordinating various events that highlighted the Izborskii Klub's vision. On December 9, 2023, Polosin, alongside the deputy minister of science and higher education, participated in a conference at Saint Petersburg State University, where Averianov presented the "Worldview" document.[121] The dissemination and promotion of the document continued into January 2024, featuring a series of events, including a conference at Ural Federal University in Ekaterinburg, with Polosin's participation. Most importantly, Averianov addressed the "Education and Worldview" conference, convened by the Ministry of Education at the Space Pavilion of VDNKh in Moscow with the aim to provide an overview of the initial implementation of teaching the module "Fundamentals of Russian Statehood" in Russian universities. Addressing a large audience of teachers from across Russia, Averianov presented the "Worldview of Russian Civilization" doctrine, emphasizing its ambition to guide a "paradigm change in the Russian education system," the establishment of a "value vector in the teaching of humanities," and the adoption of a "civilizational approach."[122] At a subsequent conference held in Moscow, Polosin expressed his profound "gratitude" to the Izborskii Klub for taking on the endeavor of establishing a "common language" within Russian philosophy and affirmed his dedication to ongoing collaboration.[123]

The promotional efforts surrounding the "Worldview of Russian Civilization" document shed light on the Izborskii Klub's strategic engagements with key centers of scientific activity. For instance, on January 18, 2024, the club organized a conference to introduce the doctrine in the science city of Koltsovo, situated in the Novosibirsk region. The event was attended by notable figures including the deputy

121 "K russkoi filosofskoi simfonii," December 9, 2023, https://izborsk-club.ru/25060.

122 Vitalii Averianov, "Vrata v mir samosoznaniia. V. V. Averianov na konferentsii 'Obrazovanie i mirovozzrenie,'" February 20, 2024, https://izborsk-club.ru/25392.

123 "Itogovaia konferentsiia po russkomu kanonu," March 8, 2024, https://izborsk-club.ru/25420.

prime minister of the Novosibirsk Region, the mayor of Koltsovo, and members of the Russian Academy of Sciences. Furthermore, on January 19, members of the Izborskii Klub visited the renowned science city of Akademgorodok, where they engaged in discussions with scientists at the Institute of Nuclear Physics of the Siberian Branch of the Russian Academy of Sciences. Following this visit, the club announced the establishment of a Novosibirsk branch, highlighting the expansion of its reach and influence within academic and scientific circles.[124]

The acknowledgment of Izborskii Klub members attaining the status of recognized experts, actively contributing to state-endorsed public platforms for idea generation, is further supported by additional evidence. Dugin, for instance, leads the Higher Political School named after Ivan Ilin, founded in 2024 at the Russian State University for the Humanities. Additionally, Metropolitan Tikhon Shevkunov chairs the expert council of the project titled "The Russian State-Civilization. History. Institutions. People," based at the Higher School of Economics and dedicated to the creation of a seven-volume publication spotlighting a "gallery of historical figures … whose unwavering commitment to serving the beloved Fatherland was central to their lives."[125]

The period of wartime has therefore coincided with the Izborskii Klub's attainment of official expert status, contributing to the formulation of the state's ideological frameworks. Despite receiving acknowledgment, however, the club continues to contend for status recognition within a polarized intellectual landscape.

8.3 War Ideology versus Exile Philosophy: Intellectual Polarization Maintained

8.3.1 IF RAN as a Battleground for Intellectual Confrontations

The Institute of Philosophy of the Russian Academy of Sciences (IF RAN), Russia's most prestigious academic institution, has become

[124] On these events, see Izborskii Klub's journal, issue no. 1 (2024): 147–48.

[125] "NIU VSHE stanet kliuchevym uchastnikom proekta 'Rossiiskoe gosudarstvo-tsivilizatsiia. Istoriia. Institutsii. Liudi,'" hse.ru, September 20, 2023, www.hse.ru/news/expertise/860738604.html.

the focal point of a crusade by hawkish ideologues aiming to assert dominance within cultural and intellectual spheres.

Even before the outbreak of the war, IF RAN was targeted in 2021 by far-right groups, including the Patriot media group, led by Prigozhin, and the online news channel Tsargrad, owned by monarchist oligarch Konstantin Malofeev.[126] These media outlets have portrayed the institute as the "brain of the liberal-destructive, dissident, and cosmopolitan movement in Russia," accusing it of "undermining the national, spiritual, and state foundations of Russia."[127] Scholars at the institute have faced personal attacks, accused of prioritizing the study of foreign philosophies over Russian philosophy, collaborating with Western academic institutions, and receiving funding from various American organizations, such as George Soros's Open Society Foundation.[128] The media outlet Insider suggested that one motivation for these attacks could have been the competition between the "Russian Dream – 2050" development strategy, created by the World Russian People's Council under Malofeev's leadership,[129] and the "Russian Project for Civilizational Development," spearheaded by Andrei Smirnov, the director of IF RAN.[130]

Alongside the media attacks on the institute, this coalition of ideological groups sought to overthrow the institute's governance, with the aim of securing resources and recognition within the Russian intellectual community. In December 2021, they gained the support of the minister of science and higher education, Valerii Falkov, who appointed the researcher Anatolii Cherniaev as the interim director of the institute. This promotion represented a significant political victory for the hawks. While Cherniaev had previously been removed from his

126 "Reidery protiv filososov. Kak ultrapravye konservatory vo glave s Malofeevym zakhvatyvaiut Institut filosofii RAN," *The Insider*, March 7, 2023, https://theins.ru/obshestvo/259245.

127 Andrei Samokhin, "Tsentr razrusheniia Rossii. Struktury Sorosa vrutsia k upravleniiu institutom filosofii RAN," December 14, 2021, https://tsargrad.tv/articles/centr-razrushenija-rossii-struktury-sorosa-rvutsja-k-upravleniju-institutom-filosofii-ran_462002.

128 Andrei Samokhin, "Tainye pisma 'diversantov' v mantiiakh: Gotovitsia udar po russkoi nauke," April 29, 2022, https://tsargrad.tv/articles/tajnye-pisma-diversantov-v-mantijah-gotovitsja-udar-po-russkoj-nauke_539510.

129 See Chapter 7 in this book, Section 7.3.

130 "Reidery protiv filososov. Kak ultrapravye konservatory vo glave s Malofeevym zakhvatyvaiut Institut filosofii RAN."

administrative responsibilities within the institute, his appointment was clearly intended to advance his research interests in "Russian culture within the Eurasian civilization," "the philosophical and theological thought of the 20th-century Russian diaspora," and "the relationship between the Church and society in Russia."[131] As noted by Yulia Sineokaia, who was deputy director of the Institute until her emigration to France in 2022, "the new director's task was to transform an academic institution into an ideological bulwark against Russia's imminent invasion of Ukraine."[132] This shift in leadership aimed to align the institute more closely with nationalist and conservative ideologies, reflecting broader efforts to consolidate ideological control and promote a unified, state-sanctioned narrative in anticipation of the war.

This attempt, however, faced internal opposition within the institute. Shortly after Cherniaev's appointment, the Scientific Council of the Institute released a statement expressing "categorical disagreement" with his selection.[133] They decried the appointment process as hasty, secretive, and covert, while also highlighting Cherniaev's incapacity to take on the role as a former employee dismissed due to his "inability to perform administrative work within a scientific team." Furthermore, they emphasized the significant reputational and status setbacks Cherniaev faced following his endorsement of the defamatory campaign led by Tsargrad against the institute. The public statement was accompanied by a personal plea directed at Vladimir Putin, in which the Scientific Council stressed that institute's work had been dedicated to "fulfilling the state task with an emphasis on the study of traditions and identity, value foundations, and civilizational prospects for the development of Russian society." The statement further underscored the alignment between the institute's research and the official norms and concepts promoted in political discourse, including the multipolarity of the world order and Russia's identity as a distinct civilization.[134]

131 "Cherniaev Anatolii Vladimirovich," Institut Filosofii Rossiiskoi Akademii Nauk, https://iphras.ru/chernyaev.htm.

132 Yulia Sineokaya, "Le jdanovisme est de retour : la chasse aux philosophes," Desk Russie, January 27, 2024, https://desk-russie.eu/2024/01/27/le-jdanovisme-est-de-retour.html.

133 "Zaiavlenie uchenogo soveta Instituta filosofii RAN v sviazi s naznacheniem vvemenno ispolniaiushchego obiazannosti direktora Instituta," Institut Filosofii Rossiiskoi Akademii Nauk, https://iphras.ru/22_12_2021.htm.

134 "Zaiavlenie uchenogo soveta Instituta filosofii RAN v sviazi s naznacheniem vremenno ispolniaiushchego obiazannosti direktora Instituta."

The mobilization of the Scientific Council bore fruit, leading to Cherniaev's replacement with Academician Abdusalam Guseinov,[135] who had previously served as the director of the institute from 2006 to 2015. While this achievement demonstrated the institute's scientific staff's continued agency, it was contingent upon its compliance with research directions imposed by political and administrative authorities. Indeed, a few months later, in March 2022, amid weeks of ongoing war, a general meeting of the institute's staff was convened to emphasize the "new rules of the game." According to reports from the newspaper *Argumenti Nedeli*, the leadership of the institute clarified that, subsequent to a meeting with the presidential administration, they had been charged with formulating Russia's philosophy, "our philosophy," distinct from Western philosophy.[136]

8.3.2 War Ideology against Exile Philosophy: A Persistent Divide

Although the political-administrative supervision of the institute has become evident, the continuing struggles for influence that the institute is entangled in reveal the persisting polarization within the Russian intellectual field. Two distinct factions have emerged in the war context, both seeking to establish alternative spaces for philosophical discourse beyond IF RAN.

On one side, hawkish groups, including the Izborskii Klub, Sun of the North, the Zinovev Club, and Tsargrad, are actively formulating a "philosophy of the front" to legitimize imperialism and wartime violence. As highlighted earlier in this chapter, some activities of these entities are funded by the presidential administration. Their campaign against IF RAN has intensified with the onset of war. In the fall of 2022, Prokhanov's newspaper *Zavtra* published a series of articles scrutinizing the institute's activities since the dissolution of the Soviet Union, critically focusing on its international engagements. *Zavtra* bluntly described the institute as "the center of propaganda of postmodernist philosophy in Russia," specifically targeting research fields like feminism, multiculturalism, gender studies, and environmental ethics as

135 "Guseinov Abdusalam Abdulkerimovich," https://iphras.ru/guseinov.htm.

136 "Institut filosofii RAN ukhodit v intellektualnoe podpole?," *Argumenty nedeli,* April 1, 2022, https://argumenti.ru/opinion/2022/04/766103.

efforts "aimed at undermining Russia's traditional values."[137] These ideas were later echoed on the newspaper's YouTube channel "Den," which boasts 1.5 million subscribers, amplifying the campaign's reach and impact. Furthermore, these groups are actively engaged in organizing online philosophical courses. For instance, Sun of the North offers courses on topics ranging from Russian military philosophy to the "philosophy of war and death," the history of Russian philosophy, the metaphysics of empire, the history of Christianity, and the history and philosophy of esoteric studies.[138]

On the opposing side, intellectuals who have left Russia are actively engaged in laying the foundation for restructuring a critical practice of intellectual discourse in opposition to war.

Even predating the war, the Free University emerged in 2020, founded by a collective of professors from HSE who, having experienced online teaching due to Covid-related restrictions, decided to use these new teaching methods to develop their own university. Designed as an independent and self-governed online educational institution, the Free University boasts a faculty of over a hundred professors and offers courses across various social and natural sciences. Diverging from the philosophical landscape in Russia, the curriculum includes offerings such as an introduction to the history of feminist ideas of the twentieth century, as well as courses on Western Marxism and existentialism.[139]

Russia's invasion of Ukraine sparked a new wave of philosophical emigration, leading to the creation of two significant collective endeavors. The first of these was the production of a collective volume in Russian, titled *Pered litsom katastrofy* (*Facing Catastrophe*), which was released in 2023 by the German publisher Lit Verlag, based in Berlin. Coordinated by the philosopher Nikolai Plotnikov, the book comprises 15 chapters authored by intellectuals from the Russian diaspora or those who recently emigrated. Drawing on the lineage of past publications of philosophical emigration during the Soviet era, the volume aims to offer a collective "philosophical and historical understanding of the ongoing catastrophe."[140]

137 Aleksei Goncharov, "Troianskie Koni. Chem zanimaetsia Institut filosofii RAN," *Zavtra*, September 15, 2022, https://zavtra.ru/blogs/filosofiya_dvojnogo_naznacheniya.

138 See the course offer here: https://solsevera.ru/#rec353203651.

139 "Tsekh filosofii i religiovedeniia," Svobodnyi Universitet, https://freemoscow.university/school/czeh-filosofii-i-religovedeniya/.

140 Nikolai Plotnikov, *Pered Litsom Katastrofy* (Berlin: Lit Verlag, 2023), 6.

The second prominent collective of intellectuals in exile is the Institute of Independent Philosophers, established as an association based in Paris in 2023 by Yulia Sineokaia, former deputy director of IF RAN. The institute brings together an intergenerational cohort of more than 100 scholars, primarily located in Europe, Central Asia, and the Caucasus.

These three initiatives share a common dedication to developing an alternative space for free, independent, and critical intellectual discourse. The Free University's declaration of values, which places a strong emphasis on academic freedom and autonomy, is positioned as a response to "government intervention in humanities teaching," "censorship and restriction of academic freedom," "repressive education laws," and "political repression."[141] Similarly, the Institute of Independent Philosophers is committed to fostering "free philosophical thought" and promoting "critical philosophical views."[142]

In contrast to the historical waves of intellectual emigration under the Soviet Union, which often followed up on prerevolutionary Russian thought's reflection on Russian identity, history, and Orthodoxy, the Russian nationalist framework of thought no longer serves as a defining factor for this contemporary wave of intellectual emigration. Instead, they fully embrace their place within a globalized intellectual landscape. The decision of both the Free University and the Institute of Independent Philosophers to avoid using the term "Russian" in their self-designation signifies their desire to integrate into cosmopolitan intellectual communities. In this regard, the Institute of Independent Philosophers envisions the future of the Russian philosophical community as an integral part of the global "Republic of Scholars." Sineokaia has further emphasized that among one of the beneficial outcomes of the conflict was the opportunity to enrich Russian intellectual discourse through an expanded comprehension of "homeland, philosophical horizons, and dialogue."[143]

The collective volume *Facing Catastrophe* represents a different approach regarding the relationship with the Russian language and

[141] See the "about" section of their website: https://freemoscow.university/about/ and the "values" section: https://freemoscow.university/values/.

[142] See the institute's website: https://independentphilosophers.com/en.

[143] "Iuliia Sineokaia: 'Na samom dele russkaia filosofiia ne izuchena,'" *Radio Sbododa*, December 24, 2023, www.svoboda.org/a/yuliya-sineokaya-na-samom-dele-russkaya-filosofiya-ne-izuchena-/32744271.html.

thought. In his foreword, Plotnikov underscored the necessity for intellectuals in exile to write in Russian, preserving a "discursive space of freedom ... where public intellectual discourse published in Russian could thrive without concern for censorship and self-censorship."[144] In an interview, he further emphasized the importance of working in Russian to maintain a continuity of reflection and semantic resources of resistance within the language:

> It was crucial for me to publish the collection *Facing Catastrophe* in Russian, even though it might have been easier to publish it in German or English. It is important that this reflection occurs in the language where orders for the shelling and bombing of Ukrainian cities are currently issued, so that the intellectual resource of resistance is strengthened within this language.[145]

These various groups of exiled intellectuals, intersecting with each other, unite around a common research agenda: the critical confrontation of the "war philosophy" emanating from Moscow. In *Facing Catastrophe*, Plotnikov asserts:

> It is imperative to deconstruct all historical, political and philosophical myths – such as "traditional values," "unlimited sovereignty," "identity," "Russian civilization," "empire," "Great Russia" and dozens of other large and small myths of national superiority that have served as discursive justification for Russia's military aggression and have fostered a consciousness of imperial hubris."[146]

One of the research projects of the Institute of Independent Philosophers, named "Dictionary of the Political Language of Putin's Russia," shares a similar objective. Likewise, the Free University's journal, entitled *Palladium*, has dedicated multiple issues to critically assessing concepts such as "Russian world" and "Z ideology,"[147] while also developing the epistemological frameworks for a "sociology of war."[148]

144 Plotnikov, *Pered Litsom Katastrofy*, 6.
145 "Nikolai Plotnikov: 'U filosofii v Rossii nikogda ne bylo institutsionalnogo khrebta," *T-invariant*, July 31, 2023, www.t-invariant.org/2023/07/nikolaj-plotnikov-u-filosofii-v-rossii-nikogda-ne-bylo-institutsionalnogo-hrebta/
146 Plotnikov, *Pered Litsom Katastrofy*, 7.
147 See *Palladium*, issue no 9 (2023): https://freeuniversity.pubpub.org/palladium-8.
148 See *Palladium*, issue no 3 (2022): https://freeuniversity.pubpub.org/palladium-3.

In a parallel manner to their active management of domestic ideological production through promotion and demotion tools, state authorities also endeavor to regulate the influence of intellectuals in exile. They employ censorship mechanisms that prohibit the publication of works like *Facing Catastrophe* and any discourse or critique of such works in internet and media spheres. Additionally, certain intellectuals in exile, like Sineokaia, have been labeled as foreign agents by the Ministry of Justice, aiming to intimidate their actions and impede their engagement with the domestic public sphere.

Moreover, proponents of war ideology seek to established a militarized division between those supporting war efforts and intellectuals in exile, whom they label as traitors aligned with Western interests. Commenting on Cherniaev's dismissal from his role as a researcher at IF RAN in December 2023, Dugin disseminated conspiracy theories alleging that this event was part of a "broader global strategy involving the infiltration of the Academy of Sciences, orchestrated under the influence of figures like Sineokaia and the CIA."[149]

Thus, despite their geographical separation, the ongoing confrontation between hawkish ideologues and exiled intellectuals challenges the hegemony of war ideology and maintains polarization within the country's intellectual sphere.

8.4 Conclusion

This chapter has explored the evolving role of Russian hawks in shaping ideological production in the context of Russia's war against Ukraine. It has illustrated how the regime has deployed Soviet-style "vertical" mechanisms for propagating norms and principles through bureaucratic channels, legislative measures, and policy documents. Notably, educational programs have been instrumentalized as vehicles for disseminating narratives rationalizing the war, such as the concept of Novorossiia to justify the annexation of Ukrainian territories and the notion of "state-civilization" to assert Russia's leadership role on the global stage as a civilizational pole contesting Western hegemony.

[149] Aleksandr Dugin, "Poteria Cherniaeva Eto Sdacha Khersona...," Telegram, December 24, 2023, https://t.me/Agdchan/13289.

Two significant conclusions arise from this analysis. First, the regime retains adaptability in its doctrinal framework through sustained engagement with a variety of nonstate ideological actors. State sponsorship of hawkish groups like the Izborskii Klub has shown their consistent alignment with official views on the war since 2022. However, the transactional nature of the state's support for these groups allows for a degree of flexibility, enabling the promotion or demotion of their ideological production in response to changing strategic circumstances.

Second, this chapter underscored the perpetuation of intellectual polarization and contradiction within Russia's public sphere, even amid the backdrop of wartime conditions and authoritarian repression. This phenomenon is primarily driven by the interference and confrontation between Russia-based ideological centers and intellectual emigration, which seeks to foster alternative, critical perspectives opposing the war.

9 Conclusion

Instead of the common historiographical divide between the Soviet and the post-Soviet period, this book covers a wide historical timeline spanning from the 1970s until today. During these years, a group of ideologues, designated as the "Russian hawks," have developed and consolidated a new conservative language, which I have termed "modernist conservatism," as it claims that technological progress can marry Russia-specific cultural and religious values and buttress authoritarian state power.

By looking at the Soviet genesis of their worldviews, I have found that what these ideologues "were *doing* in writing" was to oppose Western modernization theories, according to which postindustrial advancements would eventually lead developed societies to adopt the same set of liberal economic and political institutions.[1] In contrast to this convergence horizon, hawks argued that the Soviet system would remain distinct from the West by integrating technological modernization with specifically Russian cultural and religious values. Russian modernist conservatism, in this respect, serves as a case study of the concept of "multiple modernities" coined by sociologist Shmuel Eisenstadt to describe the proliferation, from around the 1960s, of understandings of modernity emancipated from the sociocultural dimensions of the Western liberal model.[2]

The hawks' call for the reenchantment of Soviet modernity, encapsulated by the motto "spiritualization of technology," departed from orthodox Marxism–Leninism. Instead, it drew on the informal development of the philosophy of Russian cosmism, which, inspired by

1 On the contextualist analysis of the performativity of texts and the need to understand what authors do when they write, see Quentin Skinner, "General Preface," in *Visions of Politics: Volume 1; Regarding Method* (Cambridge: Cambridge University Press, 2002), vii.

2 S. N. Eisenstadt, "Multiple Modernities," *Daedalus* 129, no. 1 (2000): 1–29.

prerevolutionary authors, advocated the use of technoscientific progress to orient the evolution of the universe toward the achievement of a Christian-inspired eschatological goal.

Over the period 1970–2024, modernist conservatism was not devised as an abstract theoretical system but rather consolidated as a collective language coalescing various groups and generations united by their common opposition to Russia's convergence with the West. Starting in the late Soviet Union, modernist conservatism provided a rallying "magnet"[3] sealing a common group identity for the first generation of hawks, which aggregated conservative intellectuals nostalgic for the tsarist empire with pro–status quo members of the Soviet politico-military establishment. Despite its social and ideological diversity, this group shared common experiences of struggle against liberal reformists through practices such as the publication of group manifestos, the creation of electoral coalitions, and, in 1991, the organization of a military coup against Mikhail Gorbachev. Although it lacked electoral successes and it eventually failed to prevent the collapse of the Soviet Union, the platform represented by modernist conservatism was sustained as an ideological language organizing and maintaining the identity of this antiliberal coalition across the transition to post-Soviet Russia. Throughout the 1990s, modernist conservatism continued to be framed as this coalition's common "group style"[4] against liberal "others."

A second generation of hawks, the "Young Conservatives," consolidated as a group toward the end of the 1990s and the beginning of the 2000s. They upheld a similar critique of the convergence horizon in the context of increased contestation of Western hegemony over the international order and of Russia's transition toward liberal economic and political institutions. The same type of relational processes of group identification and intergroup competition forged the Young Conservatives' cohesion, despite the ideological variety of its members, which ranged from Orthodox imperialism to secular ethnic nationalism. The unity of the group was formed as much on a set of

[3] On "coalition magnets," see Daniel Béland and Robert Henry Cox, "Ideas as Coalition Magnets: Coalition Building, Policy Entrepreneurs, and Power Relations," *Journal of European Public Policy* 23, no. 3 (2016): 429.

[4] The term "group style" is used by Nina Eliasoph and Paul Lichterman in "Culture in Interaction," *American Journal of Sociology* 108, no. 4 (2003): 737.

common ideas and beliefs as on a common pledge to gain hegemony over liberal-inclined groups.

Professionalized as public intellectuals through their formation as social scientists and their careers as online media journalists, Young Conservatives further entrenched their elders' blend of traditionalist conservatism with technological modernism into a formal ideological doctrine, which they named "dynamic conservatism." As they viewed it, dynamic conservatism's synthesis of traditional values and technological might should become Russia's new state ideology.

In 2012, the fusion of hawks of both generations into the Izborskii Klub institutionalized the existence of an idea network advocating the restoration of Russia's imperial, great-power status in cultural and military confrontation with the West.

The primacy of the interactional dimension of ideological group identity-building over inner theoretical consistency in the formation of the first and second generations of hawks highlights a shift in the use of ideology. Instead of a rigid macro-belief system aimed at mass audiences, modernist conservatism was conceived as a group label to build a coalition within an interelite competition for influence over policy decisions. This aspect of the production of modernist conservatism, aimed at reaching ruling circles, relates to the second central argument of the book on the role that hawks came to play in shaping and legitimizing the Kremlin's policy choices.

To understand the rise of the hawks' ideas to political prominence, I have examined the successive steps of their formation and institutionalization as an idea network cutting across intellectual and political elites. This analysis has been based on a combination of discourse analysis and socioempirical research on the conditions of idea formation and circulation within an intellectual production space structured by power relations between competing groups. Beyond analyzing the rhetoric of Russian hawks, I have explored the range of symbolic and material resources (generation, education, professional occupation, institutional affiliations, publication venues, funding) that have enabled them to gain recognition, legitimacy, and visibility in this competitive space. Additionally, I have sought to highlight the political performativity of their ideas, not only by examining the parallels between their discourse and official speech but also by tracing the actual circulation of ideas through interactions between intellectual circles and ruling elites.

The major finding of my research is that, despite the prohibition of state ideology in the Russian constitution of 1993, the Russian regime, from the mid-1990s onward, has progressively revived Soviet practices of sponsorship of ideology production. Instead of the Soviet institutionalization of an ideological apparatus, however, the current regime has outsourced it to clubs and think tanks outside party institutions.

This challenges the common narrative that identifies a distinct conservative turning point in the Russian regime from 2012 onward. Instead, I argue that this shift should be viewed within a broader and more gradual evolution of the relationship between decision-makers and "ideas networks." The second implication is that regime support for ideology production aimed not at consolidating a unique state ideology but at cultivating and authoritatively controlling a certain degree of ideological pluralism. While an ideological core consolidated over the years in official discourse around key concepts such as strong state power and the multipolarity of the world order, additional ideological content remained fluid. This practice of "managed ideological pluralism" through the promotion or demotion of different idea networks maintained a range of lines and narratives available to justify various policy courses.

This diversity facilitated a flexible policy agenda, encompassing the implementation of neoliberal economic reforms leading to Russia's accession to the World Trade Organization in 2012, alongside foreign and security policies challenging liberal norms of the international order. Moreover, this variability elucidates significant shifts in Russia's foreign policy, particularly the evolution of the Kremlin's Ukraine policy, which transitioned from engaging in diplomatic negotiations to resolve the Donbass conflict in 2014 to a fully revisionist use of force in 2022.

In addressing the question of whether ideas are influential in Russian politics, my research affirms their significant impact. Ideology plays a pivotal role within the Russian political system by shaping the collective language constitutive of elite groups. The competition of these groups, in turn, shapes the set of policy options available. However, contrary to the notion of the Russian regime adhering to a singular ideological paradigm, my research reveals a different approach. Instead of favoring a specific ideological framework, the Russian regime employs a distinctive approach to managing the sphere of ideological production. I have highlighted the functioning of the Russian political system as a "network state," where hawks have been increasingly able to compete against more liberal idea networks to establish connections with ruling circles. Their ascension stems both from the bottom-up strategies they deployed to reach out to policy circles and from state-led cooptation of ideological resources that align with the regime preferences.

On the one hand, I have demonstrated that the hawks adopted a Gramscian strategy of influence, according to which they sought to inform ruling elites' policy decisions by gaining cultural hegemony in the public sphere rather than investing in party politics. This strategy, endorsed by the first generation of hawks in the 1970s, was characteristic of late Soviet intellectuals' practice of "politics by culture," using literary magazines as substitute forums for sociopolitical debates to express nonconformist views while sticking to the constraining rules of an authoritarian public sphere and a one-party system.[5] This mixed position of nonconformism and loyalism, aimed at changing the views and policies of the ruling elites, was subsequently taken up by the second generation of hawks. As they started their careers in the 2000s, Young Conservatives faced an increasingly authoritarian public sphere constraining the development of independent, partisan agency. By contrast with their elders, however, Young Conservatives relied on the internet as their primary medium for cultural influence, through which they became online opinion-makers.

Second, the hawks relied on organizational strategies aimed at building networks aggregating members of various professional milieus in transpartisan, interelite places of ideology production. Toward the end of the Soviet Union and in the following decade of the 1990s, the newspapers *Den* (1990–93) and *Zavtra* (1993–) played a nodal role as the social and doctrinal space ensuring the group's cohesion and visibility in the public sphere. Starting from the 2000s, the Young Conservatives further professionalized the practice of ideological entrepreneurship. Their academic training in the social sciences and their knowledge of Western intellectual milieus enabled them able to organize collective doctrinal works, attract financial resources from

[5] On the Soviet practice of "politics by culture," see Yitzhak M. Brudny, *Reinventing Russia: Russian Nationalism and the Soviet State, 1953–1991*, Russian Research Center Studies 91 (Cambridge, MA: Harvard University Press, 1998).

conservative business circles, and establish institutional representation in the public sphere through intellectual societies and think tanks, such as the Institute of Dynamic Conservatism.

Their integration with the elder generation of hawks within the Izborskii Klub in 2012 embedded modernist conservatism in institutions that outlasted the original historical conjuncture that had instigated it. This institutional foundation facilitated the aggregation of members, resources, and funding to compete with concurrent liberal groups in the field of public expertise. The growing visibility, recognition, and legitimation of hawks in the public sphere over the period demonstrate that their discursive and organizational strategies played a significant role in reshaping value hierarchies and norms defining authorized public discourse.

On the other hand, modernist conservatism rose to political prominence through top-down mechanisms of state cooptation of ideological resources. These mechanisms were progressively put into place in reaction to a series of turning points that challenged the legitimacy of the Russian regime and/or its distinction vis-à-vis Western liberal societies and consequently reconfigured the relationship between ruling elites and conservative circles of ideology production.

The first such turning point followed the October 1993 constitutional crisis, in the aftermath of which some of the key ideas of conservative ideologues such as the need for strong state power and the promotion of Russia's "national idea" were appropriated by Boris Yeltsin to justify the authoritarian superpresidentialization of the Russian regime and the construction of a new post-Soviet state patriotism.

The years 1998–99 – marked by Russia's economic crisis, NATO's extension to Poland, Hungary, and the Czech Republic, NATO's intervention in the Kosovo crisis without a UN mandate, and Russia's launch of the Second Chechen War – represented a second landmark moment that led to a general cultural backlash to Russia's economic liberalization and cultural Westernization. The beginning of Putin's presidency in 2000 was paired with a partial rejection of the liberal legacy of the 1990s through the authoritarian consolidation of strong state power based on notions such as the "dictatorship of law" and the "power vertical." In this context, modernist conservatives gained official institutional recognition as legitimate public intellectuals with access to mass audience TV media. Some of their ideas – such as their critique of Western liberal modernity, post-Soviet democracy, the market economy, and Western hegemony over the international order, as well as their nostalgia for Russia's great-power status and their promotion of Russia-specific traditional values – therefore moved from the fringes to the mainstream of the public sphere.

The spread of colored revolutions in the post-Soviet space in the 2000s and, most notably, Ukraine's Orange Revolution in 2004, marked a third turning point. As the Russian regime feared the domestic reproduction of a revolutionary scenario, the ruling party, United Russia, partnered with hawkish ideologues to organize a counterreaction, mostly aimed at the youth, against liberal and nationalist opposition movements. High-ranking officials in charge of ideological provision for the party granted increased visibility and resources, including financial support, to proregime modernist conservatives. In addition, President Putin himself delivered ideological speeches endorsing the hawks' critique of Western liberal modernity and seeking to legitimize Russia's distinctiveness based on the promotion of concepts such as "sovereign democracy," spiritual sovereignty, and the contestation of unipolarity in the international order.

Finally, the 2011–12 cycle of mass street protests against electoral fraud publicly staged the ideological polarization of ruling elites between supporters of demands for liberalizing reforms and advocates of authoritarian consolidation. Building on these dividing lines, the creation of the Izborskii Klub in 2012 institutionalized the existence of an interelite network across hawkish ideologues and members of the ruling elite aimed at promoting dynamic conservatism as Russia's strategic ideological basis for the achievement of its national interests. In this position, dynamic conservatism settled in the policy expertise landscape as the strategic subculture of conservative elite groups. These groups were alternatively promoted or demoted relative to other more liberal groups through the distribution of state resources based on their alignment with the presidential administration's interpretation of Russia's strategic priorities. In particular, ideas originating from the Izborskii Klub were used to support the Kremlin's conservative domestic turn imposing social discipline based on traditional values and to justify its expansionist foreign policy.

The overall trend of consolidation, over the post-Soviet period, of a partnership between hawks and ruling elites highlights the increasing contribution of their ideology as a set of actionable ideas contextually used by the Russian regime to frame and legitimize policy decisions. However, my research also demonstrates that this trend of state support for the hawks experienced cycles of expansion and contraction, and that it had significantly reduced ahead of Russia's invasion of Ukraine.

Following the annexation of Crimea in 2014, the Russian regime pursued engagement with Ukraine to resolve the Donbass conflict through the Minsk agreements, thereby departing from the hawks' calls for full-scale invasion and integration of Donbass into Russia. On my latest trip to Moscow, which ended in December 2019, Izborskii Klub ideologues unanimously complained about their isolation and alienation from influential power centers. These testimonies were verified by the fact that the presidential administration put in place in 2016 had persistently declined the club's applications for financial grants.

However, Putin's decision to launch a war of aggression against Ukraine on February 24, 2022, signaled a pivotal shift in strategic thinking, whereby the preference went from diplomatic negotiations to an unconstrained, revisionist use of force. Since the outbreak of the war against Ukraine, justification for the use of armed force and rejection of the international order has dominated all sectors of state policies. The adoption of a blend of revisionist geopolitical worldviews, anti-Western sentiments, and conservative traditionalism by figures previously regarded as liberal, including Dmitrii Medvedev and Sergei Kirienko, suggests a shift away from acknowledging various idea networks among policy elites to establishing the hawks' ideas as the dominant discourse.

The Russian regime's wartime mobilization has revived elements of the Soviet-era "vertical" structure, facilitating the dissemination of norms through a bureaucratic hierarchy. However, it has not fully reconstructed a cohesive ideological apparatus, maintaining flexibility in its doctrinal framework. Alongside state initiatives, the regime continues to shape ideology production through interactions with nonstate ideological entrepreneurs. Moreover, despite wartime conditions and authoritarian repression, intellectual polarization persists within Russia's public sphere, driven by the opposition between domestic ideological centers and intellectual émigrés promoting alternative, critical perspectives against the war.

To conclude, it is crucial to continue investigating the interaction between ideology and politics in the wartime context to understand the mechanisms shaping the regime's strategic thinking and their implications for regional and global security. Moreover, questioning the resilience of the managed ideological pluralism identified in this book is essential for assessing the evolution and stability of the regime's current foundations.

Annex 1

List of Interviews

Izborskii Klub Members

Ageev, Aleksandr. Moscow, July 13, 2019.
Averianov, Vitalii. Moscow, July 4, 2018.
  Moscow, July 28, 2019.
Averianov, Vitalii and Aleksandr Nagornii. Moscow, February 20, 2019.
Cherniakhovskii, Sergei. Moscow, July 11, 2019.
Dugin, Aleksandr. Moscow, February 26, 2019.
Egorchenkov, Egor. Moscow, July 16, 2019.
Khazin, Mikhail. Moscow, July 10, 2019.
Korovin, Valerii. Moscow, July 13, 2019.
Pisarev, Sergei. Ekaterinburg, September 11, 2019.
Prokhanov, Aleksandr. Moscow, February 18, 2019.
Rozanov, Oleg. Moscow, September 19, 2019.

Young Conservatives

Kholmogorov, Egor. Moscow, July 5, 2018.
  Moscow, September 16, 2019.
Krylov, Konstantin. Moscow, November 28, 2019.
Mezhuev, Boris. Moscow, October 31, 2019.
Remizov, Mikhail. Moscow, June 19, 2018.
  Moscow, February 21, 2019.

Others

A., political consultant, former employee of the Foundation for Effective Politics. Moscow, November 6, 2019.
B., former department head, Molodaia Gvardiia. Moscow, November 8, 2019.
C., Soviet scholar of cosmism. Zoom, December 18, 2020.

Afanasiev, Andrei, journalist, Tsargrad. Moscow, November 29, 2019.
Aksiuchits, Viktor, politician. Moscow, November 19, 2019.
Kopeikin, Kirill, archpriest, Russian Orthodox Church. Moscow, February 28, 2019.
Kozyrev, Aleksei, associate professor, MGU. Moscow, February 21, 2019.
Melville, Andrei, professor, HSE. Moscow, December 3, 2019.
Orlov, Dmitrii, political consultant. Moscow, November 13, 2019.
Poliakov, Leonid, professor, HSE. Moscow, June 28, 2017.
Skurlatov, Valerii, philosopher. Email, January 19, 2021.
Sushentsov, Andrei, associate professor, MGIMO. Moscow, December 7, 2019.
Verkhovskii, Aleksandr, director of the research center SOVA. Moscow, July 31, 2019.
Volodikhin, Dmitrii, professor, MGU. Moscow, October 1, 2019.

Annex 2

Professional Occupation and Network Connections of the Izborskii Klub's Founding Members (2012–2013)

Professional category	Members	Position	Universities	Publications/media	Partisan activities	Responsibility in state institutions	Religious organizations
Economists	Aleksandr Ageev (1962–)	Doctor in Economics, expert at the Russian Academy of Sciences, director of the Institute for Economic Strategies of the Russian Academy of Sciences.	Head of the department of business projects management at the National Research Nuclear University "MEPhI," professor at the public administration faculty of Lomonosov Moscow State University and professor at MGIMO.	Author of over 500 scientific papers, including 28 monographs. Editor-in-chief of the journals *Economic Strategies* (*Ekonomicheskie strategii*) and *Partnership of Civilizations* (*Partnerstvo tsivilizatsii*).		Member of the Economic Council under the President of the Russian Federation, member of the expert council under the Chairman of the College of the Military-Industrial Commission, member of expert council under the Russian Emergencies Ministry.	President of the Club of Orthodox Entrepreneurs.

Professional category	Members	Position	Universities	Publications/media	Partisan activities	Responsibility in state institutions	Religious organizations
	Sergei Batchikov (1953–)	Economist and entrepreneur. Chairman of the Board of the Russian Trade and Financial Union. Director of the Center for Management Problems in Large Socio-Economic Systems of the International Research Institute for Management Problems.		Author of over 100 articles on socioeconomic topics and international economic relations. A regular contributor to the *Russian Economic Journal (Rossiiskiii ekonomicheskii zhurnal)*, *Economic Strategies (Ekonomicheskie Strategii)* and *Zavtra*. Author. Coauthor, with Sergei Glazev and Sergei Kara-Murza, of several books.			Member of the Club of Orthodox Entrepreneurs. He took part in the preparation of the Club's report "On the Strategy for Transforming Russia: Spiritual Principle, Goals, Risks and Opportunities."
	Sergei Glazev (1961–)	Doctor in Economics, academician of the Russian Academy of Sciences.	Head of the Department of Theory and Methodology of State and Municipal Administration at the Faculty of Public Administration, Moscow State University.	Author of more than 150 scientific papers and 20 books.	In the 2003 elections to the State Duma, he organized and headed the electoral bloc of the Rodina party. 2003–2007 – Deputy of the State Duma.	Adviser to the President of the Russian Federation on Eurasian economic Integration. Former executive secretary of the Commission of the Customs Union of the Republic of Belarus, the Republic of Kazakhstan and the Russian Federation.	

Mikhail Deliagin (1968–)	Doctor in Economics, scientific director of the autonomous nonprofit organization Institute of Globalization's Problems.		Author of more than 900 articles, author of 12 monographs. Editor-in-chief of the magazine *Svobodnaia Mysl*. Host of a number of television and radio programs.	Chairman of the Ideology council of Rodina party (2004–2006). Member of the permanent political conference of the party Other Russia (2006–2007).	Member of the Scientific Council under the Security Council of the Russian Federation.
Andrei Kobiakov (1961–)	Candidate in Economics. Chairman of the Board of the Institute of Dynamic Conservatism.	Associate professor at Moscow's State University.	Author of about 700 publications, including the book *The Decline of the Dollar Empire and the End of Pax Americana* (2003, coauthored with Mikail Khazin, 5,000 copies). Deputy editor-in-chief of the weekly sociopolitical magazine *Odnako* (*However*). Former editor-in-chief of the business magazine *Russian Entrepreneur*.		

Professional category	Members	Position	Universities	Publications/media	Partisan activities	Responsibility in state institutions	Religious organizations
	Mikhail Khazin (1962–)	Economist, television and radio host. President of the expert consulting company Neocon.		Author of numerous publications in the magazines *Profil*, *Ekspert*, and *Odnako*. In 2003, in coauthorship with A. Kobyakov, he wrote a book, *The Decline of the Dollar Empire and the End of Pax Americana* (5,000 copies). One of the presenters of the *Economics* program on the radio station Govorit Moskva. As an invited expert, he has repeatedly appeared on the radio program *Echo of Moscow* and the television program *Odnako*.		Former deputy head of the Economic Department of the President of the Russian Federation (1997–98).	Member of the Expert Council "Economics and Ethics" under the Patriarch of the Russian Orthodox Church.
Philosophers	Vitalii Averianov (1973–)	Doctor in Philosophy. Deputy chairman of the Izborskii Klub.	Former researcher at the Institute of Philosophy of the Russian Academy of Sciences (2002–2006).	Authors of many articles in academic journals and newspapers.			Member of the Inter-Council Presence of the Russian Orthodox Church of the first convocation (2009–14).

Aleksandr Dugin (1962–)	Doctor in Political Science.	Head of the Department of Sociology of International Relations of the Faculty of Social Sciences at Moscow's State University and head of the Center for Conservative Research at Moscow's State University.	Regular columnist for *Izvestia*, *Krasnaya Zvezda*, *Literaturnaya Gazeta*, *Komsomolskaya Pravda*, *Argumenty i Fakty*, and others. Regular guest on TV channels (Pervii Kanal, NTV, TVT). Host of the program *Russian Veshch* on the radio Russian News Service.	In 2000, he created the Eurasia Party. Since 2003, he has been the leader of the International Eurasian Movement.	Former adviser to the chairman of the State Duma of the Russian Federation (1998–2003).	In 2005, editor-in-chief of the Orthodox TV channel Spas; host of the weekly analytical program *Vekhi*.
Valerii Korovin (1977–)	Journalist, essayist. Director of the Center for Geopolitical Expertise.	Deputy head of the Center for Conservative Research at the Sociological Faculty of Moscow State University.	He has actively published in various newspapers (*Russkii Zhurnal*, *Strana.ru*, *Gazeta*, *Vedomosti*, *Nezavisimoe Obozrenie*, *Krasnaia Zvezda*…). Former author and presenter of the "Reaction" column on the *Vekhi* program on the Spas TV channel. Editor-in-Chief of the Eurasia Information and Analytical Internet Portal.	Deputy head of the International Eurasian Movement.		

Professional category	Members	Position	Universities	Publications/media	Partisan activities	Responsibility in state institutions	Religious organizations
	Shamil Sultanov (1952–)	Candidate in history. President of the Center for Strategic Studies "Russia – Islamic World."		Deputy editor-in-chief of *Zavtra*. Regular columnist for the "new right" magazine *Elementy* and the Palestinian newspaper *Al-Quds*.	Deputy of the State Duma (2003–2007), elected on the list of the Rodina party.		President of the Center for Strategic Studies "Russia – Islamic World."
Journalists	Maksim Kalashnikov (1966–)	Journalist and writer of science fiction.		Author of more than 30 books. Worked as a journalist for *Russian Entrepreneur*, *RPMonitor*, the *Globoscope* web magazine and the *Supernova Reality* magazine.	Secretary for strategic development of the Central Council of the party "Motherland: Common Sense."		
	Mikhail Leontev (1958–)	Head of the Copyright Programs Department of the Information Programs Directorate of Channel One.		Leading political and economic columnist for TV Channel One (Pervii Kanal). Head of the TV program *Odnako* and the sociopolitical magazine of the same name. Conducts radio programs on Vesti FM and Maiak Radio.	Member of the political council of Eurasia. In 2002 he became a member of United Russia.		
	Maksim Shevchenko (1966–)	Journalist.		Host of TV programs on Channel One (Pervii Kanal). Regular columnist for *Nezavisimaya Gazeta*.	Member of the Anti-Orange Committee.	Member of the Federal Civic Chamber. Member of the Presidential Council for the Development of Civil Society and Human Rights.	Head of the Center for Strategic Studies of Religion and Politics of the Modern World.

	Vladislav Shurygin (1963–)	Journalist.		Editor of department for military issues and deputy editor-in-chief of *Zavtra*; member of the editorial board of APN.ru. Host of the program *Curfew* on the Internet TV channel "Den."	Member of the National-Bolshevik Party since 2002.		
Historians	Nataliia Narochnitskaia (1948–)	Doctor in History. Head of the European Institute for Democracy and Cooperation (Paris).	Senior researcher at the Institute of World Economy and International Relations of the Russian Academy of Sciences.	Authors of multiple articles and monographs, among them the widely distributed book on the Second World War *For What and With Whom We Fought* (2005, 27,000 copies).	Deputy of the State Duma (2003–2007), elected on the list of the Rodina party.	Member of the Commission under the President of the Russian Federation to counter attempts to falsify history to the detriment of Russia's interests. In 2008, appointed by Putin as the head of the European Institute for Democracy and Cooperation (Paris), one of two Russian nongovernmental organizations abroad funded by the Russian Federation.	Member of Russian Orthodox Church's Inter-Council Presence. One of the initiators and active leaders of the World Russian People's Council. Recipient of Order of St. Olga Equal to the Apostles of the Russian Orthodox Church and of the Order of St. Great Martyr Barbara of the Ukrainian Orthodox Church of the Moscow Patriarchate.

Professional category	Members	Position	Universities	Publications/media	Partisan activities	Responsibility in state institutions	Religious organizations
	Nikolai Starikov (1970–)	Essayist.		Author of 20 books and several best-sellers: *Crisis$: How It Is Done* (2009, 12, 000 copies), *Nationalization of the Ruble – the Way to Russia's Freedom* (2011, 20, 000 copies); *Stalin. Remembering Together* (2012, 20, 000 copies). Well-known blogger, regular guest on TV and radio broadcasts.	Founder and leader of the public organization Patriots of the Great Fatherland (PVO). One of the leaders of the Anti-Maidan movement. Member of the "All-Russian Popular Front" in Saint Petersburg.		
	Andrei Fursov (1951–)	Candidate in History. Head of the Asia and Africa Department of the Institute of Scientific Information on Social Sciences of the Russian Academy of Sciences.	Associate professor of the Department of History of the Near and Middle East at the Institute of Asian and African Countries in Moscow State University.	Author of 250 works, including 9 monographs. Regular contributors in both academic and journalistic publications (*Voprosy Filosofii*, *Vostok*, *Russian Historical Journal*, *Sociological Research*) and in newspapers (*Literaturnaya Gazeta*, *Moskovskie Novosti*, *Zavtra*, etc.).			

Writers	Aleksandr Prokhanov (1938–)	Writer. Chairman and founder of the Izborskii Klub.		Writer of more than 30 novels and political essays. Editor-in-chief of the newspaper *Zavtra*.	Deputy chairman of the Public Council under the Ministry of Defense and member of the Council on Public Television.
	Iurii Poliakov (1954–)	Writer.		Author of more than 20 novels. Laureate of several literary prizes: Gogol Prize (2005), Bunin Prize (2008). Editor-in-chief of *Literaturnaya Gazeta*. Host of the program *Context* on the TV channel Russia-Culture.	Former member of the Presidential Council for the Development of Civil Society Institutions and Human Rights (2005–2009). Recipient of the state's Order of Friendship (2008) and Order of Honor (2010). Recipient of the Gratitude of the President of the Russian Federation (April 30, 2008).
Political scientists	Aleksandr Nagornii (1947–2020)	Candidate in Political Science. Deputy chairman of the Izborskii Klub.		Deputy editor-in-chief of *Zavtra*.	

Professional category	Members	Position	Universities	Publications/media	Partisan activities	Responsibility in state institutions	Religious organizations
	Sergei Cherniakhovskii (1956–)	Doctor in Political Science.	Professor at Moscow State University.	Author of about 1,000 scientific and analytical works, including monographs. Regular host on the TV programs *Press Center* (ORT), *Nothing Personal* (TVC), *Glas Naroda* (NTV), and *What Is to Be Done?* (Kultura) and on the radio stations Maiak Radio, BBC Russian service.		Member of the Public Council of the Ministry of Culture of the Russian Federation.	
Businessman	Aleksandr Notin (1953–)	Candidate in history. Head of the investment group Monolith.				Former first secretary of the Department of the Middle East and North Africa of the Ministry of Foreign Affairs of the Russian Federation. Assistant to the governor of the Nizhny Novgorod region V.P. Shantsev.	Founder of an Orthodox cultural and educational community Crossing.

Politician	Iurii Lastochkin (1965–)	Candidate in Economics. City mayor of Rybinsk.			Former deputy of the State Duma of the Iaroslavl Region of the III and IV convocations.		Recipient of the Order of Saint Reverend Seraphim of Sarov, third degree for assistance to the Iaroslavl diocese and in connection with the 1,000th anniversary of Iaroslavl.
Military	Leonid Ivashov (1943–)	Doctor of History. Colonel general. President of the Academy of Geopolitical Problems.	Professor at the Moscow State Institute of International Relations.	Regular guest on central TV channels.		Former head of the Main Directorate of International Military Cooperation of the Ministry of Defense (1996–2001).	
Clergy	Mitropolit Tikhon (Shevkunov) (1958–)	Metropolitan of Pskov and Porkhov.		Author of multiple publications. Editor-in-chief of the Orthodox Internet portal Pravoslavie.Ru. Film director of the movie *The Fall of an Empire: The Lesson of Byzantium* (2008), winner of the Golden Eagle Award for Best Documentary.		Member of the Council for Culture and Arts under the President of the Russian Federation.	Member of the Supreme Church Council of the Russian Orthodox Church. Executive Secretary of the Patriarchal Council for Culture.

Annex 3

Professional Occupation and Biographical Details of the Izborskii Klub Members Added in the Period 2013–2021

Type of capital	Members added 2013–October 2021	Profession	Biographical details
Financial resources	Oleg Rozanov (1969–)	Businessman	President of the METR holding.
			Since 2015, executive secretary of the Izborsk Club for Regional and International Activities. Since 2016, first deputy chairman of the Izborskii Klub.
	Sergei Pisarev (1960–)	Entrepreneur	Entrepreneur, president of the Russian Entrepreneur Foundation.
Public outreach	Episkop Avgustin (Anisimov) (1945–)	Clergy	Bishop of Gorodetskii and Vetluzhskii.
	Vladimir Bortko (1946–)	Film director	Film director and producer. People's Artist of the Russian Federation (2000), Honored Artist of the Russian Federation (1994), People's Artist of Ukraine (2003), laureate of the State Prize of the RSFSR (1988), recipient of the Order of Honor (2006). Deputy of the State Duma (elected on the list of the KPRF party) and deputy chairman of the State Duma Committee on Culture (2011–16).
	Andrei Kovalev (1957–)	Musician, businessman	Russian businessman and musician. Leader of the Pilgrim rock group, TV and radio host, music producer, organizer of rock festivals, owner of the development company Ecooffis.
			Former head of the Main Directorate of the Forest Fund of the Ministry of Natural Resources of the Russian Federation (2000), Former Deputy Minister of the Forest Industry of the Russian Federation (1994–95), deputy chairman of the Russian State Timber Company Roslesprom and vice president of the joint stock company Russian Timber Industrialists; deputy of the Moscow State Duma (2004–2009).

Type of capital	Members added 2013–October 2021	Profession	Biographical details
	Albir Krganov (1976–)	Clergy	Mufti of the CRO Spiritual Assembly of Muslims of Russia, chairman of the CRO Spiritual Administration of Muslims of the city of Moscow and the Central region “Moscow Muftiat,” muft of the CRO Spiritual Administration of Muslims of the Chuvash Republic. Member of the Civic Chamber of the Russian Federation.
	Ivan Okhobystin (1966–)	Actor and film director	Russian actor, film director, screenwriter, journalist and writer.
	Zakhar Prilepin (1975–)	Writer	Writer, deputy editor-in-chief of the news portal Svobodnaia mysl.
	Konstantin Semin (1980–)	Journalist	Russian journalist, TV presenter of the All-Russian State Television and Radio Broadcasting Company.
	Karen Shakhnazarov (1952–)	Film director	Film director and producer. People’s Artist of the Russian Federation (2002). Recipient of the Order of Honour (2008). Recipient of the Golden Eagle Award (2008, 2009, 2012, 2017). Laureate of the Lenin Komsomol Prize (1986), the State Prize of the RSFSR named after the Vasiliev brothers (1988), two State Prizes of the Russian Federation (2003, 2013)
	Dzhuletto Keza (1940–2020)	Politician	Italian journalist and politician. Member of the European Parliament in 2004–2009.
Public outreach, analytical expertise	Zhores Alferov (1930–2019)	Physicist	Physicist and Nobel Prize Laureate. Academician of the Russian Academy of Sciences (RAS). Member of the KPRF, deputy of the State Duma of the Russian Federation (1995–2019). Cochairman of the Scientific Advisory Council of the Skolkovo Foundation, head of the Skolkovo Innovation Center (2010–19).

Analytical expertise	Bardan Bagdasarian (1971–)	Historian	Doctor in History. Dean of the Faculty of History, Political Science and Law of the Moscow State Regional University (MGOU), professor of the Department of Public Policy of Moscow State University.
	Sergei Baranov (1967–)	Sociologist	Candidate in Sociology. Analyst at the Expert Institute for Social Research. Former head of the analytical department of the NGO Combat Brotherhood (2005–2008). Former head of the Trade Representation of the Yamal-Nenets Autonomous Okrug in Kiev (2011–16).
	Vladimir Bolshakov (1951–)	Philosopher	Doctor in Philosophy. Professor at the Department of Philosophy and Socio-Political Technologies of the Russian State University of Oil and Gas named after I.M. Gubkin.
	Dmitrii Egorchenkov (1980–)	Researcher	Director of the Institute for Strategic Studies and Forecasts of the RUDN University.
	Elena Larina (1964–)	Researcher	Entrepreneur, analyst. Professor at the Institute of Economic Strategies and the Academy of Information Systems.
	Georgii Malinetskii (1956–)	Mathematician	Head of the department for modeling nonlinear processes at the Institute of Applied Mathematics of the Russian Academy of Sciences. Full member of the Academy of Military Sciences, member of the Public Council on the problems of the military-industrial complex under the deputy prime minister of the Russian Federation (since 2012).
	Vladimir Ovchinskii (1955–)	Police major general	Russian criminologist, retired police major general, Doctor in jurisprudence. Former head of the Russian Bureau of Interpol (1997–99).

Type of capital	Members added 2013–October 2021	Profession	Biographical details
	Iurii Tavrovskii (1949–)	Orientalist, journalist	Professor at the Peoples' Friendship University of Russia, member of the Presidium of the Eurasian Academy of Television and Radio. Since 1996, he has been the head of the department of public relations in the large oil trading corporation RAO International Economic Cooperation. Former advisor to the head of the Main Directorate for Servicing the Diplomatic Corps under the Russian Foreign Ministry, in charge of press relations and editor-in-chief of *Diplomat* magazine (1999–2009).
	Georgii Filimonov (1980–)	Political scientist	Doctor in Political Science, professor of the RUDN University.
	Roman Lazuka (1984–)	Manager	Lawyer and environmental auditor. He works for the top management of industrial companies of large Russian business in the mining sector (coal, oil). He is involved in the control of processes in the field of ecology and industrial safety. Since 2021, he has held the position of deputy general director – executive director at the Investment Development Agency.
	Vasilii Simchera (1940–2020)	Economist	Doctor in Economics, professor. Vice president of the Academy of Economic Sciences.
Advocacy	Gennadii Zhivotov (1946–)	Cartoonist	Graphic artist, Honored Artist of the Russian Federation. Employee-cartoonist of the newspaper *Zavtra*, member of the Union of Artists of the Russian Federation.
	Pavel Karpov (1970–)	Manager	Head of the industrial and economic section of the Izborskii Klub. He has held managerial positions in industrial enterprises and large chemical holdings.

	Mikhail Kildiashov (1986–)	Writer	Poet, publicist, literary critic. Candidate in Philology. Secretary of the Union of Writers of Russia, member of the Civic Chamber of the Orenburg region. Chairman of the Orenburg regional branch of the Izborskii Klub.
	Oleg Platonov (1950–)	Writer, editor	Doctor in Economic. Chief editor of the publishing house Russian Civilization, which published the Izborskii Klub's essays.
	Sergei Ushkalov (1969–)	Historian	Chairman of the Bryansk regional branch of the Izborskii Klub.
Relations with the political establishment	Dmitrii Aiatskov (1950–)	Politician	Doctor in History. Former governor of the Saratov Region (1996–2005). Former assistant to the head of the Presidential Administration of the Russian Federation (2006–11). Active State Councilor of the Russian Federation, 2nd class. Founder of the Volga branch of the Izborskii Klub.
	Murat Ziazikov (1957–)	Politician	Deputy plenipotentiary representative of the President of the Russian Federation in the Central Federal District.
	Tatiana Kravchuk (1981–)	Politician	Deputy minister of physical culture and sports of the Moscow Region, chairman of the Board of Trustees of the All-Russian Public Organization Russian World.
	Aleksandr Mazharov (1960–)	Politician	Candidate in Economics. Deputy governor of the Yamal-Nenets Autonomous Okrug, director of the Department of External Relations of the Yamal-Nenets Autonomous Okrug.
	Georgii Muradov (1954–)	Politician	Deputy chairman of the Council of Ministers of the Republic of Crimea – Permanent Representative of the Republic of Crimea under the President of the Russian Federation.
	Sergei Potemkin (1988–)	Politician	Head of the Office of the Oryol Regional Council of People's Deputies, current Corresponding Member of the Russian Municipal Academy.

Type of capital	Members added 2013–October 2021	Profession	Biographical details
	Sergei Tsekov (1953–)	Politician	Member of the Federation Council from the Republic of Crimea. Former chairman of the Standing Committee on Culture of the Supreme Council of the Autonomous Republic of Crimea (2010–14). Former first deputy chairman of the Supreme Council of the Autonomous Republic of Crimea (2006–10).
	Viacheslav Shtyrov (1953–)	Politician	Member of the Federation Council Committee on Defense and Security, Chairman of the Council for the Arctic and Antarctic under the Federation Council, member of the Presidium of the State Commission on the Development of the Arctic. Former deputy chairman of the Federation Council of the Federal Assembly of the Russian Federation (2010–14). Former president of the Republic of Sakha (Yakutia) (2002–10).

Bibliography

Archives

Literaturnaia gazeta (1968–85)
Den (1990–93)
Zavtra (1993–)
dynacon.ru (2009–12)
izborsk-club.ru (2012–)
Izborskii Klub. Russkie strategii (2012–)

Primary Sources

Ageev, Aleksandr. "Golod 72. Prakticheskaia gastroenterologiia Chteniia." *Russkii zhurnal*, April 17, 2002. https://web.archive.org/web/20050219000911/http:/geksogen.ru/r42.html.

"Akhmadinezhad v Izborskom Klube." *Izborskii Klub. Russkie strategii,* no. 6 (2013): 2.

Aleksandrov, Nikolai. "Beda, chto skuchen tvoi roman. Geksogennyi nadezhdy patrioticheskoi belletristiki." gazeta.ru, April 9, 2002. https://web.archive.org/web/20050218090239/http:/geksogen.ru/r23.html.

"'Gospodin Geksogen' podelilsia s gospodinom Limonovym." gazeta.ru, June 3, 2002. https://web.archive.org/web/20060529204255/http:/geksogen.ru/r65.html.

Alekseev, Mikhail, and Konstantin Krylov. *Osobennosti natsionalnogo povedeniia*. Moscow: Art-Biznes-Tsentr, 2001.

Aleshkovskii, Petr. "Esli skrestit Zhirinovskogo s Glazunovym." *Vremia MN*, April 12, 2002. https://web.archive.org/web/20050218173528/http:/geksogen.ru/r31.html.

"Vpechatleniia nedeli." *Obshchaia gazeta*, April 2002. https://web.archive.org/web/20050218173354/http:/geksogen.ru/r27.html.

Anachenkov, Boris. "Kak zerkalo NTR." *Literaturnaia gazeta*, no. 42 (October 17, 1979): 4.

"Antikrizisnye mery i energetike: Vopros natsionalnogo budushchego." dynacon.ru, October 5, 2009. www.dynacon.ru/content/articles_idk/353/.

"Antivaldaiskaia vozvyshennost." *Kommersant*, September 10, 2012. www.kommersant.ru/doc/2019043.

Atlas Russkoi Mechty. Russkaia mechta, 2021. https://izborsk-club.ru/files/Atlas_rusdream.pdf.

Averianov, Vitalii. "Doklad v Pekine." *Izborskii Klub*, May 20, 2015. https://izborsk-club.ru/5604.

"Dvusmyslennost prezidentskogo poslaniia." *Russkii obozrevatel*, December 1, 2010. http://averianov.net/sii/438/?h=619.

"Fenomenologia smutnogo vremeni: Otkuda zhdat Minina i Pozharskogo?" *Obshchestvennie Nauki i Sovremennost* 3 (1996): 95–103.

"Gensek Vladimir Groznyi." APN.ru, August 20, 2004. http://averianov.net/sii/463/?h=670.

"Izborskii Klub i glavnyi vopros epokhi." *Izborskii Klub. Russkie strategii*, no. 6 (2013): 18–28.

"Izborskii Klub provodit psikhoterapiiu." *Izborskii Klub*, June 4, 2013. https://izborsk-club.ru/1317.

"Kastratsia germafrodita – Konetz postmoderna?" *Volshebnaia Gora* VIII (2002). http://averianov.net/sii/472/?h=478.

"Kogda bog izbiraet nemoshch… (Otets Dimitrii Dudko i ego propoved 'Cherez pozor')." *Pravoslavnoe Knizhnoe Obozrenie* 1–2 (1999). http://averianov.net/sii/483/?h=670.

"Konservatizm – Ochishchenie ot illiuzii (programma kluba konservativnykh analitikov)." *Zolotoi Lev, no.* 11–12 (2000). http://averianov.net/sii/477/?h=670.

"Konservatizm v otdelno vziatoi strane." *Volshebnaia Gora* XII (2006). http://averianov.net/sii/501/?h=670.

"Korporatizm – Novaia mifologiia." *Filosofskaia gazeta*, 2001. http://averianov.net/sii/535/?h=670.

"Krytyi Krest (osnovy filosofii bogochelovecheskoi kultury)." *Volshebnaia Gora*, no. 6 (1997).

"Metafizika nichego. Ob opyte sviashchennogo pisaniia bezdny G. Dzhemalia." metacultura.ru, 1999. http://averianov.net/sii/482/?h=670.

"Mezhdu tsarstvom i diktaturoi. Sravnivaia 'Proekt Rossiia' i Russkuiu Doktrinu." KM.ru, August 30, 2007. http://averianov.net/sii/490/?h=674.

"Mysliashchaia korporatsiia." Moskovskie novosti, September 14, 2007. http://averianov.net/sii/?h=619.

"Neoborimaia krotost. Ob o. Dimitrii Dudko." *Pravoslavnoe Knizhnoe Obozrenie*, December 1998. http://averianov.net/sii/538/?h=670;%20 http://averianov.net/sii/483/?h=670.

"Nevidimaia os mira. Nam nuzhen orden mechtanostsev." *Izborskii Klub*, January 3, 2020. https://izborsk-club.ru/18514.

"Nuzhno stat zavisimymi ot budushchego Rossii." APN.ru, December 7, 2005.
Nuzhnye drugie liudi. *Zavtra*, July 14, 2010. https://zavtra.ru/blogs/2010-07-1431.
"O politicheskikh itogakh serafimovskikh torzhestv." APN.ru, July 30, 2004. http://averianov.net/sii/465/?h=670.
"O 'sinteze' pravoslavnoi ideologii." *NG religii*, March 7, 2000. http://averianov.net/sii/479/?h=639.
"Obrashchenie k 'reshitelnomu menshinstvu.'" APN.ru, 07 2005. http://averianov.net/sii/450/?h=670.
"Ot Dumy k soboru (politologicheskaia fantastika blizhnego deistviia)." *Russkii zhurnal*, December 29, 2003. http://averianov.net/sii/468/?h=478.
"Otchaiane Brillianta." *Ekspert* 1–2, no. 309 (2002). http://averianov.net/sii/471/?h=478.
Piat let Russkoi Doktrine. *Zavtra*, December 29, 2010. https://zavtra.ru/blogs/2010-12-2973.
"Posle sobornykh slushanii opponenty zabespokoilis." *Narodnoe radio*, August 4, 2007. http://averianov.net/sii/493/?h=674.
Priroda Russkoi Ekspansii. Moscow: Lenta-Press, 2003.
"Putin slishkom tiazhelo rasstaetsia s zastarelymi illiuziiami." *Izborskii Klub*, December 20, 2014. https://izborsk-club.ru/4397.
"Rassypavshaiasia matreshka." *RPmonitor*, December 2006. http://averianov.net/sii/526/?h=630.
"Raznye konservatizmy, raznye traditsionalizmy." pravoslavie.ru, September 4, 2001. http://averianov.net/sii/475/?h=670.
"Rossiia – Ne ot mira sego." *Zavtra*, no. 425 (January 8, 2002). http://averianov.net/sii/?h=478.
"Rossiia i chelovechestvo." *Russkii zhurnal*, 2002. http://averianov.net/sii/470/?h=478.
"Russkaia Doktrina – Eto sobiraiushchii, a ne razdeliaiushchii dokument." *Interfaks-religiia*, August 20, 2007. http://averianov.net/sii/491/?h=635.
"Russkaia istoricheskaia traditsiia v neokonservatizme I. A. Ilina." *Istoriia Filosofii* 9 (2002): 110–19.
"Segodnia russkoi tserkvi 'bolshe vsekh nado.'" *NG religii*, October 11, 2000. http://averianov.net/sii/479/?h=670.
"Traditsiia i traditsionalizm v nauchnoi i obshchestvennoi mysli Rossii (60-e–90-e gg. XX veka)." *Obshchestvennie nauki i sovremennost no.* 1 (2000): 68–77.
"Traditsiia kak preemstvennost i sluzhenie." *Chelovek, no.* 2 (2000): 38–51.

"Tretii polius." *Ekspert* 10, no. 317 (2002). http://averianov.net/sii/532/?h=478.

"Tsivilizatsiia v labirintakh kosmizma." *Ekspert* 5 (2003). http://averianov.net/sii/528/?h=478.

"Ukraina – Lish povod dlia velikogo sobytiia." *Izborskii Klub*, April 4, 2022. https://izborsk-club.ru/22582.

"U ministra obrazovaniia, pokhozhe, kartblansh." *Izborskii Klub*, February 7, 2022. https://izborsk-club.ru/10118.

"Vavilonskoe osvobozhdenie." *Ekspert* 33, no. 339 (2002). http://averianov.net/sii/533/?h=478.

"Vdokh i vydokh Rossii." *Ekspert* 30, no. 337 (2002). http://averianov.net/sii/527/?h=478.

"Vesna ochistitelnaia." *Izborskii Klub*, March 18, 2022. https://izborsk-club.ru/22500.

"Vrata v mir samosoznaniia. V. V. Averianov na konferentsii 'Obrazovanie i mirovozzrenie.'" February 20, 2024. https://izborsk-club.ru/25392.

"V.V. Khlebnikov: Traditsionalizm v avangarde." *Volshebnaia gora* V (1996). http://averianov.net/sii/484/?h=478.

"Zhitie Veniamina Blazhennogo." *Voprosy literatury* 6 (1994). http://averianov.net/sii/?h=478.

Baidin, Valerii. *Nepodvizhnoe stranstvie, povest-vospominanie*. Moscow: Vikmo-M, 2018.

Bitov, Andrei, Oleg Volkov, Iurii Dmitriev, Petr Dudochkin, Leonid Korobkov, Aleksandr Prokhanov, and Vladimir Chivilikhin. "Kruglii stol – I hram, i masterskaia!" *Literaturnaia gazeta,* no. 14 (April 5, 1978): 4–5.

Bondarenko, Vladimir. "Prokhanovskii proryv." *Sovetskaia Rossiia*, April 27, 2002. https://web.archive.org/web/20060507143320/http:/geksogen.ru/r70.html.

"V novuiu derevniu – Na telege?" *Literaturnaia gazeta,* no. 49 (December 5, 1979): 4.

"Volshebnaia Gora." *Zavtra*, October 24, 2012. https://zavtra.ru/blogs/volshebnaya-gora-2012-10-24-000000.

Brazhnikov, Ilia. "Vopreki nazvaniiu doklad nes v sebe dukh istinnoi reformatsii." *politconservatism.ru*, September 2, 2015. https://politconservatism.ru/prognosis/vopreki-nazvaniyu-doklad-nyes-v-sebe-dukh-istinnoy-reformatsii.

Bychkov, Sergei. "V Rossii postroiat suverennuiu teokratiiu?" *Moskovskii komsomolets*, September 12, 2007. www.rusdoctrina.ru/page95794.html.

Chemezov, Sergei. "'Otkuda prenebrezhenie k rossiiskomu?' Glava 'Rostekha' ob importozameshchenii." RBC, June 15, 2022. www.rbc.ru/opinions/economics/15/06/2022/62a87e589a7947cbf332c253.

"Cherniaev Anatolii Vladimirovich." *Institut Filosofii Rossiiskoi Akademii Nauk*, https://iphras.ru/chernyaev.htm.

Cherniakhovskii, Sergei. "Izborsk i Ulianovsk." APN.ru, January 21, 2013. www.apn.ru/publications/article28236.htm.

Chernyshev, Sergei. "Vmesto manifesta. Predpinimatel: Novoe slovo. Novoe soslovie. Novoe remeslo." *Russkii zhurnal*, September 11, 2000. http://old.russ.ru/ist_sovr/ckp/20000904_I.html.

"Concept of the Foreign Policy of the Russian Federation," March 31, 2023. https://mid.ru/en/foreign_policy/fundamental_documents/1860586/.

"Conception of State Nationality Policy in the Russian Federation." *Statutes and Decisions* 33, no. 6 (November 1997): 80.

"Council Implementing Regulation (EU) No 826/2014 of 30 July 2014 Implementing Regulation (EU) No 269/2014 Concerning Restrictive Measures in Respect of Actions Undermining or Threatening the Territorial Integrity, Sovereignty and Independence of Ukraine." *Official Journal of the European Union*, July 30, 2014. https://eur-lex.europa.eu/legal-content/EN/TXT/?uri=CELEX:32014R0826.

"Crimea Referendum: Voters 'Back Russia Union,'" March 16, 2014. www.bbc.com/news/world-europe-26606097.

Danilkin, Lev. "Tovarishch Dante. 'Gospodin Geksogen' Aleksandr Prokhanov." afisha.ru, March 2002. https://web.archive.org/web/20050218001108/http:/geksogen.ru/r11.html.

"Uroki 'Astorii.'" Vedomosti, June 3, 2002. https://web.archive.org/web/20060529204238/http:/geksogen.ru/r63.html.

Dedkov, Igor. "'Totalnye argumenty' Aleksandra Prokhanova, ili zhizn 'po-novomu.'" *Literaturnaia ucheba*, no. 3 (1980). https://ru-prokhanov.livejournal.com/110015.html.

Deliagin, Mikhail. "Russkaia kultura i sposob proizvodstva." dynacon.ru, December 3, 2009. www.dynacon.ru/content/articles_idk/362/.

Demidov, Ivan. "Russkii proekt vo Vsemirnoi pautine." sostav.ru. May 18, 2007. www.sostav.ru/news/2007/05/18/27/.

"Demografiia, narodosberezhenie i nravstvennost: Zamglavy VRNS Malofeev o sudbonosnoi dlia strany 'Russkoi Mechte – 2050.'" https://vrns.ru/news/demografiya-narodosberezhenie-i-nravstvennost-zamglavy-vrns-malofeev-o-sudbonosnoy-dlya-strany-russk/.

"Dmitry Medvedev's Article, Go Russia!" September 10, 2009. http://en.kremlin.ru/events/president/news/5413.

"Doktrina Russkogo Mira," September 26, 2016. https://izborsk-club.ru/10269.

Dugin, Aleksandr. "Faktor 'Vagnera' i tezis spravedlivosti." *Izborskii Klub*, April 10, 2023. https://izborskclub.ru/24137.

"Kherson–Poslednii rubezh otstupleniia," tsargrad.tv, November 11, 2022. https://tsargrad.tv/articles/aleksandr-dugin-herson-poslednij-rubezh-otstuplenija_662480?fbclid=IwZXh0bgNhZW0CMTAAAR1VnobbqQLX-52LdgGMaKjI2a5H22i6awa2oDf1tyKzDt9YDQFB9O3z6bc_aem_AZbR0oFQxeBHz9tX_dqK1I_qiPDMkpOPPRFGFCWEGngL_Oeb7r2pG3EUR0pZ_hDcWiGi3CDngMpMtOMAoAalithz.

"Novaia formula Putina." *Izborskii Klub. Russkie strategii*, no. 2 (2014): 20.

"Ocherednaia oshibka Fukuiamy." *Izborskii Klub*, March 20, 2022. https://izborsk-club.ru/22508.

"Posle miatezha. Tochka bifurkatsii." *Izborskii Klub*, June 28, 2023. https://izborsk-club.ru/24505.

"Poteria Cherniaeva eto sdacha Khersona..." Telegram, December 24, 2023. https://t.me/Agdchan/13289.

"Putin provozglasil Russkuiu Ideiu." *Izborskii Klub*, October 4, 2022. https://izborsk-club.ru/23400.

"Rossii nuzhna totalnaia militarizatsiia." *Izborskii Klub*, March 11, 2024. https://izborsk-club.ru/25427.

"Russkii otvet na vyzov zapada." *Izborskii Klub. Russkie strategii*, no. 1 (2013).

"Vragi Rossii podlo, ispodtishka ubili moiu doch." *Izborskii Klub*, August 22, 2022. https://izborsk-club.ru/23224.

"Dve traditsii dosudarstvennosti: Put k primireniiu." *Izborskii Klub. Russkie strategii*, no. 3 (2013): 22.

Filosokskii Sobor. Velikoe russkoe ispravlenie imen, 2022. www.youtube.com/watch?v=CVBMI5wvWWg.

Frolov, Sergei. "Stanet li 'doktrina' panatseei?" *Russkii kurer*, October 24, 2005.

Gavrilov, Aleksandr. "Radi krasno-korichnevogo slovtsa." grani.ru, June 4, 2002. https://graniru.org/Culture/m.750.html.

Gavriushin, Nikolai. "A byl li 'russkii kosmizm'?" *Voprosy istorii estestvoznaniia i tekhniki*, no. 3 (1993).

"Iz istorii russkogo kosmizma." *Trudy V i VI chtenii, posviashchennykh razrabotke nauchnogo nslediia i razvitiiu tvorchestva K. E. Tsiolkovskogo*, 1972.

"General Assembly Adopts Resolution Calling upon States Not to Recognize Changes in Status of Crimea Region," March 27, 2014. www.un.org/press/en/2014/ga11493.doc.htm.

Glazev, Sergei. "Nasledie 'Rodiny.'" APN.ru, September 4, 2007. www.apn.ru/index.php?newsid=17727.

"Takie sobytiia, kak seichas, proiskhodiat raz v stoletie." *Izborskii Klub*, March 28, 2022. https://izborsk-club.ru/22542.

Glazev, Sergei, and Aleksandr Prokhanov. "Eto – Nashi idei." *Zavtra*, no. 26 (2006).

Gligach, Vladimir. "Tolko svadby? Postavte vopros chire." *Literaturnaia gazeta*, no. 38 (September 16, 1970): 2.

Golyshev, Vladimir. "Adresaty nashego doklada nakhodilis v Kremle i na staroi ploshchadi." politconservatism.ru, September 7, 2015. https://politconservatism.ru/thinking/adresaty-nashego-doklada-nakhodilis-v-kremle-i-na-staroy-ploshchadi.

Goncharov, Aleksei. "Troianskie koni. Chem zanimaetsia Institut Filosofii RAN." *Zavtra*, September 15, 2022. https://zavtra.ru/blogs/filosofiya_dvojnogo_naznacheniya.

"Guseinov Abdusalam Abdulkerimovich." *Institut Filosofii Rossiiskoi Akademii Nauk*, https://iphras.ru/guseinov.htm.

Gusev, Vladimir. "Zemlia i nebo." *Literaturnaia gazeta*, no. 38 (September 19, 1979): 4.

Iakubov, Adyl. "V ozhidanii analiticheskogo romana." *Literaturnaia gazeta*, no. 43 (October 24, 1979): 4.

"Itogovaia konferentsiia po russkomu kanonu." *Izborskii Klub*, March 8, 2024. https://izborsk-club.ru/25420.

"Itogovyi Protokol Sobornykh Slushanii Vsemirnogo Russkogo Narodnogo Sobora Po Teme 'Russkai Doktrina,'" www.rusdoctrina.ru/page95520.html.

"Iuliia Sineokaia: 'Na samom dele russkaia filosofiia ne izuchena,'" svoboda.org, December 24, 2023, www.svoboda.org/a/yuliya-sineokaya-na-samom-dele-russkaya-filosofiya-ne-izuchena-/32744271.html.

Iurgens, Igor. "My proigrali okhraniteliam." *The New Times*, March 5, 2012. https://newtimes.ru/articles/detail/50506.

Iuzefovich, Galina. "S parokhoda sovremennosti." *Ezhenedelnyi zhurnal*, June 11, 2002. https://web.archive.org/web/20060529204740/http:/geksogen.ru/r95.html.

Ivanov, Aleksandr. "Prokhanov kak pevets ruinirovannoi sovetskoi imperii." *Interview by Nikolai Aleksandrov*. gazeta.ru, April 9, 2002. https://web.archive.org/web/20050218173300/http://geksogen.ru/r24.html.

"Vopros kak otvet." *Zavtra*, no. 476 (December 30, 2002). https://web.archive.org/web/20080831151656/http:/www.zavtra.ru/cgi/veil/data/zavtra/03/476/62.html.

Ivanov, Aleksandr, and Mikhail Kotomin. "'Kultura dvizhetsia vzryvami.' Beseda s glavnoi Ad Marginem Aleksandrom Ivanovym i vedushchim redaktorom izdatelstva Mikhailom Kotominym." *Interview by*

Andrei Smirnov. Zavtra, May 2002. https://web.archive.org/web/20060507143406/http://geksogen.ru/r61.html.

"Iz zhzh-dnevnika Egora Kholmogorova," www.rusdoctrina.ru/page95544.html.

"Izborskii Klub prinial uchastie v I Moskovskom Ekonomicheskom Forume." dynacon.ru, May 2013. www.dynacon.ru/content/articles/1111/.

"Izborskii Klub vzialsia za prakticheskoe voploshchenie Russkoi Mechty," May 20, 2021. https://izborsk-club.ru/21120.

"K publikatsii knigi 'Gospodin Geksogen' A. Prokhanova v izdatelstve Ad Marginem. Obsuzhdenie v sektore 'Analticheskoi Antropologii' IF RAN," June 13, 2002. https://web.archive.org/web/20080407224154/http:/anthropology.rinet.ru/drupal/node.php?id=56.

"K russkoi filosofskoi simfonii." *Izborskii Klub*, December 9, 2023. https://izborsk-club.ru/25060.

Kalashnikov, Maksim. "Magiia i fabrika Russkoi Mechty." *Izborskii Klub. Russkie Strategii* 2, no. 78 (2020): 7–12.

Karaganov, Sergei. "A Difficult but Necessary Decision." *Russia in Global Affairs*, June 13, 2023. https://eng.globalaffairs.ru/articles/a-difficult-but-necessary-decision/.

"Soiuz Evropy: Poslednii shans?" Rossiia v Globalnoi Politike, July 9, 2010. https://globalaffairs.ru/articles/soyuz-evropy-poslednij-shans/.

Karaganov, Sergei, Dmitry Trenin, and Alexander Kramarenko. "Russia's Policy towards World Majority." *Report under the Auspices of the Ministry of Foreign Affairs of the Russian Federation*, 2023, www.mid.ru/upload/medialibrary/c98/cjmfdf73760bme0y99zqllj51zzllrvs/Russia%E2%80%99s%20Policy.pdf.

Kenzheev, Bakhyt. "Lobstery s Borneo, ili khoroshii pisatel Prokhanov." *Russkii zhurnal*, June 14, 2002. https://web.archive.org/web/20060507143317/http:/geksogen.ru/r104.html.

Kholmogorov, Egor. "Dvenadtsatii k 'Pismu Odinnadtsati'. Solzhenitsyn i 'Russkaia Partiia': Aspekty ideologicheskogo sosedstva." *Tetradi po konservatizmu* 66 (2019): 177–220.

"Eto bylo vremia, kogda liudi sogrevali drug druga." *Vzgliad*, September 22, 2015.

"'Kontrreformatsiia': Zhizn bez maiatnika." politconservatism.ru, September 10, 2015. https://politconservatism.ru/thinking/kontrreformatsiya-zhizn-bez-mayatnika.

Russkii Proekt: Restavratsiia Budushchego. Moscow: Eksmo, 2005.

Kobiakov, Andrei. "Doktrina – sobornyi trud." *Zavtra* (no. 39), September 2007.

Kobiakov, Andrei, and Vitalii Averianov. "Idei Russkoi Doktriny o reformirovanii strany vsego za god poluchili priznanie i u vlasti i u obshchestva." *Interview by Igor Pushkarev*. API, November 14, 2006. www.rusdoctrina.ru/page95822.html.

Kolesnikov, Andrei. "Kapituliatsiia pered istoriei." Izvestiia, April 23, 2002. https://web.archive.org/web/20050219000850/http:/geksogen.ru/r44.html.

"Maskonskoe lozhe." gazeta.ru, September 11, 2012. www.gazeta.ru/column/kolesnikov/4764101.shtml?updated.

Komogortsev, Aleksei. "Russkii kosmizm i novaia mifologiia razvitiia." *Zavtra*, December 27, 2019. https://zavtra.ru/blogs/russkij_kosmizm_i_novaya_mifologiya_razvitiya.

"Konferentsiia v MGIMO." dynacon.ru, December 2013. www.dynacon.ru/content/articles/2376/.

"Kontrreformatsiia." *Russkii obozrevatel*. www.rus-obr.ru/ru-club/4066.

"Kontseptsiia gosudarstvennoi semeinoi politiki do 2025 goda," August 29, 2014. https://rg.ru/2014/08/29/semya-site-dok.html.

Korovin, Valerii. "O Surkove i ego agenture." *Izborskii Klub*, March 31, 2014. https://izborsk-club.ru/2905.

Kovalenko, Viktor. "Etot strogii sudiia – vremia." *Literaturnaia gazeta*, no. 46 (October 3, 1979): 4.

"'Krasno-belyi' soiuz-budushchee Rossii." *Izborskii Klub. Russkie strategii*, no. 3 (2013): 38.

Kriuchkov, Vladimir, and Aleksandr Prokhanov. "Bezopasnost strany – Nuleva." *Zavtra*, April 1994.

"Krizis russkogo natsionalizma." *Russkii obozrevatel*, October 11, 2007. www.rus-obr.ru/ru-club/91.

Krug, Pavel. "Komu liazhet na stol 'Russkaia Doktrina'?" Nezavisimaia gazeta, September 5, 2007. www.rusdoctrina.ru/page95798.html.

"Kruglyi stol o 'russkom pravoslavnom bolshinstve.'" dynacon.ru, October 21, 2009. www.dynacon.ru/content/articles_idk/357/.

Krupin, Vladimir. "Nanolevshchee." *Literaturnaia gazeta*, no. 40 (October 3, 1979): 4.

Krylov, Konstantin. "'Kontrreformatsiia': Predystoriia i posleslovie." politconservatism.ru, September 10, 2015. https://politconservatism.ru/experiences/kontrreformatsiya-predystoriya-i-posleslovie.

"Obo mne." https://krylov.cc/about.php?id=72.

"Rossiiane i russkie." Traditio. Accessed August 11, 2020. https://traditio.wiki/krylov/rossian.html.

"Rus i Nerus." *Russkii zhurnal*, October 7, 2003. http://old.russ.ru/politics/20031007-kryl.html.

"Staropatriotizm." APN.ru, June 9, 2011. www.apn.ru/index.php?newsid=24317.

"Vseobshchii sinopsis ili sistema mnenii." krylov.livejournal.com. https://krylov.livejournal.com/2853229.html?thread=143227757#t143227757.

"Kto zashchitit russkikh? Stal izvesten sostav VRNS," April 11, 2019. https://tsargrad.tv/news/novye-soborjane_194068.
Kulikov, Ivan. "Mutant chetyrekh." Nezavisimaia gazeta, March 29, 2002. www.ng.ru/neiro/2002-03-28/4_prohanov.html.
Kurginian, Sergei. "Na voine kak na voine." *Zavtra*, February 27, 2012. https://zavtra.ru/blogs/na-vojne-kak-na-vojne.
Kuritsyn, Viacheslav. "Geksogen bez ssylok." *Russkii zhurnal*, June 10, 2002. https://web.archive.org/web/20050211182431/http:/geksogen.ru/r82.html.
Kyrlezhev, Aleksandr. "Tupiki provintsialnogo myshleniia." Nezavisimaia gazeta, October 18, 2000. www.ng.ru/ideas/2000-10-18/8_tupik.html.
Leontev, Mikhail. "O mitinge na Poklonnoi." *Zavtra*, February 3, 2012. https://zavtra.ru/blogs/o-mitinge-na-poklonnoj.
Likhachev, Dmitrii. "Gomosfera – Termin nashikh dnei." *Ogonek*, no. 36 (1984): 17–19.
Makarkin, Aleksei. "Pravoslavnyi stalinizm." *Ezhednevnyi zhurnal*, September 5, 2007. www.rusdoctrina.ru/page95797.html.
Maler, Arkadii. "Nasledniki vekhovskoi traditsii." politconservatism.ru, September 3, 2015. https://politconservatism.ru/thinking/nasledniki-vekhovskoy-traditsii.
"Traektorii mladokonservatizma." *Russkii zhurnal*, May 15, 2009. http://russ.ru/Mestnyj-vzglyad/Traektorii-mladokonservatizma.
"Manifest ottsov-osnovatelei," September 8, 2012. www.dynacon.ru/content/articles/887/.
Medvedev, Dmitrii. "Eshche raz o primenenii iadernogo oruzhiia..." Telegram, September 27, 2022. https://t.me/medvedev_telegram/181.
"Menia chasto sprashivaiut..." Telegram, June 7, 2022. https://t.me/medvedev_telegram/105.
"Pochemu nashe delo pravoe..." Telegram, November 4, 2022. https://t.me/medvedev_telegram/206.
"Ukrainian criminals have announced that..." X (formerly Twitter), August 29, 2023. https://x.com/MedvedevRussiaE/status/1696537158465851619.
"WHY WILL UKRAINE DISAPPEAR? BECAUSE NOBODY NEEDS IT." *X (formerly Twitter)*, April 8, 2023. https://x.com/MedvedevRussiaE/status/1644669039095037953. Patriarchia.ru.
"Meeting on Socioeconomic Support for Regions," March 16, 2022. http://en.kremlin.ru/events/president/news/67996.
"Memorandum, priniatyi uchastnikami ekspertnoi vstrechi 'Kto i zachem vtiagivaet Rossiiu v VTO.'" dynacon.ru, February 22, 2011. www.dynacon.ru/content/articles_idk/499/.

Mezhuev, Boris. "Amerikanskii fundamentalizm i russkaia 'Konservativnaia Revoliutsiia.'" *Logos*, no. 1 (2003). https://magazines.gorky.media/logos/2003/1/amerikanskij-fundamentalizm-i-russkaya-8220-konservativnaya-revolyucziya-8221.html.

"Konflikt vneshnepoliticheskikh ideologii." APN.ru, October 8, 2004. www.apn.ru/index.php?newsid=1130.

"Neokonservativnii proekt dlia Rossii." APN.ru, March 16, 2007. www.apn.ru/opinions/article11658.htm.

Politicheskaia Kritika Vadima Tsymburskogo. Evropa, 2011.

"Poniatie 'natsionalnii interes' v rossiiskoi obshchestvenno-politicheskoi zhizni." *Polis*, no. 1 (1997): 5–31.

"Prezident razocharovanii." APN.ru, April 27, 2005. www.apn.ru/index.php?newsid=1375.

"'Russkaia ideia' pered vyzovom sovremennosti." *Vestnik Moskovskogo Universiteta*, no. 6 (1993): 29–34.

"Migratsiia i derussifikatsiia v sovremennoi Rossii." *Russkii obozrevatel*, August 2, 2007. www.rus-obr.ru/ru-club/86.

Mikhalskii, Vatslav. "Boi s teniu." *Literaturnaia gazeta*, no. 45 (November 7, 1979): 6.

Militarev, Viktor. "Doklad 'Kontrreformatsiia' v moei lichnoi istorii." politconservatism.ru, September 4, 2015. https://politconservatism.ru/thinking/doklad-kontrreformatsiya-v-moey-lichnoy-istorii.

"Mobilizatsionnyi proekt – Osnovnaia predposylka strategii 'Bolshogo Ryvka.'" dynacon.ru, 2013. www.dynacon.ru/content/articles/976/.

Morozov, Aleksandr. "'Novyi kurs' i moskovskaia patriarkhiia'." Nezavisimaia gazeta, August 9, 2000. www.ng.ru/facts/2000-08-09/2_new.html.

Moskovskaia dukhovnaia akademiia. "O Russkoi Doktrine," www.rusdoctrina.ru/page95538.html.

"Moskovskoe 'Iabloko' podderzhalo provedenie 'Russkogo Marsha.'" *Radio sbododa*, November 1, 2006. www.svoboda.org/a/269476.html.

Multatuli, Petr. "'Rediska naoborot'. Kuda vedet Izborskii Klub?" *Religare.ru*, January 29, 2013. www.religare.ru/2_99349.html.

"My verim v Rossiiu." In *My verim v Rossiiu. Ot Russkoi Doktriny k Izborskomu Klubu*. Moscow: Russkaia tsivilizatsiia, 2019.

"Na Iamale otkrylos otdelenie Izborskogo kluba," April 1, 2019. https://izborsk-club.ru/16727.

"Nachalo," September 2012. www.dynacon.ru/content/articles/886/.

Nagornii, Aleksandr. "Akademiki trepeshchut pered vlastiu." *Izborskii Klub*, December 1, 2016. https://izborsk-club.ru/11258.

"Ot Miunkhena k Valdaiu." *Izborskii Klub*, October 3, 2013. https://izborsk-club.ru/1897.

"Putin: Vneshnepoliticheskii vektor," no. 2 (2014): 35.
"Stalinskii retsept." *Izborskii Klub*, June 25, 2014. https://izborsk-club.ru/3409.

"Nakaz XXV Vsemirnogo russkogo naradnogo sobora 'Nastoiashchee i budushchee russkogo mira,'" March 27, 2024. www.patriarchia.ru/db/text/6116189.html.

"National Security Concept of the Russian Federation," January 10, 2000. www.mid.ru/foreign_policy/official_documents/-/asset_publisher/CptICkB6BZ29/content/id/589768.

"Natsionalnaia model ekonomiki." dynacon.ru, April 2013. www.dynacon.ru/content/articles/1295/.

Nemzer, Andrei. "Geksogen s vami." *Vremia Novostei*, June 3, 2002. https://web.archive.org/web/20060529204319/http:/geksogen.ru/r69.html.

"NIU VSHE stanet kliuchevym uchastnikom proekta 'Rossiiskoe gosudarstvo-tsivilizatsiia. Istoriia. Institutsii. Liudi.'" hse.ru, www.hse.ru/news/expertise/860738604.html.

Notin, Aleksandr. "Valdaiskii signal." *Izborskii Klub. Russkie strategii*, no. 3 (2014).

"Novaia staraia kholodnaia voina: Zakliuchenie." dynacon.ru, 2014. http://dynacon.ru/content/articles/4409/#a6.

Novikova, Liza. "Knigi za nedeliu." *Kommersant*, April 10, 2002. https://web.archive.org/web/20050216130611/http://geksogen.ru/r26.html.

"Novye konservatory: Budushchee Rossii?" *Moskovskii Vestnik*, no. 4 (2004). http://averianov.net/sii/458/?h=670.

"O klube." *Izborskii Klub*. https://izborsk-club.ru/about.

"O modernizatsii na slovakh i na dele." dynacon.ru, November 27, 2009. www.dynacon.ru/content/articles_idk/361/.

"O nas." https://admarginem.ru/o-nas/.

"O sobore – Ustav," http://web.archive.org/web/20150509105311/http://vrns.ru/o_sobore/ustav.php.

"O spetsoperatsii na Ukraine." *Komsomolskaia Pravda*, February 26, 2022. www.kp.ru/daily/27369.5/4551490/.

"Obrazovana rabochaia gruppa po podgotovke predlozhenii o vnesenii popravok v konstitutsiiu," January 15, 2020. http://en.kremlin.ru/events/president/news/18089.

Okara, Andrei. "Nezrimoe siianie 'Volshebnoi Gory.'" *Russkii zhurnal*, October 12, 2009. http://russ.ru/Mirovaya-povestka/Nezrimoe-siyanie-Volshebnoj-Gory.

Olshanskii, Dmitrii. "Kak ia stal chernosotentsiem." *Novaia gazeta*, 2002. www.ng.ru/ng_exlibris/2002-04-11/2_black.html.
"Ot Geksogena do galliutsinogena." *Vremia MN*, April 5, 2002. https://web.archive.org/web/20050218090249/http:/geksogen.ru/r16.html.

"Osnovnye poniatiia i terminy Russkoi Doktriny," www.rusdoctrina.ru/page95513.html.

"Otkliki i publikatsii," www.rusdoctrina.ru/page95510.html.

Ovchinskii, Vladimir, and Elena Larina. "Kholodnaia voina 2.0." *Izborskii Klub*, November 11, 2014. https://izborsk-club.ru/4224.

Pirogov, Lev. "Na komsomolskom prospekte sostaialas 'Vstrecha na Elbe.'" *Ex Libris*, November 6, 2001. https://web.archive.org/web/20050103233314/http:/www.geksogen.ru/r1.html.

Plotnikov, Nikolai. *Pered litsom katastrofy*. Berlin: Lit Verlag, 2023.

Pogribnii, Anatolii. "Gde iskat orientiry?" *Literaturnaia gazeta*, no. 48 (November 28, 1979): 6.

"Polozhenie o premii." www.natsbest.ru/polozhenie-o-premii/.

Poroskov, Nikolai. "Novye odissei." *Vremia novostei*, no. 198 (October 25, 2005).

"Pravitelstvo Rossiiskoi Federatsii. Postanovlenie ot 30 dekabria 2015 goda n 1493. O gosudarstvennoi programme 'Patrioticheskoe vospitanie grazhdan Rossiiskoi Federatsii na 2016–2020 gody,'" https://docs.cntd.ru/document/420327349?marker=6560IO.

"Predotvratit voinu – Pobedit v voine," September 30, 2014. https://izborsk-club.ru/3963.

"Predsevatel pravitelstva Rossisskoi Federatsii V. V. Putin vstretilsia s politologami," February 6, 2012. http://archive.government.ru/docs/18008/.

"Prezentatsiia knigi 'Verouchenie Russkoi Mechty. Ideologiia gosudarstva rossiiskogo,'" December 16, 2019. http://pressmia.ru/pressclub/20191216/952558794.html.

Prilepin, Zakhar. "Demonam soobshchaiu: Vy nikogo ne zapugaete." *Izborskii Klub*, May 7, 2023. https://izborsk-club.ru/24289.

"Grekh" zhalovatsia. Rossiiskaia gazeta, June 6, 2011. https://rg.ru/2011/06/06/reg-privolzhe/prilepin.html.

"Nasha elita po-prezhnemu sostoit iz bolshikh sprutoobraznykh mafioznykh soobshchestv." *Izborskii Klub*, October 23, 2023. https://izborsk-club.ru/24860.

Prisco, Giulio. "Maximum Jailbreak, and the Legacy of Stephen Hawking." *Turingchurch.net*, October 22, 2018. https://turingchurch.net/maximum-jailbreak-and-the-legacy-of-stephen-hawking-3a5773b9e6df.

Prokhanov, Aleksandr. "Akademiia Russkoi Mechty." *Izborskii Klub*, February 20, 2019. https://izborsk-club.ru/16525.

"Angola – Novyi Vetnam?" *Literaturnaia gazeta*, no. 33 (September 16, 1981): 9.

"Baptisty – Ochen tikhii, krotkii narod, tam net nikakikh enteo." *Izborskii Klub*, August 22, 2017. https://izborsk-club.ru/13904.

"Chasha siia." *Zavtra*, February 15, 2012. https://zavtra.ru/blogs/chasha-siya.

"Chto tvoriat bandity." *Literaturnaia gazeta*, no. 9 (February 27, 1980): 9.

"Dolgozhdannii avangard." *Izborskii Klub*, February 1, 2024. https://izborsk-club.ru/25276.

"Edinye v revoliutsii." *Literaturnaia gazeta*, no. 19 (May 7, 1980): 14.

"Ei, ukhnem!" *Izborskii Klub*, July 28, 2022. https://izborsk-club.ru/23128.

"Eltsin, zachem razbombil Belgrad?" *Zavtra*, March 1999.

"Eshche odna neobiavlennaia." *Literaturnaia gazeta*, no. 23 (June 3, 1981): 14.

"Eskadra." *Literaturnaia gazeta*, no. 38 (September 19, 1984): 11.

"Golos russkoi istorii." *Izborskii Klub*, March 5, 2022. https://izborsk-club.ru/22430.

"Gosudarstvu byt!" Izborskii Klub, December 23, 2013. https://izborsk-club.ru/2384.

"Iadernii shchit." *Literaturnaia gazeta*, no. 46 (November 17, 1982): 10.

"Intelligent v derevne." *Literaturnaia gazeta*, no. 26 (June 25, 1969): 10.

"Iz plamia i sveta pozhdennoe slovo." *Zavtra*, March 27, 2014. https://zavtra.ru/blogs/iz-plamya-i-sveta-rozhdyonnoe-slovo.

"Khozhdenie v ogon." *Zavtra*, December 10, 2011. http://zavtra.ru/blogs/hozhdenie-v-ogon.

"Krasnye zvezdy nad okeanom." *Literaturnaia gazeta*, no. 29 (July 21, 1982): 10.

"Krymskoe vino pobedy." *Zavtra*, March 13, 2014. https://zavtra.ru/blogs/kryimskoe-vino-pobedyi.

"Kultura khram, a ne strelbishche." *Literaturnaia Rossiia*, January 22, 1988.

"Mechta neiziasnimaia." *Izborskii Klub*, December 27, 2018. https://izborsk-club.ru/16324.

"Metafora sovremennosti." *Literaturnaia gazeta*, no. 37 (September 12, 1979): 4.

"Muchketovskii rudnik: Spustia polveka." *Literaturnaia gazeta*, no. 45 (November 5, 1969): 10.

"My zhili v unison s epokhoi." *Izborskii Klub*, December 26, 2015. https://izborsk-club.ru/8084.

"Na novykh rubezhakh: Reportakh iz raiona manevrov 'Dvina.'" *Literaturnaia gazeta*, no. 13 (March 25, 1970): 11.

"Namibiia, ty budesh svobodnoi!" *Literaturnaia gazeta*, no. 26 (June 24, 1981): 15.

"Nash desant v Damask." dynacon.ru, July 2013. www.dynacon.ru/content/articles/1463/.

"Nasha rabota tolko nachinaetsia." *Izborskii Klub*, February 28, 2019. https://izborsk-club.ru/16571.
"Ne oshibitsia v diagnoze." *Literaturnaia Ucheba*, no. 3 (1980).
"Novosibirsk – Gorod-tsivilizatsiia." April 27, 2015. dynacon.ru. www.dynacon.ru/content/articles/5506/.
"Nuzhny li svadby?" *Literaturnaia gazeta*, no. 34 (August 19, 1970): 12.
"Ot partii vlasti – K partii Russkoi Mechty." *Zavtra*, September 24, 2018. https://zavtra.ru/blogs/ot_partii_vlasti_-_k_partii_russkoj_mechti.
"Plemena i puli." *Literaturnaia gazeta*, no. 5 (January 28, 1981): 14.
"Pobedy trudnii put." *Literaturnaia gazeta*, no. 52 (December 24, 1980): 14.
"Poklonobortsy vs Bolotokhodtsy." *Zavtra*, February 16, 2012. https://zavtra.ru/blogs/poklonobortsyi-vs-bolotohodtsyi.
"Poliarnii kupol." *Literaturnaia gazeta*, no. 36 (September 7, 1983): 12.
"Polk prikhodit v gorodok." *Literaturnaia gazeta*, no. 8 (February 18, 1970): 11.
"Polkhovskii Maidan." *Literaturnaia gazeta*, no. 44 (October 1968): 11.
"Posle boia." *Literaturnaia gazeta*, no. 34 (August 20, 1969): 3.
"Posredi Sibiri." *Literaturnaia gazeta*, no. 22 (April 13, 1977): 10.
"Povrat s odinochestvom." *Literaturnaia gazeta*, no. 6 (February 9, 1977): 12.
"Prekrashchenie gubitelnoi raspri." *Izborskii Klub. Russkie strategii*, no. 3 (2013): 17.
"Pust rasisty ne mykaiut nochami glaz." *Literaturnaia gazeta*, no. 15 (April 14, 1982): 14.
"Putin – Russkii mechtatel." *Izborskii Klub*, January 31, 2019. https://izborsk-club.ru/16446.
"Puzyri zemli." *Izborskii Klub*, June 27, 2023. https://izborsk-club.ru/24498.
"Razgromlena banda." *Literaturnaia gazeta*, no. 2 (January 7, 1981): 14.
"Rodina – Dalnii vostok." *Literaturnaia gazeta*, no. 33 (August 12, 1970): 10.
"Rossiia – Imperiia sveta." *Zavtra*, June 11, 2001. http://zavtra.ru/blogs/2001-06-1211.
"Rossiia: Atomnii vektor." *Zavtra*, July 17, 2007. http://zavtra.ru/blogs/2007-07-1841.
"Russkii OPK – Sol soli zemli." *Zavtra*, February 22, 2012. https://zavtra.ru/blogs/russkij-opk-sol-soli-zemli.
"Russkoe omovenie." *Izborskii Klub*, March 18, 2022. https://izborsk-club.ru/22501.
"S kholma vidna vsia Rossiia." *Zavtra*, October 2, 2007. http://zavtra.ru/blogs/2007-10-0311.
Simfoniia "Piatoy Imperii." Moscow: Eksmo, 2007.

"Sokhi i puli." *Literaturnaia gazeta*, no. 30 (June 28, 1982): 14.
"Soldaty revoliutsii." *Literaturnaia gazeta*, no. 16 (April 16, 1980): 14.
"Strategicheskii bombardirovshchik 'Izborskii Klub.'" *Zavtra*, August 21, 2014. https://zavtra.ru/blogs/strategicheskij-bombardirovschik-izborskij-klub.
"Sviashchenny tvoi granitsy, Rodina!" *Literaturnaia gazeta*, no. 11 (March 12, 1969): 15.
"Tobolsk: Novye ritmy." *Literaturnaia gazeta*, no. 51 (December 22, 1976): 10.
"Umer glavnii 'metafizicheskii realist.'" *Izborskii Klub*, October 28, 2015. https://izborsk-club.ru/7534.
"V sorochintsakh iarmarka." *Literaturnaia gazeta*, no. 38 (September 18, 1968): 13.
"Vozduchnye proselki." *Literaturnaia gazeta*, no. 32 (August 6, 1969): 12.
"Vremia pakhoty i seba." *Literaturnaia gazeta*, no. 12 (March 19, 1980): 9.
"Vstaiushchaia iz prakha." *Literaturnaia gazeta*, no. 23 (June 9, 1982): 14.
"Vstrechi na maivande." *Literaturnaia gazeta*, no. 17 (April 12, 1981): 7.
"Vybor – Revoliutsiia." *Literaturnaia gazeta*, no. 33 (June 18, 1980): 14.
"Vystoiat!" *Literaturnaia gazeta*, no. 50 (December 15, 1982): 14.
"Za nami – Rossiia!" Izborskii Klub, October 4, 2022. https://izborsk-club.ru/23399.
"Za plugom." *Literaturnaia gazeta*, no. 7 (February 11, 1981): 15.
"Zashchitniki kamennoi sopki." *Literaturnaia gazeta*, no. 36 (September 3, 1969): 2.
Interview by Vladimir Pozner. Efir 1, 2010. www.1tv.ru/shows/pozner/vypuski/gost-aleksandr-prohanov-pozner-vypusk-ot-18-05-2010?start=0.

Prokhanov, Aleksandr, and Vladimir Gusev. "Iz reki po imeni – 'Fakt,'" no. 2 (January 9, 1974): 5.

Prokhanov, Aleksandr, and Konstantin Pchelnikov. "Gorod vverkh." *Literaturnaia gazeta*, no. 40 (September 30, 1970): 11.

Proskurin, Oleg. "Natsionalnyi Bestseller-2001, ili apofeoz Prokhanova." *Russkii zhurnal*, June 4, 2002.

"Puti i stsenarii samoorganizatsii russkikh patrioticheskih sil v 2011-2012 gg." dynacon.ru, April 28, 2011. www.dynacon.ru/content/articles_idk/520/.

Putin, Vladimir. "Address by President of the Russian Federation." Website of the President of Russia, March 18, 2014. http://en.kremlin.ru/events/president/news/20603.
"Address by the President of the Russian Federation." Website of the President of Russia, February 21, 2022. http://en.kremlin.ru/events/president/news/67828.

"Address by the President of the Russian Federation." Website of the President of Russia, February 24, 2022. http://en.kremlin.ru/events/president/news/67843.

"Address on Day of Reunification of the Donetsk People's Republic, Lugansk People's Republic and the Zaporozhye and Kherson Regions with Russia." Website of the President of Russia, October 2, 2023. http://en.kremlin.ru/events/president/news/72403.

"Annual Address to the Federal Assembly." Website of the President of Russia, May 10, 2006. http://en.kremlin.ru/events/president/transcripts/23577.

"Annual Address to the Federal Assembly of the Russian Federation." Website of the President of Russia, April 25, 2005. http://en.kremlin.ru/events/president/transcripts/22931.

"Direct Line with Vladimir Putin." Website of the President of Russia, April 17, 2014. http://en.kremlin.ru/events/president/news/20796.

"Meeting of the Valdai International Discussion Club." Website of the President of Russia, September 19, 2013. http://en.kremlin.ru/events/president/news/19243.

"Meeting with Government Members." Website of the President of Russia, August 4, 2023. http://en.kremlin.ru/events/president/news/71892.

"Meeting with State Duma Party Leaders." Website of the President of Russia, December 19, 2023. http://en.kremlin.ru/events/president/news/73000.

"On the Historical Unity of Russians and Ukrainians." Website of the President of Russia, July 12, 2022. http://en.kremlin.ru/events/president/news/66181.

"President of Russia Vladimir Putin Addressed Novorossiia Militia." Website of the President of Russia, August 29, 2014. http://en.kremlin.ru/events/president/transcripts/46506.

"Presidential Address to the Federal Assembly." Website of the President of Russia, April 26, 2007. http://en.kremlin.ru/events/president/transcripts/24203.

"Presidential Address to the Federal Assembly." Website of the President of Russia, December 12, 2012. http://en.kremlin.ru/events/president/news/17118.

"Presidential Address to the Federal Assembly." Website of the President of Russia, December 12, 2013. http://en.kremlin.ru/events/president/news/19825.

"Presidential Address to the Federal Assembly." Website of the President of Russia, December 4, 2014. http://en.kremlin.ru/events/president/news/47173.

"Presidential Address to the Federal Assembly." Website of the President of Russia, March 1, 2018. http://en.kremlin.ru/events/president/news/56957.

"Rossiia Na Rubezhe Tysiacheletii." Nezavisimaia gazeta, December 30, 1999. www.ng.ru/politics/1999-12-30/4_millenium.html.

"Security Council Meeting." Website of the President of Russia, February 22, 2022. http://en.kremlin.ru/events/president/news/67825.

"Security Council Meeting." Website of the President of Russia, April 13, 2023. http://en.kremlin.ru/events/president/news/70870.

"Signing of Treaties on Accession of Donetsk and Lugansk People's Republics and Zaporozhye and Kherson Regions to Russia." Website of the President of Russia, October 5, 2022. http://en.kremlin.ru/events/president/news/69465.

"St Petersburg International Economic Forum Plenary Session." Website of the President of Russia, June 22, 2022. http://en.kremlin.ru/events/president/news/68669.

"United Russia Party Congress." Website of the President of Russia, December 19, 2023. http://en.kremlin.ru/events/president/news/73013.

"Valdai International Discussion Club Meeting." Website of the President of Russia, October 31, 2022. http://en.kremlin.ru/events/president/news/69695.

"Radio 'Svoboda,'" August 20, 2007. www.rusdoctrina.ru/page95813.html.

"Razgovor po sushchestvu." *Portal "Mir Rossii,"* December 30, 2005. www.rusdoctrina.ru/page95545.html.

"Realnyie innovatsii i ikh imitatsii v Rossii." dynacon.ru, June 10, 2009. www.dynacon.ru/content/articles_idk/331/.

"Reindustrializatsiia. Chelovek truda." dynacon.ru, April 2013. www.dynacon.ru/content/articles/1294/.

Remizov, Mikhail. "Konservatizm segodnia: Analiticheskii obzor." APN.ru, January 30, 2006. https://apn-nn.com/analytic/konservatizm-segodnya-analiticheskiy-obzor/.

"Rossiia i mirovoi krizis: Prognozy i stsenarii." dynacon.ru, August 27, 2009.

"RTR programma 'Natsionalnyi Interes,'" May 14, 2006. www.rusdoctrina.ru/page95537.html.

"Speech and the Following Discussion at the Munich Conference on Security Policy." Website of the President of Russia, February 10, 2007. http://en.kremlin.ru/events/president/transcripts/24034.

"Transcript of Press Conference with the Russian and Foreign Media." Website of the President of Russia, February 1, 2007. http://en.kremlin.ru/events/president/transcripts/24026.

Russkaia Doktrina. Moscow: Iauza-Press, 2007.

"Russkie v natsionalnoi politike RF." *Russkii Obozrevatel*, July 19, 2007. www.rus-obr.ru/ru-club/85.

"Russkii kovcheg. Alternativnaia strategiia mirovogo razvitiia," February 18, 2020. https://izborsk-club.ru/18825.

"Russkii mif kak osnavanie russkoi idei." *Zavtra*, November 27, 2023, https://zavtra.ru/blogs/russkij_mif_kak_osnovanie_russkoj_idei.

"Russkoe zavtra: Natsionalnoe gosudarstvo, imperiia ili rasseiane? Stenogramma kruglogo stola." dynacon.ru, March 22, 2011. www.dynacon.ru/content/articles_idk/512/.

Sakharov, Andrei. "Rasmyshleniia o progresse, mirnom sosushchestvovanii i intellektualnoi svobode." In *Trevogo i Nadezhda*, 11–47. Moscow: Inter-Verso, 1968.

Samokhin, Andrei. "Tainye pisma 'diversantov' v mantiiakh: Gotovitsia udar po russkoi nauke," tsargrad.tv, April 29, 2022. https://tsargrad.tv/articles/tajnye-pisma-diversantov-v-mantijah-gotovitsja-udar-po-russkoj-nauke_539510.

"Tsentr razrusheniia Rossii. Struktury Sorosa vrutsia k upravleniiu institutom filosofii RAN," tsargrad.tv, December 14, 2021. https://tsargrad.tv/articles/centr-razrushenija-rossii-struktury-sorosa-rvutsja-k-upravleniju-institutom-filosofii-ran_462002.

"Sberezhenie, razvitie i preumnozhenie natsii," 2006. http://averianov.net/doc/618/?h=635.

Semenova, Svetlana. Filosofstvovat – znachit uchitsia ne umirat. *Interview by Aleksandr Iakovkev. Literaturnaia gazeta*, Vol. 10 no 5870, March 19, 2002.

"Sergievskii Proekt." www.rusdoctrina.ru/page95505.html.

Shebarshin, Leonid, and Aleksandr Prokhanov. "Shef razvedki v gostiakh u 'Dnia.'" *Zavtra*, August 1991.

Skurlatov, Valerii. "Interviu so mnoi o filosofii." *Livejournal*, May 18, 2011. https://skurlatov.livejournal.com/1229402.html.

"Perechityvaia 'Ustav nrava.'" *Livejournal*, November 4, 2006. https://skurlatov.livejournal.com/148680.html.

Politik ne dolzhen dumat o dengakh i smerti. Interview by Aleksei Alikin. Russkaia Planeta, March 13, 2014. https://rusplt.ru/policy/interview-Skurlatov-8611.html.

"Pravaia vera i odin iz ee provozvestnikov Nikolai Fedorovich Fedorov (1829–1903)." *Livejournal*, October 9, 2019. https://skurlatov.livejournal.com/5683435.html.

"Universitet Molodogo Marksista: Ego kratkaia istoriia i Programma." *Livejournal*, April 30, 2010. https://skurlatov.livejournal.com/899852.html.

"Vspominaia Igoria Kolchenko." *Livejournal*, May 29, 2012. https://skurlatov.livejournal.com/1509991.html.
Shurygin, Vladislav. "Dvazhdy predatel." *Izborskii Klub*, June 28, 2023. https://izborsk-club.ru/24504.
Sineokaya, Yulia. "Le jdanovisme est de retour: la chasse aux philosophes." *Desk Russie*, January 27, 2024. https://desk-russie.eu/2024/01/27/le-jdanovisme-est-de-retour.html.
Slavnikovaia, Olga. Ia – odinokii chelovek v literature. Interview by Oleg Proskurin. Russkii zhurnal, May 28, 2002.
Soldatov, Aleksandr. "Atomnoe pravoslavie." *Ogonek*, no. 37 (September 2007). www.rusdoctrina.ru/page95795.html.
Solntse Severa. "Sbornik filosofskogo sobora 'Velikoe russkoe ispravlenie imen' za 2022 God." VK. https://vk.com/@solsevera-sbornik-filosofskogo-sobora-velikoe-russkoe-ispravlenie-imen.
"Sovremennyi konservatizm v Rossii – Neklassicheskoe mirovozzrenie. Stenogramma ekspertnoi vstrechi." dynacon.ru, May 20, 2009. www.dynacon.ru/content/articles_idk/337/.
"Spasti Ukrainu!" February 13, 2014. https://izborsk-club.ru/2602.
"Stenogramma kruglogo stola Izborskogo Kluba 'V poiskakh Russkoi Mechty i obraza budushchego,'" October 10, 2018. https://izborsk-club.ru/15978.
"Strategiia 'Bolchogo Ryvka,'" January 30, 2013. https://izborsk-club.ru/975.
Surkov, Vladislav. "Nasha rossiiskaia model demokratii nazyvaetsia 'suverennoi demokratiei.'" *Edinaia Rossiia*, June 28, 2006. https://web.archive.org/web/20080430012854/http://www.edinros.ru/news.html?id=114108.
"Sviashchennaia istoriia – Zdes i seichas," December 30, 2018. https://izborsk-club.ru/16343.
Sviatenkov, Pavel. "Veselaia semeika." politconservatism.ru, September 25, 2015. https://politconservatism.ru/thinking/veselaya-semeyka.
Svobodnyi universitet. "Tsekh filosofii i religiovedeniia." https://freemoscow.university/school/czeh-filosofii-i-religovedeniya/.
Tavrovskii, Iurii. *Kitai, Rossiia i sosedi. Novoe tysiacheletie.* Moscow: Vostochnaia kniga, 2015.
Novyi shelkovyi put. Glavnyi proekt XXI veka. Moscow: Eksmo, 2017.
Si Tszinpin. Novaia epokha. Moscow: Eksmo, 2018.
Si Tszinpin: Po stupeniam kitaiskoi mechty. Moscow: Eksmo, 2015.
"Tezisy Russkoi Doktriny," November 2005. http://averianov.net/sii/510/?h=604.
"Transchelovek protiv cheloveka," October 31, 2020. https://izborsk-club.ru/20212.

Trofimenkov, Mikhail. "Roman meniaet chitatelskoe zrenie." *Zavtra*, June 2002. https://web.archive.org/web/20050211181402/http:/geksogen.ru/r93.html.

Tsipko, Aleksandr. "V ozhidanii Gagarina." *Literaturnaia gazeta*, no. 1 (2006). www.rusdoctrina.ru/page95540.html.

"Ukaz Prezidenta Rossiiskoi Federatsii No 809," November 9, 2022. http://kremlin.ru/acts/bank/48502.

"Ukaz Prezidenta Rossisskoi Federatsii No 611," September 5, 2022. http://kremlin.ru/acts/bank/48280.

"Ukraine-Related Designations. Specially Designated Nationals List Update." U.S. Department of the Treasury, March 11, 2015. https://home.treasury.gov/policy-issues/financial-sanctions/recent-actions/20150311.

"Ulianovskaia deklaratsiia Izborskogo Kluba." *Izborskii Klub. Russkie strategii*, no. 3 (2013): 46.

Ustinov, Albert. "Kto 'pervii paren na derevne'?" *Literaturnaia gazeta*, October 19, 1979, 4.

"V gosudarstvennoi Dume predstavili dokumentalknii film 'Narod mechty,'" July 22, 2019. http://duma.gov.ru/news/45809/.

"V poiskakh russkoi mechty. Gorst zemli.," September 17, 2018. https://izborsk-club.ru/15849.

"V pskovskoi oblasti osviatili krest 'sviashchennogo kholma,'" September 27, 2007. https://regnum.ru/news/economy/891482.html.

Vinnikov, Vladimir. "'Russkii reaktor' na VDNKh." *Zavtra*, September 12, 2019. https://zavtra.ru/blogs/pyatij_stalin_gryadyot.

"Voennaia reforma kak sostavnaia chast kontseptsii bezopasnosti RF: Sistemno-dinamicheskaia otsenka," February 6, 2013. https://izborsk-club.ru/994.

"Vruchenie premii 'Nastionalnyi bestseller' Aleksandru Prokhanovu," June 4, 2002. www.svoboda.org/a/24186346.html.

"Vsemirnyi Russkii Narodnyi Sobor rassmatrivaet 'Russkuiu Doktrinu' v kachestve natsionalnogo proekta," June 28, 2007. www.rusdoctrina.ru/page95531.html.

"Vsia khronika," www.rusdoctrina.ru/page95504.html.

"Vzaimodeistvie Kitaia i Rossii i budushchee initsiativy 'Odin poias, odin put,'" May 16, 2017. https://ru.valdaiclub.com/events/posts/foreign/prezentatsiya-doklada-valday-kitai-kazakhstan/?sphrase_id=135663.

"XXI vek: Bratanie krasnykh i belykh," December 21, 2012. https://izborsk-club.ru/898.

Yermolov, Fedor. "Free Speech and the Attack on Vladimir Sorokin." *Ofitsialnyi sait Vladimira Sorokina*, August 13, 2002. https://srkn.ru/criticism/yermolov.shtml.

"Zaiavlenie uchenogo soveta Instituta Filosofii RAN v sviazi s naznacheniem vremenno ispolniaiushchego obiazannosti direktora Instituta." *Institut Filosofii Rossiiskoi Akademii Nauk*, https://iphras.ru/22_12_2021.htm.

"Zakat zapada i natsionalizm slobod." *Russkii obozrevatel*, October 25, 2007. www.rus-obr.ru/ru-club/92.

"Zasedanie kluba na 'Energomashe,'" September 21, 2012. https://izborsk-club.ru/889.

"Zasedanie Zinoveskogo kluba. Novoia dekolonizatsiia kak dezapadnizatsiia," September 26, 2023. https://pressria.ru/20230926/955466392.html.

"Zasedanie Zinoveskogo kluba. Pochemu Rossiia prava: rusofobiia kak novii kholokost," April 22, 2022. https://pressria.ru/20220422/953612214.html.

"Zasedanie Zinoveskogo kluba. Pochemu Rossiia prava: sviashchennaia voina," July 26, 2023. https://pressria.ru/20230726/955003264.html.

"Zhizn i sudba." *Rossiia-1*, December 7, 2022. https://smotrim.ru/video/2525882.

Zolotonosov, Mikhail. "Operatsiia 'Prokhanov.'" *Moskovskie novosti*, June 13, 2002. https://web.archive.org/web/20060507143444/http://geksogen.ru/r105.html.

Secondary Sources

Abbott, Andrew. *Department and Discipline: Chicago Sociology at One Hundred*. Chicago: University of Chicago Press, 1999.

Adamsky, Dima. "Christ-Loving Warriors: Ecclesiastical Dimension of the Russian Military Campaign in Syria." *Problems of Post-Communism* 67, no. 6 (2020): 433–45.

Russian Nuclear Orthodoxy: Religion, Politics, and Strategy. Stanford, CA: Stanford University Press, 2019.

Agadjanian, Alexander. "Tradition, Morality and Community: Elaborating Orthodox Identity in Putin's Russia." *Religion, State and Society* 45, no. 1 (2017): 39–60.

"Vulnerable Post-Soviet Secularities: Patterns and Dynamics in Russia and Beyond." In *Multiple Secularities beyond the West: Religion and Modernity in the Global Age*, edited by Marian Burchardt, Monika Wohlrab-Sahr, and Matthias Middell, 241–60. Boston: De Gruyter, Inc., 2015.

Allensworth, Wayne. *The Russian Question: Nationalism, Modernization, and Post-Communist Russia*. Lanham, MD: Rowman & Littlefield, 1998.

Andersson, Jenny. "Bridging the Iron Curtain. Futurology as Dissidence and Control." In *The Future of the World: Futurology, Futurists, and the Struggle for the Post Cold War Imagination*, edited by Jenny Andersson, 122–51. Oxford: Oxford University Press, 2018.

The Future of the World: Futurology, Futurists, and the Struggle for the Post Cold War Imagination. New York, NY: Oxford University Press, 2018.

Androsenko, Nataliia. "Publitsistika mladokonservatorov v sovremennom kommunikativnom prostranstve Rossii." *Kommunikologiia* 4, no. 1 (2016): 160–72.

Arnason, Johann P. "Communism and Modernity." *Daedalus* 129, no. 1 (2000): 61–90.

Åslund, Anders. "Sergey Glazyev and the Revival of Soviet Economics." *Post-Soviet Affairs* 29, no. 5 (September 2013): 375–86.

Atnashev, Timur. "Perekliuchaia rezhimy publichnosti: Kak Nina Andreeva sodeistvovala prevrashcheniiu glasnosti v svobodu slova." *Novoe literaturnoe obozrenie* 151, no. 3 (2018): 447–78.

"Utopicheskii konservatizm v epokhu pozdnei perestroiki: Otpuskaia vozhzhi istorii." *Sotsiologiia Vlasti* 29, no. 2 (2017): 12–53.

Autio-Sarasmo, Sari. "Stagnation or Not?: The Brezhnev Leadership and East-West Interaction." In *Reconsidering Stagnation in the Brezhnev Era: Ideology and Exchange*, edited by Dina Fainberg and Artemy Kalinovsky, 87–104. Lanham, MD: Lexington Books, 2016.

Bacon, Edwin. "Policy Change and the Narratives of Russia's Think Tanks." *Palgrave Communications* 4, no. 1 (December 2018): 94.

"Putin's Crimea Speech, 18 March 2014: Russia's Changing Public Political Narrative." *Journal of Soviet and Post-Soviet Politics and Society* 1, no. 1 (2015): 13–36.

Bacon, Edwin, and Mark Sandle, eds. *Brezhnev Reconsidered*. Houndsmills, UK and New York: Palgrave Macmillan, 2002.

Balzacq, Thierry, and Pablo Barnier-Khawam. "Ideas and Ideology in Grand Strategy." In *The Oxford Handbook of Grand Strategy*, edited by Thierry Balzacq and Ronald R. Krebs, 158–72. Oxford: Oxford University Press, 2021.

Balzacq, Thierry, and Ronald R. Krebs. "The Enduring Appeal of Grand Strategy." In *The Oxford Handbook of Grand Strategy*, edited by Thierry Balzacq and Ronald R. Krebs, xx–21. Oxford: Oxford University Press, 2021.

Balzer, Harley. "Managed Pluralism: Vladimir Putin's Emerging Regime." *Post-Soviet Affairs* 19, no. 3 (2003): 189–227.

Beck, Ulrich, Wolfgang Bonss, and Christoph Lau. "The Theory of Reflexive Modernization: Problematic, Hypotheses and Research Programme." *Theory, Culture & Society* 20, no. 2 (2003): 1–33.

Beck, Ulrich, Anthony Giddens, and Scott Lash. *Reflexive Modernization: Politics, Tradition and Aesthetics in the Modern Social Order*. Stanford, CA: Stanford University Press, 1994.

Behr, Valentin. "Towards a Transnational and Social History of Anti-Liberalism. Insights from the Trajectory of Ryszard Legutko." *European Politics and Society*, 24, no. 1: (2023): 22–39.

Béland, Daniel, and Robert Henry Cox. "Ideas as Coalition Magnets: Coalition Building, Policy Entrepreneurs, and Power Relations." *Journal of European Public Policy* 23, no. 3 (March 15, 2016): 428–45.

"Belarus Becomes Unlikely Refuge for Wagner's Boss," *Le Monde*, August 8, 2023. www.lemonde.fr/en/international/article/2023/06/26/belarus-becomes-an-unlikely-refuge-for-wagner-s-boss_6037745_4.html.

Bell, Daniel. *The Coming of Post-Industrial Society: A Venture in Social Forecasting*. New York, NY: Basic Books, 1973.

"The 'End of Ideology' in the USSR?" In *Marxist Ideology in the Contemporary World: Its Appeals and Paradoxes*, edited by Milorad Drachkovich, 76–113. Stanford: F.A. Praeger Pall Mall Press, 1966.

Berelowitch, Alexis. "Préface." In *Entre le passé et l'avenir. L'homme soviétique ordinaire*, edited by Iurij Levada, 9–25. Paris: Presses de la Fondation nationale des sciences politiques, 1993.

Berger, Peter L., ed. *The Desecularization of the World: Resurgent Religion and World Politics*. Washington, DC: Ethics and Public Policy Center W. B. Eerdmans, 1999.

Bernstein, Anya. "Freeze, Die, Come to Life: The Many Paths to Immortality in Post-Soviet Russia." *American Ethnologist* 42, no. 4 (2015): 766–81.

The Future of Immortality: Remaking Life and Death in Contemporary Russia. Princeton: Princeton University Press, 2019.

Bhabha, Homi K. *The Location of Culture. Routledge Classics*. London and New York: Routledge, 2004.

"Biznesmen Prigozhin prishel na proshchanie s ubitoi Darei Duginoi s med-aliu Geroia Rossii," dailystorm.ru, April 23, 2022. https://dailystorm.ru/news/biznesmen-prigozhin-nazval-ubituyu-daryu-duginu-kamnem-v-osnove-rossiyskogo-velichiya.

Blakkisrud, Helge. "*Russkii* as the New *Rossiiskii*? Nation-Building in Russia after 1991." *Nationalities Papers* (2022): 1–16.

Blic, Damien de, and Cyril Lemieux. "The Scandal as Test: Elements of Pragmatic Sociology." *Politix* 71, no. 3 (2005): 9.

Blondiaux, Loïc. "Les clubs: sociétés de pensée, agencement de réseaux ou instances de sociabilité politique ?" *Politix* 1, no. 2 (1988): 29–42.

Bloomfield, Alan. "Time to Move On: Reconceptualizing the Strategic Culture Debate." *Contemporary Security Policy* 33, no. 3 (2012): 437–61.

Bluhm, Katharina. "Modernization, Geopolitics and the New Russian Conservatives." *Arbeitspapiere Des Osteuropa-Instituts (Abteilung Soziologie), Freie Universität Berlin* 1: (2016): 3–38.

"Postmodernity and Modernity as Political Terms." In *Contemporary Russian Conservatism. Problems, Paradoxes, and Perspectives*, edited by Mikhail Suslov and Dmitry Uzlaner, 153–76. Leiden and Boston, MA: Brill, 2020.

Bluhm, Katharina, and Mihai Varga, eds. *New Conservatives in Russia and East Central Europe*. Abingdon and New York, NY: Routledge, 2019.

Bokhanov, Aleksandr, ed. *Rossisskie konservatory*. Moscow: Russkii mir, 1997.

Boldyrev, Aleksei. "Averianov." In *Russkaia Filosofiia. Entsiklopediia*, edited by Mikhail Maslin, 9–10. Moscow: Mir filosofii Moskva, 2019.

"Russkaia Doktrina." In *Russkaia Filosofiia. Entsiklopediia*, 595–96. Mir filosofii Moskva, 2019.

Boobbyer, Philip. "Russian Liberal Conservatism." In *Russian Nationalism, Past and Present*, edited by Geoffrey Hosking and Robert Service, 36–37. Basingstoke: Macmillan Press, 1998.

Boumaza, Magali. "L'expérience d'une jeune chercheuse en 'milieu extrême': Une enquête au Front National." *Regards sociologiques*, no. 22 (2001): 105–21.

Boumaza, Magali, and Aurélie Campana. "Enquêter n milieu 'difficile'. Introduction." *Revue francaise de science politique* 57, no. 1 (2007): 5–25.

Bourdieu, Pierre. "Champ intellectuel et projet créateur." *Les temps modernes*, no. 246 (1966): 865–906.

Distinction: A Social Critique of the Judgement of Taste. Routledge Classics. London: Routledge, 2010.

"Le fonctionnement du champ intellectuel." *Regards sociologiques*, no. 17/18 (1999): 5–27.

Questions de sociologie. Paris: Minuit, 1981.

The Rules of Art: Genesis and Structure of the Literary Field. Stanford, CA: Stanford University Press, 1996.

Sociologie générale. Volume 1. Cours au Collège de France (1981–1983). Points Essais. Paris: Éditions Points, 2019.

Brady, Anne-Marie, ed. *China's Thought Management*. Routledge Studies on China in Transition 40. Abingdon and New York: Routledge, 2012.

Marketing Dictatorship: Propaganda and Thought Work in Contemporary China. Lanham, MD: Rowman & Littlefield Publishers, 2009.

Briggle, Adam. "Bioconservatism as Customized Science." In *The Customization of Science: The Impact of Religious and Political Worldviews on Contemporary Science*, edited by Steve Fuller, Mikael Stenmark, and Ulf Zackariasson, 176–90. London: Palgrave Macmillan UK, 2014.

Brown, Archie. *Seven Years That Changed the World: Perestroika in Perspective*. Oxford and New York: Oxford University Press, 2007.

Brown, Kerry, and Una Aleksandra Bērziņa-Čerenkova. "Ideology in the Era of Xi Jinping." *Journal of Chinese Political Science* 23, no. 3 (September 2018): 323–39.

Brudny, Yitzhak M. *Reinventing Russia: Russian Nationalism and the Soviet State, 1953–1991*. Cambridge, MA: Harvard University Press, 1998.

Bullough, Oliver. *The Last Man in Russia: The Struggle to Save a Dying Nation*. New York: Basic Books, 2013.

Burchardt, Marian, Monika Wohlrab-Sahr, and Matthias Middell. *Multiple Secularities beyond the West: Religion and Modernity in the Global Age*. Boston: De Gruyter, 2015.

Bursa-Millet, Zeynep. "Le foyer des intellectuels. Sociohistoire d'un club d'influence de droite dans la Turquie du XXe siècle." *Doctoral Dissertation in Sociology, Ecole des hautes études en sciences sociales*, 2020.

Buzogány, Aron, and Mihai Varga. "Illiberal Thought Collectives and Policy Networks in Hungary and Poland." *European Politics and Society* 24, no. 1 (2021): 40–48.

Camic, Charles, and Neil Gross. "The New Sociology of Ideas." In *The Blackwell Companion to Sociology*, edited by Judith R. Blau, 236–49. Oxford, UK: Blackwell Publishing Ltd, 2001.

Carman, Douglas. "Translation and Analysis of the Doctrine of Information Security of the Russian Federation: Mass Media and the Politics of Identity." *Washington International Law Journal* 11, no. 2 (2002): 339.

Cefaï, Daniel. "Expérience, culture et politique." In *Cultures politiques*, edited by Daniel Cefaï, 93–116. Paris: Presses Universitaires de France, 2001.

Chaubet, François. "Sociologie et histoire des intellectuels." In *L'histoire des intellectuels aujourd'hui*, edited by Michel Leymarie and Jean-François Sirinelli, 183–200. Paris: Presses universitaires de France, 2003.

Chebankova, Elena. "The State and the Public Sphere in Russia." *Demokratizatsiya: The Journal of Post-Soviet Democratization* 19, no. 4 (2011): 317–42.

Checkel, Jeffrey T. "The Constructive Turn in International Relations Theory." *World Politics* 50, no. 2 (January 1998): 324–48.

Chekov, Alexander D., Anna V. Makarycheva, Anastasiia M. Solomentseva, Maxim A. Suchkov, and Andrei A. Sushentsov. "War of the Future: A View from Russia." *Survival* 61, no. 6 (November 2, 2019): 25–48.

Chernyshova, Natalya. "Consumers as Citizens: Revisiting the Questions of Public Disengagement in the Brezhnev Era." In *Reconsidering Stagnation in the Brezhnev Era: Ideology and Exchange*, edited by Dina Fainberg and Artemy Kalinovsky, 3–20. Lanham, MD: Lexington Books, 2016.

Chnirelman, Viktor. *Russkoe rodnoverie. Neoiazychestvo i natsionalizm v sovremennoi Rossii*. Moscow: BBI, 2012.

Chuprinin, Sergei. "Posle draki. Urok prikladnoi konspirologii." *Znamia*, no. 10 (2002). https://magazines.gorky.media/znamia/2002/10/posle-draki.html.

Clark, Katerina. "The Changing Image of Science and Technology in Soviet Literature." In *Science and the Soviet Social Order*, edited by Loren R. Graham. Cambridge, MA and London: Harvard University Press, 1990.

Clowes, Edith. "Provinces, Piety, and Promotional Putinism: Mapping Aleksandr Prokhanov's Counter-Utopian Russia'." In *The Post-Soviet Politics of Utopia: Language, Fiction and Fantasy in Modern Russia*, edited by Mikhail Suslov and Per-Arne Bodin, 2020.

Coalson, Robert. "Kalashnikov in the Kremlin." Radio Free Europe, December 9, 2009. www.rferl.org/a/1899581.html.

Coman, Ramona, Valentin Behr, and Jan Beyer. "The Shaping Power of Anti-Liberal Ideas." *European Politics and Society* 24, no. 1 (2023): 1–4.

Coman, Ramona, and Clara Volintiru. "Anti-Liberal Ideas and Institutional Change in Central and Eastern Europe." *European Politics and Society* 24, no. 1 (2023): 5–21.

Curanović, Alicja. "Domestic Lobbyists and Conservatism in Russian Foreign Policy." In *Russia's Foreign Policy: The Internal-International Link*, edited by Aldo Ferrari and Eleonora Tafuro Ambrosetti, 37–64. Milan: Ledizioni LediPublishing, 2021.

The Religious Factor in Russia's Foreign Policy. London: Rouledge, 2012.

The Sense of Mission in Russian Foreign Policy: Destined for Greatness! Abingdon and New York, NY: Routledge, 2021.

Danilkin, Lev. *Chelovek s iaitsom, zhizn i mnenie Aleksandra Prokhanova*. Moscow: Ad Marginem, 2007.

David-Fox Michael. *Crossing Borders: Modernity, Ideology, and Culture in Russia and the Soviet Union*. Pittsburgh, PA: University of Pittsburgh Press, 2015.

Denisova, Anastasia. "Democracy, Protest and Public Sphere in Russia after the 2011–2012 Anti-Government Protests: Digital Media at Stake." *Media, Culture & Society* 39, no. 7 (2017): 976–94.

Dennes, Maryse. "Étapes d'un renouveau de la philosophie en Russie (des Années 1960 aux années 1990)." *Conference paper*. Inalco, Paris, 2022.

"Deux ans de guerre en Ukraine: En Russie, la militarisation à marche forcée de l'éducation." *Le Monde*, February 23, 2024. www.lemonde.fr/international/article/2024/02/23/deux-ans-de-guerre-en-ukraine-en-russie-la-militarisation-a-marche-forcee-de-l-education_6218077_3210.html.

Dézé, Alexandre. "Justifier l'injustifiable. Fondements, place et donctions du discours scientifique dans la propagande xénophobe du Front National." In *Discours savants, discours militants: Mélange des genres*, edited by Philippe Hamman, Jean-Matthieu Méon, and Benoît Verrier, 57–83. Paris: L'Harmattan, 2002.

Diesen, Glenn. *Russian Conservatism: Managing Change under Permanent Revolution*. Lanham, MD: Rowman & Littlefield, 2021.

Diunov, Mikhail. "Mladokonservatizm. Ego istoriia ego znachenie." *Russkii zhurnal*, December 5, 2009. www.russ.ru/pole/Mladokonservatizm.-Ego-istoriya-ego-znachenie.

Dobry, Michel. *Sociologie des crises politiques: La dynamique des mobilisations multisectorielles*. Paris: Presses de la Fondation nationale des sciences politiques, 1986.

Domushchii, Sergei. "Naklikali pobedu. Kak FEP igral na vyborakh v 90-kh i vyigryval." *Secretmag*, November 15, 2019. https://secretmag.ru/stories/naklikali-pobedu-kak-fep-igral-na-vyborakh-v-90-kh-i-vyigryval.htm?fbclid=IwAR2_uo0m8g6DebDFVlNbtxtmLF9B7ff6z8tkEeJ7h2VCRJ1alUBOngZCRsg.

Donovan, Victoria. "Militarized Memory." In *Russia's Regional Identities: The Power of the Provinces*, edited by Edith W. Clowes, Gisela Erbslöh, and Ani Kokobobo, First edition, 73–95. London and New York: Routledge Taylor & Francis Group, 2018.

Dosse, François. "De l'histoire des idées à l'histoire intellectuelle." In *L'histoire des intellectuels aujourd'hui*, edited by Michel Leymarie and Jean-François Sirinelli, 161–82. Paris: Presses universitaires de France, 2003.

Dukalskis, Alexander. *The Authoritarian Public Sphere: Legitimation and Autocratic Power in North Korea, Burma, and China*. Abingdon and New York, NY: Routledge, 2017.

Duller, Matthias. "Internationalization of Cold War Systems Analysis: RAND, IIASA and the Institutional Reasons for Methodological Change." *History of the Human Sciences* 29, no. 4–5 (2016): 172–90.

Dunlop, John B. "Aleksandr Dugin's 'Neo-Eurasian' Textbook and Dmitrii Trenin's Ambivalent Response." *Harvard Ukrainian Studies* 25, no. 1/2 (2001): 91–127.

The Rise of Russia and the Fall of the Soviet Empire. Princeton, NJ: Princeton University Press, 1993.

Eatwell, Roger, and Matthew Goodwin. *National Populism: The Revolt against Liberal Democracy*. London, UK: Pelican, 2018.

Eisenstadt, Shmuel N. "Multiple Modernities." *Daedalus* 129, no. 1 (2000): 1–29.

"Multiple Modernities in an Age of Globalization." *The Canadian Journal of Sociology/Cahiers Canadiens de Sociologie* 24, no. 2 (1999): 283–95.

Eliasoph, Nina, and Paul Lichterman. "Culture in Interaction." *American Journal of Sociology* 108, no. 4 (2003): 735–94.

Engerman, David C. "The Soviet Union as a Modern Society." In *Know Your Enemy: The Rise and Fall of America's Soviet Experts*, 180–205. Cary, NC: Oxford University Press USA – OSO, 2009.

English, Robert. *Russia and the Idea of the West: Gorbachev, Intellectuals, and the End of the Cold War*. New York: Columbia University Press, 2000.

Engström, Maria. "Contemporary Russian Messianism and New Russian Foreign Policy." *Contemporary Security Policy* 35, no. 3 (2014): 356–79.

"Telluro-Cosmic Imperial Utopia and Contemporary Russian Art." In *The Post-Soviet Politics of Utopia: Language, Fiction and Fantasy in Modern Russia*, edited by Per-Arne Bodin and Mikhail Suslov, 61–80. London and New York: I.B. Tauris, 2019.

Epstein, Mikhail. *After the Future: The Paradoxes of Postmodernism and Contemporary Russian Culture*. Amherst: University of Massachusetts Press, 1995.

Ideas against Ideocracy: Non-Marxist Thought of the Late Soviet Period (1953–1991). New York: Bloomsbury Academic, 2022.

"Minimal Religion (1982)." In *Russian Postmodernism: New Perspectives on Post-Soviet Culture*, edited by Mikhail Epstein, Alexander Genis, and Slobodanka Vladiv-Glover, 296–306. New York and Oxford: Berghahn Books, 2016.

The Phoenix of Philosophy: Russian Thought of the Late Soviet Period (1953–1991). New York, NY: Bloomsbury Academic, 2019.

Etkind, Alexander. "The Decay of the Russian Public Sphere." *Current History* 114, no. 774 (2015): 278–81.

Fainberg, Dina, and Artemy Kalinovsky, eds. *Reconsidering Stagnation in the Brezhnev Era: Ideology and Exchange*. Lanham, MD: Lexington Books, 2016.

Farman, Abou. "Re-Enchantment Cosmologies: Mastery and Obsolescence in an Intelligent Universe." *Anthropological Quarterly* 85, no. 4 (2012): 1069–88.

Farrell, Theo. "Constructivist Security Studies: Portrait of a Research Program." *International Studies Review* 4, no. 1 (2002): 49–72.

Fauconnier, Clémentine. "Enquêter sur le parti Russie unie: de la défiance politique à l'illégitimité scientifique? L'apport critique de l'étude des objets antipathiques." *Terrains/Théories*, no. 10 (2019).

"Organisation partisane et exercice du pouvoir dans la Russie de Poutine: Les paradoxes de la fabrication de Russie Unie (2001–2012)." *Doctoral Dissertation in Political Science, Institut d'études politiques de Paris*, 2015.

Faure, Juliette. "A Russian Version of Reactionary Modernism: Aleksandr Prokhanov's 'Spiritualization of Technology.'" *Journal of Political Ideologies* 26, no. 3 (2021): 365–79.

"Définir le conservatisme russe. Un enjeu d'historiographie et de méthode pour l'histoire des idées politiques." *Cahiers du monde russe. Russie – Empire russe – Union soviétique et États indépendants* 61, no. 3–4 (2020): 573–84.

"L'idée politique de tradition dans les discours du régime russe contemporain (2012–2018)." *Institut d'études politiques*, 2018.

Filatova, Olga. "Discursive Practices in the Digital Public Sphere of Modern Russia: Results and Directions of Research', *Administrative Consulting*, no. 11 (2019): 180–92.

Filipov, Ivan, and Yevgeny Senshen. "'The Z-Space has Unexpectedly Become a Place for Political Thought.'" *Russia Post*, November 14, 2023. https://russiapost.info/society/zchannel.

Freeden, Michael. "Confronting the Chimera of a 'Post-Ideological' Age." *Critical Review of International Social and Political Philosophy* 8, no. 2 (2005): 247–62.

Ideologies and Political Theory: A Conceptual Approach. Oxford: Clarendon Press, 1996.

"Ideology and Political Theory." *Journal of Political Ideologies* 11, no. 1 (2006): 3–22.

"Segments and Modules: The Micro-Ideologies." In *Ideology: A Very Short Introduction*, 94–102. Oxford: Oxford University Press, 2003. www-veryshortintroductions-com.ezp-prod1.hul.harvard.edu/view/10.1093/actrade/9780192802811.001.0001/actrade-9780192802811-chapter-7.

"From Accepting NATO Aspirations to 'Denazifying': 20+ Years of Putin's Changing Views on Ukraine." *Russia Matters*, June 16, 2022. www.russiamatters.org/analysis/accepting-nato-aspirations-denazifying-20-years-putins-changing-views-ukraine.

Fukuyama, Francis. "Reflections on the End of History, Five Years Later." *History and Theory* 34, no. 2 (May 1995): 27.

The End of History and the Last Man. Toronto and New York: Free Press; Maxwell Macmillan Canada; Maxwell Macmillan International, 1992.

"'Fundamentals of Homeland Security' How Russia Is Turning Schools into Training Grounds for Future Soldiers." *Meduza*, April 1, 2024. https://meduza.io/en/feature/2024/04/01/fundamentals-of-homeland-security.

Gacheva, Anastasiia. *Russkii kosmizm v ideiakh i litsakh*. Moscow: Akademicheskii Proekt, 2019.

Galeotti, Mark. *Putin's Wars: From Chechnya to Ukraine*. Oxford: Osprey Publishing, 2022.
German, Tracey. "Harnessing Protest Potential: Russian Strategic Culture and the Colored Revolutions." *Contemporary Security Policy* 41, no. 4 (2020): 541–63.
Gerovitch, Slava. *From Newspeak to Cyberspeak: A History of Soviet Cybernetics*. Cambridge, MA: MIT Press, 2002.
Gilburd, Eleonory. "Picasso in Thaw Culture." *Cahiers du monde russe. Russie – Empire russe – Union soviétique et États indépendants* 47, no. 47/1–2 (June 1, 2006): 65–108.
Gill, Graeme. *Symbolism and Regime Change in Russia*. Cambridge and New York: Cambridge University Press, 2013.
Gouarné, Isabelle. "L'introduction du marxisme en France: philosoviétisme et sciences humaines, 1920–1939." Presses universitaires de Rennes, 2013.
Gouarné, Isabelle and Olessia Kirtchik. "La 'modernité' des sciences sociales soviétiques." *Revue d'histoire des sciences humaines*, no. 40 (2022): 5.
Graef, Alexander. "Influential or Irrelevant? The Role of Foreign Policy Think Tanks in Russia." In *Russia's Foreign Policy: The Internal-International Link*, edited by Aldo Ferrari and Eleonora Tafuro Ambrosetti, 12–36. Milan: Ledizioni LediPublishing, 2021.
Graef, Alexander, and Anton Barbashin. "Thinking Foreign Policy in Russia: Think Tanks and Grand Narratives." *The Atlantic Council*, November 12, 2019. www.atlanticcouncil.org/in-depth-research-reports/report/thinking-foreign-policy-in-russia-think-tanks-and-grand-narratives/.
Graham, Loren R. "Introduction: The Impact of Science and Technology on Soviet Politics and Society." In *Science and the Soviet Social Order*, edited by Loren R. Graham, 1–16. Cambridge, MA: Harvard University Press, 1990.
"Granty ot Putina dadut za propagandu russkogo mira i borbu s pedofilami," December 8, 2015. www.rbc.ru/politics/08/12/2015/5666f9cf9a7947d88622c924.
Gray, Colin S. "National Style in Strategy: The American Example." *International Security* 6, no. 2 (1981): 21–47.
Greene, Samuel A. *Moscow in Movement: Power and Opposition in Putin's Russia*. Stanford, CA: Stanford University Press, 2014.
Greene, Samuel A. and Graeme B. Robertson, "State-Mobilized Movements after Annexation of Crimea: The Construction of Novorossiya." In *Ruling by Other Means: State-Mobilized Movements*, edited by Elizabeth J. Perry, Grzegorz Ekiert, and Xiaojun Yan, Cambridge Studies in Contentious Politics, Cambridge: Cambridge University Press, 2020, 193–216.

Gross, Neil. *Richard Rorty: The Making of an American Philosopher*. Chicago: University of Chicago Press, 2008.

Grosul, Vladislav, ed. *Russkii konservatizm XIX stoletiia. Ideologiia i praktika*. Moscow: Progress-Traditsiia, 2000.

Gusev, Vladimir. *Russkii konservatizm: Osnovnye napravleniia i etapy razvitiia*. Tver: Tverskoi gosudarstvennyi universitet, 2001.

Haas, Mark L. *The Clash of Ideologies: Middle Eastern Politics and American Security*. New York: Oxford University Press, 2012.

Habermas, Jürgen. *The Structural Transformation of the Public Sphere: An Inquiry into a Category of Bourgeois Society*. Cambridge, MA: MIT Press, 1999.

Hagemeister, Michael. "Konstantin Tsiolkovskii and the Occult Roots of Soviet Space Travel." In *The New Age of Russia – Occult and Esoteric Dimensions, Glatzer Rosenthal, Hagemeister, Menzel*. Ithaca and London: Cornell University Press, 1997.

"Le 'Cosmisme Russe', 'philosophie de l'avenir'?" *Slavica Occitania* 46 (December 2018): 49–68.

Nikolaj Fedorov: Studien zu Leben, Werk und Wirkung. München: Otto Sagner, 1989.

"Russian Cosmism in the 1920s and Today." In *The Occult in Russian and Soviet Culture*, edited by Bernice G. Rosenthal, 185–202. Ithaca and New York: Cornell University Press, 1997.

"The Conquest of Space and the Bliss of Atoms: Konstantin Tsiolkovskii." In *Cosmic Enthusiasm: The Cultural Impact of Soviet Space Exploration since the 1950s*, edited by Eva Maurer, Julia Richers, Monica Rüthers, and Carmen Scheide, 27–41. New York: Palgrave Macmillan, 2011.

The Hybrid Ideology: Historian Michael Hagemeister Traces the Trajectory of Russian Cosmism. Interview by Shental Andrey. INRUSSIA. http://inrussia.com/the-hybrid-ideology.

Hanson, Stephen. *Post-Imperial Democracies: Ideology and Party Formation in Third Republic France, Weimar Germany, and Post-Soviet Russia*. Cambridge and New York: Cambridge University Press, 2010.

Haraway, Donna. *Simians, Cyborgs, and Women: The Reinvention of Nature*. New York: Routledge, 1991.

Harding, Susan. "Representing Fundamentalism: The Problem of the Repugnant Cultural Other." *Social Research* 58, no. 2 (1991): 373–93.

Haslam, Jonathan. *No Virtue Like Necessity: Realist Thought in International Relations since Machiavelli*. New Haven: Yale University Press, 2014.

Hauchecorne, Mathieu. *La Gauche américaine en France: La réception de John Rawls et des théories de la justice (1971–2010)*. Paris: CNRS éditions, 2019.

"L'histoire sociale des idées peut-elle s'en tenir aux intentions? Une analyse comparée de l'histoire intellectuelle skinnérienne et de la sociologie des idées." In *Vers une histoire sociale des idées politiques*, edited by Chloé Gaboriaux and Arnault Skornicki, 129–46. Espaces Politiques. Villeneuve-d'Ascq, France: Presses universitaires du Septentrion, 2017.

Hauchecorne, Mathieu, and Frédérique Matonti. "Actualité de l'histoire sociale des idées politiques." *Raisons politiques* 67, no. 3 (October 24, 2017): 5–10.

Hay, Colin. "Ideas and the Construction of Interests." In *Ideas and Politics in Social Science Research*, edited by Daniel Béland and Robert Henry Cox, 65–81. Oxford: Oxford University Press, 2010.

Herf, Jeffrey. *Reactionary Modernism: Technology, Culture, and Politics in Weimar and the Third Reich*. Cambridge: Cambridge University Press, 2003.

Hermansson, Patrick, David Lawrence, Joe Mulhall, and Simon Murdoch. "The Dark Enlightenment: Neoreaction and Silicon Valley." In *The International Alt-Right*. London and New York: Routledge, 2020.

Hervieu-Léger, Danièle. *La religion pour mémoire*. Paris: Cerf, 2008.

Hill, Fiona, and Angela Stent. "The World Putin Wants: How Distortions about the Past Feed Delusions about the Future." *Foreign Affairs* 101 (October 2022). www.foreignaffairs.com/russian-federation/world-putin-wants-fiona-hill-angela-stent.

Hoffmann, David L. *Cultivating the Masses: Modern State Practices and Soviet Socialism, 1914–1939*. Ithaca: Cornell University Press, 2011.

Hoffmann, Stanley. "Clash of Globalizations." *Foreign Affairs* 81, no. 4 (2002): 104–15.

Holbig, Heike. "Ideology after the End of Ideology. China and the Quest for Autocratic Legitimation." *Democratization* 20, no. 1 (2013): 61–81.

Hopf, Ted. *Social Construction of International Politics: Identities & Foreign Policies, Moscow, 1955 and 1999*. Ithaca: Cornell University Press, 2002.

"How Putin's Right-Hand Man Took Out Prigozhin." *The Wall Street Journal*, December 22, 2023, www.wsj.com/world/russia/putin-patrushev-plan-prigozhin-assassination-428d5ed8.

Human Rights Watch. "Russia Criminalizes Independent War Reporting, Anti-War Protests," March 7, 2022. www.hrw.org/news/2022/03/07/russia-criminalizes-independent-war-reporting-anti-war-protests.

"Institut Filosofii RAN ukhodit v intellektualnoe podpole?" *Argumenty nedeli*, April 1, 2022. https://argumenti.ru/opinion/2022/04/766103.

Institute for the Study of War. "Russian Offensive Campaign Assessment," December 6, 2022. http://dev-isw.bivings.com/.

International Crisis Group. "Rebels without a Cause: Russia's Proxies in Eastern Ukraine." *Europe & Central Asia*, no. 254 (2019): 1–25.

Ivanov, Sergey. "What Russia's New History Textbook Reveals." *Russia Post*, August 18, 2023. https://russiapost.info/politics/new_history.

Jasanoff, Sheila, and Sang-Hyun Kim, eds. *Dreamscapes of Modernity: Sociotechnical Imaginaries and the Fabrication of Power*. Chicago and London: The University of Chicago Press, 2015.

Jones, Polly. "Introduction: The Dilemmas of De-Stalinization." In *The Dilemmas of De-Stalinization: Negotiating Cultural and Social Change in the Khrushchev Era*, edited by Polly Jones, 1–18. London and New York: Routledge, 2006.

Josephson, Paul R. *New Atlantis Revisited: Akademgorodok, the Siberian City of Science*. Princeton, NJ: Princeton University Press, 1997.

"Rockets, Reactors and Soviet Culture." In *Science and the Soviet Social Order*, edited by Loren Graham, 141–67. Cambridge, MA: Harvard University Press, 1990.

"Soviet Scientists and the State: Politics, Ideology, and Fundamental Research from Stalin to Gorbachev." *Social Research* 59, no. 3 (1992): 589–614.

Kartsov, Aleksei. *Pravovaia ideologiia konservatizma*. Moscow: Moskovskii obshchestvennyi nauchnyi fond, 1999.

Kasper, Karlheinz. "Russische Literaturpreise 2002 im Widerstreit der Ideologien." *Osteuropa* 53, no. 6 (2003): 839–57.

Katzenstein, Peter J., ed. *The Culture of National Security: Norms and Identity in World Politics*. New York, NY: Columbia University Press, 1996.

Kharkhordin, Oleg. *The Collective and the Individual in Russia*. Berkeley, Los Angeles and London: University of California Press, 1999.

Kirtchik, Olessia, and Mariana Heredia. "Social and Behavioral Sciences under Dictatorship." In *International Encyclopedia of the Social & Behavioral Sciences (Second Edition)*, edited by James D. Wright, 139–46. Oxford: Elsevier, 2015.

Kipp, Jacob. "Aleksandr Dugin and the Ideology of National Revival: Geopolitics, Eurasianism and the Conservative Revolution." *European Security* 11, no. 3 (2002): 91–125.

Klumbyte, Neringa, and Gulnaz Sharafutdinova. "Introduction: What Was Late Socialism?" In *Soviet Society in the Era of Late Socialism, 1964–1985*, edited by Neringa Klumbyte and Gulnaz Sharafutdinova, 6–18. Blue Ridge Summit, PA: Lexington Books, 2012.

Knorre, Boris. "Fedorovskoe Religiozno-Filosofskoe Dvizhenie Kak Primer Religioznogo Modernizma." *The Russian Review* 10 (2006).

Kolstø, Pål, and Helge Blakkisrud, eds. *The New Russian Nationalism: Imperialism, Ethnicity and Authoritarianism 2000–15*. Edinburgh: Edinburgh University Press, 2016.

Kononenko, Vadim, and Arkadii Moshes. *Russia as a Network State: What Works in Russia When State Institutions Do Not?* Houndmills, Basingstoke and New York: Palgrave Macmillan, 2011.

Kostiuk, Konstantin. "Tri portreta. Sotsialno-eticheskie vozzreniia v russkoi pravoslavnoi tserkvi kontsa XX veka." *Kontinent*, no. 113 (2002). https://magazines.gorky.media/continent/2002/113/tri-portreta.html.

Koveneva, Olga. "Les communautés politiques en France et en Russie. Regards croisés sur quelques modalités du 'vivre ensemble'." *Annales. Histoire, sciences sociales* 66, no. 3 (2011): 787–817.

Kryshtanovskaya, Olga, and Stephen White. "Inside the Putin Court: A Research Note." *Europe-Asia Studies* 57, no. 7 (2005): 1065–75.

"Kto takaia Olga Vasileva: Chto izvestno o novom ministre obrazovaniia," August 19, 2016. https://tass.ru/politika/3551544.

Kukulin, Ilia. "Excerpts from 'The Legitimization of Ultra-Right Discourse in Contemporary Russian Literature.'" In *Late and Post Soviet Literature: A Reader*, edited by Mark Lipovetsky and Lisa Ryoko Wakamiya, 337–47. Boston: Academic Studies Press, 2014.

"Nostalgicheskaia Modernizatsiia, Ili: Rossiia, Vpered!" *Neprikosnovennyi Zapas*, no. 6 (2010).

"Reaktsiia Dissotsiatsii: Legitimatsia Ultrapravogo Diskursa v Sovremennoi Rossiiskoi Literature." In *Russkii Natsionalizm: Sotsialnyi i Kulturnyi Kontekst*, edited by Marlène Laruelle, 257–338. Moscow: Novoe literaturnoe obozrenie, 2008.

"Sentimentalnaia tekhnologiia: Pamiat o 1960-kh v diskussiiakh o modernizatsii 2009–2010 godov." *Neprikosnovennyi zapas*, no. 6 (2010). https://magazines.gorky.media/nz/2010/6/sentimentalnaya-tehnologiya-pamyat-o-1960-h-v-diskussiyah-o-modernizaczii-2009-2010-godov.html.

Kurenov, Denis. "Szhech, utopit i zapretit. Kto i pochemu zhaluetsia na khudozhestvennuiu literaturu v Rossii XXI veka?" yuga.ru, October 16, 2016. www.yuga.ru/articles/culture/7577.html.

Lamont, Michèle. "Meaning-Making in Cultural Sociology: Broadening Our Agenda." *Contemporary Sociology* 29, no. 4 (2000): 602–7.

Laqueur, Walter. *Black Hundred: The Rise of the Extreme Right in Russia.* New York: HarperCollins, 1993.

Laruelle, Marlène. "Alexandre Dugin: Esquisse d'un eurasisme d'extrême-droite en Russie post-soviétique." *Revue d'études comparatives Est-Ouest* 32, no. 3 (2001): 85–103.

"Alexei Navalny and Challenges in Reconciling 'Nationalism' and 'Liberalism.'" *Post-Soviet Affairs* 30, no. 4 (2014): 276–97.

"Conservatism as the Kremlin's New Toolkit: An Ideology at the Lowest Cost." *Russian Analytical Digest*, no. 138 (2013): 2–4.

In the Name of the Nation: Nationalism and Politics in Contemporary Russia. Sciences Po Series in International Relations and Political Economy. New York, NY: Palgrave Macmillian, 2009.

"Inside and around the Kremlin's Black Box: The New Nationalist Think Tanks in Russia." *Institute for Security and Development Policy*, no. Stockholm Paper (October 2009).

ed. *Le rouge et le noir: Extrême droite et nationalisme en Russie*. CNRS Science Politique. Paris: CNRS Éditions, 2007.

"Making Sense of Russia's Illiberalism." *Journal of Democracy* 31, no. 3 (July 2020): 115–29.

"Putin's Regime and the Ideological Market: A Difficult Balancing Game." Carnegie Endowment for International Peace, March 16, 2017. https://carnegieendowment.org/2017/03/16/putin-s-regime-and-ideological-market-difficult-balancing-game-pub-68250.

"Russia as a 'Divided Nation,' from Compatriots to Crimea: A Contribution to the Discussion on Nationalism and Foreign Policy." *Problems of Post-Communism* 62, no. 2 (2015): 88–97.

Russian Eurasianism: An Ideology of Empire. Washington, DC and Baltimore, MD: Woodrow Wilson Center Press; Johns Hopkins University Press, 2008.

Russian Nationalism: Imaginaries, Doctrines, and Political Battlefields. London and New York: Routledge, 2019. http://search.ebscohost.com/login.aspx?direct=true&scope=site&db=nlebk&db=nlabk&AN=1925259.

"Russia's Ideological Construction in the Context of the War in Ukraine." *Russie.Eurasie.Reports (IFRI)* 46 (March 2024).

"The Iuzhinskii Circle: Far-Right Metaphysics in the Soviet Underground and Its Legacy Today." *The Russian Review* 74, no. 7 (2015): 563–80.

"The Izborsky Club, or the New Conservative Avant-Garde in Russia." *The Russian Review* 75 (2016): 626–44.

"The Kremlin's Ideological Ecosystems. Equilibrium and Competition." *PONARS Eurasia Policy Memo*, no. 493 (2017): 1–6.

"The 'Russian World'. Russia's Soft Power and Geopolitical Imagination." *Center on Global Interests*, 2015.

"The Three Colors of Novorossiya, or the Russian Nationalist Mythmaking of the Ukrainian Crisis." *Post-Soviet Affairs* 32, no. 1 (2016): 55–74.

Laruelle, Marlène, and Laura Howells. "Ideological or Pragmatic? A Data-Driven Analysis of the Russian Presidential Grant Fund." *Russian Politics* 5, no. 1 (2020): 29–51.

Lash, Scott. "Reflexivity and Its Doubles: Structures, Aesthetics, Community." In *Reflexive Modernization: Politics, Tradition and Aesthetics in the Modern Society*, by Ulrich Beck, Anthony Giddens, and Scott Lash, 110–73. Stanford, CA: Stanford University Press, 1994.

Laurinavicius, Marius. “Dmitry Rogozin’s Clan: Visionaries and Executors behind Aggression towards Ukraine.” *Delfi.En*, August 19, 2014. www.delfi.lt/en/politics/dmitry-rogozins-clan-visionaries-and-executors-behind-aggression-towards-ukraine.d?id=65585356.

Ledeneva, Alena V. *Can Russia Modernise?: Sistema, Power Networks and Informal Governance*. Cambridge and New York: Cambridge University Press, 2013.

Lemieux, Cyril. “À quoi sert l’analyse des controverses?” *Mil Neuf Cent. Revue d’histoire Intellectuelle* 1, no. 25 (2007): 191–212.

“Le crépuscule des champs: Limites d’un concept ou disparition d’une réalité historique?” In *Bourdieu: Théoricien de La Pratique*, edited by Michel de Fornel and Albert Ogien, 75–100. Paris: Editions de l’Ecole des hautes études en sciences sociales, 2011.

Levitsky, Steven and Lucan A. Way. *Competitive Authoritarianism: Hybrid Regimes after the Cold War*. Cambridge: Cambridge University Press, 2010.

Lipovetskii, Mark. *Paralogii. Transformatsii (post)modernistkogo diskursa v russkoi kulture 1920–2000-kh godov*. Moscow: Novoe literaturnoe obozrenie, 2008.

Lipovetskii, Mark, and Aleksandr Etkind. “Vozvrashchenie tritona: Sovetskaia katastrofa i postsovetskii roman.” *Novoe literaturnoe obozrenie* 94, no. 6 (2008): 174–206.

Livers, Keith. “The Tower or the Labyrinth: Conspiracy, Occult, and Empire-Nostalgia in the Work of Viktor Pelevin and Aleksandr Prokhanov.” *The Russian Review* 69, no. 3 (2010): 477–503.

Luehrmann, Sonja. “The Spirit of Late Socialism and the Value of Transformation: Brezhnevism through the Lens of Post-Soviet Religious Revival.” *Cahiers du monde russe* 54, no. 54/3–4 (2013): 543–63.

Lukoianov, Igor. *Rossiiskie konservatory (konets XIX – nachalo XX vv.). Posobie k lektsionnomu kursu*. Sankt-Peterburg: Nestor-Istoriia, 2003.

Magnúsdóttir, Rósa. “‘Be Careful in America, Premier Khrushchev!’” *Cahiers du monde russe. Russie – Empire russe – Union soviétique et États indépendants* 47, no. 47/1–2 (June 1, 2006): 109–30.

Magun, Artemii. “Perestroika kak konservativnaia revoliutsiia?” *Neprikosnovennyi zapas*, no. 6 (2010). https://magazines.gorky.media/nz/2010/6/perestrojka-kak-konservativnaya-revolyucziya.html.

Negative Revolution: Modern Political Subject and Its Fate after the Cold War. New York: Bloomsbury Academic, 2013.

Malyarenko, Tatyana, and Stefan Wolff. “The Logic of Competitive Influence-Seeking: Russia, Ukraine, and the Conflict in Donbas.” *Post-Soviet Affairs* 34, no. 4 (2018): 191–212.

Mannheim, Karl. *Essays on the Sociology of Knowledge*. London: Routledge & Kegan Paul, 1972.

Ideology and Utopia: An Introduction to the Sociology of Knowledge. Mansfield Centre, Mansfield Center, CT: Martino Publishing, 2015.

March, Luke. "Nationalism for Export? The Domestic and Foreign-Policy Implications of the New 'Russian Idea.'" *Europe-Asia Studies* 64, no. 3 (2012): 401–25.

Markiewicz-Lagneau, Janina. "La fin de l'intelligentsia? Formation et transformation de l'intelligentsia soviétique." *Revue d'études comparatives Est-Ouest* 7, no. 4 (1976): 7–71.

Marples, David R. *The War in Ukraine's Donbas: Origins, Contexts, and the Future*. Budapest: Central European University Press, 2022.

Matonti, Frédérique. *Intellectuels communistes: essai sur l'obéissance politique. La nouvelle critique (1967–1980)*. Paris: Éditions La Découverte, 2005.

"Plaidoyer pour une histoire sociale des idées politiques." *Revue d'histoire moderne et contemporaine* 5, no. 59–4bis (2012): 85–104.

Mélat, Hélène. "Du traumatisme à l'évasion: les premiers pas de la littérature postsoviétique (1992–2005)." *La Revue russe* 26, no. 1 (2005): 9–24.

Mespoulet, Martine. "La 'renaissance' de la sociologie en URSS (1958–1972). Une voie étroite entre matérialisme historique et 'recherches sociologiques concrètes.'" *Revue d'histoire des sciences humaines* 16, no. 1 (2007): 57–86.

Mikkonen, Simo. "In the Shadow of Technology: The Anatomy of East–West Scholarly Exchanges in the Late Soviet Period." *History of the Human Sciences* 29, no. 4–5 (2016): 151–71.

Minakov, Arkadii, ed. *Konservatizm v Rossii i mire. Proshloe i nastoiashchee. Sbornik nauchnykh trudov*. Voronezh: Voronezhskii gosudarstvennyi universitet, 2001.

"Ministr Iustitsii Nachal Diskussiiu Ob Otmene Zapreta Na Ideologiiu." *Vedomosti*, May 12, 2023. www.vedomosti.ru/politics/articles/2023/05/12/974675-ministr-yustitsii-nachal-diskussiyu-ob-otmene-zapreta-na-ideologiyu.

Minkenberg, Michael. "The Renewal of the Radical Right: Between Modernity and Anti-modernity." *Government and Opposition* 35, no. 2 (April 2000): 170–88.

Mitrokhin, Nikolai. *Russkaia Partiia: Dvizhenie russkikh natsionalistov v SSSR 1953–1985 gody*. Moscow: Novoe literaturnoe obozrenie, 2003.

Momzikoff-Markoff, Sophie. *Les hommes de Gorbatchev: Influences et réseaux, 1956–1992*. Paris: Éditions de la Sorbonne, 2020.

Mondon, Aurelien, and Aaron Winter. *Reactionary Democracy: How Racism and the Populist Far Right Became Mainstream*. London and New York: Verso Books, 2020.

Moyn, Samuel. "Imaginary Intellectual History." In *Rethinking Modern European Intellectual History*, edited by Darrin M. McMahon and Samuel Moyn. Oxford: Oxford University Press, 2014.

Nathans, Benjamin. "The Dictatorship of Reason: Aleksandr Vol'Pin and the Idea of Rights under 'Developed Socialism.'" *Slavic Review* 66, no. 4 (2007): 630–63.

Nettleton, Nordica. "Driving towards Communist consumerism." *Cahiers du monde russe* 47, no. 1–2 (2006): 131–51.

Neumann, Iver B. *Russia and the Idea of Europe: A Study in Identity and International Relations*. 2nd edition. The New International Relations Series. London and New York: Routledge, Taylor & Francis Group, 2017.

Nikerov, Viktor A. *Kto est kto. Russkoe izdanie. Biograzicheskii innovatsionnii spravoshnik*. Moscow: Astreia, 2009.

Nikolski, Véra. "La critique des notions politiques occidentales en Russie contemporaine: Entre rejet et réappropriation." *Institut Européen Est-Ouest*, 2008. http://institut-est-ouest.ens-lyon.fr/spip.php?article149.

"La valeur heuristique de l'empathie dans l'étude des engagements « répugnants »." *Genèses* 84, no. 3 (2011): 113–26.

National-bolchevisme et néo-eurasisme dans la Russie contemporaine: La carrière militante d'une idéologie. Media Critic. Paris: Mare & Martin, 2013.

Noble, Ben. "'Traditional Values' and the Limits of Civic Unity." *Russia Post*, November 21, 2022. https://russiapost.info/politics/traditional_values.

Noordenbos, Boris. *Post-Soviet Literature and the Search for a Russian Identity*. New York: Palgrave Macmillan, 2016.

Norris, Pippa, and Ronald Inglehart. *Cultural Backlash: Trump, Brexit, and Authoritarian Populism*. New York, NY: Cambridge University Press, 2019.

Okunev, Igor. "Barriers to the Development of Independent Foreign Policy Think-Tanks in Russia." *Institute of Public Affairs (Warsaw)*, no. Policy Papers 2/11 (2011).

Orlov, Dmitrii. "ONF i vyzov razvitiia." Nezavisimaia gazeta, May 12, 2011. www.ng.ru/politics/2011-05-12/3_kartblansh.html.

Orlov, Dmitrii, Dmitrii Badovskii, and Mikhail Vinogradov. "Konservativnaia modernizatsiia – 2010: Konfiguratsiia vlasti i novaia politicheskaia povestka dnia." Regnum.ru, January 13, 2010. https://regnum.ru/news/polit/1241073.html.

"Oruzhie massovogo raziasneniia." *Kommersant*, April 22, 2022. www.kommersant.ru/doc/5326305.

Oswald, Ingrid, and Viktor Voronkov, "The 'Public-Private' Sphere in Soviet and Post-Soviet Society Perception and Dynamics of 'Public' and 'Private' in Contemporary Russia." *European Societies* 6, no. 1 (2004): 97–117.

Ottaway, Marina. *Democracy Challenged: The Rise of Semi-Authoritarianism*. Washington, DC: Carnegie Endowment for International Peace, 2003.

Oushakine, Serguei. "In the State of Post-Soviet Aphasia: Symbolic Development in Contemporary Russia." *Europe-Asia Studies* 52, no. 6 (2000): 991–1016.

Paretskaya, Anna. "A Middle Class without Capitalism? Socialist Ideology and Post-Collectivist Discourse in the Late-Soviet Era." In *Soviet Society in the Era of Late Socialism, 1964–1985*, edited by Neringa Klumbyte and Gulnaz Sharafutdinova, 45–67. Blue Ridge Summit, PA: Lexington Books, 2012.

Parland, Thomas. *The Extreme Nationalist Threat in Russia: The Growing Influence of Western Rightist Ideas*. London and New York: Routledge Curzon, 2004.

Parthé, Kathleen F. *Russian Village Prose: The Radiant Past*. Course Book. Princeton Paperbacks. Princeton, NJ: Princeton University Press, 1992.

"Peredelat Patsifista." *Novaya gazeta,* April 7, 2024. https://novayagazeta.eu/articles/2024/04/07/peredelat-patsifista.

Pertsev, Andrey. "An 'Experienced Strategist' The Man behind Russia's New Ideological Course for University Students." *Meduza*, June 10, 2023. https://meduza.io/en/feature/2023/06/10/an-experienced-strategist.

"From Kremlin Courtiers to Propaganda Serfdom." *Riddle Russia*, April 6, 2022. https://ridl.io/from-kremlin-courtiers-to-propaganda-serfdom/.

"'Hawkish Times Need Hawkish People' How the Death of Daria Dugina Helped Her Father, Alexander Dugin, Rise from Ultraconservative Fringe Philosopher to Key Kremlin Ideologue." *Meduza*, November 3, 2022. https://meduza.io/en/feature/2022/11/03/hawkish-times-need-hawkish-people.

"'In Public There Are Only Jingoistic Voices' How Russia's War against Ukraine Continues to Divide Putin's Elites." *Meduza*, June 17, 2022. https://meduza.io/en/feature/2022/06/17/in-public-there-are-only-jingoistic-voices.

"Sergei Kirienko's New Sphere of Influence." *Riddle Russia*, May 18, 2022. https://ridl.io/sergei-kirienko-s-new-sphere-of-influence/.

Peters, Michael A. "The Chinese Dream: Xi Jinping Thought on Socialism with Chinese Characteristics for a New Era." *Educational Philosophy and Theory* 49, no. 14 (2017): 1299–304.

Pipes, Richard. *Russian Conservatism and Its Critics: A Study in Political Culture*. New Haven: Yale University Press, 2005.

Plokhy, Serhii. *The Russo-Ukrainian War: The Return of History*. New York: W. W. Norton & Company, 2023.

Pogue, James. "Inside the New Right, Where Peter Thiel Is Placing His Biggest Bets." *Vanity Fair*, April 20, 2022, www.vanityfair.com/news/2022/04/inside-the-new-right-where-peter-thiel-is-placing-his-biggest-bets.

Poliakov, Leonid. "Liberalnyi konservator." Nezavisimaia gazeta, February 2, 2000. www.ng.ru/ideas/2000-02-02/8_conserve.html.

Polowy, Teresa. "Twenty Years Later: Russian Literature and Literary Studies since 1991." *Canadian Slavonic Papers/Revue Canadienne Des Slavistes* 53, no. 2/4 (2011): 527–44.

Popov, Vladimir. "Sibirskaya utopiia Baptistov." *Nezavisimaia gazeta*, October 20, 2010. www.ng.ru/ng_religii/2010-10-20/7_sibir.html.

Preobrazhenskii, Ivan. "Imperiia bet po liberalam," September 10, 2012. www.rosbalt.ru/blogs/2012/09/10/1032462.html.

Prigogine, Ilya, and Isabelle Stengers. *The End of Certainty*. New York: Simon and Schuster, 1997.

"Prigozhin Asks Prosecutors to Probe 'crime' by Top Russian Defence Officials." *Reuters*, May 31, 2023. www.reuters.com/world/europe/prigozhin-asks-prosecutors-investigate-crimes-by-top-russian-defence-officials-2023-05-31/.

Pringle, Heather. *Master Plan: Himmler's Scholars and the Holocaust*. New York: Hyperion, 2007.

Prozorov, Sergei. "Russian Conservatism in the Putin Presidency: The Dispersion of a Hegemonic Discourse." *Journal of Political Ideologies* 10, no. 2 (2005): 121–43.

Pudal, Bernard. "De l'histoire des idées politiques à l'histoire sociale des idées politiques." In *Les formes de l'activité politique: Éléments d'analyse sociologique, du XVIIIe siècle à nos jours*, edited by Antonin Cohen, Bernard Lacroix, and Philippe Riutort, 185–92. Paris: Presses universitaires de France, 2006.

Pudal, Bernard and Pennetier Claude. *Le souffle d'octobre 1917: l'engagement des communistes français*. Ivry-sur-Seine: Les Editions de l'Atelier, 2017.

Pushkin, Sergei. *Istoriosofiia russkogo konservatizma XIX v.* Nizhnii Novgorod: Volgo-Viatskaia akademiia gosudarstvennoi sluzhby, 1998.

"Putin podpisal ukaz o prazdnovanii v 2022 godu stoletiia so dnia rozhdeniia filosofa Zinoveva." *TASS,* October 1, 2021. https://tass.ru/obschestvo/12558461.

Rakhshmir, Pavel, ed. *Istoricheskie metamorfozy konservatizma*. Perm: Permskii gosudarstvennyi universitet, 1997.

Ramadan-Alban, Wendy, and Thierry Balzacq. "Pivotal Powers – Iran." In *Comparative Grand Strategy: A Framework and Cases*, edited by

Thierry Balzacq, Peter Dombrowski, and Simon Reich, 192–216. Oxford: Oxford University Press, 192AD.

Razuvalova, Anna. "Conspiracy Theory and Neoconservative PR Strategies in the 2000–2010s: The Case of Aleksandr Prokhanov." In *'Truth' and Fiction. Conspiracy Theories in Eastern European Culture and Literature*, edited by Peter Deutschmann, Jens Herlth, and Alois Woldan, 145–68. Münster: transcript Verlag, 2020.

"The Plot Device of Conspiracy in Nikolay Burlyaev's Film Lermontov and A Director's Diary: On the 'Ethnography of the Emotions' of the National-Conservative Community." *Forum for Anthropology and Culture*, no. 12 (2016): 161–85.

Reid, Susan E. "Khrushchev Modern." *Cahiers du monde russe. Russie – Empire Russe – Union Soviétique et États Indépendants* 47, no. 47/1–2 (2006): 227–68.

"Reidery protiv filososov. Kak ultrapravye konservatory vo glave s Malofeevym zakhvatyvaiut Institut Filosofii RAN." *The Insider*, March 7, 2023. https://theins.ru/obshestvo/259245.

"Rektor MGU uvolil Aleksandra Dugina," June 27, 2014. https://lenta.ru/news/2014/06/27/dugin/.

Repnikov, Aleksandr. *Konservativnaia kontseptsiia rossiiskoi gosudarstvennosti*. Moscow: Svobodnaia mysl, 1999.

"Reziume. Vladimirov Aleksandr Ivanovich." www.kadet.ru/lichno/vlad_v/vlad_in1.htm.

Ricœur, Paul. *L'idéologie et l'utopie*. Points Essais. Paris: Éditions Points, 2016.

Rich, Andrew. *Think Tanks, Public Policy, and the Politics of Expertise*. Cambridge: Cambridge University Press, 2004.

Rindzevičiūtė, Egle. "The Future as an Intellectual Technology in the Soviet Union – From Centralised Planning to Reflexive Management." *Cahiers du monde russe* 56, no. 1 (March 2015): 111–34.

The Power of Systems: How Policy Sciences Opened Up the Cold War World. Ithaca and London: Cornell University Press, 2016.

"Toward a Joint Future beyond the Iron Curtain: East-West Politics of Global Modelling." In *The Struggle for the Long-Term in Transnational Science and Politics: Forging the Future*, edited by Jenny Andersson and Egle Rindzeviciute, 115–43. London: Taylor & Francis Group, 2015.

Robinson, Paul. *Russian Conservatism*. Ithaca and New York: Northern Illinois University Press, an imprint of Cornell University Press, 2019.

Romanovskii, Nikolai. "The First Director: Academician A.M. Rumiantsev." *Sociological Research* 48, no. 5 (2009): 55–64.

Rousselet, Kathy. "Dukhovnost' in Russia's Politics." *Religion, State and Society* 48, no. 1 (2020): 38–55.

"Russia's Technocrat-in-Chief How Sergey Kiriyenko Transformed the Kremlin's Domestic Policy and Quietly Gained Influence within the Putin Administration," October 11, 2019. https://meduza.io/en/feature/2019/10/11/russia-s-technocrat-in-chief.

Sakwa, Richard. "Modernisation, Neo-modernisation, and Comparative Democratisation in Russia." *East European Politics* 28, no. 1 (2012): 43–57.

Putin and the Oligarch: The Khodorkovsky-Yukos Affair. London: I.B. Tauris, 2014.

Putin Redux: Power and Contradiction in Contemporary Russia. Abingdon and Burlington, VT: Routledge, 2014.

Putin: Russia's Choice. London and New York: Routledge, 2004.

"Putin's Leadership: Character and Consequences." *Europe-Asia Studies* 60, no. 6 (2008): 879–97.

The Putin Paradox. London, New York, Oxford, New Delhi and Sydney: I.B. Tauris, 2020.

Samarina, Aleksandra. "Apostoly konservativnogo patriotizma." Nezavisimaia gazeta, September 10, 2012. www.ng.ru/politics/2012-09-10/1_apostoly.html.

Sandle, Mark. "A Triumph of Ideological Hairdressing? Intellectual Life in the Brezhnev Era Reconsidered." In *Brezhnev Reconsidered*, edited by Edwin Bacon and Mark Sandle, 1–21. London: Palgrave Macmillan UK, 2002.

Sauer, Pjotr. "Wagner Chief Accuses Moscow of Lying to Public about Ukraine." *The Guardian*, June 23, 2023, sec. World news. www.theguardian.com/world/2023/jun/23/wagner-chief-accuses-moscow-of-lying-to-public-about-ukraine-yevgeny-prigozhin.

Sauvé, Guillaume. "La morale à l'épreuve de la politique: La pensée politique de l'intelligentsia libérale soviétique de l'époque de la Perestroïka." *Doctoral Dissertation in Political Science*. Institu d'études politiques de Paris, 2016.

Scanlan, James P., ed. *Russian Thought after Communism: The Recovery of a Philosophical Heritage*. Armonk, NY: M.E. Sharpe, 1994.

Schwartz, Matthias. "A Dream Come True: Close Encounters with Outer Space in Soviet Popular Scientific Journals of the 1950s and 1960s." In *Soviet Space Culture. Cosmic Enthusiasm in Socialist Societies*, edited by Eva Maurer, Julia Richers, Monica Rüthers, and Carmen Scheide, 232–65. New York: Palgrave Macmillan, 2011.

Seddon, Max. "The Russian Oligarch Who Wants Vladimir Putin to Be a Tsar." *Financial Times*, March 13, 2020.

Semenova, Svetlana, and Anastasiia Gacheva, eds. *Russkii kosmizm: Antologiia filosofskoi mysli*. Moscow: Pedagogika Press, 1993.

Sergeev, Mikhail, Alexander Nikolaevich Chumakov, Mary Elizabeth Theis, and Alyssa DeBlasio, eds. *Russian Philosophy in the Twenty-First Century: An Anthology*. Leiden and Boston: Brill Rodopi, 2021.

Shekhovtsov, Anton. "The Palingenetic Thrust of Russian Neo-Eurasianism: Ideas of Rebirth in Aleksandr Dugin's Worldview." *Totalitarian Movements and Political Religions* 9, no. 4 (2008): 491–506.

Shekhovtsov, Anton, and Andreas Umland. "Is Aleksandr Dugin a Traditionalist? 'Neo-Eurasianism' and Perennial Philosophy." *The Russian Review* 68, no. 4 (2009): 662–78.

Shishkov, Andrey. "Eastern Orthodoxy, Conservatism, and (Neo) Palamite Tradition in Post-Soviet Russia." In *Contemporary Russian Conservatism. Problems, Paradoxes, and Perspectives*, edited by Mikhail Suslov and Dmitry Uzlaner, 321–46. Leiden and Boston, MA: Brill, 2020.

Shlapentokh, Dmitry. "Alexander Dugin's Views of Russian History: Collapse and Revival." *Journal of Contemporary Central and Eastern Europe* 25, no. 3 (September 2, 2017): 331–43.

Shneidman, Norman N. *Russian Literature, 1988–1994: The End of an Era*. Toronto: University of Toronto Press, 2016.

Shnirelman, Victor. "Russian Neoconservatism and Apocalyptic Imperialism." In *Contemporary Russian Conservatism. Problems, Paradoxes, and Perspectives*, edited by Mikhail Suslov and Dmitry Uzlaner, 347–78. Leiden and Boston, MA: Brill, 2020.

Siddiqi, Asif A. "Imagining the Cosmos: Utopians, Mystics, and the Popular Culture of Spaceflight in Revolutionary Russia." *Osiris* 23, no. 1 (2008): 260–88.

"Spaceflight in the National Imagination." In *Remembering the Space Age*, edited by Steven J. Dick, 17–35. Washington, DC: National Aeronatuics and Space Administration Office of External Relations History Division, 2008.

Siegelbaum, Lewis H. *Cars for Comrades: The Life of the Soviet Automobile*. Ithaca, NY: Cornell University Press, 2008.

Sigman, Carole. *Clubs politiques et perestroïka en Russie: Subversion sans dissidence*. Paris: Karthala, 2009.

Simakova, Marina, Anton Vidokle, and Arseny Zhilyaev. "Cosmic Doubts." In *Art without Death: Conversations on Russian Cosmism*, edited by Bart de Baere, 109–29. E-Flux Journal. Berlin: Sternberg Press, 2017.

Sirinelli, Jean-François. "Le hasard ou la nécessité? une histoire en chantier: l'histoire des intellectuels." *Vingtième siècle. Revue d'histoire* 9, no. 1 (1986): 97–108.

Skinner, Quentin. *Visions of Politics. Volume 1: Regarding Method*. Cambridge and New York: Cambridge University Press, 2002.

Skocpol, Theda. *The Tea Party and the Remaking of Republican Conservatism*. New York: Oxford University Press, 2016.

Skornicki, Arnault. "De Skinner à Weber. Contextualisme et sociologie." In *Vers une histoire sociale des idées politiques*, edited by Chloé Gaboriaux and Arnault Skornicki, 111–28. Villeneuve-d'Ascq, France: Presses universitaires du Septentrion, 2017.

L'économiste, la cour et la patrie: l'économie politique dans la France des Lumières. Paris: CNRS éditions, 2011.

Skornicki, Arnault, and Jérôme Tournadre. *La nouvelle histoire des idées politiques*. Paris: la Découverte, 2015.

Snegovaya, Maria. *Putin's Information Warfare in Ukraine: Soviet Origins of Russia's Hybrid Warfare*. Vol. 1, 1. Washington, DC: Institute for the Study of War, 2015.

Snyder, Jack L. "The Soviet Strategic Culture: Implications for Limited Nuclear Operations." *Rand Corporation*, no. R-2154-AF (September 1977).

"'Soiuz tirana s sofistom zhdut tiazhelye vremena.' Filosofy i sotsiologi — o voine." *T-invariant*, June 16, 2023. www.t-invariant.org/2023/06/soyuz-tirana-s-sofistom-zhdut-tyazhelye-vremena-filosofy-i-sotsiologi-o-vojne/.

Sommer, Vitezslav. "'Are We Still Behaving as Revolutionaries?': Radovan Richta, Theory of Revolution and Dilemmas of Reform Communism in Czechoslovakia." *Studies in East European Thought* 69 (2017): 93–110.

Starobinets, Anna. "The Real Russia." *New Statesman* 16, no. 742 (February 3, 2003): XVI–XVII.

"State-Controlled 'Autonomy' How the Kremlin Uses "Independent Organizations" to Do Its Propaganda Dirty Work." *Meduza*, February 26, 2024. https://meduza.io/en/feature/2024/02/27/state-controlled-autonomy.

Stone, Diane. *Capturing the Political Imagination: Think Tanks and the Policy Process*. London and Portland, OR: Frank Cass, 1996.

Suslov, Mikhail. "Geographical Metanarratives in Russia and the European East: Contemporary Pan-Slavism." *Eurasian Geography and Economics* 53, no. 5 (2012): 575–95.

Putinism – Post-Soviet Russian Regime Ideology. London and New York: Routledge, 2024.

"The Fundamentalist Utopia of Gennady Shimanov from the 1960s–1980s." *Demokratizatsiya: The Journal of Post-Soviet Democratization* 17, no. 4 (2009): 324–49.

"The Production of 'Novorossiya': A Territorial Brand in Public Debates." *Europe-Asia Studies* 69, no. 2 (2017): 202–21.

Suslov, Mikhail, and Dmitry Uzlaner, eds. *Contemporary Russian Conservatism: Problems, Paradoxes, and Perspectives*. Eurasian Studies Library: History, Societies & Cultures in Eurasia, volume 13. Boston and Leiden: Brill, 2020.

Taillandier, Apolline. "In the Name of Posthumanity. Visions and Justifications of Liberal Order in Contemporary Anglophone Transhumanism." *Doctoral Dissertation in Political Science*. Institut d'études politiques de Paris, 2021.

Tait, Joshua. "Mencius Moldbug and Neoreaction." In *Key Thinkers of the Radical Right: Behind the New Threat to Liberal Democracy*, edited by Mark Sedgwick, 187–203. Oxford University Press, 2019.

Thorun, Christian. *Explaining Change in Russian Foreign Policy: The Role of Ideas in Post-Soviet Russia's Conduct towards the West*. Basingstoke and New York: Palgrave Macmillan, 2009.

Tournadre-Plancq, Jérôme. *Au-delà de la gauche et de la droite, une troisième voie britannique? Science Politique*, v. 6. Paris: Dalloz, 2006.

Trenin, Dmitri. "Russia's Conservative Modernization: A Mission Impossible?" Carnegie Moscow Center, May 25, 2010. https://carnegiemoscow.org/2010/05/25/russia-s-conservative-modernization-mission-impossible.

Tsygankov, Andrei. "Crafting the State-Civilization Vladimir Putin's Turn to Distinct Values." *Problems of Post-Communism* 63, no. 3 (2016): 146–58.

Russia's Foreign Policy: Change and Continuity in National Identity. Lanham: Rowman & Littlefield, 2016.

The Strong State in Russia: Development and Crisis. Oxford and New York: Oxford University Press, 2014.

Umland, Andreas. "Vers une société incivile? Contextualisation du déclin des partis politiques d'extrême droite en Russie post-soviétique." In *Le rouge et le noir. Extrême droite et nationalisme en Russie*, edited by Marlène Laruelle, 139–72. Paris: CNRS Éditions.

Uvarchev, Leonid. "Gosduma priniala v 2022 godu rekordnoe chislo zakonov — 653." *Kommersant*, December 22, 2022. www.kommersant.ru/doc/5736100.

Uzlaner, Dmitry. "Russian Conservatism as an Ideology: The Logic of Isolationism." In *Contemporary Russian Conservatism*, edited by Mikhail Suslov and Dmitry Uzlaner, 103–28. Leiden and Boston: Brill, 2020.

Varga-Harris, Christine. "Forging Citizenship on the Home Front: Reviving the Socialist Contract and Constructing Soviet Identity during the Thaw." In *The Dilemmas of De-Stalinization: Negotiating Cultural *and Social Change in the Khrushchev Era*, edited by Polly Jones, 101–16. London and New York: Routledge, 2006.

Vasileva, Anna. "Istoriia stanet tsaritsei nauk." *Kommersant*, February 2, 2023. www.kommersant.ru/doc/5798930.

Ven Bruusgaard, Kristin. "Russian Nuclear Strategy and Conventional Inferiority." *Journal of Strategic Studies* 44, no. 1 (2021): 3–35.

Vendil Pallin, Carolina, and Susanne Oxenstierna. "Russian Think Tanks and Soft Power." *Swedish Defence Research Agency (FOI-R)*, August 2017.

Vitkine, Benoît. "En Russie, Anatoli Tchoubaïs, conseiller de Poutine et figure libérale, fait défection." *Le Monde*, March 24, 2022. www.lemonde.fr/international/article/2022/03/24/en-russie-anatoli-tchoubais-conseiller-de-poutine-et-figure-liberale-fait-defection_6118948_3210.html.

Vormann, Boris, and Michael D. Weinman, eds. *The Emergence of Illiberalism: Understanding a Global Phenomenon*. New York: Routledge, 2020.

Walicki, Andrzej. *The Flow of Ideas: Russian Thought from the Enlightenment to the Religious-Philosophical Renaissance*, Eastern European Culture, Politics, and Societies, volume 7. New York: Peter Lang Edition, 2015.

Wang, Zheng. "The Chinese Dream: Concept and Context." *Journal of Chinese Political Science* 19 (2014): 1–13.

Weaver, R. Kent. "The Changing World of Think Tanks." *PS: Political Science and Politics* 22, no. 3 (1989): 563–78.

Weiss, Andrew S. "With Friends Like These: The Kremlin's Far-Right and Populist Connections." Carnegie Endowment for International Peace, February 27, 2020. https://carnegieendowment.org/2020/02/27/with-friends-like-these-kremlin-s-far-right-and-populist-connections-in-italy-and-austria-pub-81100.

Weiss, Daniel. "The New Russian Legislation on Blasphemy and Swearing: The Parliamentary Debates." *Zeitschrift Für Slavische Philologie* 72, no. 2 (2016): 289–321.

Wenger, Agnès. "Return of the Voenkor: The Military as a New Opinion Leader in Russia?" *Russia Post*, August 14, 2022. https://russiapost.info/politics/voenkor.

Wolfe, Tom, and E. W. Johnson. *The New Journalism*. New York: Harper & Row, 1973.

Xufeng, Zhu. "The Influence of Think Tanks in the Chinese Policy Process: Different Ways and Mechanisms." *Asian Survey* 49, no. 2 (2009): 333–57.

Yanov, Alexander. *The Russian Challenge and the Year 2000*. New York: Blackwell Publishers, 1987.

The Russian New Right: Right-Wing Ideologies in the Contemporary USSR. Research Series – Institute of International Studies, University of California, Berkeley; No. 35. Berkeley: Institute of International Studies, University of California, 1978.

Yaszek, Lisa. "Afrofuturism, Science Fiction, and the History of the Future." *Socialism and Democracy* 20, no. 3 (November 1, 2006): 41–60.

Yurchak, Alexei. *Everything Was Forever, until It Was no More: The Last Soviet Generation*. Princeton, NJ: Princeton University Press, 2005.

"Zakharchenko Vasilii Dmitrievich – Bolchaia Entsiklopediia russkogo naroda." https://web.archive.org/web/20120417200250/http://www.rusinst.ru/articletext.asp?rzd=1&id=5816&abc=1.

Zakharova, Larissa. "Soviet Public Spheres." *Politika*, 2017, www.politika.io/en/notice/soviet-public-spheres.

Zhegulev, Ilia. "Samye vliiatelnye v RPTs – O glvanykh deistvuiushchikh litsakh russkoi pravoslavnoi tserkvi." *Meduza*, November 26, 2015. https://meduza.io/feature/2015/11/26/samye-vliyatelnye-v-rpts.

Zhuk, Sergei I. "'Academic Détente': IREX Files, Academic Reports, and 'American' Adventures of Soviet Americanists during the Brezhnev Era." *Cahiers du monde russe. Russie – Empire russe – Union Soviétique et états indépendants* 54, no. 54/1–2 (2013): 297–328.

Zubok, Vladislav. "Can Putin Survive? The Lessons of the Soviet Collapse Essays." *Foreign Affairs* 101, no. 4 (2022): 84–96.

Zhivago's Children: The Last Russian Intelligentsia. Cambridge, MA: Belknap Press of Harvard University Press, 2009.

Zygar, Mikhail. *All the Kremlin's Men: Inside the Court of Vladimir Putin*. New York: PublicAffairs, 2016.

Index

For EU product safety concerns, contact us at Calle de José Abascal, 56–1°, 28003 Madrid, Spain or eugpsr@cambridge.org.

www.ingramcontent.com/pod-product-compliance
Ingram Content Group UK Ltd.
Pitfield, Milton Keynes, MK11 3LW, UK
UKHW020114190126
467120UK00020B/719
* 9 7 8 1 0 0 9 5 4 2 6 4 7 *